THE PSYCHOLOGY OF COMPUTER VISION

McGraw-Hill computer science series

RICHARD W. HAMMING
Bell Telephone Laboratories

EDWARD A. FEIGENBAUM
Stanford University

Bell and Newell *Computer Structures: Readings and Examples*
Cole *Introduction to Computing*
Donovan *Systems Programming*
Gear *Computer Organization and Programming*
Givone *Introduction to Switching Circuit Theory*
Hamming *Computers and Society*
Hamming *Introduction to Applied Numerical Analysis*
Hellerman *Digital Computer System Principles*
Hellerman and Conroy *Computer System Performance*
Kain *Automata Theory: Machines and Languages*
Kohavi *Switching and Finite Automata Theory*
Liu *Introduction to Combinatorial Mathematics*
Madnick and Donovan *Operating Systems*
Manna *Mathematical Theory of Computation*
Newman and Sproull *Principles of Interactive Computer Graphics*
Nilsson *Artificial Intelligence*
Ralston *Introduction to Programming and Computer Science*
Rosen *Programming Systems and Languages*
Salton *Automatic Information Organization and Retrieval*
Stone *Introduction to Computer Organization and Data Structures*
Stone and Siewiorek *Introduction to Computer Organization and Data Structures* PDP-11 edition
Tonge and Feldman *Computing: An Introduction to Procedures and Procedure-Followers*
Tremblay and Manohar *Discrete Mathematical Structures with Applications to Computer Science*
Watson *Timesharing System Design Concepts*
Wegner *Programming Languages, Information Structures, and Machine Organization*

Winston *The Psychology of Computer Vision*

THE PSYCHOLOGY OF COMPUTER VISION

Patrick Henry Winston
Editor

With contributions from

Berthold Horn
Massachusetts Institute of Technology

Marvin Minsky
Massachusetts Institute of Technology

Yoshiaki Shirai
Electro-Technical Laboratory, Tokyo

David Waltz
University of Illinois

Patrick Henry Winston
Massachusetts Institute of Technology

McGRAW-HILL BOOK COMPANY
New York St. Louis San Francisco Auckland Düsseldorf Johannesburg
Kuala Lumpur London Mexico Montreal New Delhi Panama Paris
São Paulo Singapore Sydney Tokyo Toronto

Library of Congress Cataloging in Publication Data

Winston, Patrick Henry.
The psychology of computer vision.

(McGraw-Hill computer science series)
Includes index.
1. Pattern perception. 2. Artificial intelligence.
I. Horn, Berthold. II. Title.
Q327.W56 001.53'5 74-22334
ISBN 0-07-071048-1

THE PSYCHOLOGY OF COMPUTER VISION

1 2 3 4 5 6 7 8 9 0 K P K P 7 9 8 7 6 5

ACKNOWLEDGMENTS

Much of the research reported in this book was supported by the Advanced Research Projects Agency of the Department of Defense and monitored by the Office of Naval Research.

Chapter 3, Analyzing Intensity Arrays Using Knowledge about Scenes, by Yoshiaki Shirai, was previously published in *Artificial Intelligence* under the title A Context Sensitive Line Finder for Recognition of Polyhedra and is reprinted with permission from North-Holland Publishing Company.

This book was set in Press Roman, designed, and illustrated by Scripta Graphica. The editors were Albrecht von Hagen and Evelyn Walters Pettit.
Kingsport Press, Inc., was printer and binder.

CONTENTS

1 MACHINE VISION

Patrick Henry Winston

1.1 THE BOOK

1.1.1 Content

This book is about machine vision research. The chapters are slightly abridged Ph.D. theses or other similarly major works, all from the M.I.T. Artificial Intelligence Laboratory. The central themes are as follows:

1. Horn demonstrates how the coordinates of a curved surface can be derived from surface intensity variation.
2. Shirai shows how knowledge about blocks can help drive a line finder over an intensity array in order to find objects and create a line drawing.
3. Waltz confirms that the structure of a line drawing forces conclusions about which lines separate bodies and about which lines are shadows or cracks.
4. Winston explains how a machine can quickly learn the essence of concepts involving simple configurations like that of an "arch."

5. Minsky discusses a theory of abstract symbolic representation designed to cope with movement in and reasoning about three-dimensional space.

The theories of Horn, Shirai, Waltz, and Winston are all supported by experiments with program implementations. Minsky's theory is ready to be filled out and refined through such implementations.

1.1.2 Purpose

I have several objectives in assembling these works:

1. I want to provide easy access to the particular material in the collection. Most of the papers have appeared in the accessible literature only in synopsis form or not at all. None of the material is yet treated in existing textbooks and most students, particularly undergraduates, do far too little direct reading from original papers.
2. I want to show the breadth of machine vision research. The spectrum stretches from frontal confrontation with light intensity arrays to extremely knotty questions of knowledge representation and manipulation. These papers are representative of our best work along this spectrum.
3. I want to promote a new way of approaching traditional puzzles. Making machines see is an important way to understand how we animals see, and I hope these studies will be refreshing and stimulating to those who have a serious interest in the psychology of seeing, learning, and knowledge representation.
4. I want to encourage more work. Each of the chapters could eventually prove to be prefaces to other volumes. Much remains to be done.

I have selected only M.I.T. work for this volume and have thus excused myself from the difficult job of selecting a representative set of papers from the literature at large. Too much has been done at Stanford, Stanford Research Institute, Carnegie, Edinburgh, Maryland, and elsewhere to allow a more general selection that would seem satisfactory to all the people of the machine vision community who have contributed in a major way. I certainly acknowledge that many of the papers here could be replaced by some other paper with equal quality and significance.

Some of these are cited in the papers included here but we are not particularly good bibliographers. The natural and unfortunate result is that we sometimes reinvent some ideas and sometimes fail to properly acknowledge earlier origins and sometimes do not provide useful pointers to further study. For this we are justly scolded. The references given are not meant to exhaustively circumscribe any particular area, but are meant to indicate particular known sources of inspiration or illuminating reference. Many readers should certainly examine more thorough listings like those of Azriel Rosenfeld mentioned in the bibliography and the lists of publications available from the various artificial intelligence laboratories.

1.2 THE WORK

It sometimes makes sense to think of a complicated system as a collection of modules, especially at the beginning. Thus a robot given a visually presented sample structure and told to copy it using blocks and wedges might need a vision system composed of the following specialists:

Line finder: To look for lines in the array of picture points
Region grouper: To decide how regions in a line drawing fit together to form bodies
Body identifier: To identify the blocks and wedges once bodies are collected out of regions
Support analyzer: To speculate on how the bodies support one another
Position locator: To nail down the coordinates of the objects

Once such a set of specialists exists, one should be able to paste them together using a simple executive program that runs each in turn over an evolving data base. It is now well known that the pasting is far from easy and we still wait for complete vision systems that are scientifically satisfactory. Early work on vision properly concentrated on line finding and region grouping, treating them independently, in the expectation that solutions would become part of a bigger system. Both problems seemed easy. Both proved difficult. Indeed, it was not until many people had worked several years that enough progress had been made to support the successful demonstration by Horn, Binford, Winston, and Freuder of their system to copy blocks structures in December, 1970.

1.2.1 Waltz

Waltz's work deals with analyzing completed line drawings. He builds on earlier work of Huffman[1] and Clowes[2] to demonstrate that the physical world severely constrains the way lines and vertexes can fit together in line drawings. He shows that deciding if a particular line in a drawing is a shadow, crack, obscuring edge, or internal seam can be done in a way analogous to the solution of sets of algebraic equations. In algebra, one has variables together with constraints in the form of equations. In scene analysis, each line corresponds to a variable, and determining the lines' physical origins corresponds to solving algebra equations for variable values. The constraints analogous to equations turn out to be given by the vertexes. Figure 1.1 shows a scene typical of those easily analyzed by a program embodiment of Waltz's theory together with the symbols Waltz uses to denote category membership.

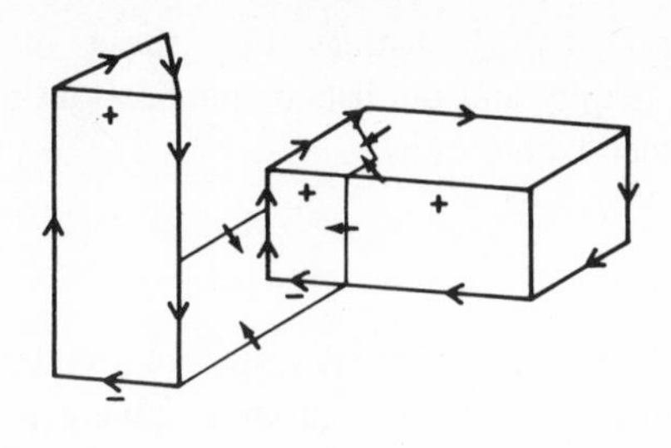

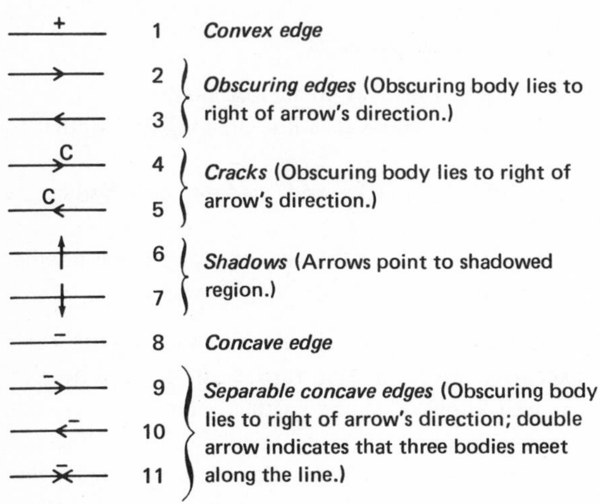

Fig. 1.1

To show how Waltz's theory works, suppose we divide all possible lines into categories. Altogether Waltz recognizes eleven possible interpretations for lines, given that interpretations like that of shadow are allotted two slots in the list according to which side of the line the darker region lies on. But certainly the arrangement of lines around a single vertex is limited. We cannot, for example, allow the combination given in Fig. 1.2 for an L-type vertex

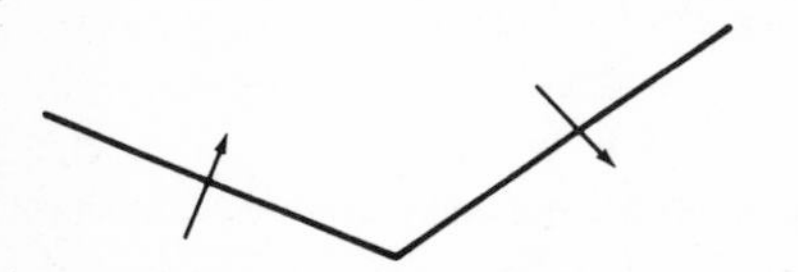

Fig. 1.2

since it is physically absurd for two regions each to be darker than the other as the sense of the shadow labels indicates.

It is reasonable to suppose such forbidden combinations might be rare. In fact, the physically possible combinations are the rare ones as indicated in Fig. 1.3.

By the time Waltz fully expanded his interpretation set to include information about illumination on both sides of the lines, only 3 percent to 3×10^{-6} percent of the total combinations are legal for the common vertex types!

Further constraint emerges when vertexes are put together. Clearly a line cannot change its identity from one end to another—a line cannot be a shadow on one end only to become a crack on the other. The net effect of this point is that scene analysis reduces to searching for a set of line labels providing physically realizable configurations at each of the vertexes.

Although this all seems straightforward enough, it was not clear in the beginning that Waltz would succeed at all, much less succeed to such an astonishing degree. Let us look at a summary of the strongest features of Waltz's theory, which, taken together, constitute what we have come to call "The Waltz Effect:"

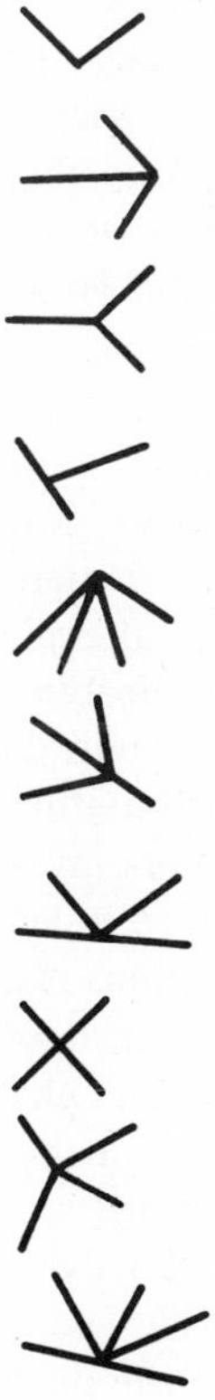

	Approximate number of combinatorially possible labelings	Approximate number of physically possible labelings
	3,249	92
	185,000	86
	185,000	826
	185,000	623
	11×10^6	10
	11×10^6	435
	11×10^6	213
	11×10^6	128
	11×10^6	160
	600×10^6	20

Fig. 1.3

The finite size of the task: Waltz ends with a need to enumerate a few thousand vertex possibilities. A project of such scope is large enough to frighten away anyone who spends only a few hours looking at the problem because the job seems too big for all practical purposes. Yet, as often seems to be the case in exploring the knowledge required by those parts of intelligence that seem most mysterious, the apparent infinity turns out to be quite manageable.

Lack of ambiguity in analysis: Generally the Waltz procedure converges on one interpretation for each line in a scene. Only a few lines will have more than one interpretation, and then usually only two or three. This seems in part a result of the constraint contributed by observed shadows. Curiously, early work was made more difficult by the supposition that shadows were only an annoying complication!

Rapid convergence: Potentially, the known nature of a particular line could propagate its influence over a considerable distance and be required at a considerable distance to effect some final interpretation decision. This does not seem to be the case for two reasons: First, influence does not readily pass through the T-joints proliferate on object boundaries. Second, the physical constraints seem powerful enough to fully disambiguate the identity of a line after only a few vertexes near it are explored. Waltz's work suggests that scene analysis on this level is to a large extent a local phenomenon, and incidentally, it should be amenable to parallel processing.

Description refinement simplifies analysis: Surely proper refinement of one's descriptive base should always lead to better, faster analysis. Waltz's result is indeed a crisp demonstration of that end of a spectrum: instead of combinatorial explosion and deductive chaos, we see good description forcing analysis. But arbitrary refinement will not work. For example, subdividing the lines according to their length would not add much useful constraint.

Explanation of older work: Waltz's work gives theoretical substance to a good bit of prior work conducted in an exploratory, often ad hoc mode. Older empirical observations based on experiments with functioning programs are now explained in terms of understood particulars of Waltz's catalog of physical constraints. Indeed Waltz's theory is so well worked out that the knowledge needed in analyzing drawings is reduced in his system to a sort of compiled form, with the major procedural activities being table look up and straightforward comparisons. Now less seems required of sophisticated problem solving to handle the problem.

The last point can be amplified by comparing Waltz's results with the earlier work of Guzman.[3] Guzman is famous for a program which merged regions into bodies using evidence from the vertexes. Each vertex may suggest that one or more pairs of regions around it belong together according to the rules given in Fig. 1.4. This table is empirically derived and reflects only commonsense judgment about vertexes frequently seen in line drawings.

The program worked fairly well, especially after some study of good ways to keep score of suggestions from the vertexes, but it remained clear that more work was to be done: the program could not handle shadows and it did poorly if there were holes in objects or missing lines in the drawing. Also it had a distinctly ad hoc flavor. Nevertheless, it did work, and it did support some experiments that are interesting to reflect on now.

For one thing Guzman's program always found forks less reliable than arrows. This makes good sense now because Waltz demonstrated that in his refined categorization there are almost ten times as many types of forks as there are arrows. Forks are less reliable because there are simply more ways for a fork to be something other than the junction of convex edges on a single body!

Another example lies in the observation that Guzman's program worked best when no region was too far removed from the outline of the scene against the table or other background. The Waltz explanation is that the existence of background at a vertex induces even more than the normal constraint, with the consequence being a smaller table of vertex possibilities to work from. Working in from the extreme outline is simply a good idea because typically the outline vertexes are a priori the most likely to force quick conclusions.

On another level, an important point emerges in connection with how better description obviates the need for complicated mechanisms for using the description. A series of blunder-evoking counterexamples eventually forced Guzman into a complicated program for weighing together the advice from the vertexes. He elected to follow mainly the more-evidence path rather than

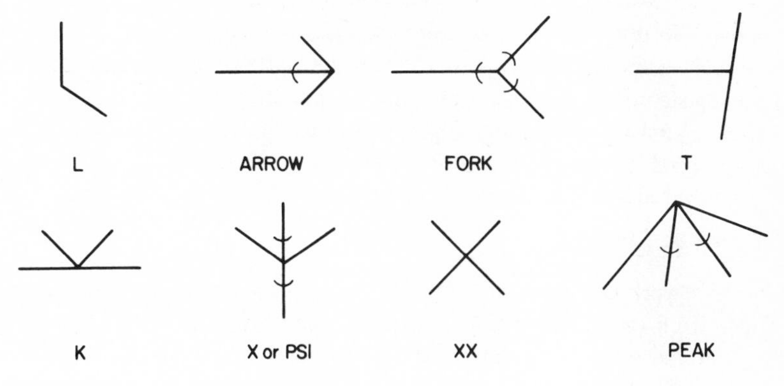

Fig. 1.4

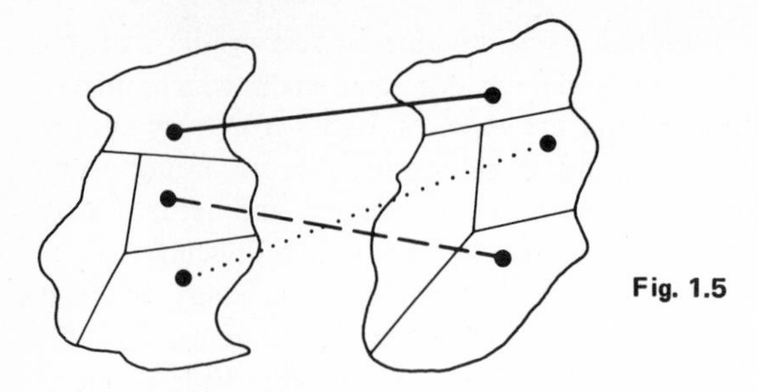

Fig. 1.5

try for improving the quality of evidence. Waltz uses much better evidence derived from more beautiful descriptions, and the question of how to weigh evidence is not even perceptible as an issue. The process naturally and quickly converges on either a unique interpretation or a small number of scene interpretations, each as good as the next with respect to the information available to Guzman's and Waltz's programs.

Figure 1.5 shows my view of what seems to have happened on a certain abstract level in going from Guzman to Waltz. There are observations of the interaction of some vaguely defined things–in the case at hand Guzman observed the interaction of vertex types and region affinities. There is perhaps a temptation to work out a probabilistic theory in view of the somewhat random and diverse interactions. Another approach, however, is to partition the things into subcategories such that the apparent statistical nature of the interaction dissolves into precisely defined and fully constrained interaction between the subcategories. This is the route Waltz took. Waltz found the subcategories for line drawings to be his shadow, crack, concave, convex, and boundary lines. In terms of the abstraction I am arguing for, this subcategorization of Waltz's was the right one to break up the diffuse irregular interaction of the blobs into the well-defined and strongly constrained relations between the blobs' subdivisions. In some of the recent studies of case grammar, we again find that proper subdivision of categories reduces the variability observed in how the categories are signalled syntactically. In view of such examples, it is wrong to think of Waltz's work as only a statement of the epistemology of line drawings of polyhedra. Instead I think it is an elegant case study of a paradigm we can expect to see again and again, and as such, it is a strong metaphoric tool for guiding our thinking, not only in vision but also in the study of other systems involving intelligence.

1.2.2 Shirai

Shirai's work complements Waltz's: Shirai works toward a line drawing rather than from one. Since Shirai is centrally concerned with how intensity arrays from some sort of camera can be understood, we tend to speak of the work as lying in the direction of "picture analysis" rather than "scene analysis," but it should be understood that the terms represent only a rough categorization preferable to the obsolete "high-level" and "low-level" terminology previously used.

One might think that picture analysis would involve inherently little problem solving and that it might therefore be the easier area to work in. But facing facts, pulling something meaningful from an array of picture points is already a problem, bigger than most novices imagine and unworthy of the casual notice usually given to it by the uninformed. The edges themselves often generate only very small intensity differences that are hard to deal with because information from television cameras and other sensors is noisy and distorted beyond belief. As Horn shows,[4] sensors supply some of the degradation and the objects themselves contribute more in the form of dirt, texture, shadows, and multiple reflections. If a line finder is too sensitive, all of these problems create a jungle of falsely perceived edges. If the line finder is not sensitive enough, some legitimate lines will be missing from the drawing.

Unfortunately these difficulties cannot be handled by careful tuning of sensitivity parameters. Some noise-produced lines are stronger than real ones and cannot be properly disregarded without an introduction of genuine world knowledge in the line-finding process. By knowing or hypothesizing that a particular object is a brick, one can use the strong lines to guide a search for the weak ones. Shirai's work represents a step towards a picture-point analyzing system that understands what it sees. His system is one that understands facts about the world in general and that can use those facts to understand a particular scene in it. Such a strategy brings problem solving down into an area that one might prefer to think of as a domain for filtering theory, but filtering theory unfortunately lacks power in picture processing because the noise lacks the nice properties that underlie the linear filtering approach. Shirai's line finder is the most successful so far and it uses none of the sophisticated filtering techniques.

Graphically Shirai's, like many other modern products of artificial intelligence research, looks more like a network of procedures rather than an executive with subroutines, each called in an orderly, immutable sequence. Each procedure is connected to others via potential control-transfer links. In practice which of these links are used depends on the context in which the various procedures are used, the context being the joint product of the system and the problem undergoing analysis.

As such, the work moves toward what Minsky and Papert have called the heterarchical approach to thinking about complex problem solving tasks. Briefly, the approach involves the following notions, some of which are just restatements and refinements of some of the classical rules of good programming practice:

1. A complex system should be goal oriented. Procedures at all levels should be short and associated with some definite goal. Goals should normally be satisfied by invoking a small number of subgoals for

other procedures or by directly calling a few primitives. A corollary is that the system should be top down. For the most part nothing should be done unless necessary to accomplish something at a higher level.

2. The executive control should be distributed throughout the system. In a heterarchical system, the modules interact not like a master and slaves but more like a community of experts.
3. Programmers should make as few assumptions as possible about the state the system will be in when a procedure is called. The procedure itself should contain the necessary machinery to set up whatever conditions are required before it can do its job. This is obviously of prime importance when many authors contribute to the system, for they should be able to add knowledge via some new code without completely understanding the rest of the system. In practice this usually works out as a list of goals lying like a preamble near the beginning of a routine. Typically these goals are satisfied by simple reference to the data base, but if not, notes are left as to where help may be found in the Planner[5] or Conniver style.[6]
4. A system should contain a considerable amount of knowledge about the domain in either declarative or procedural form. Great performance cannot be expected from systems that do not know much about what they are working with.
5. The system should contain some knowledge of itself. It is not enough to think of executives and primitives. There should be modules that act as critics and complain when something looks suspicious. Others must know how and when the primitives are likely to fail. Communication among these modules should be more colorful than the mere flow of data and command. It should include what in human discourse would be called advice, suggestions, remarks, complaints, criticism, questions, answers, lies, and conjectures.
6. A system should have facilities for tentative conclusions. The system will detect mistakes as it goes. When this happens, it needs to know what facts in the data base are most problematical, it needs to know how to try to fix things, and it needs to know how far ranging the consequences of a change are likely to be.

Although Shirai's system lacks strength in some of these areas it is nevertheless an outstanding demonstration that the heterarchy metaphor can be dramatically useful in dealing with picture intensities.

1.2.3 Horn

Horn's work also lies in the domain of picture analysis as distinct from scene analysis. Straightforwardly speaking, the problem is to understand in mathematical terms how the observed shading of smoothly curved objects forces conclusions about precisely where the surfaces lie in three-dimensional space. Horn takes us through an adventure in applied mathematics, with matrix partial differential equations lurking everywhere, to find the answer, expressible either as a set of difference equations or as a functioning program. Figure 1.6 shows an example of how, under reasonable lighting conditions, numerical integration of Horn's equations can derive the shape of a complicated curved object, in this case a human nose.

On a certain level Horn's work is the same story told again: the physical world severely constrains what we see, and understanding those constraints allows us to write analysis programs. We are properly reminded of Waltz's work where the theme of constraint exploitation also predominates.

Incidentally, the programs often display the same talents and failings that we humans have. Horn recalls, for example, that the effectiveness of the facial cosmetic art in part follows straightforwardly from the way shadings suggest shapes. Cheeks that are too round or perhaps not round enough can be helpfully altered by a deft application of rouge, fooling both human and machine observers. But of course Horn's theory goes considerably beyond giving a precise explanation of why makeup works and illuminates more puzzling phenomena, such as why the full moon's overall shape seems so much more like a flat disk than a sphere.

Curiously, serious work on the detailed shape of the moon provides a historically interesting antecedent to Horn's study. Before moon missions became commonplace, there was considerable interest in working out the contours of the maria, using the shading idea and presumptions about regularity of reflectivity. Prior to Horn's general solution to the problem, the moon stimulated important work, but solutions were restricted to simplifying special case conditions found in the moon problem.[7-10]

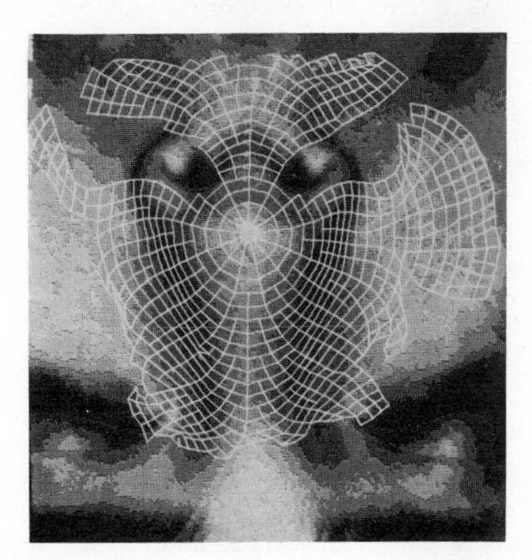
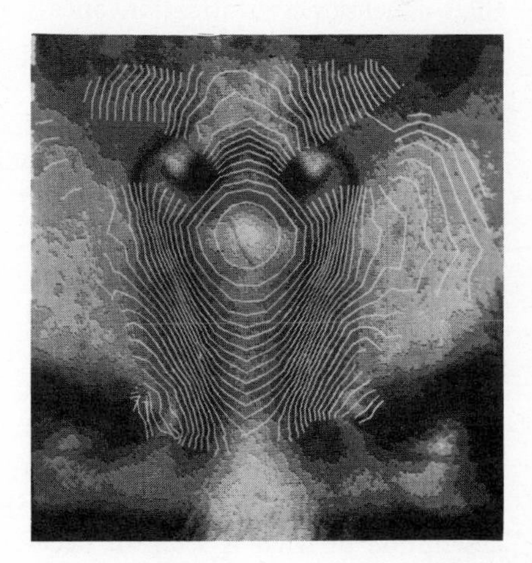

Fig. 1.6

This work of Horn thankfully steps out of the plane-faced polyhedra domain. But since Horn was so successful and since one might question the importance of the world of blocks and wedges, it is important perhaps to recall that any domain is good only insofar as it contains manageable forms of the central questions–where "manageable" means that the overall problem is not so hard as to force unsatisfyingly particular solutions and the "central questions" addressed are those for which the community at large has genuine interest. By these standards the blocks world has done admirably well. In artificial intelligence the central questions of the past often have had to do with problem solving, and we have therefore more strongly pursued the problem-solving aspects of vision, leaving some of the more basic picture analysis and object representation aspects temporarily out to pasture. Consequently, the blocks world, simple as it is in its requirements for representational sophistication, has been the right and proper domain.

But it has served its time. If we are to say that we understand vision, we must be able to reach the whole way around with a comprehensive theory that embraces the processing of pictures as well as the understanding of scenes. It is not enough to understand only the problem solving inherent in scene analysis. Everyone now agrees that the time has come to address more realistic worlds in which some simple curved objects reside and in which competence must depend on a far better understanding of how information about three-dimensional structures can be derived from picture information. Horn's work on shading as reported here, together with his previous study of focus-driven range-finding and his new work on "lightness," are all strong steps in this direction.

I should also emphasize that there is a serious representation problem to deal with, because as we learn about processing the pictures of curved-surface objects, we need a far better understanding of how to represent the three-dimensional information once we have it. Progress on the representation problem has already emerged in the generalized-cylinder concept of Binford and Agin[11] and the protrusion work of Hollerbach.[12] I expect great dividends to follow marrying such formalisms to the picture analysis work of which Horn's shading program is the outstanding example.

1.2.4 Winston

Winston shows how a machine can learn new concepts once satisfactory descriptions are brought up through picture analysis and scene analysis. The sequence shown in Fig. 1.7, by which his programs learned an "arch," is now classic.

Basically a teacher selects examples and nonexamples for the student, presenting them with no commentary other than whether they are, in fact, examples or nonexamples. It is left to the student to construct a symbolic description of what is seen, to decide why a particular sample is given as an example or as a nonexample of the concept, and to learn some new fact about the concept consequent to the analysis. There is a strong sense of student participation here, especially in comparison with earlier learning programs, in which the student learned either by a kind of statistical improvement of some internal parameters or by rote digestion of facts presented in a form near that in which they were to be remembered.

A prominent theme in the work has to do with the nonexamples, called "near misses" by Winston. These are seen to directly convey important points. The near misses allow the programs to evolve models for concepts by augmenting descriptions with information about what parts of the description are important. It is important to know, for example, that the presence of a hole in the arch is essential, whereas the color of the materials is incidental.

In this there is a strong departure from those earlier learning theories which attribute weight to descriptive features in proportion to the statistical regularity with which they appear. On the surface the statistical regularity heuristic seems logical enough, but on closer inspection it seems to wear better as a supplementary option to a learning theory rather than as a basic central component. The statistical theories, of which the psychological stimulus-response idea is a close relative, simply cannot explain how we can learn new ideas so quickly. And beyond that there is even the question of how statistical importance can be separated from repeated coincidence, be it unintentional or forced. The Winston theory, with its emphasis on intelligently selected near misses, can easily explain how the arch's hole can be taught as being important and the color incidental even if the teacher has only blocks of one color. The statistical theories are hard pressed in such situations.

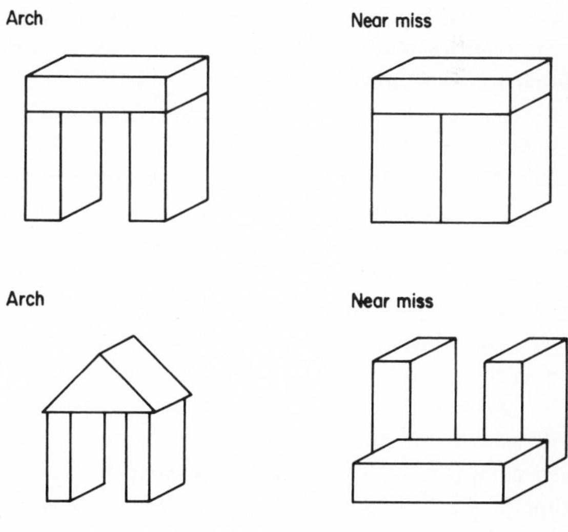

Fig. 1.7

One might suppose that there are many kinds of learning and wonder if Winston's thoughts generally apply. To explain this, suppose that learning and teaching are divided into the following categories:

Learning by discovery: There is no external teacher. Observers tend to attribute the learning to "inspiration."

Learning from sample sequences: The teacher provides study material, but certainly leaves the nontrivial situation analysis and reaction decisions to the student.

Learning by being told: The teacher informs the student about important points directly, reducing the student's work to that of assimilating the facts into previously acquired structures.

Learning by being programmed: The teacher leaves nothing or nearly nothing to the student. In the extreme, machine programs are directly altered by the "teacher," now so called only in a metaphoric sense.

The capabilities required by these various types of learning are not distinct. Indeed, I argue that the types listed form a fairly smooth continuum in which movement up the list requires supplements to the talents needed lower down. Essentially such an upward movement amounts to increasing internalization by the student of work that can be done by the teacher. I believe, however, that if we draw a line around the student and the teacher, rather than just around the student, then there is a kind of consistency to the total effort no matter which particular kind of learning we look at. The creation of good description, the manipulation of that description, and the use of near misses must go on somewhere in the total system. We humans learn most things by being told, simply because that point on the spectrum makes sense from the point of view of rapid transfer from a knowledgeable teacher to a receptive student. The learning still requires in someone the same skills illuminated in Winston's theory.

Another question asks if there is something special about learning structures. Are there substantially different requirements for learning processes? On an abstract level I think the answer is no. The work of Sussman,[13] Goldstein,[14] and Ruth[15] has demonstrated that good, purposeful description is as prerequisite to writing programs that understand and debug other programs as it was to learning about structures. And from that common base they go on to show that debugging requires close attention to comparison of what does happen against what should happen just as debugging a structure requires comparison of an evolving model against near misses.

My own thoughts in this direction, as yet purely speculative, have to do with what I call situation analysis, and again strongly rely on descriptions and their comparisons. The idea is illustrated by the problem faced by the simple robot in Fig. 1.8. At the beginning the robot is innocent of the fact that it cannot reach down and grab any object obstructed by an object on top. The teacher requires the robot to put A on top of C in Situation 1 and then also in Situation 2, but in Situation 2, B interferes. I would hope the robot could compare the two situations, note the difference in description involving B, and react accordingly. The robot should also be able to learn from Situation 3 and Situation 4 that free space is needed on the top of an object before it can support anything new. Already we can see a need in our descriptive repetoire to handle relations and properties like ON-TOP-OF and FREE-SPACE-ABOVE. And in the learning tasks given we can see a further need to handle them together, as either could be the crucial, near-miss-like difference. But before this can go much further, one would expect to require a richer domain in which to work and a far better understanding of how to represent knowledge, especially that which deals with the fuzzy boundary between physical structure and functional implication.

On another subject, it is perhaps useful to note that Winston's paper describes two theories supplementary to the learning theme. These theories, one about visual grouping and one about identifying unknowns, were

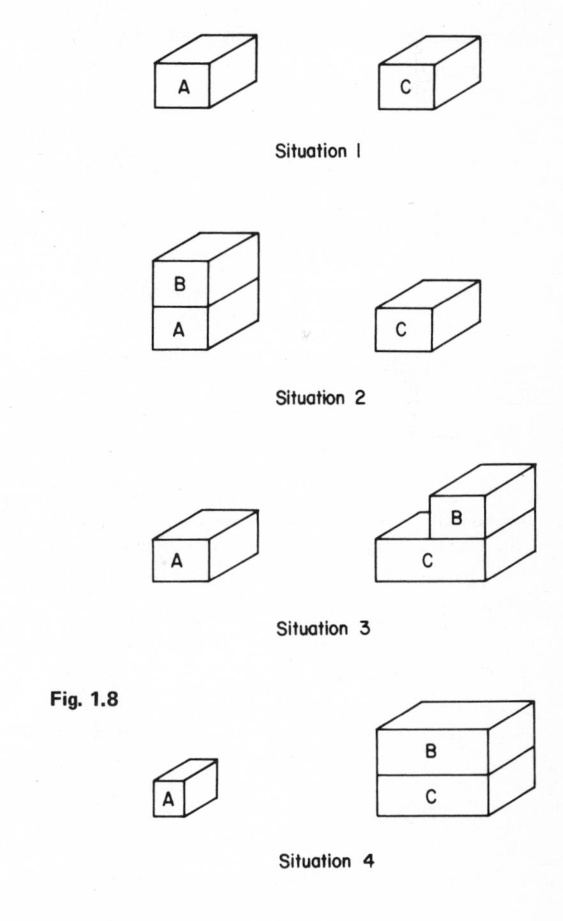

Fig. 1.8

originally thought to be secondary but have received new attention in connection with Minsky's work on representation, discussed next. It is interesting and perhaps informative to see how these ideas have matured in passing from one person to another.

1.2.5 Minsky

Suppose we are standing in an ordinary living room not previously seen. Our visual system somehow enables us to develop a model of what is in the room and where it is. That model seems sound enough to allow moving about in the room without reanalyzing the details of the visual impression with each step. Without much trouble we can even imagine what the room looks like from some viewpoint not yet experienced.

In connection with these talents, one thing seems clear: the job must be done with sophisticated interlocking symbolic structures capable of holding onto information produced from visual analysis and capable of supplying good guesses about things either partly obscured or never looked at with the complete processing associated with full attention. Additionally, the structure formalism must be accompanied by transformation functions that feed information from one structure to another as the viewpoint moves.

Minsky calls these structures "frames." His paper explores how systems of frames could be the representational foundation of truly powerful vision systems. And importantly, he goes on to show how the same frame ideas developed for natural support of vision also seem right for understanding human discourse. He shows rather clearly that understanding a room using knowledge about what to expect and hypotheses about what is obscured is not so different from understanding a children's story about buying a gift to take to a birthday party! That the same machinery could find use in such diverse tasks is a major feature of the theory—a feature not altogether unexpected if we are to presume any parsimony in the evolution of intelligence.

In any case the problem of representing knowledge seems to lie squarely across the road to continued discovery in artificial intelligence. Minsky is one of the few to face the problem directly. His frame theory as it stands offers no complete solutions, but it is a first step, a knowledge probe if you will, and we anxiously await the first programs to operate in support of the theory and to allow the experimentation so useful in debugging ideas about intelligence.

Interest is great and I believe that the frame idea will be the ancestor of a wave of progress in artificial intelligence in general, reaching beyond the boundaries of vision. As such it provides even finer hunting for research ideas than that provided by the other chapters in this book. Much remains to be done.

REFERENCES

1. Huffman, David: Impossible Objects as Nonsense Sentences, in B. Meltzer and D. Michie (eds.), "Machine Intelligence 6," Edinburgh University Press, Edinburgh, Scotland, 1971.

2. Clowes, Maxwell: On Seeing Things, *Artif. Intel.,* **2**(1):79–116 (1971).
3. Guzman, Adolfo: "Computer Recognition of Three-dimensional Objects in a Visual Scene," Ph.D. thesis, MAC-TR-59, Project MAC, Massachusetts Institute of Technology, Cambridge, Mass., 1968.
4. Horn, Berthold K. P.: The Image Dissector Eyes, *M.I.T. Artificial Intelligence Laboratory Memo* 178, 1969.
5. Hewitt, Carl: "Description and Theoretical Analysis (using schemata) of Planner: A Language for Proving Theorems and Manipulating Models in a Robot," Ph.D. thesis, AI-TR-258, Artificial Intelligence Laboratory, Massachusetts Institute of Technology, Cambridge, Mass., 1972.
6. McDermott, Drew, and Gerald Sussman: The CONNIVER Reference Manual, *M.I.T. Artificial Intelligence Laboratory Memo* 259A, 1972.
7. Fesenkov, V. P.: Photometric Investigations of the Lunar Surface, *Astronomochheskii Zh.,* **5**:219–234 (1929).
8. Van Diggelen, J.: A Photometric Investigation of the Slopes and Heights of the Ranges of Hills in the Maria of the Moon, *Bull. Astron. Inst. Netherlands,* **11**(423):283–289 (1951).
9. Willingham, D. E.: The Lunar Reflectivity Model for Ranger Block III Analysis, *Jet Prop. Lab Tech. Rept.* 32–664, Pasadena, Calif., November, 1964.
10. Rindfleisch, T.: Photometric Method for Lunar Topography, *Photometric Eng.,* **32**(2):262–276 (1966).
11. Binford, T. O. and G. J. Agin: Computer Description of Curved Objects, *3d Intern. Jt. Conf. Artif. Intel.,* Stanford Research Institute Publications Department, Menlo Park, Calif., pp. 629–640, 1973.
12. Hollerbach, John M., "Hierarchical Shape Description by Selection and Modification of Prototypes," master's thesis, Department of Electrical Engineering, Massachusetts Institute of Technology, Cambridge, Mass., 1974.
13. Sussman, Gerald: "A Computational Model of Skill Acquisition," Ph.D. thesis, AI-TR-297, Artificial Intelligence Laboratory, Massachusetts Institute of Technology, Cambridge, Mass., 1973.
14. Goldstein, Ira: "Understanding Simple Picture Programs," Ph.D. thesis, AI-TR-294, Artificial Intelligence Laboratory, Massachusetts Institute of Technology, Cambridge, Mass., 1974.
15. Ruth, Greg: "Analysis of Algorithm Implementation," Ph.D. thesis, MAC-TR-130, Project MAC, Massachusetts Institute of Technology, Cambridge, Mass., 1974.

2 UNDERSTANDING LINE DRAWINGS OF SCENES WITH SHADOWS

David Waltz

2.1 INTRODUCTION

How do we ascertain the shapes of unfamiliar objects? Why do we so seldom confuse shadows with real things? How do we "factor out" shadows when looking at scenes? How are we able to see the world as essentially the same whether it is a bright sunny day, an overcast day, or a night with only streetlights for illumination? In the terms of this paper, how can we recognize the identity of Figs. 2.1 and 2.2? Do we use learning and knowledge to interpret what we see, or do we somehow automatically see the world as stable and independent of lighting? What portions of scenes can we understand from local features alone, and what configurations require the use of global hypotheses?

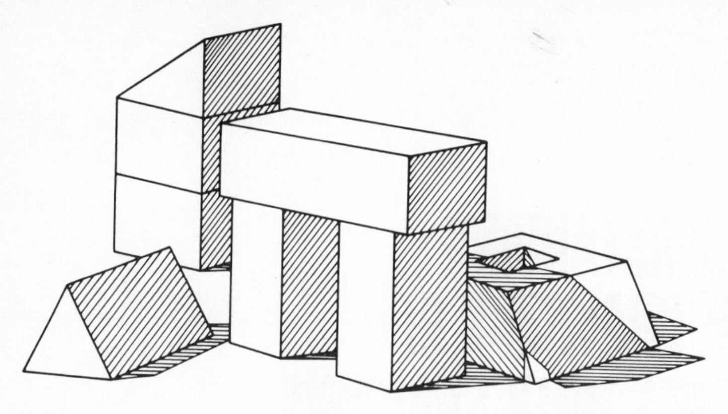

Fig. 2.1

In this essay I describe a working collection of computer programs which reconstruct three-dimensional descriptions from line drawings which are obtained from scenes composed of plane-faced objects under various lighting conditions. The system identifies shadow lines and regions, groups regions which belong to the same object, and notices such relations as contact or lack of contact between the objects, support and in-front-of/behind relations between the objects as well as information about the spatial orientation of various regions, all using the description it has generated.

2.1.1 Descriptions

The overall goal of the system is to provide a precise description of a plausible scene which could give rise to a particular line drawing. It is therefore

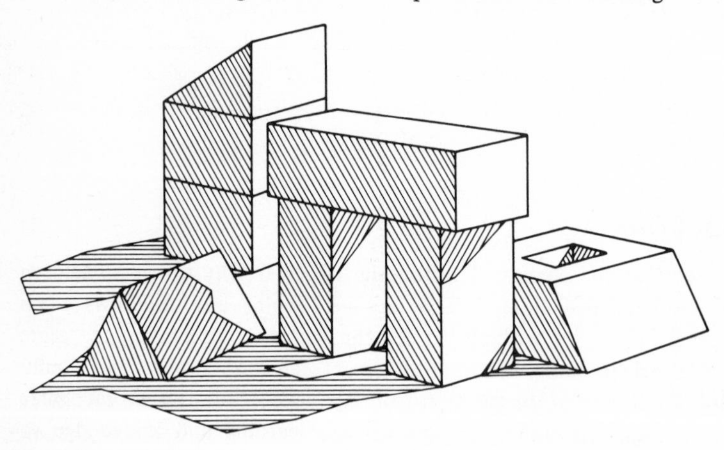

Fig. 2.2

important to have a good language in which to describe features of scenes. Since I wish to have the program operate on unfamiliar objects, the language must be capable of describing such objects. The language I have used is an expansion of the labeling system developed by Huffman[1] in the United States and Clowes[2] in Great Britain.

The language employs labels which are assigned to line segments and regions in the scene. These labels describe the edge geometry, the connection or lack of connection between adjacent regions, the orientation of each region in three dimensions, and the nature of the illumination for each region (illuminated, projected shadow region, or region facing away from the light source). The goal of the program is to assign a single label value to each line and region in the line drawing, except in cases where humans also find a feature to be ambiguous.

This language allows precise definitions of such concepts as supported-by, in-front-of, behind, rests-against, is-shadowed-by, is-capable-of-supporting, leans-on, and others. Thus, if it is possible to label each feature of a scene uniquely, then it is possible to directly extract these relations from the description of the scene based on this labeling.

2.1.2 Junction Labels

Much of the program's power is based on access to lists of possible line label assignments for each type of junction in a line drawing. Depending on the amount of computer memory available, it may either be desirable to store the complete lists as compiled knowledge or to generate the lists when they are needed. In my current program the lists are for the most part precompiled.

The composition of the dictionary is interesting in its own right. While some junction types require many dictionary entries, others require relatively few. Moreover, in some cases local information about the relative brightness of the surrounding regions and about the directions of the lines may severely limit the number of relevant dictionary entries for any particular junction. In other cases such information has little effect.

Figure 2.3 shows all the junction types which can occur in the universe of the program. The dictionary is arranged by junction type, and a standard ordering is assigned to all the line segments which make up junctions (except FORKs and MULTIs). There is a considerable amount of local information which can be used to select a subset of the total number of junction configurations which are consistent with physical reality.

For example the program can use local region brightness and line segment direction to preclude the assignment of certain labels to lines. If it

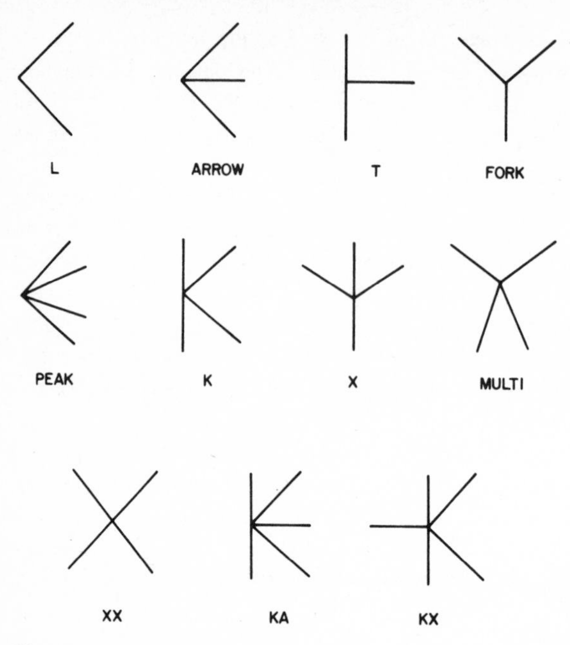

Fig. 2.3

knows that one region is brighter than an adjacent region, then the line which separates the regions can be labeled as a shadow region in only one way. There are other rules which relate region orientation, light placement and region illumination as well as rules which limit the number of labels which can be assigned to line segments which border the support surface for the scene. The program is able to combine all these types of information in finding a list of appropriate labels for a single junction.

2.1.3 Combination Rules

Combination rules are used to select the label, or labels, which correctly describe the scene features that could have produced each junction in the given line drawing. The simplest type of combination rule merely states that a label is a possible description for a junction if and only if there is at least one label which "matches" it assigned to each adjacent junction. Two junction labels "match" if and only if the line segment which joins the junctions gets the same interpretation from both of the junctions at its ends.

I thought at the outset of my work that it might be necessary to construct models of hidden vertexes or features which faced away from the eye in order to find unique labels for the visible features. The difficulty in this is that unless a program can find which lines represent obscuring edges, it cannot know where to construct hidden features, but if it needs the hidden features to label the lines, it may not be able to decide which lines represent obscuring edges. As it turns out, no such complicated rules and constructions are necessary in general; most of the labeling problem can be solved by a scheme which only compares adjacent junctions.

2.1.4 Experimental Results

The program computes the full list of dictionary entries for each junction in the scene, eliminates from the list those labels which can be precluded on the basis of local features, assigns each reduced list to its junction, and then a filtering program computes the possible labels for each line, using the fact that a line label is possible if and only if there is at least one junction label at each end of the line which contains the line label. Thus, the list of possible labels for a line segment is the intersection of the two lists of possibilities computed from the junction labels at the ends of the line segment. If any junction label would assign an interpretation to the line segment which is not in this intersection list, then that label can be eliminated from consideration. The filtering program uses a network iteration scheme to systematically remove all the interpretations which are precluded by the elimination of labels at a particular junction.

Initially I had intended to have a tree search program follow the filtering program, but to my amazement I found that in the first few scenes I tried, this program alone found a unique label for each line. Even when I tried considerably more complicated scenes, there were only a few lines in general which were not uniquely specified, and some of these were essentially ambiguous, i.e. I could not decide exactly what sort of edge gave rise to the line segment myself. The other ambiguities, i.e. the ones which I could resolve myself, in general require that the program recognize lines which are parallel or collinear or recognize regions which meet along more than one line segment and hence require more global agreement.

I have been able to use this system to investigate a large number of line drawings, including ones with missing lines and ones with numerous accidentally aligned junctions. From these investigations I can say with some certainty which types of scene features can be handled by the filtering program and which require more complicated processing. Whether or not more processing is required, the filtering system provides a computationally cheap method for acquiring a great deal of information. For example, in most scenes a large percentage of the line segments are unambiguously labeled, and more complicated processing can be directed to the areas which remain ambiguous.

Figure 2.4 shows some of the scenes which the program is able to handle. The segments which remain ambiguous after its operation are marked with stars, and the approximate amount of time the program requires to label each scene is marked below it. The computer is a PDP-10, and the program is written partially in MICRO-PLANNER[3] and partially in compiled LISP.

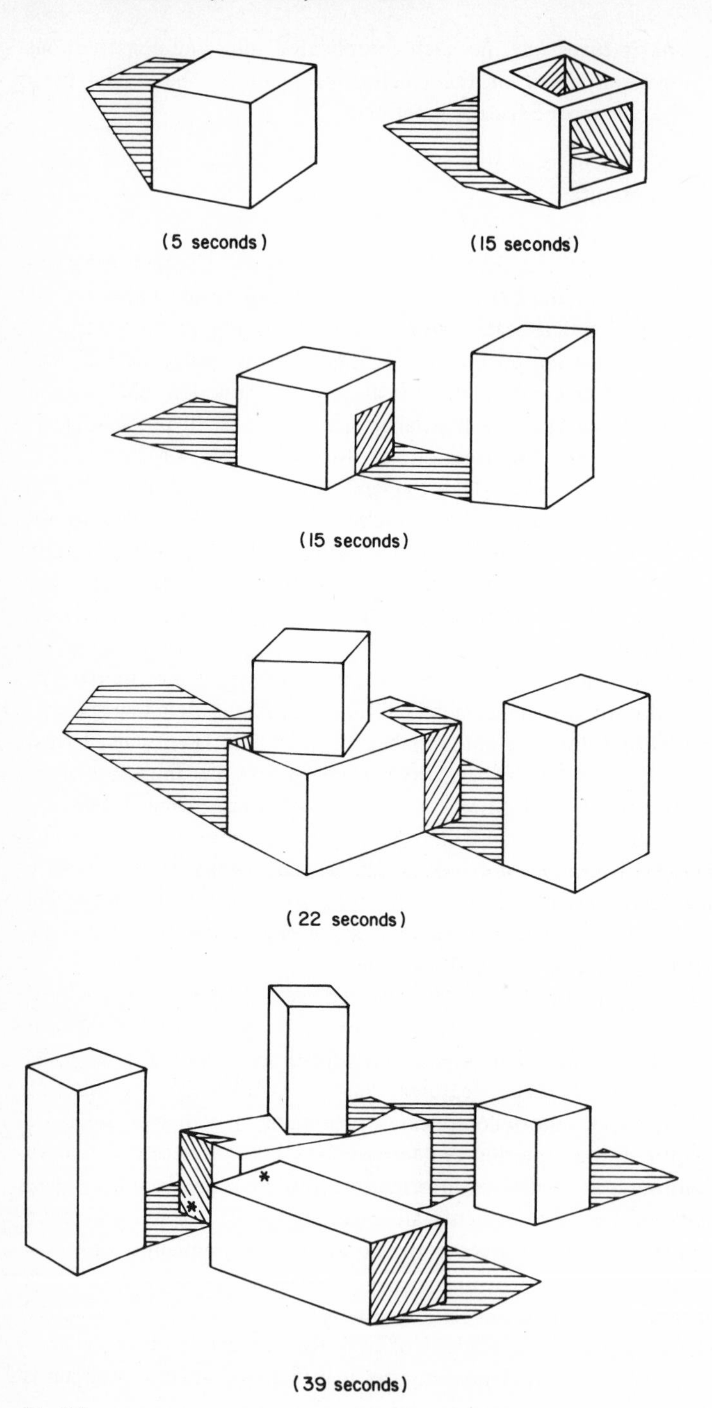

Fig. 2.4

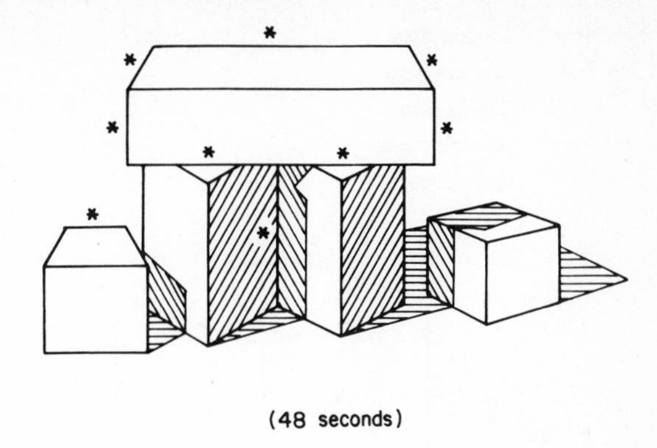

(48 seconds)

Fig. 2.4 *(continued)*

2.2 LINE LABELS

In what follows I frequently make a distinction between the scene itself (objects, table, and shadows) and the retinal representation of the scene as a two-dimensional line drawing. I will use the terms vertex, edge and surface to refer to the scene features which map into junction, line and region respectively in a line drawing.

Our first subproblem is to develop a language that allows us to relate these two worlds. I have done this by assigning names called labels to lines in the line drawing, after the manner of Huffman[1] and Clowes.[2] Thus, in Fig. 2.5 line segment J1-J2 is labeled as a shadow edge, line J2-J3 is labeled as a concave edge, line J3-J14 is labled as a convex edge, line J4-J5 is labeled as an obscuring edge and line J12-J13 is labeled as a crack edge. Thus, these terms are attached to parts of the drawing, but they designate the kinds of things found in the three-dimensional scene.

Pay particular attention to the notation used to label the lines. When I talk of junction labels I refer to the various possible combinations of such line labels around a junction. Each such combination is thought of as a particular junction labeling.

When we look at a line drawing of this sort, we usually can easily understand what the line drawing represents. In terms of a labeling scheme either (1) we are able to assign labels uniquely to each line, or (2) we can say that no such scene could exist, or (3) we can say that although it is impossible to decide unambiguously what the label of an edge should be, it must be labeled with one member of some specified subset of the total number of labels. What knowledge is needed to enable the program to reproduce such labeling assignments?

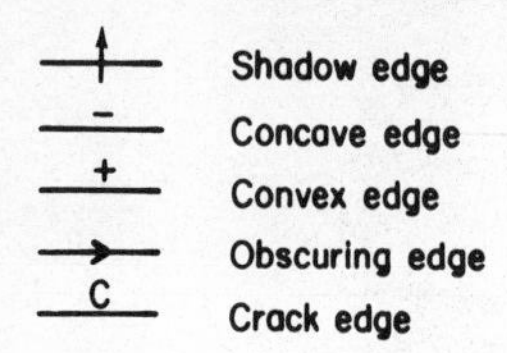

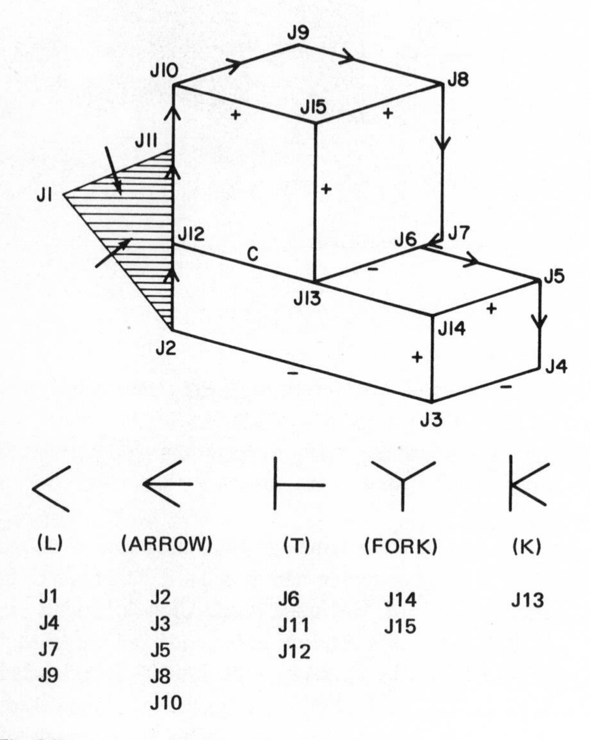

Fig. 2.5

2.2.1 System Knowledge

The knowledge of this system is expressed in several distinct forms:

1. A list of possible junction labels for each type of junction geometry includes the a priori knowledge about the possible three-dimensional interpretations of a junction.
2. Selection rules which use junction geometry, knowledge about which region is the table, and region brightness. These can easily be extended to use line segment directions to find the subset of the total list of possible junction labelings which could apply at a particular junction in a line drawing.
3. A program to find the possible labelings; it knows how to systematically eliminate impossible combinations of labels in a line drawing and, as such, contains implicit knowledge about topology.

4. Optional heuristics which can be invoked to select a single labeling from among those which remain after all the other knowledge in the program has been used. These heuristics find a "plausible" interpretation if required. For example, one heuristic eliminates interpretations that involve concave objects in favor of ones that involve convex objects, and another prefers interpretations which have the smallest number of objects; this heuristic prefers a shadow interpretation for an ambiguous region to the interpretation of the region as a piece of an object.

In this section I show how to express the first type of knowledge and give hints about some of the others. A large proportion of my energy and thought has gone into the choice of the set of possible line labels and the sets of possible junction labels. In this I have been guided by experiment with my program, since there are simply too many labels to hand simulate the program's reaction to a scene. The program, the set of edge labels, and the sets of junction labelings have each gone through an evolution involving several steps. At each step I noted the ambiguities of interpretation which remained, and then modified the system appropriately.

The changes have generally involved (1) the subdivision of one or more edge labels into several new labels embodying finer distinctions and (2) the recomputation of the junction label lists to include these new distinctions. In each case I have been able to test the new scheme to make sure that it solves the old problems without creating any unexpected new ones. For example, the initial data base contained only junctions (1) which represented trihedral vertexes (i.e., vertexes caused by the intersection of exactly three planes at a point in space) and (2) which could be constructed using only convex objects.

The present data base has been expanded to include all trihedral junctions and a number of other junctions caused by vertexes where more than three planes meet.

Throughout this evolutionary process I have tried to systematically include in the lists every possibility under the stated assumptions. In this part of the system I have made only one type of judgement: if a junction can represent a vertex which is physically possible, include that junction in the data base.

Each type of junction (L, ARROW, FORK) can only be labeled in a relatively small number of ways; thus if we can say with certainty what the label for a particular line must be, we can greatly constrain all other lines which intersect that line segment. As a specific example, if one branch of an L junction is labeled as a shadow edge, then the other branch must be labeled as a shadow edge as well.

Moreover shadows are directional, i.e., in order to specify a shadow edge, it must not only be labeled "shadow" but must also be marked to indicate which side of the edge is shadowed and which side is illuminated.

Therefore, not only the type of edge but the nature of the regions on each side can be constrained.

2.2.2 Better Edge Description

So far I have classified edges on the basis of geometry (concave, convex, obscuring, or planar) and have subdivided the planar class into crack and shadow subclasses. Suppose that I further break down each class according to whether or not each edge can be the bounding edge of an object. Objects can be bounded by obscuring edges, concave edges, and crack edges. Figure 2.6

Interpretation

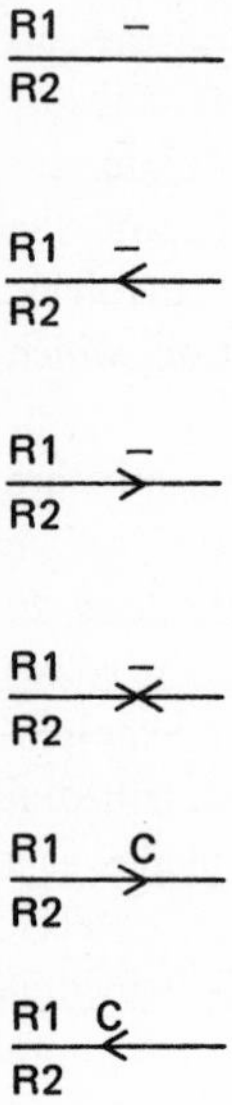

R1 –
R2
An inseparable concave edge; the object of which R1 is a part [OB(R1)] is the same as [OB(R2)].

R1 –
R2
A separable two-object concave edge; if [OB(R1)] is above [OB(R2)] then [OB(R2)] supports [OB(R1)].

R1 –
R2
Same as above; if R1 is above R2, then [OB(R2)] obscures [OB(R1)] or [OB(R1)] supports [OB(R2)].

R1 –
R2
A separable three-object concave edge; neither [OB(R1)] nor [OB(R2)] can support the other.

R1 C
R2
A crack edge; [OB(R2)] is in front of [OB(R1)] if R1 is above R2.

R1 C
R2
A crack edge; [OB(R2)] supports [OB(R1)] if R1 is above R2.

Separations

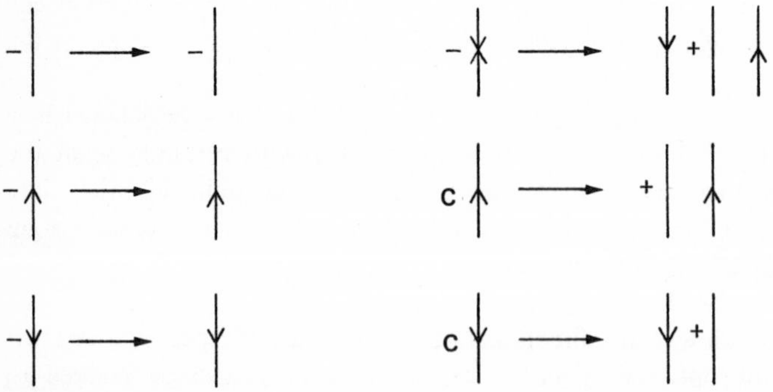

Fig. 2.6

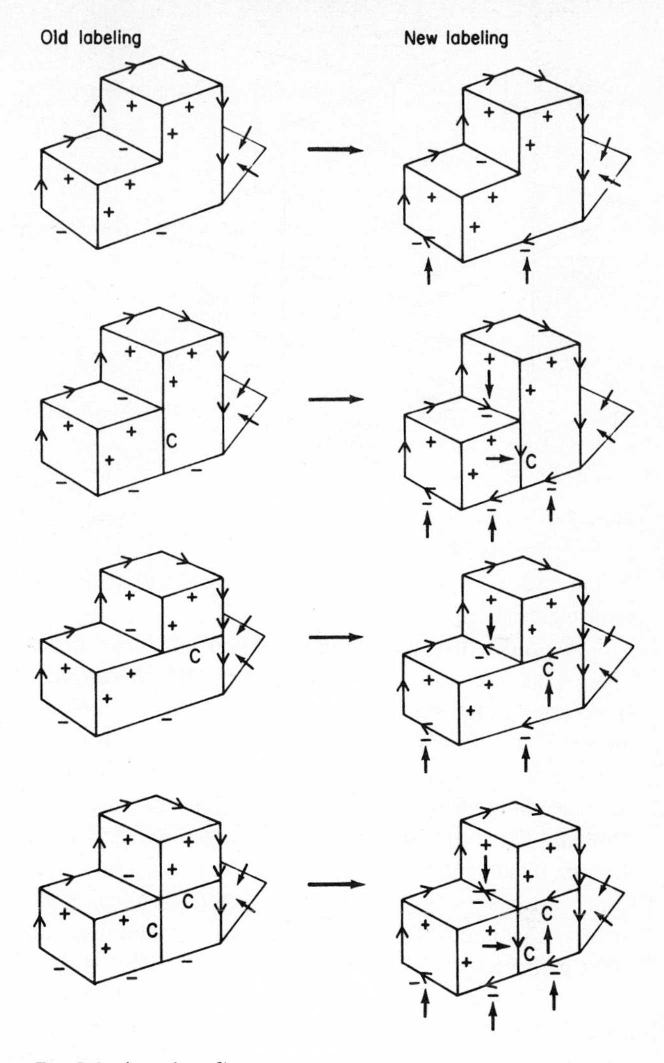

Fig. 2.6 *(continued)*

shows the results of appending a label analogous to the "obscuring edge" mark to crack and concave edges. This approach is similar to one first proposed by Freuder.[4]

2.2.3 Edge Geometry

The first problem is to find all possible trihedral vertexes. Huffman observed that three intersecting planes, whether mutually orthogonal or not, divide space into eight parts so that the types of trihedral vertex can be

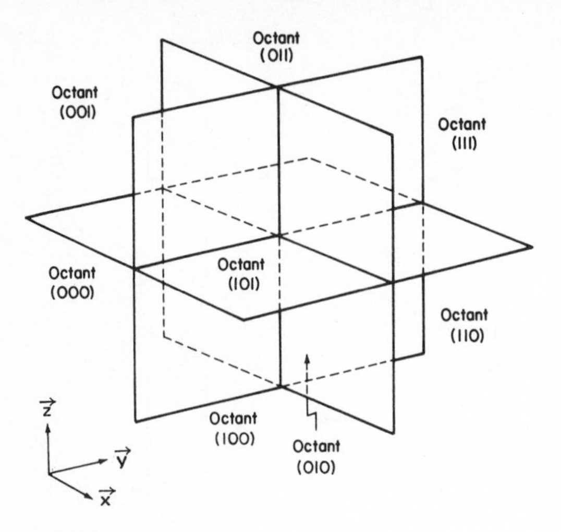

Fig. 2.7

characterized by the octants of space around the vertex which are filled by solid material.[1]

Consider the general intersection of three planes shown in Fig. 2.7. These planes divide space into octants, which can be uniquely identified by three-dimensional binary vectors **(x y z)** where the **x**, **y**, and **z** directions are specified as shown. The vectors make it easy to describe the various geometries precisely. I can then generate all possible geometries and nondegenerate views by imagining various octants to be filled in with solid material. There are junctions which correspond to having 1, 2, 3, 4, 5, 6, or 7 octants filled. Figure 2.8 shows the ten possible geometries that result from filling various octants; when considered from all possible viewing positions these ten geometries produce 196 different junction labelings. There are some other geometries which I have chosen not to use to generate junction labels. I have not included these geometries because each involves objects which touch only along one edge, and whose faces are nonetheless aligned, an extremely unlikely arrangement when compared to the other geometries. (In addition, some of the geometries are physically impossible unless one or more objects are cemented together along an edge or supported by invisible means.)

The four geometries recognized by Huffman and Clowes correspond to my numbers 1, 3, 5, and 7 in Fig. 2.8.

In Fig. 2.9 I show how the 20 different labels with type 3 geometry can be generated. Basically this process involves taking a geometry from Fig. 2.8, finding all the ways that the solid segments can be connected or separated, and finding all the possible views for each partitioning of the octants. To generate all the possible views one can either draw or imagine the particular geometry as it appears when viewed from each octant. From some viewing octants the central vertex is blocked from view by solid material, and therefore not every viewing position adds new labelings.

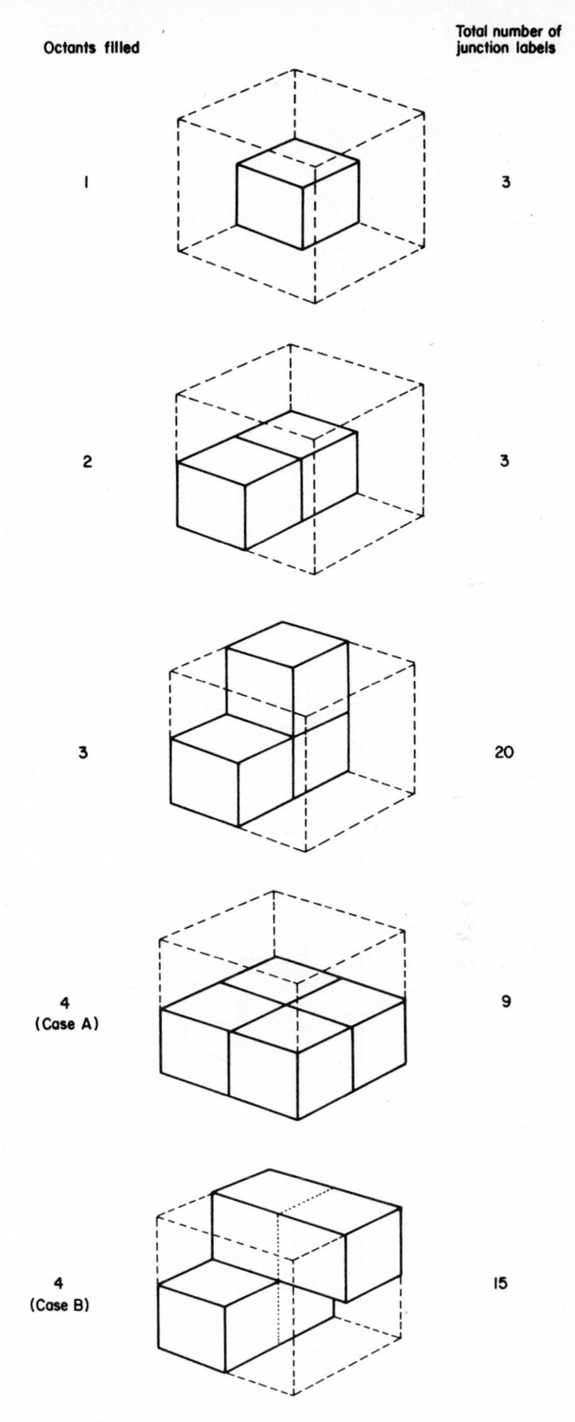
Octants filled
Total number of junction labels
1
3
2
3
3
20
4
(Case A)
9
4
(Case B)
15

Fig. 2.8

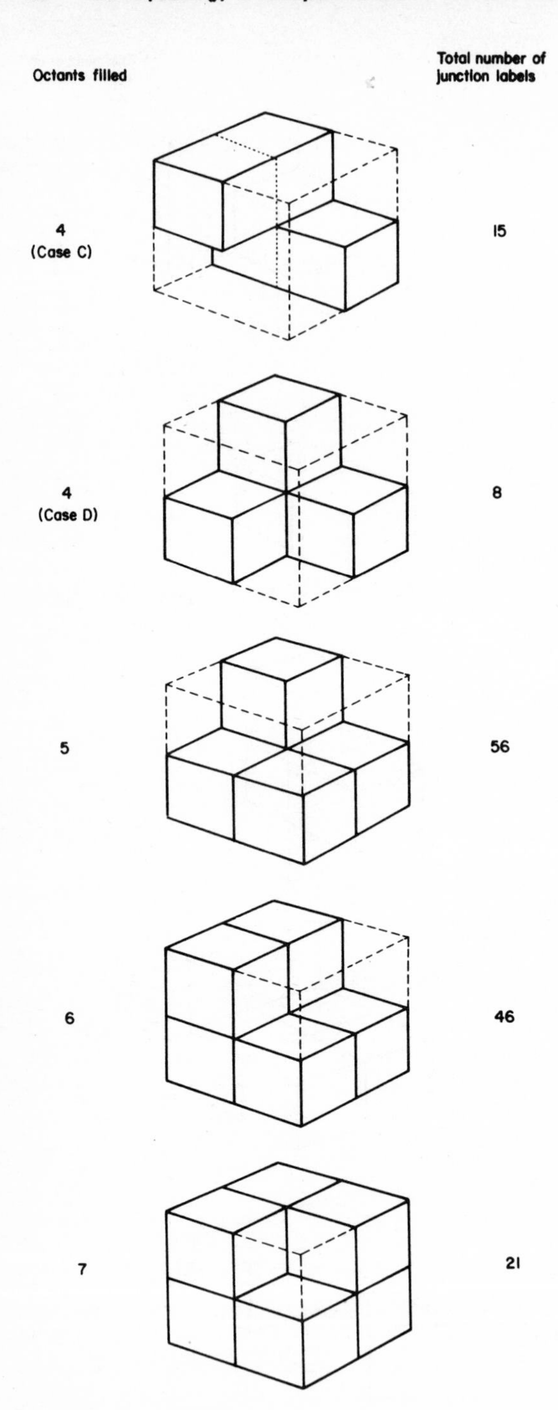

Fig. 2.8 *(continued)*

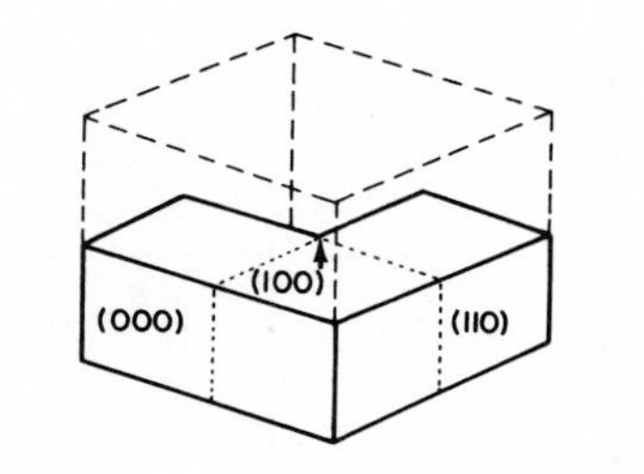

Name of junction	Appearance and labeling of junction	Number of objects at vertex	Objects at vertex are	Appearance of corresponding object(s)
L-3A	*	1	A = (000) ∪ (100) ∪ (110)	A
T-3A	* C	2	A = (000) ∪ (100) B = (110)	A B
T-3B	* C	2	A = (000) B = (100) ∪ (110)	A B
XX-3A	* A C C B C	3	A = (000) B = (100) C = (110)	A B C

Fig. 2.9

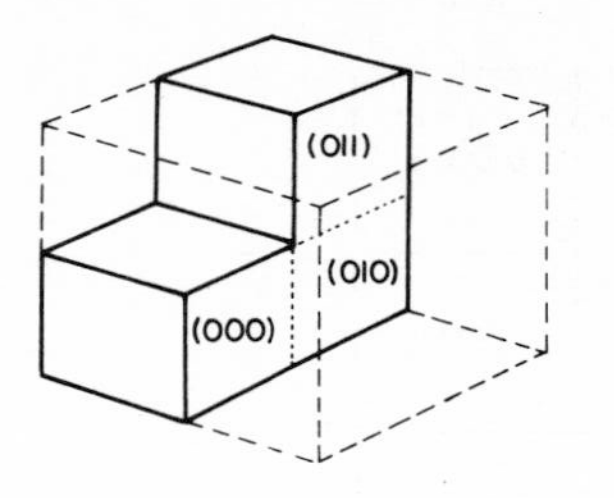

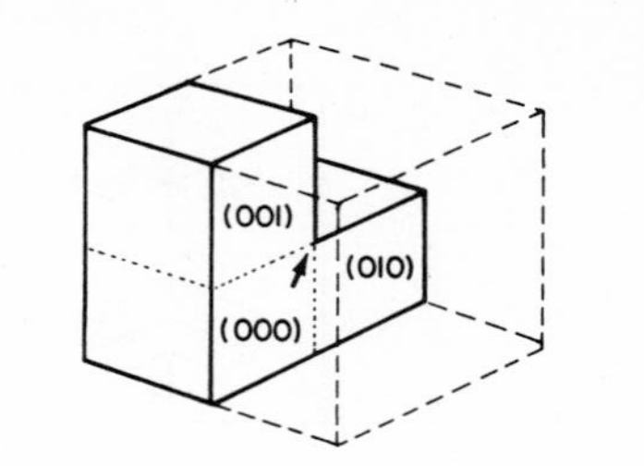

Name of junction	Appearance and labeling of junction	Number of objects at vertex	Objects at vertex are	Appearance of corresponding object(s)
Arrow-3A		1	A = (000) ∪ (010) ∪ (011)	
K-3A		2	A = (010) ∪ (011) B = (000)	
K-3B		2	A = (011) B = (000) ∪ (010)	
KXX-3A		3	A = (011) B = (010) C = (000)	

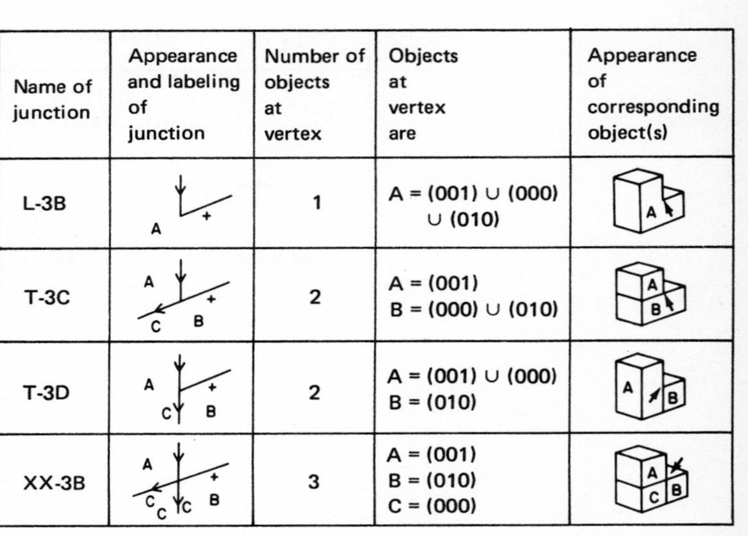

Name of junction	Appearance and labeling of junction	Number of objects at vertex	Objects at vertex are	Appearance of corresponding object(s)
L-3B		1	A = (001) ∪ (000) ∪ (010)	
T-3C		2	A = (001) B = (000) ∪ (010)	
T-3D		2	A = (001) ∪ (000) B = (010)	
XX-3B		3	A = (001) B = (010) C = (000)	

Fig. 2.9 *(continued)*

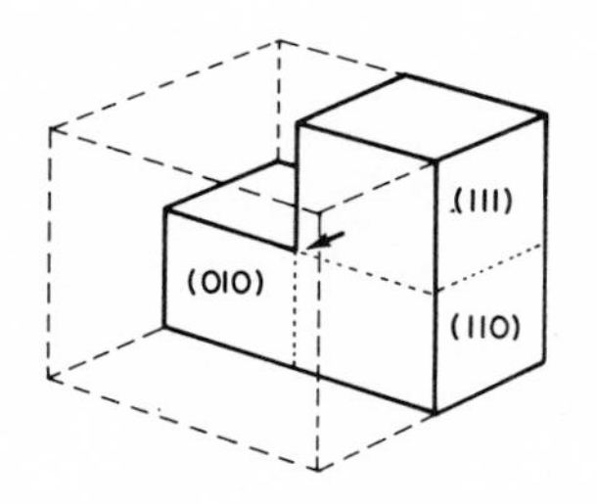

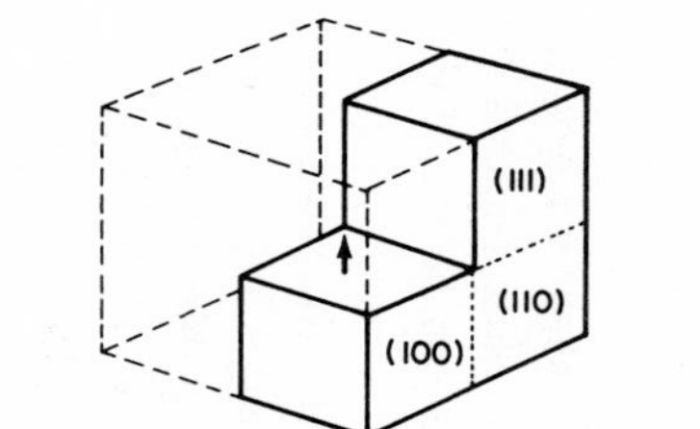

Name of junction	Appearance and labeling of junction	Number of objects at vertex	Objects at vertex are	Appearance of corresponding object(s)
L-3C		1	A = (111) ∪ (110) ∪ (010)	
T-3E		2	A = (111) B = (110) ∪ (010)	
T-3F		2	A = (111) ∪ (110) B = (010)	
XX-3C		3	A = (111) B = (010) C = (110)	

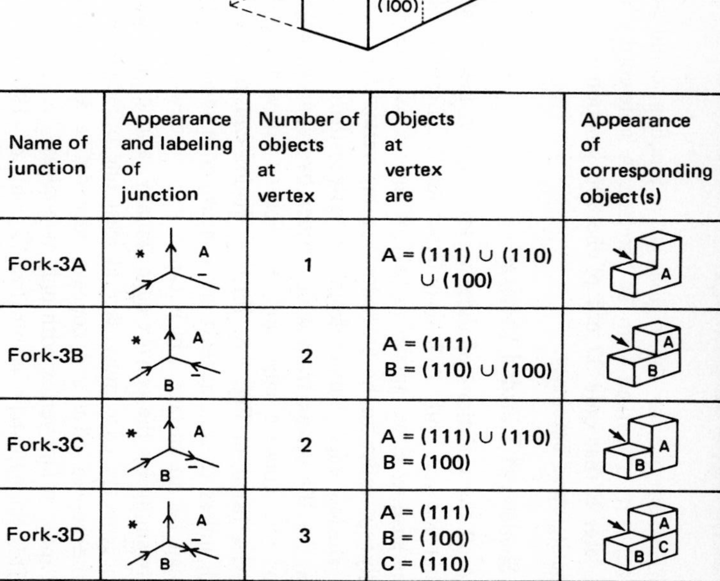

Name of junction	Appearance and labeling of junction	Number of objects at vertex	Objects at vertex are	Appearance of corresponding object(s)
Fork-3A		1	A = (111) ∪ (110) ∪ (100)	
Fork-3B		2	A = (111) B = (110) ∪ (100)	
Fork-3C		2	A = (111) ∪ (110) B = (100)	
Fork-3D		3	A = (111) B = (100) C = (110)	

Fig. 2.9 *(continued)*

Whenever one of the regions at a junction could correspond to the background it is marked with an asterisk. A noteworthy fact which I will exploit later is that only 37 out of the 196 junction labels can occur on the scene/background boundary.

2.2.4 Shadows at Trihedral Vertexes

To find all the variations of these vertexes which include shadow edges, first note that vertexes with 1, 2, 6, or 7 octants filled cannot cause shadows such that the shadow edges appear as part of the vertex. This can be stated more generally: in order to be a shadow-causing vertex (i.e., a vertex where the caused shadow edge radiates from the vertex) there must exist some viewing position for the vertex from which either two concave edges and one convex edge or one concave edge and two convex edges are visible. Consider the geometries listed in Fig. 2.8. First, a shadow-causing edge must be convex. Second, unless there is at least one concave edge adjacent to this convex edge, there can be no surface which can have a shadow projected onto it by the light streaming by the convex edge. Finally, a junction which has one convex and one concave edge must have at least one other convex or concave edge, since the convex edge and concave edge define at least three planes which cannot meet at any vertex with only two edges.

This immediately eliminates 73 out of 196 of the labelings from consideration. A listing of all the shadow-casting junctions can be constructed in the manner illustrated in Fig. 2.10; for each potential shadow-causing

To find all the shadow possibilities for a junction, first imagine it as part of an object, and define a coordinate system centered at the junction.

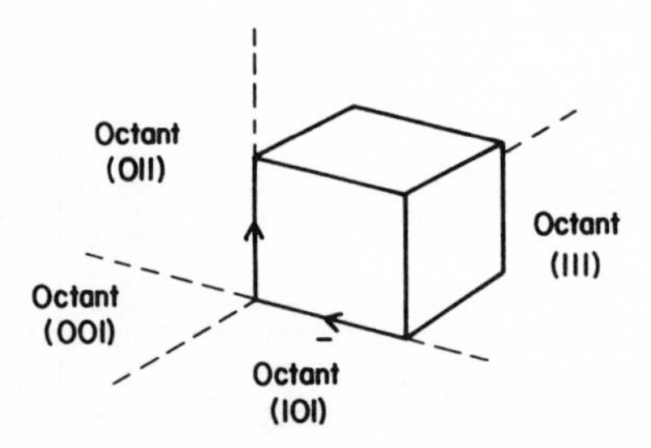

Then imagine the light source to be in each of the four octants.

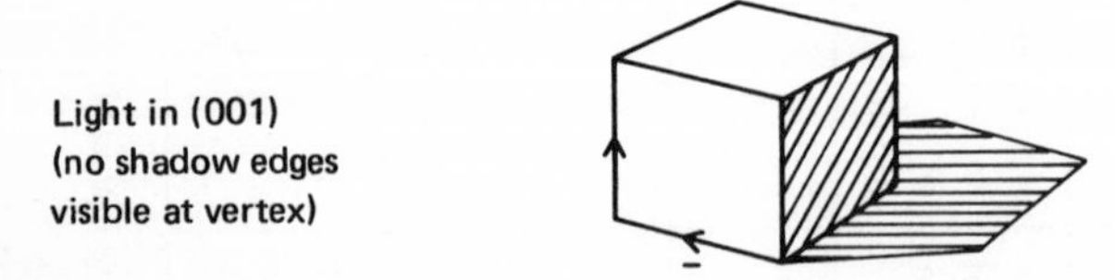

Fig. 2.10

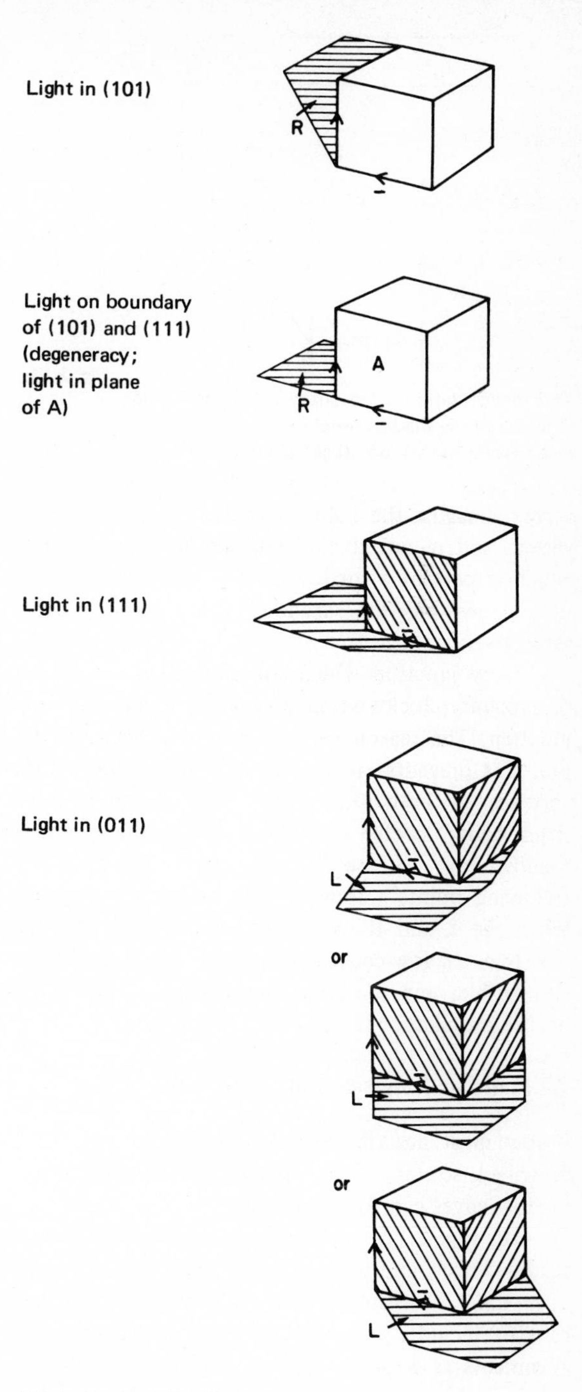

Fig. 2.10 *(continued)*

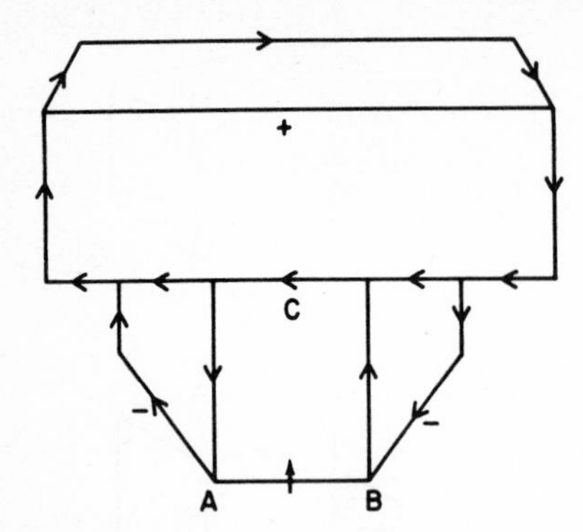

Fig. 2.11

This interpretation is prevented by adding L and R marks to the shadow junctions at A and B respectively so they no longer can match.

vertex, imagine the light source to be in each of the octants surrounding the vertex, and record all the resulting junctions. I have marked each shadow edge which is part of a shadow-causing junction with L or R, according to whether the arrow on the shadow edge points counterclockwise or clockwise respectively.

Any junction which contains either a clockwise shadow edge, marked R, or a counterclockwise shadow edge, marked L, is defined as a shadow-causing junction. The reason for distinguishing between the L and R shadow edges is that this prevents labeling an edge as if it were a shadow caused from both its vertexes. Without this device there would be no way to prevent Fig. 2.11 from being labeled as shown, with line segment L-A-B interpreted as a shadow edge. (I use L- as a prefix to mean "line segment(s) joining the following points"; thus L-A-B is the line segment joining points A and B.) When the L and R marks are attached to each shadow-causing junction, then the two shadow-causing junctions at A and B in Fig. 2.11 are no longer compatible, and therefore the labeling shown will not be considered possible by the program.

2.2.5 Other Nondegenerate Junctions

I now must describe vertexes which do not fall into the categories I have described so far. These include (1) all the rest of the combinations that shadow edges can form and (2) obscured edges.

In Fig. 2.12 I show all the other nondegenerate vertexes which involve shadow edges, and in Fig. 2.13 I show all the obscured edges.

Later I return to the topic of junction labels and show how it is possible to also include junctions representing common degeneracies and accidental alignments as well as junctions with missing lines. In the degenerate cases I do not include every labeling possibility; instead I include the most common

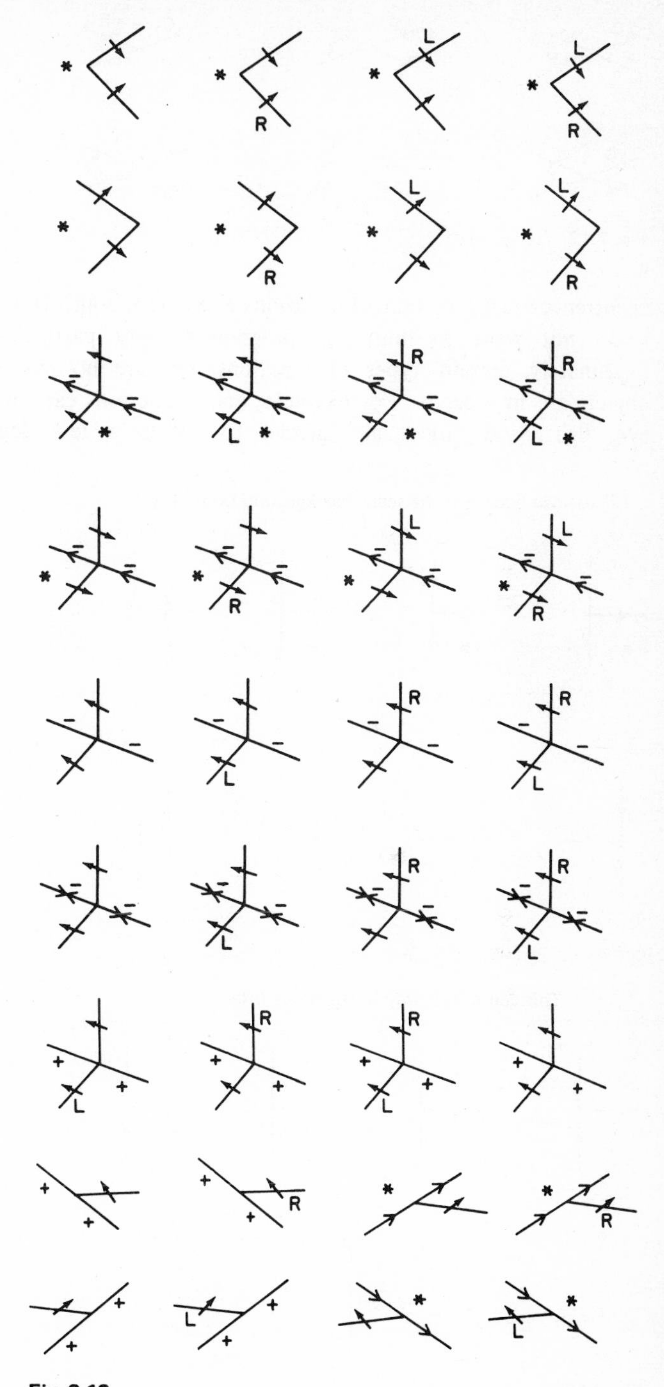

Fig. 2.12

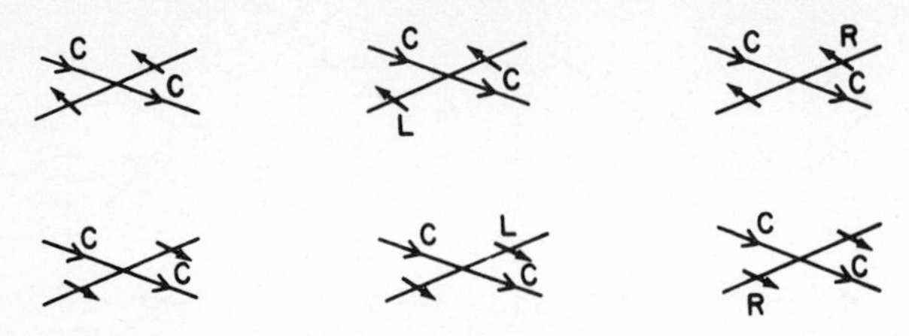

Fig. 2.12 *(continued)*

occurrences using certain observations about junctions. This is important since I do not want to limit the program to any particular set of objects. Fortunately certain types of junctions are rare no matter what types of objects are in a scene. For example, many junctions can only occur when the eye, light, and object are aligned to within a few degrees; when these

These can occur on the scene/background boundary.

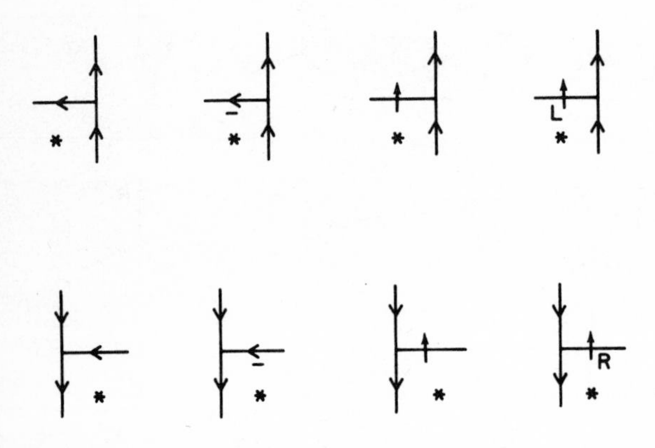

This can occur only in the scene interior.

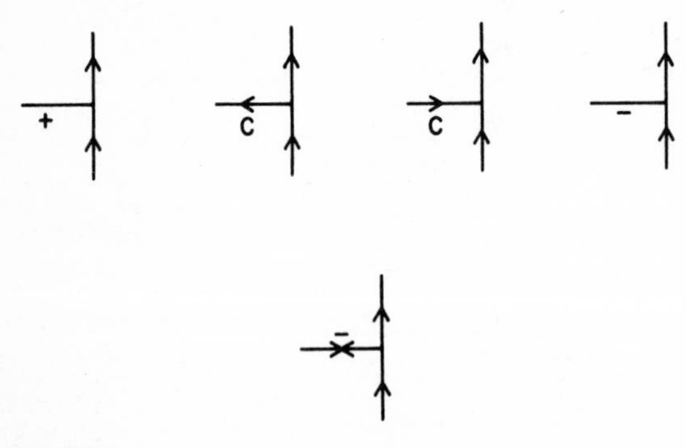

Fig. 2.13

junctions also contain unusual or aligned edges the combined likelihood of the junctions is low enough so that they can be safely omitted. It will be shown that the program can still give information about junctions even if they do not have proper labelings listed in the data base, provided that not too many of these occur together in a single scene. This approach is reasonable since any additional ability to use stereo images or to move the eye or range-finding ability will allow a program to disambiguate most of these types of features.

2.2.6 A Class of Degeneracies

As a final topic, I include one type of degeneracy which cannot be resolved by eye motion or stereo. This type of degeneracy results when the light source is placed in the plane defined by one of the faces of an object. In this case, shadows are aligned with edges to produce junctions which are unlabelable given only the normal set of labels described so far. Two examples of such alignment are shown in Fig. 2.14(*a*) and (*b*); all junctions of this type

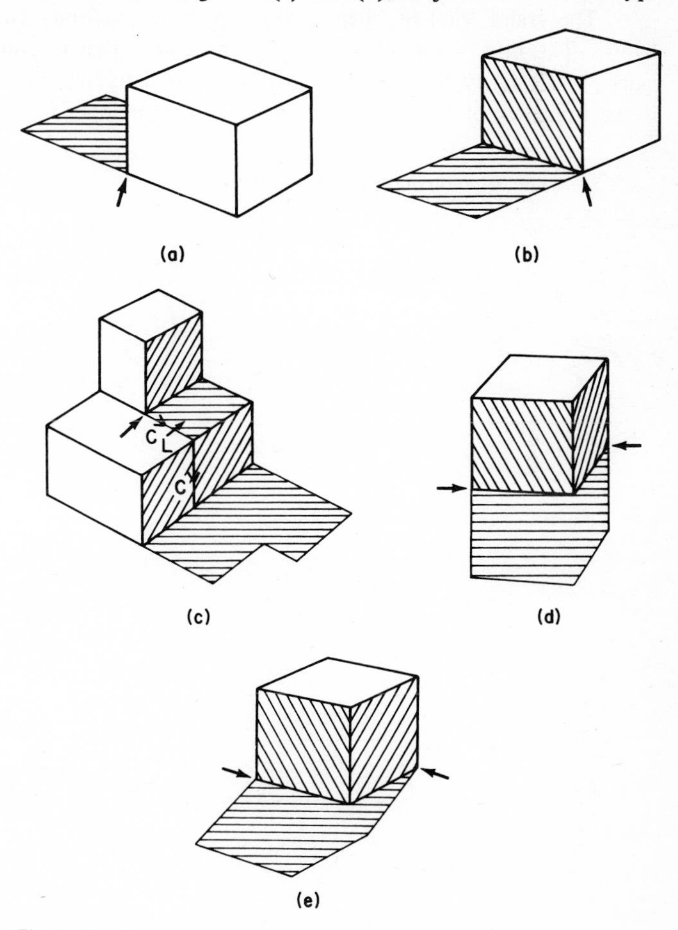

Fig. 2.14

are included in the data base except those cases where a shadow edge is projected directly onto an edge of some other type as in Fig. 2.14(*c*). These cases are excluded since they would require me to define new edge labels which are of very limited value, although there is no technical difficulty in defining such edges and junctions. I also have excluded, for the time being, cases like the one shown in Fig. 2.14(*d*), since the two junctions marked only appear to be T junctions when the eye is in the plane defined by the light source and the shadow-causing edge (L-A-B or L-C-D in Fig. 2.14(*d*). If the eye is moved to the right, the shadow-causing junctions change to ARROWs or FORKs as illustrated in Fig. 2.14(*e*). In contrast, notice that for the scenes shown in Figs. 2.14(*a*) and (*b*), no change in eye position can make any difference in the apparent geometry of the shadow-causing junctions.

Later I consider some of the common nontrihedral junctions which the program is likely to encounter. Some of these require me to define extra labels.

The grand total number of legal trihedral junctions listed in this section is 505. The interesting thing in my estimation is that the number of junction labels, while fairly large, is very small compared to the number of possibilities if the branches of these junctions were labeled independently; moreover, even

Some common nontrihedral vertexes

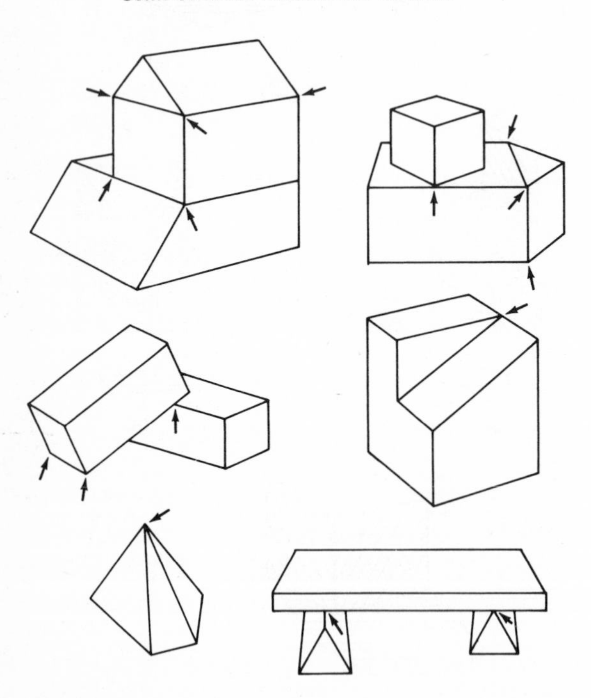

Fig. 2.15

though I have not yet shown how to include various degeneracies and alignments, the set I have described already is sufficient for most scenes which a person would construct out of plane-faced objects, provided that he did not set out to deliberately confuse the program.

Since it may not be obvious what types of common vertexes are nontrihedral, Fig. 2.15 contains a number of such vertexes. Later sections show how to handle all of them.

2.3 USING ILLUMINATION

It would be hard to devise a program which could start with a few pieces of information and eventually yield the list of junctions described in the last section. Moreover, even if such a program were written (which would indeed be theoretically interesting), it would be rather pointless to generate labels with it every time the labels are needed in an analysis. Instead the generating program could run once and save its results in a table. In this form the junction labelings table is a sort of compiled knowledge, computed once using a few general facts and methods. The knowledge in the current program is almost totally in this compiled form; this is the reason for its rapid operation, but I have paid a price for this speed in that I require a large amount of memory (about 14,000 words) to store the junction labelings. (All the rest of the labeling program occupies only about 4,000 words of memory even though it is written in MICRO-PLANNER and LISP, neither of which is particularly noted for space efficiency.)

2.3.1 Region Illumination Values

Each region can be labeled as belonging to one of the three following classes:

I–Illuminated directly by the light source.
SP–A projected shadow region; such a region would be illuminated if no object were between it and the light source.
SS–A self-shadowed region; such a region is oriented away from the light source.

Given these classes, I can define new edge labels which also include information about the lighting on both sides of the edge. Notice that in this way I can include at the edge level (a very local level) information which constrains all edges bounding the same two regions. Put another way, whenever a line can be assigned a single label which includes this lighting information, then a program has powerful constraints for the junctions which can appear around either of the regions which bound this line.

Figure 2.16 is made up of tables which relate the region illumination types which can occur on both sides of each edge type. For example, if either side of a concave or crack edge is illuminated, both sides of the edge must be illuminated.

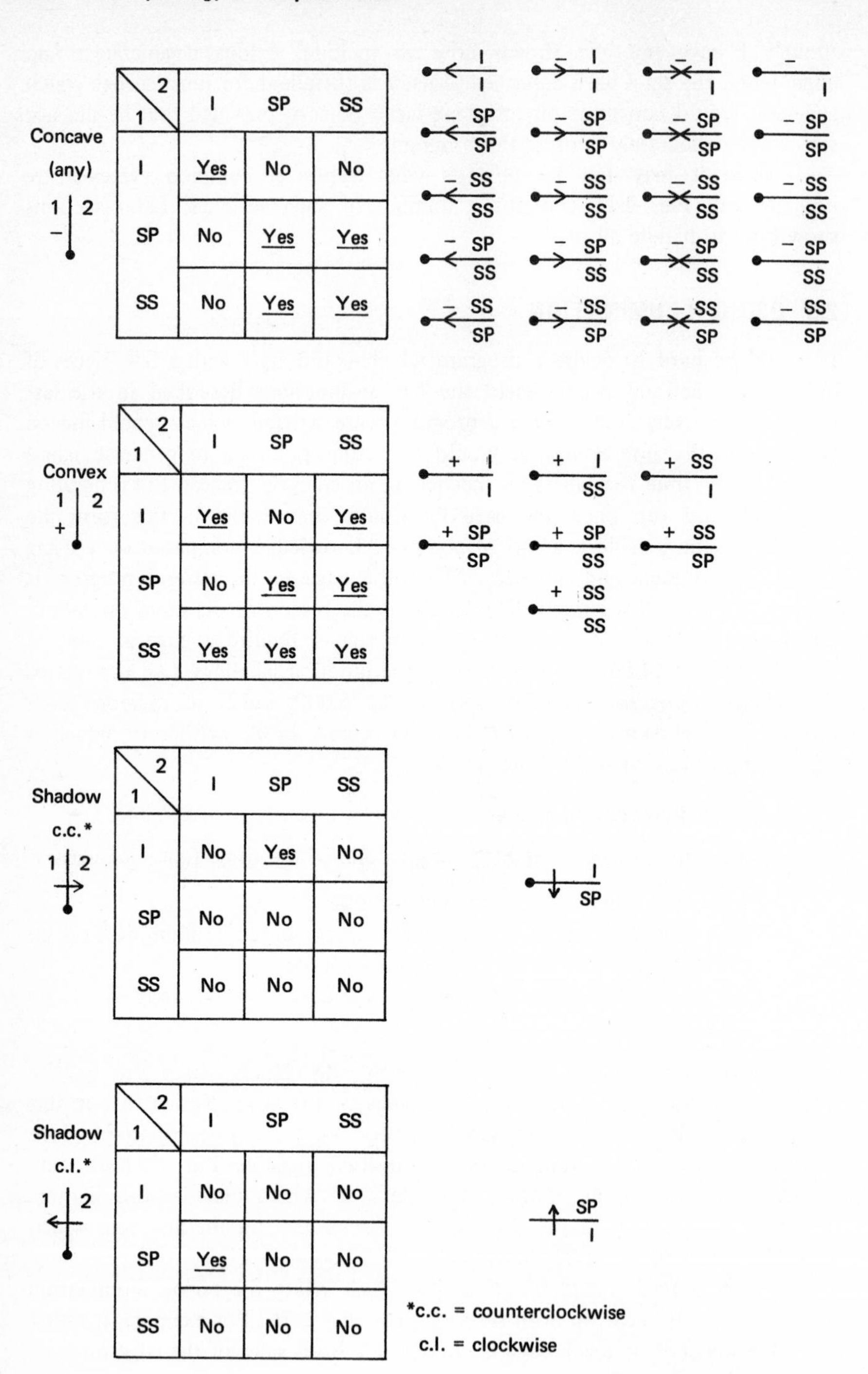

Concave (any)

1 \ 2	I	SP	SS
I	Yes	No	No
SP	No	Yes	Yes
SS	No	Yes	Yes

Convex

1 \ 2	I	SP	SS
I	Yes	No	Yes
SP	No	Yes	Yes
SS	Yes	Yes	Yes

Shadow c.c.*

1 \ 2	I	SP	SS
I	No	Yes	No
SP	No	No	No
SS	No	No	No

Shadow c.l.*

1 \ 2	I	SP	SS
I	No	No	No
SP	Yes	No	No
SS	No	No	No

Fig. 2.16

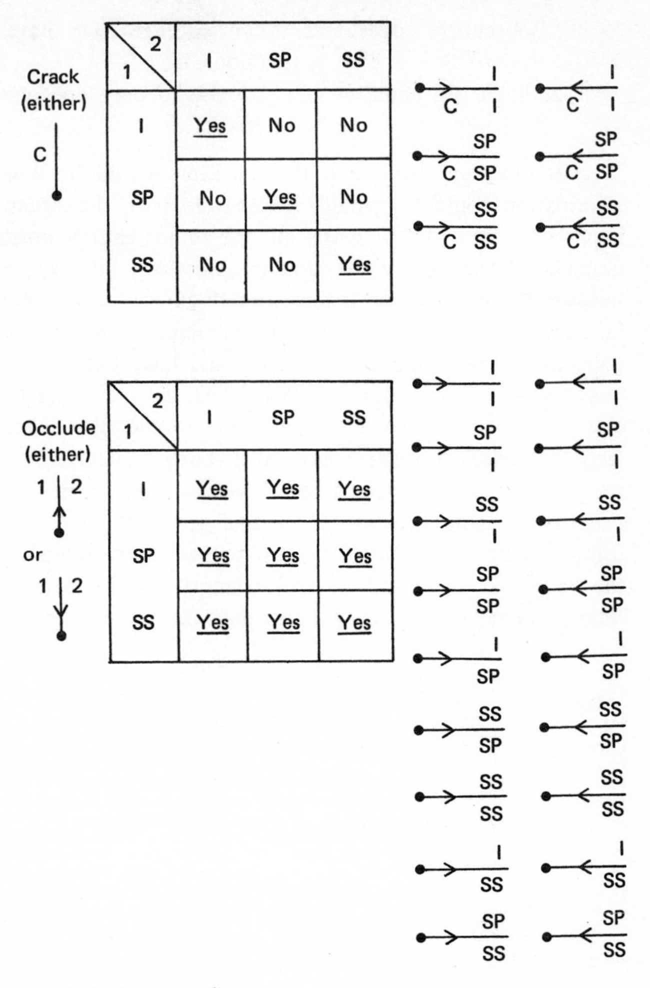

Crack (either)

1 \ 2	I	SP	SS
I	Yes	No	No
SP	No	Yes	No
SS	No	No	Yes

Occlude (either)

1 \ 2	I	SP	SS
I	Yes	Yes	Yes
SP	Yes	Yes	Yes
SS	Yes	Yes	Yes

Fig. 2.16 *(continued)*

These tables can be used to expand the set of allowable junction labels; the new set of labels can have a number of entries which have the same edge geometries but which have different region illumination values. It was very easy to write a program to expand the set of labelings; the principles of its operation are (1) each region in a given junction labeling can have only one illumination value of the three, and (2) the values on either side of each line of the junction must satisfy the restrictions in the tables of Fig. 2.16.

There are two extreme possibilities that this partitioning may have on the number of junction labelings now needed to describe all real vertexes:

1. Each old junction label which has n concave edges, m crack edges, p clockwise shadow edges, q counterclockwise shadow edges, s

obscuring edges and t convex edges will have to be replaced by $20^n 6^m 3^p 3^q 9^s 8^t$ new junctions, or

2. Each old junction will give rise to only one new junction (as in the shadow-causing junction cases).

If (1) were true then the partition would be worthless, since no new information could be gained. If (2) were true, the situation would be greatly improved, since in a sense all the much more precise information was implicitly included in the original junctions but was not explicitly stated. Because the information is now more explicitly stated, many matches between junctions can be precluded; for example, if in the old scheme some line segment L1 of junction label Q1 could have been labeled concave, as could line segment L2 of junction label Q2, a line joining these two junctions could have been labeled concave. But in the new scheme, if each junction label gives rise to a single new label, both L1 and L2 would take on one of the twenty possible values for a concave edge. Unless both L1 and L2 gave rise to the same new label, the line segment could not be labeled concave using Q1 and Q2. The truth lies somewhere between the two extremes, but the fact that it is not at the extreme of (1) means that there is a net improvement. In Fig. 2.17 I compare the number of labels before and after

Total number of labels in data base for each junction type		
Junction type	Number of labels before adding region illumination	Number of labels including region illumination
L	24	92
ARROW	24	86
T	91	623
FORK	116	826
PEAK	10	10
K	42	213
X	129	435
XX	40	128
MULTI	96	160
KA	20	20
KX	60	76
KXX	25	121
SPECIAL	40	466
Totals	717	3,256

Fig. 2.17

1 | 2

Background | Scene

Can be labeled only in one of the following ways:

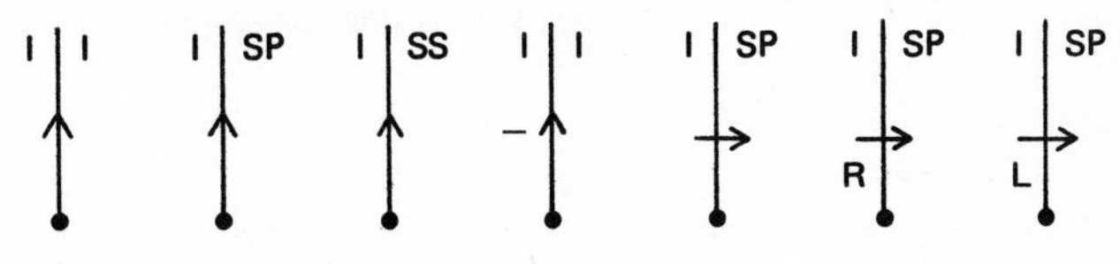

Fig. 2.18

adding region illumination information. Although there are 505 distinct labelings before adding illumination, the actual total number of labels shown in larger. This is because different permutations of labels count as different elements in some of the label lists for the junctions. The total number of list elements needed to represent the 505 labelings is 717, and this number expands to 3,256 when the region illumination information is added to the labelings.

I have also used the better descriptions to express the restriction that each scene is assumed to be on a horizontal table which has no holes in it and which is large enough to fill the retina. This means that any line segment which separates the background (table) from the rest of the scene can only be labeled as shown in Fig. 2.18, Because of this fact the number of junction labels which could be used to label junctions on the scene/background boundary can be greatly restricted.

2.3.2 Labeling Junctions with Illumination

Given tables of allowable region illumination values (Fig. 2.16), it is easy to show how to write a program which expands the data base to include this information.

In order to include illumination information in the data base, I merely append the region illumination value names to the name of each label. Thus I subdivide each label type (except shadow edge labels) into a number of possibilities. Expanding the number of line labels does not increase the total number of junction labels as much as one might imagine. (See Fig. 2.17.) The largest possible number of illumination interpretations for any junction is 3^n, where n is the number of junction branches. A number of T junctions actually have 27 interpretations (for example, this is true of any T made up of three occluding edges).

A little cleverness is required to avoid duplicate labelings when including the different permutations of X junctions. This is because some X junctions give rise to two elements in the X labelings list, while the rest add only one element. Figure 2.19(*b*) shows an X junction which requires two elements to

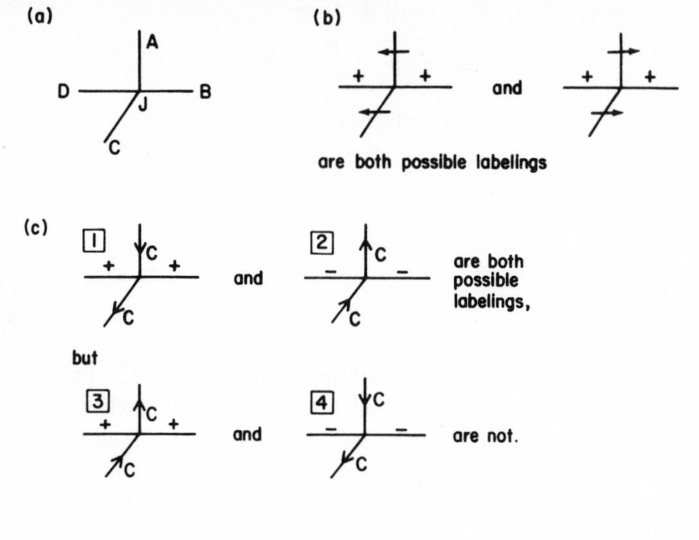

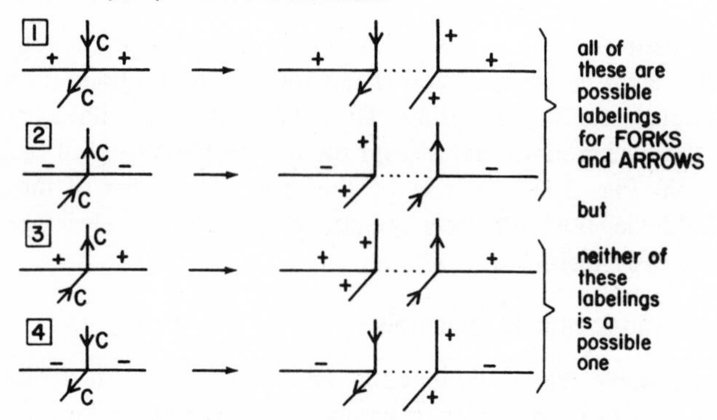

Fig. 2.19

be added to the list, while Fig. 2.19(*c*) shows two labelings which each add only one element to the data base. Most shadow X junctions give rise to two elements in the data base, and most junctions without shadows give rise to one.

It is now possible to describe how the program handles each junction it encounters:

1. If the junction is an L, ARROW, T, K, PEAK, X, KX, or KXX, it uniquely orders the junction's line segments (by choosing a particular line segment and considering the rest as ordered in a clockwise direction from this line segment).
2. If the junction is a FORK, MULTI, or XX, it chooses one line segment arbitrarily.

3. It then fetches a list of labels which contains every possible set of assignments for the lines (excluding the possibilities of accidental alignments and degeneracies and junctions with missing lines) and associates this list with the junction.

It makes absolutely no difference whether the program obtains this list from a table (the compiled knowledge case) or whether it must perform extensive computations to generate the list (the generated knowledge case). Similarly, it does not matter at all that various members of the list bear a particular relation to each other, e.g., as in the case of a FORK junction, where most elements of the list have two other elements which are permutations of the element. When I return to the issues of degeneracies, accidental alignments and missing lines, all I need to show is how the labelings corresponding to these cases can be added to the appropriate junction lists. The machinery to choose a particular element operates independently of just what the labelings actually are.

2.4 SELECTION RULES

Now that I have shown how to generate a large number of possible labels for a junction, I will show how to go about eliminating all but one of them. The strategy for doing this involves:

1. Using selection rules to eliminate as many labels as possible on the basis of relatively local information such as region brightness or line segment directions.
2. Using the main portion of the program to remove labels which cannot be part of any total scene labeling.

2.4.1 Region Brightness

If I know only that line segment L-A-B is a line in a scene, then it can theoretically be assigned any of the 57 possible labels. Once I know that L-A-B has an ARROW at one of its ends as shown in Fig. 2.20(*b*), the number of possibilities drops to 19. Suppose that I know, in addition, the relative brightness of R1 and R2 in the neighborhood of L-A-B in Fig. 2.20(*c*). There are three possibilities:

1. R1 is darker than R2,
2. R2 is darker than R1, or
3. the brightness of R1 is equal to the brightness of R2.

If (1) is true, I know for certain that if L-A-B is a shadow edge, then R1 must be the shadowed side and R2 the illuminated side. Obviously if (2) is true, then the opposite holds, i.e., R2 must be the shadowed side and R1 must be the illuminated side. If (3) is true, then it is impossible for L-A-B to be a shadow edge at all. (If I happen to also know that each object in a scene has all its faces painted identically with a nonreflective finish, then I can also

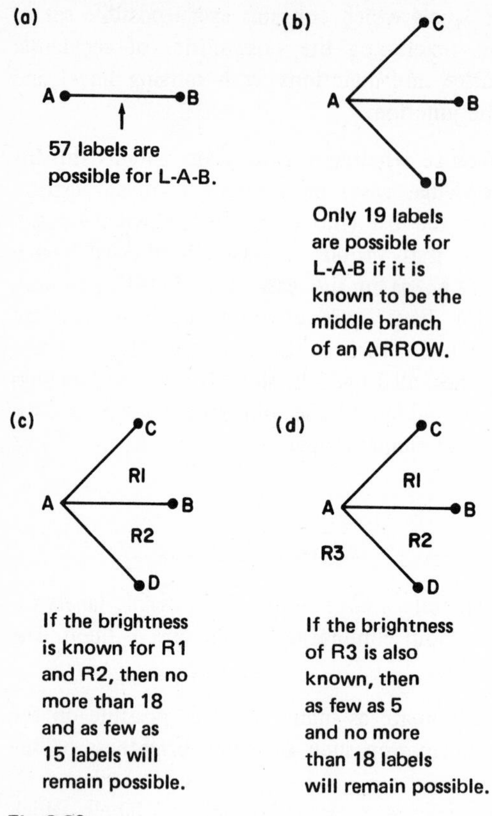

Fig. 2.20

eliminate more labels. In this case, if (1) is true, then L-A-B cannot be labeled as a convex edge with region R1 illuminated and R2 shadowed type SS; if (2) is true, then L-A-B cannot be labeled as convex with R2 illuminated and R1 shadowed type SS, and if (3) is true, then neither of these labels is possible.)

2.4.2 Scene/Background Boundary Revisited

It is easy to find all the junctions which can occur around the scene/background boundary. All that is necessary is to make a list of all the line segments which can occur along the boundary and then look for segments of junctions which are bounded by two members of this set.

Junctions which can occur on the scene/background boundary are listed separately from junctions which have the same geometry but which cannot occur on the scene/background boundary. Thus the list of ARROW labels is divided into ARROW-B, a list made up of those labels which can occur on the scene/background boundary, and ARROW-I, made up of those which

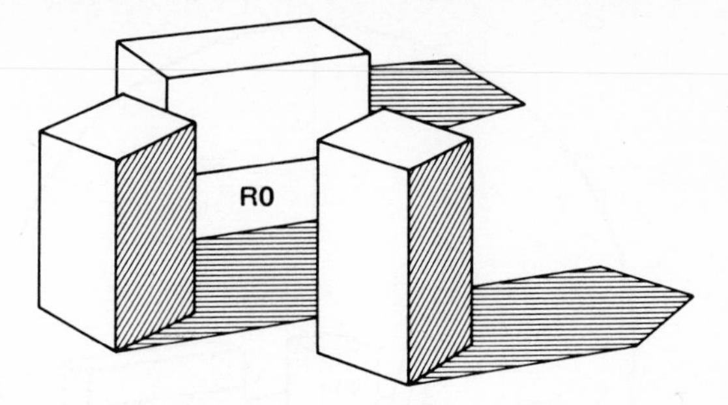

The same junctions and edges can border R0 as can appear on the scene/background boundary.

Fig. 2.21

must occur on the interior of a scene. The total list of junctions which can also appear in the interior of a scene is found by appending ARROW-B to ARROW-I, since the scene/background labelings can appear on the interior of the scene as shown in Fig. 2.21. Figure 2.22 lists the number of trihedral junction labels which can occur on the interior and on the scene/background

Fig. 2.22

	Total number of trihedral junction labelings which can appear on	
Type of junction	The interior of a scene	The scene/background boundary
L	92	16
ARROW	86	12
T	623	96
FORK	826	26
PEAK	10	2
K	213	2
X	435	72
XX	128	3
MULTI	160	8
KA	20	-
KX	76	8
KXX	121	-
SPECIAL	466	-
Totals	3,256	245

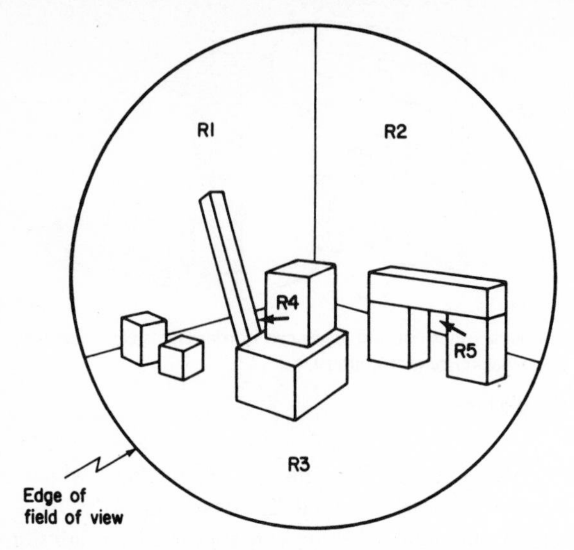

By appending all the regions which touch the edge of the field of view, we obtain all of the background except the small regions R4 and R5. By finding and continuing collinear obscured line segments (Guzman's matched Ts) these regions can be found and added to the background also.

Fig. 2.23

boundary for each type of junction. The assumption that the light source is positioned in one of the four octants of space above the support surface guarantees that the background is an illuminated region.

Obviously, if I can determine which lines in the line drawing are part of the scene/background boundary, this knowledge can be used to great advantage. It is, in fact, not difficult to determine this boundary; any of several strategies will work. Two examples are: (1) look for regions which touch the edge of the field of view and append them all together, or (2) find the contour which has the property that every junction lies on or inside it.[5]

Both of these methods require that the scene be completely surrounded by the background region or regions. As shown in Fig. 2.23, method (1) works even if the background is made up of more than one region.

Once the program has found which region is the background region, it can also find how each junction is oriented on the scene/background boundary. Some junctions always appear in the same orientation; for example, ARROW and PEAK junctions can only be oriented so that the background region is the region whose angle is greater than 180 degrees, and K junctions can only have the region whose angle is 180 degrees as the background region.

Of course there is no way to easily define the orientations of FORK, XX, or MULTI junctions. However, as shown in Fig. 2.24, the L, T, X and

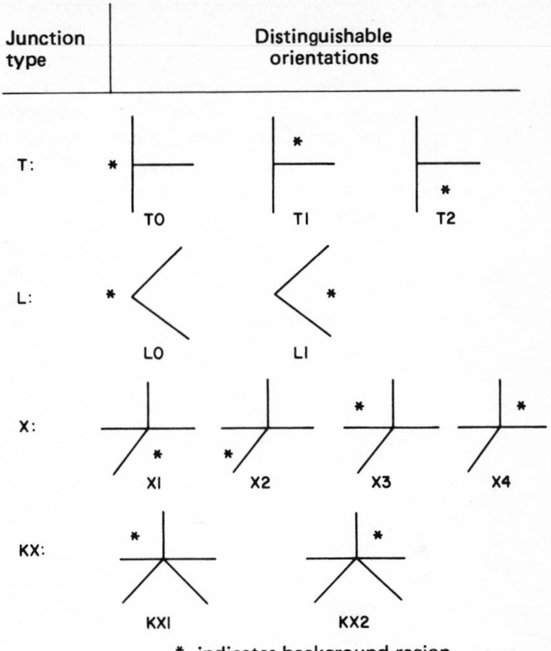

Fig. 2.24

KX junctions which appear on the scene/background boundary can be sorted according to which of their segments is the background region.

Consider Fig. 2.25. Each of the L, T, and X junctions is marked to indicate which orientation it has. Figure 2.26 shows that this distinction makes a significant reduction in the size of the starting list of label assignments for these junctions.

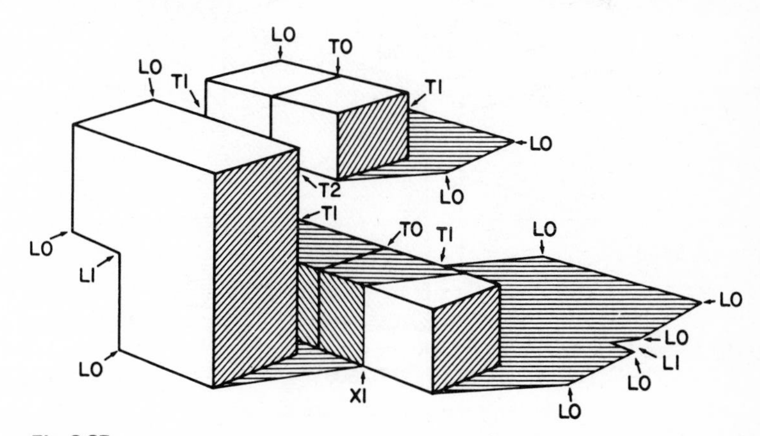

Fig. 2.25

	Number of labelings if in the scene interior	Number of labelings if on the scene/ background boundary	Number if on scene/ background boundary and orientations distinguished
T:	623	96	–
T0:	*	–	14
T1:	*	–	38
T2:	*	–	38
L:	92	16	–
L0:	*	–	9
L1:	*	–	7
X:	435	72	–
X1:	*	–	8
X2:	*	–	28
X3:	*	–	28
X4:	*	–	8
KX:	76	8	–
KX1:	*	–	4
KX2:	*	–	4

*There is no way to distinguish a preferred orientation in the interior of the scene.

Fig. 2.26

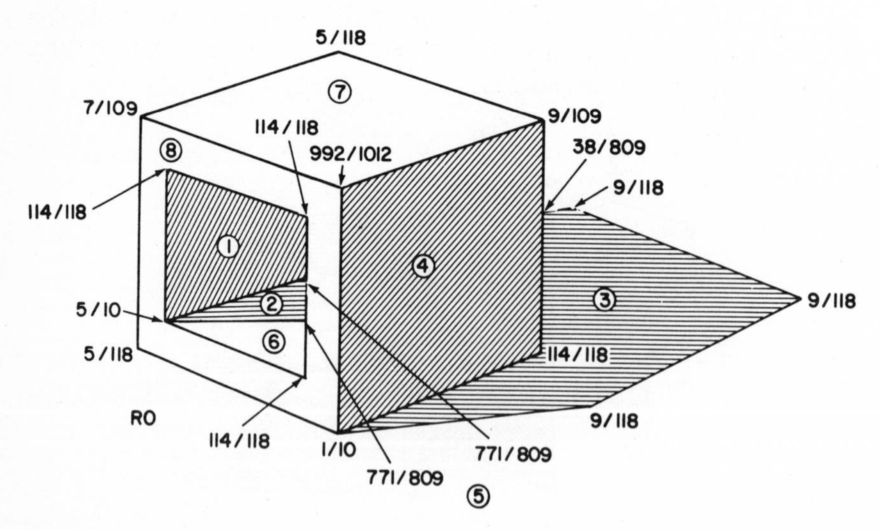

Fig. 2.27

2.4.3 An Example

I have now shown how to use selection rules to narrow down the choices for junction labels on the basis of various kinds of cues from the line drawing. To give an idea of how much these rules help, look at Fig. 2.27. Next to each junction I have listed the numbers of labels which are possible for it before and after applying the selection rules. I have assumed that the program knows that R0 is the support surface and that the circled numbers in each region indicate the relative brightness (the higher a number, the brighter the region). Notice that one junction, the peak on the scene/background boundary, can be uniquely labeled using only selection rules. Most of the interior junctions remain highly ambiguous.

2.5 THE MAIN LABELING PROGRAM

You will recall that I described at some length a "filter program" which systematically removes junction labels whenever there are no possible matches for the labels at adjacent junctions. Now that I have shown a good deal more about the junction labels and the use of the selection rules, I would like to treat this program again from a somewhat different perspective.

2.5.1 An Example

Suppose that the program is working on a scene, a portion of which is shown in Fig. 2.28. Assume that the selection rules eliminate all labels for each type of junction except those shown at the bottom of the figure. Remember that the selection rules operate only locally, i.e., they give the same list of possibilities no matter how the labeling has proceeded or in what order the junctions are taken. All the step numbers refer to Fig. 2.29, which summarizes the successive lists attached to each junction:

Step 1 Suppose that the program starts with J2, and that all of the other junctions are unlabeled. Then the program assigns list L2 to J2, and since all the other junctions are unlabeled, it has no basis on which to eliminate any of the labels in L2. As far as the program knows, all of these labelings are still possible.

Step 2 Now suppose that it next labels J1 by attaching to it the list L1. When it checks the junctions adjacent to J1 it now can see that J2 has already been labeled.

Step 3 Therefore the program looks at J2 to find what restrictions, if any, have already been placed on line segment L-J1-J2. In this case, the restrictions are that L-J1-J2 must be labeled with either B or C or A or D or F, i.e., with any letter which appears third in an element of L2. Each element of L1 which does not have B, C, A, D, or F as its first letter can then be eliminated. Therefore the program drops (G H), (E A) and (E B) as possibilities and L1 becomes

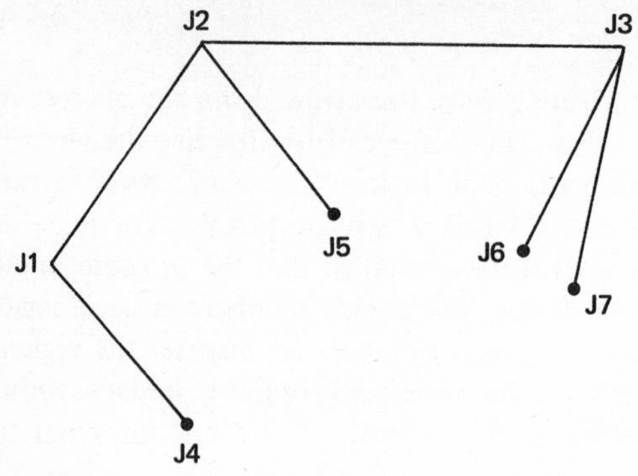

Results of selection rules for J1. (first element of each labeling refers to L-J1-J2, second to L-J1-J4)	Results of selection rules for J2. (first element refers to L-J2-J3, second to L-J2-J5, third to L-J2-J1)	Results of selection rules for J3. (first element refers to L-J3-J7, second to L-J3-J6, third to L-J3-J2)
L1 = ((A. B)	L2 = ((A B B)	L3 = ((A B A)
(A C)	(A B C)	(B C A)
(A D)	(B C A)	(G H I)
(B B)	(F A D)	(F B C)
(B E)	(D B F))	(D B F)
(C F)		(A B E)
(F A)		(D C E))
(G H)		
(E A)		
(E B))		

Fig. 2.28

((A B) (A C) (A D) (B B) (B E) (C F) (F A))

Step 4 Now the program uses this same reasoning in the opposite direction. In what ways, if any, does the fact that J1 must be labeled from the list restrict the labels of adjacent junctions? Only J2 of the adjacent junctions has been labeled so far, so only J2 can be affected. The only labels which are possible for J2 are those elements of L2 which have as a third letter A or B or C or F. Therefore, the program eliminates (F A D) as a possible label and L2 becomes

((A B B) (A B C) (B C A) (D B F))

Can the program eliminate any other labels because (F A D) has been eliminated? No, since no other neighbors of J2 except J1 have been labeled, and the reason (F A D) was eliminated was because it had no counterpart at J1.

Step 5 The program now can move on to J3 and label it with L3.

Step 6 Each label for J3 must have a third letter equal to one of the first letters from a label in L2. These letters are A, B and D. Therefore the program eliminates (G H I), (F B C), (D B F), (A B E) and (D C G) from L3 and sets L3 to

	Labels assigned to		
	L1	L2	L3
Start	–	–	–
Step 1	–	((ABB)(ABC) (BCA)(FAD) (DBF))	–
Step 2	((AB)(AC)(AD) (BB)(BE)(CF) (FA)(GH)(EA) (EB))	(unchanged)	–
Step 3	((AB)(AC)(AD) (BB)(BE)(CF) (FA))	(unchanged)	–
Step 4	(unchanged)	((ABB)(ABC) (BCA)(DBF))	–
Step 5	(unchanged)	(unchanged)	((ABA)(BCA) (GHI)(FBC) (DBF)(ABE) (DCE))
Step 6	(unchanged)	(unchanged)	((ABA)(BCA))
Step 7	(unchanged)	((ABB)(ABC))	(unchanged)
Step 8	((BB)(BE)(CF))	(unchanged)	(unchanged)
	No more labelings can be eliminated		
Final Result	((BB)(BE)(CF))	((ABB)(ABC))	((ABA)(BCA))
Time			

Fig. 2.29

((A B A) (B C A))

Step 7 What labels now are possible for J2? Since the only remaining labels for J3 both set L-J2-J3 to A, the program eliminates (B C A) and (D B F) from L2 so that L2 becomes

((A B B) (A B C))

Step 8 This time, a neighbor of J2, namely J1, has been labeled already, so the program must check to see whether eliminating the element of L2 has placed further restrictions on L1. Only elements of L1 which have a first letter B or C are possible labels now, so the program eliminates (A B), (A C), (A D), and (F A). L1 thus becomes

((B B) (B E) (C F))

Since no other neighbors of J1 are labeled, the effects of this change cannot propagate any further.

2.5.2 Discussion

I think it is easiest to view the process of the program at each junction as having three actions:

1. attaching labels,
2. removing any of these labels which are impossible given the current context of this junction, and
3. iteratively removing labelings from the context by allowing the new restrictions embodied in the list of labels for the junction to propagate outward from the junction until no more changes in the context can be made.

There are two points of importance:

1. The solution the program finds is the same no matter where it begins in the scene, and
2. the program is guaranteed to be finished after one pass through the junctions, where it performs the three actions listed above at each junction.

Given a line drawing with N junctions, a data base which has no more than M possible labelings for any junction, and a situation where any number of junctions from 0 to N have already been labeled, let condition C be one where for each possible line label which can be assigned to a line segment either

1. there is at least one matching line label assigned to the junction at the other end of this line segment, or else
2. the junction at the other end of the line segment has not been labeled.

Condition C must be satisfied before the program moves on to a new junction; the program keeps track of the line segments on which the condition may not be satisfied.

When the program begins labeling a junction J, assume that C holds throughout the line drawing. When the junction, previously unlabeled, has labels added, the only line segments along which C can be violated are the line segments which join J to its neighbors, and it is possible for C to be unsatisfied in both directions on these segments (i.e., both J and J's neighbors may have unmatched line labels). Therefore, to make sure that the program needs to consider each line segment a minimum number of times, the program first uses the lists of possible labels specified by J's neighbors to eliminate all impossible labels from J.

To see why this is the correct way to proceed, suppose that the program used J's initial set of labels to eliminate some labels from one of J's neighbors, J1. It is then possible that the set of labels for J can be reduced further because neighbor J2 has no match for one or more labels still attached to J. The program would then have to go back to line L-J-J1 again to see whether more labels could be eliminated from J1. By considering the effects of each of J's neighbors on J's labels first, the program guarantees that as many labels as possible have been eliminated from J's label list before using this list to recompute the lists for J's neighbors.

Condition C can now only be untrue along line segments joining J with its neighbors and, moreover, can only be untrue in one direction, i.e., J's neighbors may have unmatched labels, but not vice versa. When the program eliminates the unmatched labels from each of J's neighbors, C is now satisfied on each line segment joining J to its neighbors and C can only be unsatisfied along the line segments joining J's neighbors with the neighbors of J's neighbors, and again only in an "outward" direction, i.e., the junctions two line segments away from J can have unmatched labels, but all those junctions one line segment away (J's neighbors) cannot have unmatched labels.

The line segments on which C does not hold continue to spread outward to the neighbors of junctions two segments away from J, then junctions three segments away from J, etc., but only as long as labels are being removed from any junctions. As soon as the program reaches a step where no labels are removed from any junction, then the program knows that condition C must be satisfied everywhere in the scene, and it can move on to the next unlabeled junction.

The violations of C can spread outward to eventually touch any line segment of a line drawing, but only if the number of labels can be reduced at each junction on some path between the junction the program is currently labeling and the line segment.

One final point: the process is guaranteed to terminate, since if there are N junctions and no more than M labels possible for any one junction, the process can never go on for more than M × N steps at the very worst. This is important since the restrictions can propagate back to the junction which initiated the process. To see that the possibility of cycles does not create any difficulties, consider the following trick. Suppose that as soon as the starting junction has been checked against each of its neighbors, that all the remaining labels are removed from it. The restrictions can then spread outward only until no more changes can be made; now look at the process as though the junction were being labeled for the first time with the set of junctions just removed as its starting junction set. This process can then be repeated as often as necessary, but the number of times can never be greater than the initial number of labelings assigned to the junction, since the process terminates if no more labels can be removed from the list of possibilities.

2.5.3 Control Structure

While the program can start at any junction and still arrive at the same solution, the amount of time required to understand a scene does depend on the order in which the junctions are labeled. The basic heuristic for speeding up the program is to eliminate as many possibilities as early as possible. Two techniques which help accomplish this end are to

1. label all the junctions on the scene/background boundary first, since these have many fewer interpretations than interior junctions do, and
2. next label all junctions which bound regions that share an edge or junction with the background.

I mentioned at the beginning of this paper that the amount of time (and therefore computation) is roughly proportional to the number of line segments in a scene. This may not seem to fit with the obvious fact that there is really nothing to prevent the effects caused by labeling a single junction to propagate to every portion of a line drawing.

There are good physical reasons why this seldom happens. The basic reason is that some junctions simply do not propagate effects to all their neighbors, and so the effects tend to die out before getting too far. The prime type of junction which stifles the spreading effects is the T junction.

In most T junctions, the labelings of the upright and crossbar portions are independent. Even if we know the exact labeling of the crossbar portion we are unlikely to be able to draw any conclusions about the labeling of the upright and vice versa. Since objects are most commonly separated by T junctions, the effects of labeling a junction are for the most part limited to the object of which the junction is a part and to the object's shadow edges, if any.

Another reason why effects do not propagate far is that when junctions are unlabeled or when they are uniquely labeled, they do not propagate effects at all. Thus when few junctions are labeled and when most junctions are labeled the effects of adding restrictions tend to be localized.

2.5.4 Program Performance

The program portions I have now described are adequate for labeling scenes without accidental alignments, nontrihedral vertexes or missing lines. Within this range there are still certain types of features which confuse the program, but before showing its limits, I will show some of its complete successes. In all the scenes which follow, I assume that the program knows which region is the background region, and that it also knows the relative brightness of various regions. The program operates nearly as well without these facts but not as rapidly. Figure 2.30 shows a number of scenes for which the program produces unique labelings or is only confused about the illumination type of one or two regions as in Fig. 2.30(*d*) and (*i*). By varying some of the region brightness values or omitting them, the program could also be confused in a similar way about the tops of objects in Fig. 2.30(*a*), (*b*), (*e*), (*g*), and (*h*). In general, the program is not particularly good at finding the illumination types

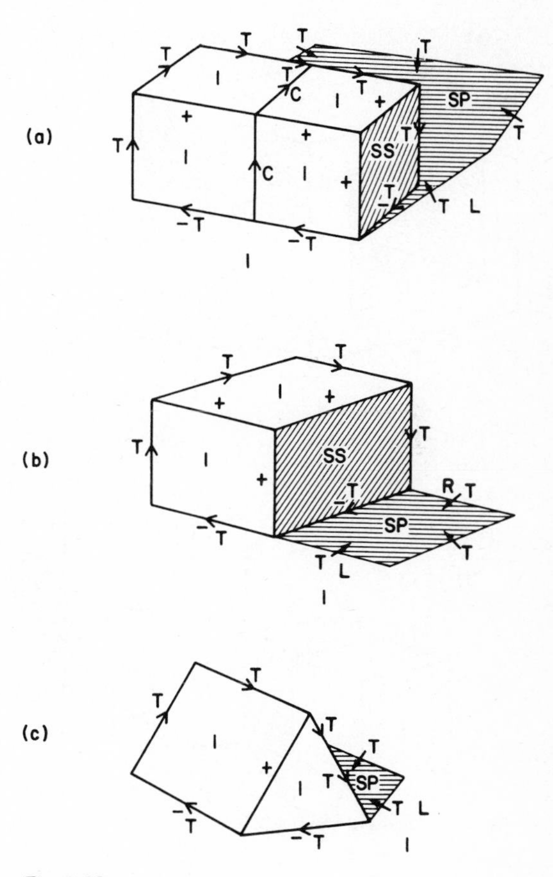

Fig. 2.30

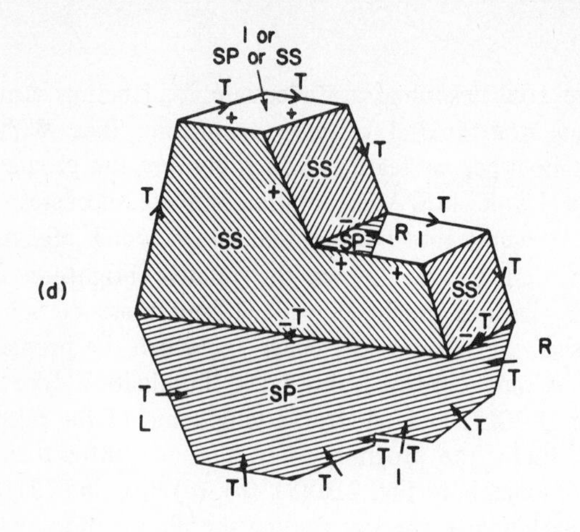

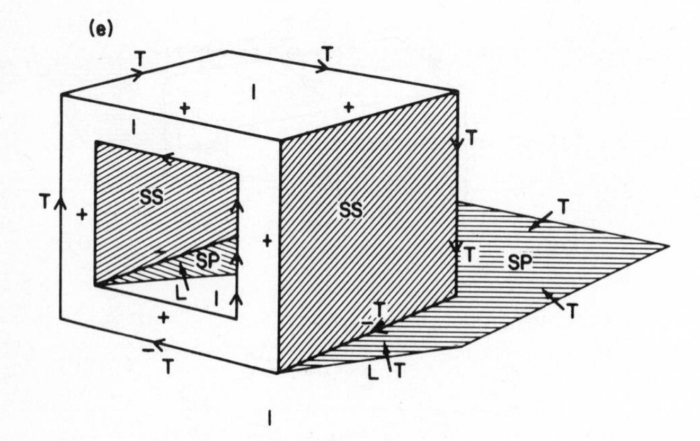

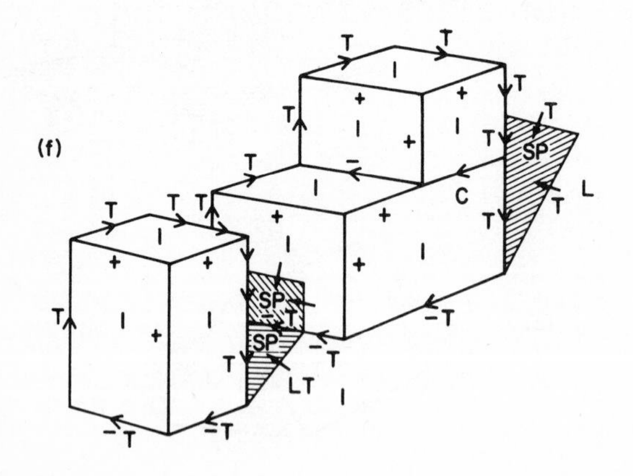

Fig. 2.30 *(continued)*

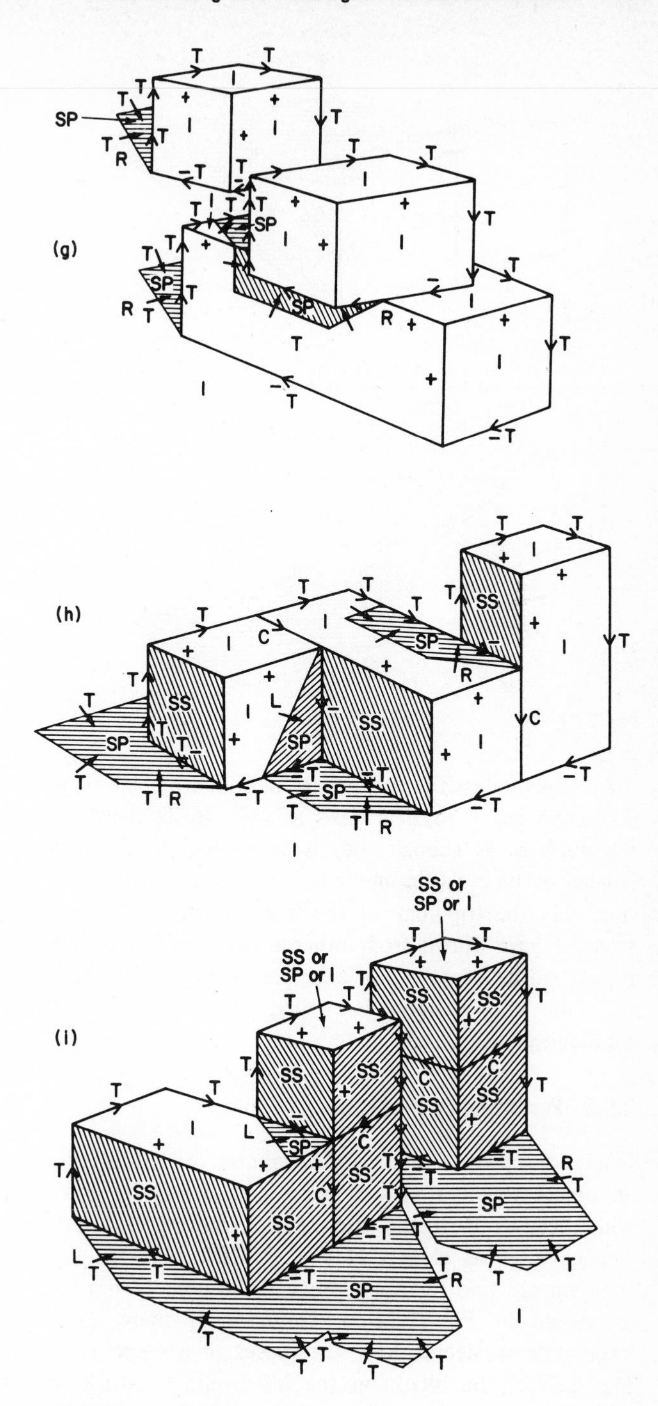

Fig. 2.30 *(continued)*

(a)

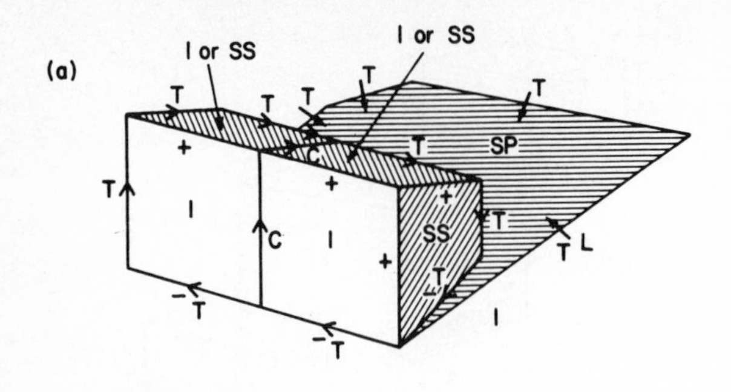

(b)

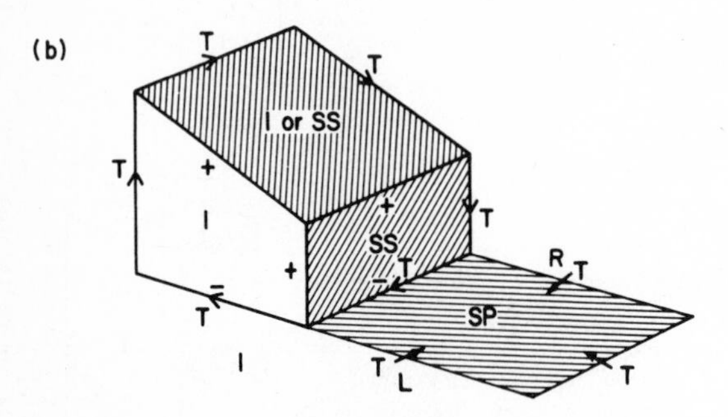

Fig. 2.31

for regions unless the regions are bounded by one or more concave edges. This confusion has a physical basis as well. In all these diagrams I have drawn the top surfaces as though they were parallel to the table so they all should be labeled as type I (illuminated), but since the program I have described so far uses only the topology of the line drawings, it has no way to distinguish the scenes I have drawn from other topologically equivalent scenes which should be labeled differently. For example, in Fig. 2.31 I have redrawn (*a*) and (*b*) so that the top surfaces are type SS (self-shadowed), but the figures are topologically identical.

2.5.5 Performance Problems

Shadows convey a considerable amount of information about which edges of an object touch a surface since a shadow edge can only intersect the edge which causes it if the surface the shadow is cast on touches the shadow-causing edge as shown in Fig. 2.32(*a*). As long as shadows are present, a program can find relations between the objects in a scene and the background, as shown in Fig. 2.32(*b*). However, if there are no shadows, then it is impossible to decide how the pieces of a scene are related. For example, in Fig. 2.32(*c*) the block on the left could be stuck to a wall, or sitting on a table, or sitting on a smaller block which suspends it off the table; there is simply no way to tell which of these cases is the true one given only a shadow-free line drawing. Moreover, the program does not use (at this point) knowledge of the line segment directions in a scene, so it cannot even distinguish which way is up. If you turn Fig. 2.32(*c*) about one-third of a turn clockwise, there is a reasonable interpretation of the two blocks where A is supported by B. Without line segment direction information the program finds all these interpretations in the absence of shadows.

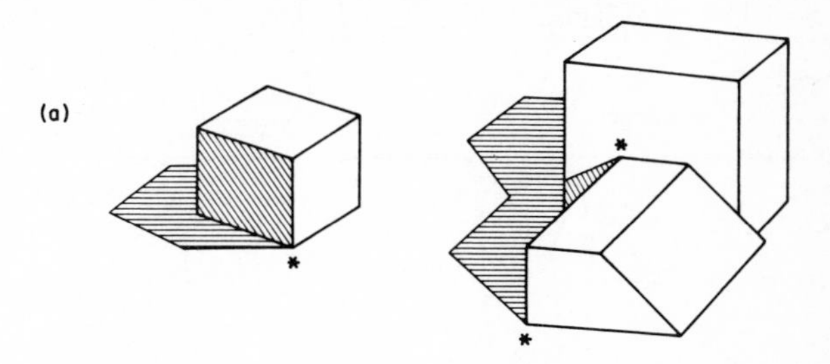

In these scenes the starred junctions provide evidence the two objects or the object and table *touch:*

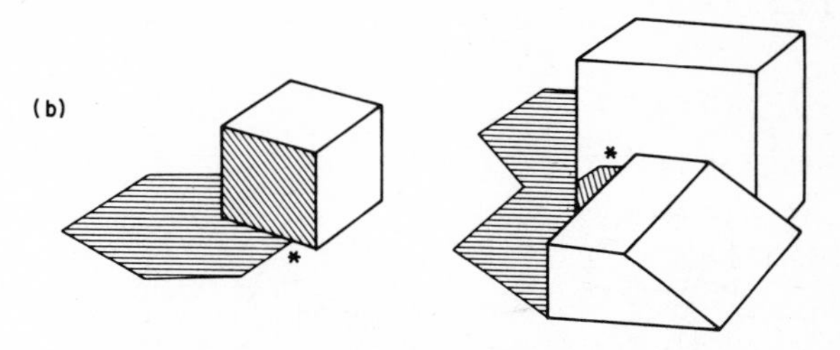

In these scenes the starred junctions provide evidence that the two objects or the object and table *do not touch.*

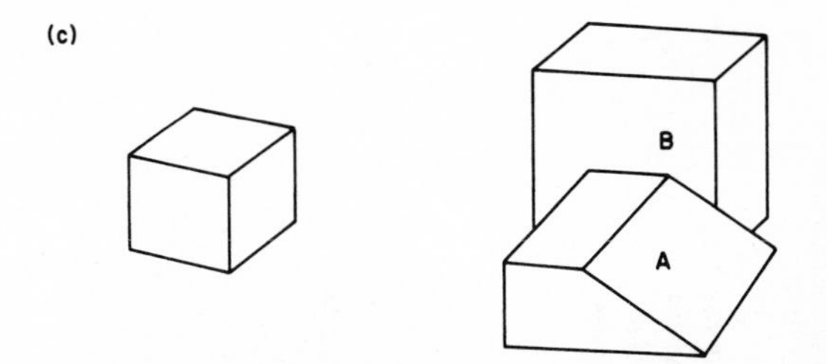

In these scenes there is no evidence to use to relate the objects to each other or to the table; it is not possible to decide whether they touch or not.

Fig. 2.32

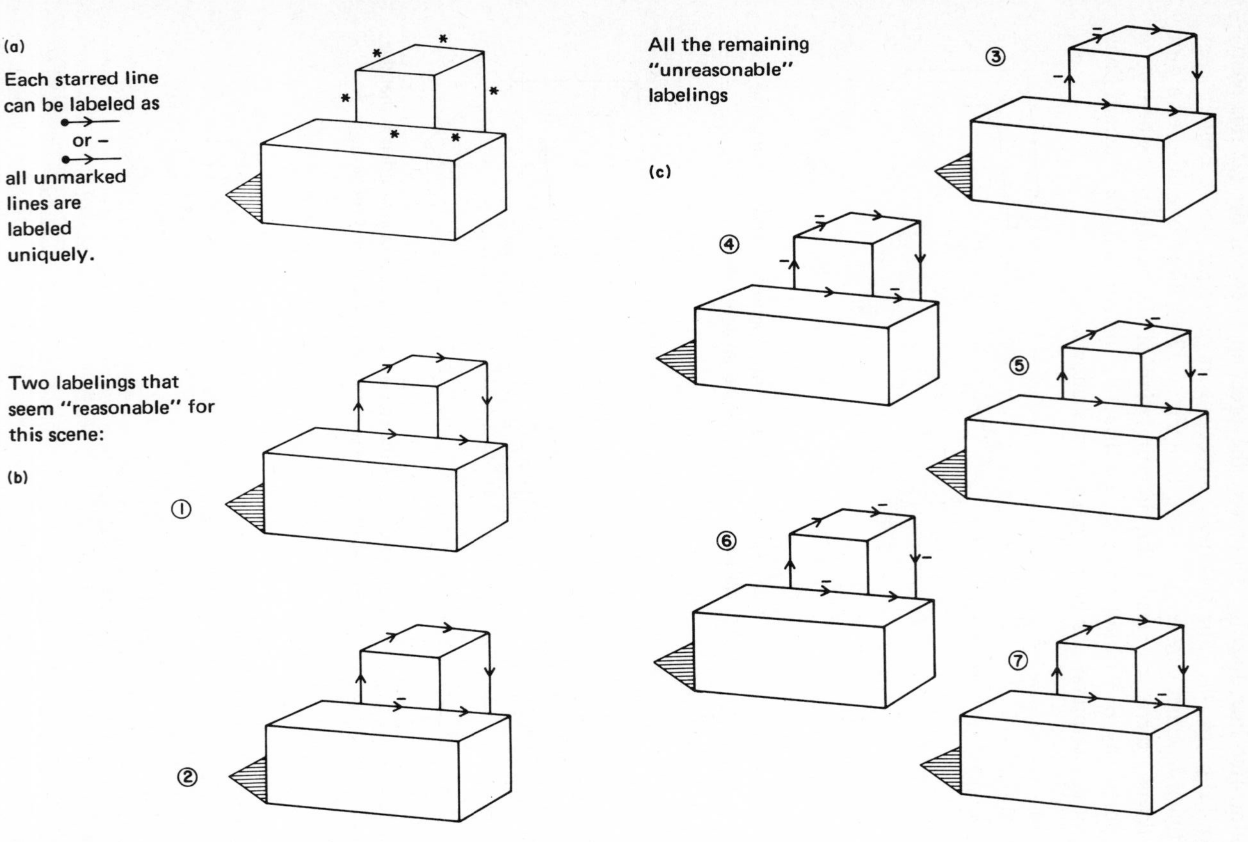
(a)
Each starred line
can be labeled as
or –
all unmarked
lines are
labeled
uniquely.
Two labelings that
seem "reasonable" for
this scene:
(b)
①
②
All the remaining
"unreasonable"
labelings
(c)
③
④
⑤
⑥
⑦

Fig. 2.33

In Fig. 2.33, each of the segments marked with a star can be interpreted either as an obscuring edge or as a concave edge, though in most cases choosing one or the other for some line segment forces other segments to be interpreted uniquely, as shown in Fig. 2.33(*b*) and (*c*). To show why the program finds all these labelings as reasonable interpretations, I have constructed the five scenes in Fig. 2.34 to be topologically identical to the scenes in Fig. 2.33(*c*); this time, however, the labelings shown seem at least plausible if not the most reasonable.

Figure 2.35 shows another problem case. Such a case occurs when we can only see enough of an object so that it is not possible to tell whether the region is a shadow or an object. If it happens that the ambiguous region is brighter than the background (or what would be the illuminated portion of a partly shadowed surface if the feature occurs on the interior of a scene), then the program can eliminate the possibility that the region is a shadow. Unfortunately, if the ambiguous region is darker than its neighbor, the program cannot tell whether the region is a shadow or a dark object. In Fig.

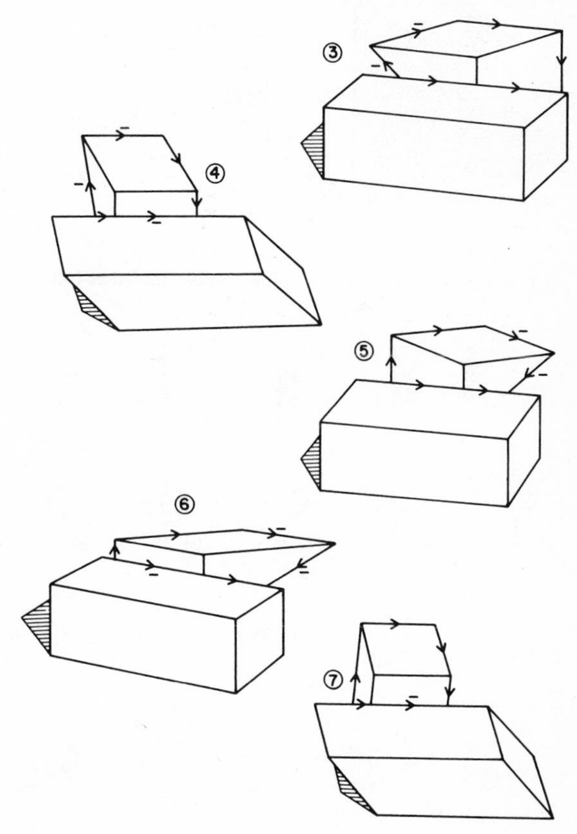

Fig. 2.34

2.35 do you think that both A and B should really be labeled as shadow regions? In fact neither A nor B can be shadows! You can prove this for yourself by finding the characteristic light source slope for the scene, using the front object and its shadow. Then note that there can be no hidden objects which could project A and B.

The labelings which the program finds must be made up of local features, each one of which is physically possible, but it is not obvious that the features which remain should each be part of a total labeling of the scene which is physically possible. After all, the only conditions I impose are that each of these features must agree with at least one other feature at each neighboring junction. On the basis of the fact that the main labeling program does not leave extraneous labels on junctions, it seems clear that topology provides a major portion of the cues necessary to understand a scene.

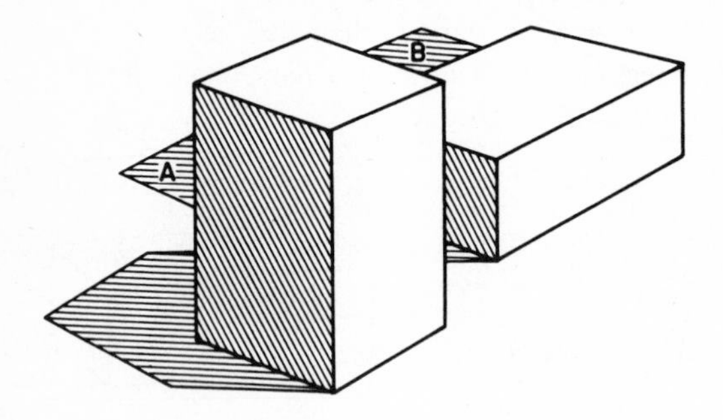

According to the program A and B can be labeled as follows:

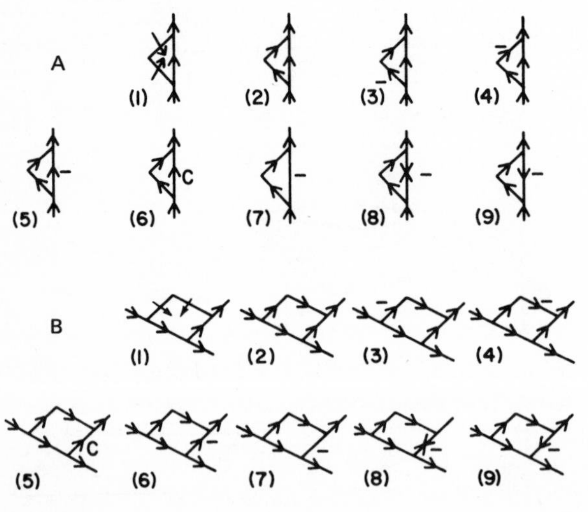

Fig. 2.35

In the next section I show some heuristic rules which can be used to eliminate some of the labelings which people usually consider unlikely. In fact the true case is that these labelings are not unlikely, but the scenes which have these labelings as reasonable ones (to our eyes) do not often arise in our experience. Unfortunately, heuristics sometimes reject real interpretations, and indeed would reject each of the interpretations shown in Fig. 2.34 in favor of the ones in Fig. 2.33(*b*). Nonetheless, in the absence of solid rules, these heuristics can be useful. In the last section I will deal with techniques which enable a program to find the labelings which we would assign to these line drawings without resorting to heuristics.

2.6 NONTRIHEDRAL VERTEXES AND RELATED PROBLEMS

So far I have assumed that all the junctions I am given are normal trihedral junctions and essentially that the line drawing which I am given is "perfect." When a program has to be able to accept data from real line finders and from aribitrarily arranged scenes, these criteria are rather unrealistic.

In this section, I show how to correct some of these problems in a passive manner. By passive I mean that the program is unable to ask a line finding program to look more carefully or to use alternative predicates at a suspicious junction, and similarly that it cannot move its eye or camera, or direct a hand to rearrange part of a scene.

Instead I handle these types of problems by including labels for a number of the most common of these junctions in the regular data base. In cases where the program confuses these junction labelings with the regular labelings and where I want a single parsing, I can easily remove these new types of junction labels first, since I have included special markers for each labeling of this type. Moreover, depending on the reliability of the program which generates the line drawing, I may wish to remove labels in different orders. For example, if a line finding program rarely misses edges, missing edge interpretations can be removed first; if a line finding program tends to miss short line segments, then accidental alignments are probably being generated by the program, and these interpretations can be retained until last. Therefore the labels for each type of problem are marked with different indicators in the data base.

2.6.1 Nontrihedral Vertexes

Some nontrihedral vertexes must be included in the data base; indeed some are much more common than many of the trihedral vertexes. I will limit the number by including only those nontrihedral vertexes which can be formed by convex trihedral objects.

The first type of vertex is formed by the alignment of a vertex with a convex edge as shown in Fig. 2.36(*a*) and (*b*). In Fig. 2.36(*c*) a similar set of

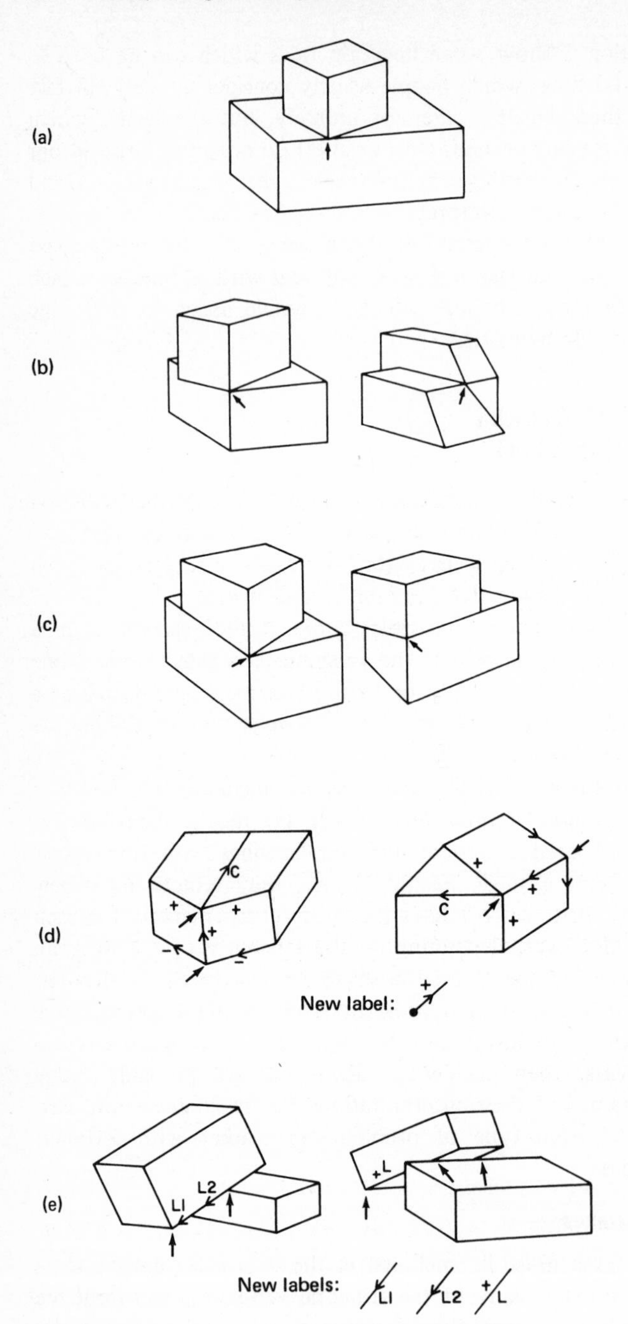

Fig. 2.36

junctions is shown for objects which MARRY (i.e., have coplanar faces separated by a crack edge; see Winston[6]) along one edge, but which have different face angles.

Figure 2.36(*d*) illustrates another common nontrihedral vertex which again results from objects with dissimilar face angles. This time I need a new type of edge (a separable convex edge) labeled as shown in that figure.

Figure 2.36(*e*) illustrates the types of non-trihedral vertexes which can occur when one block leans on another. In order to keep these cases from being confused with other trihedral junctions, I have introduced three new edge types. These types only can occur in a very limited number of contexts.

In the data base each of the labelings of the types shown in Fig. 2.36, and any other junction labels involving the leaning edges or the separable convex edges, are marked as nontrihedral. Later, if I wish to find a single parsing for a scene where there are still ambiguous labels, removing these nontrihedral junctions, if possible, may be a good heuristic.

2.6.2 Accidental Alignments (First Type)

In this section I have not attempted to exhaustively list every possible junction labeling which results from accidental alignment, but have concentrated on including only the most common cases. There is some justification for this, in that ambiguities caused by accidental alignments can be resolved by simply moving with respect to the scene.

Figure 2.37 lists all the junctions which can take part in the first type of accidental alignment I will consider. This type of alignment occurs when a vertex is closer to the eye than an edge which appears to be but is not part of the vertex. Thus the set of vertexes in Fig. 2.37 is exactly that subset of the scene/background boundary junctions which contain only obscuring edges on the scene/background boundary. Figure 2.37 shows only those junctions which I include as sufficiently common. The rest are excluded because they involve unusual concave geometries like those found in Soma cube pieces (Soma cubes are the three-dimensional puzzles manufactured by Parker Bros., Inc., Salem, Mass.) or because they involve three-object edges or because the resulting junction would have enough line segments to require a designation of SPECIAL or because the junction would require the alignment of the eye with three points in space.

At this writing, I have not included all these accidental alignment types in the program's data base, but I have included most of the scene/background boundary cases and a number of the interior cases. In general, I have assumed that no nontrihedral edges or three-object edges will be among those obscured since both the alignment itself and the edge types are relatively unlikely, so their coincidence at a single junction is extremely unlikely.

Junctions which are used to make up accidental alignment list

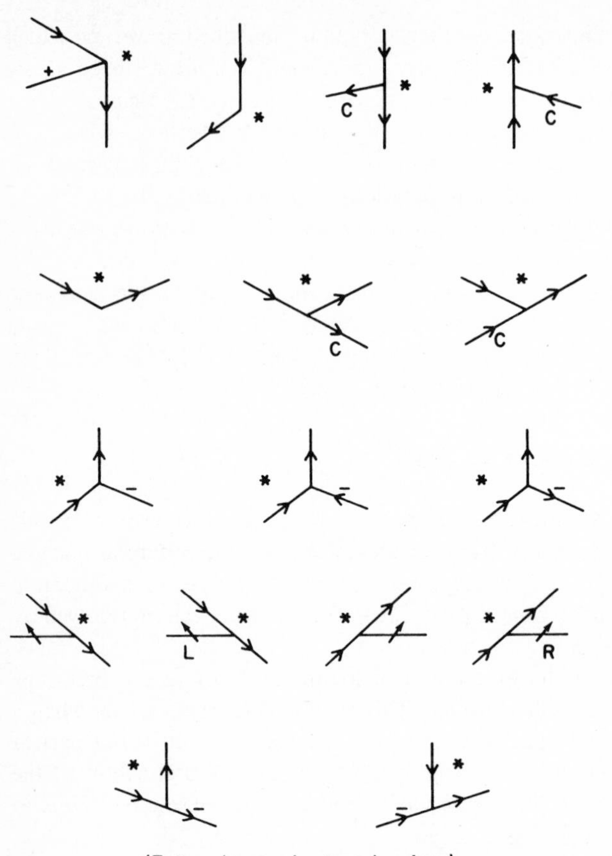

Fig. 2.37

2.6.3 Accidental Alignment (without Obscuring Edges)

Figure 2.38 shows some alignments which have shown up frequently in scenes I have worked with. These junctions have occurred because (1) our line finding program misses short line segments (and therefore tends to include more lines than it should in a single junction), (2) our line finding program has a tolerance angle within which it will call edges collinear, so some edges are called collinear even when they are not, and (3) edges which lie in a plane parallel to the surface on which they cast shadows are parallel to the shadows they cast, so that alignments become particularly likely when we use bricks, cubes, and prisms.

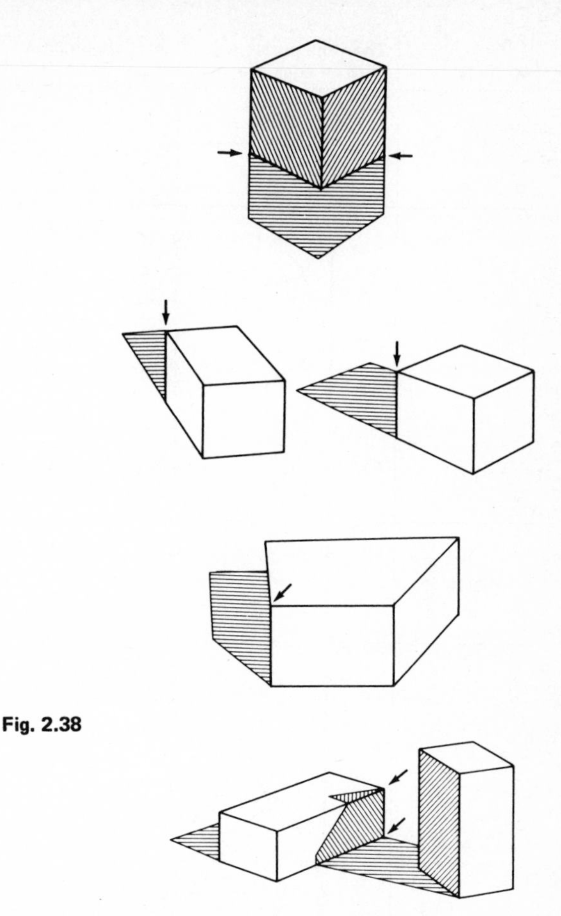

Fig. 2.38

2.6.4 Accidental Alignments (Third Type)

The worst type of accidental alignment, in terms of the number of new junctions it can introduce, occurs when an edge between the eye and a vertex appears to be part of the vertex. Fortunately, all of the types of junctions which these alignments introduce are either Ks, KAs or SPECIALs. To see why this is so, look at Fig. 2.39. All these labelings can be quite easily generated by a program which operates on the regular data base. Notice that for each obscured vertex labeling three new labelings are generated since the near region can have any of the three illumination values.

Also notice that any of these junctions which appear on the scene/background boundary can only be oriented with the background in a junction segment type K1, K2, K3, KA1, KA2, KA3, or KA4. (See Fig. 2.40.) Therefore it is not difficult to recognize the cases where accidental alignments of this type occur on the scene/background boundary since none of the regular trihedral junctions can ever appear on the scene/background boundary in any of these

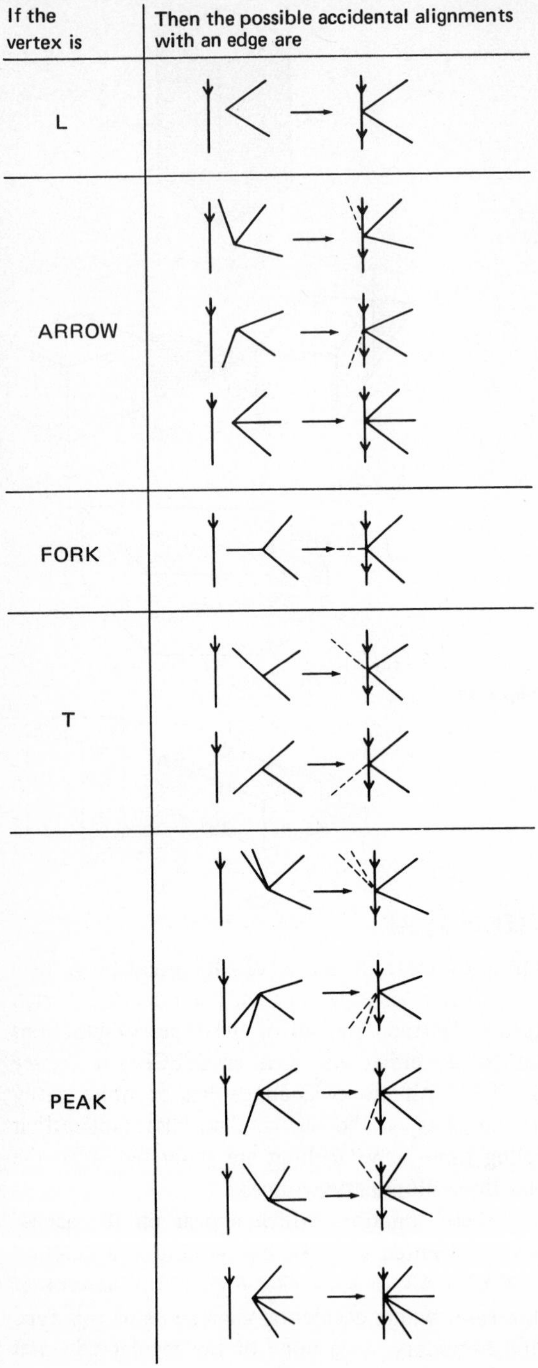

If the vertex is	Then the possible accidental alignments with an edge are
L	
ARROW	
FORK	
T	
PEAK	

Fig. 2.39

If the vertex is	Then the possible accidental alignments with an edge are
MULTI	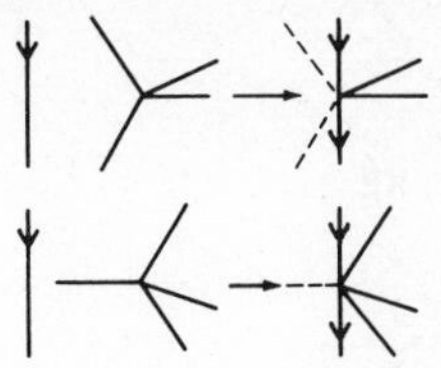
XX	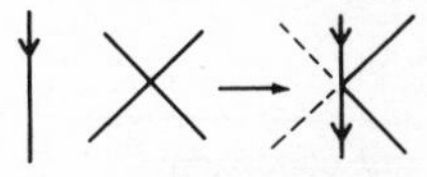
X	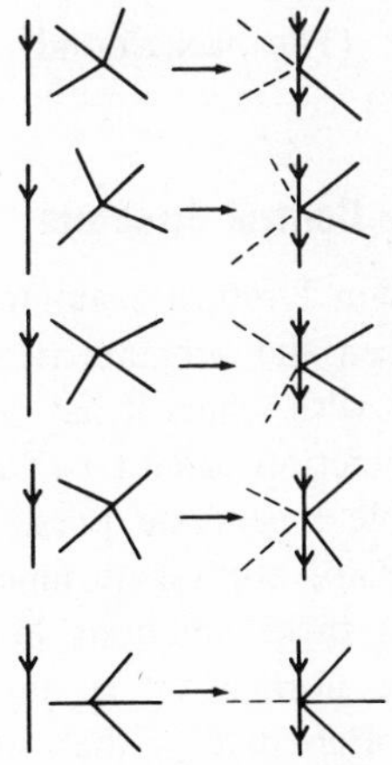
K	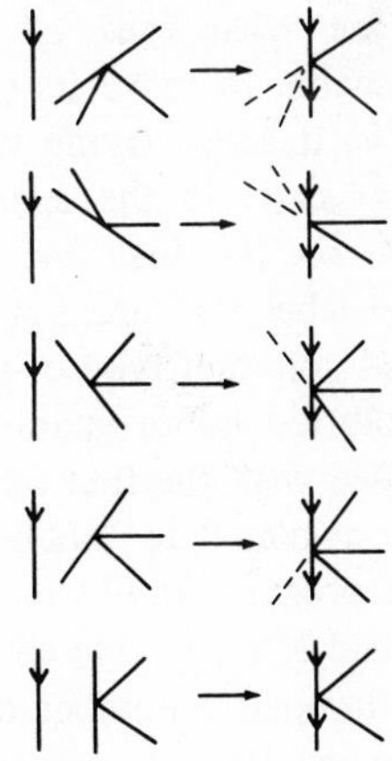

Fig. 2.39 *(continued)*

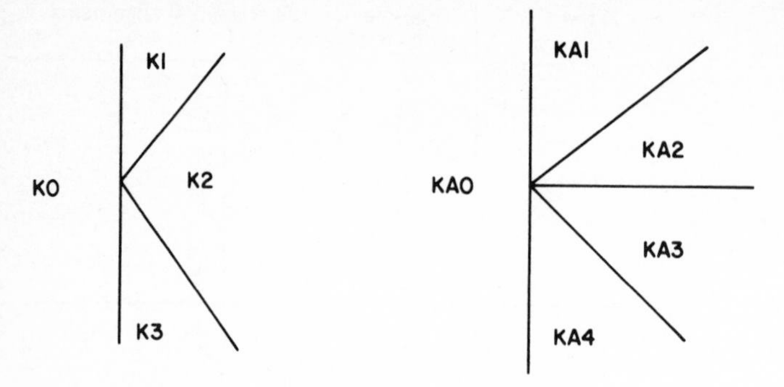

Fig. 2.40 Default condition.

orientations. (The background can only appear normally in segments of type K0 of KA0.)

2.6.5 More Control Structure

In this section I return again to the main labeling program and describe what happens when the program is unable to label a scene consistently, using the set of labels with which it has been equipped.

If a junction cannot be labeled from the normal set, instead of marking it unlabelable I generate possible labelings by modifying the line drawing so that it contains equivalent junctions which are not accidentally aligned, and then I label these junctions in the normal manner. Thus, as shown in Fig. 2.41, if the normal set of junctions is inadequate to label a K, the most reasonable alternative is that the junction is actually an obscured L vertex. Therefore I change the line drawing (saving the original of course) and try to label the new line drawing. This change is equivalent to moving the eye slightly to see what type of junction is obscured, except that since the program is unable to move its eye and therefore does not know what the real vertex type is, it keeps trying various alternatives until one works, or until it hits a default case. In the example shown, the program finds a reasonable interpretation on the first try. If it had not, then the program would next have tried to label the junction as an obscured ARROW, since ARROWs are the next most common type of junction after Ls.

This solution is not guaranteed to contain the correct one; the program will be satisfied with the first set of modifications for the K and KA junctions which gives a complete labeling. To be certain of including the correct solution, the program would have to try every combination of interpretations for every K and KA and save all the ones which give complete labelings.

I have lumped a number of junction types together into a default case for two reasons: this lessened the possibility of stopping before getting the desired "correct" solution, and it enabled the program to run much faster and

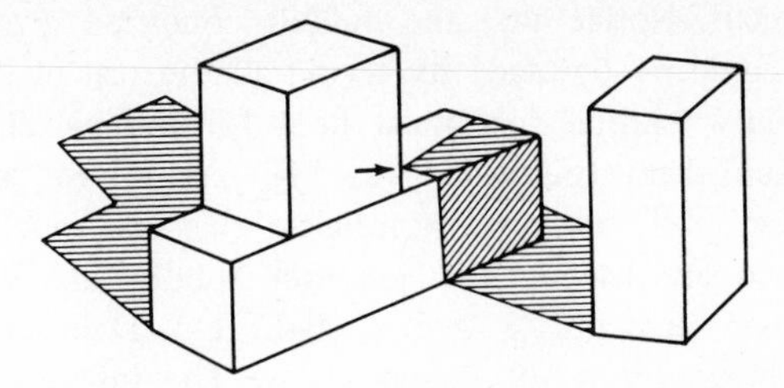

This K junction cannot be labeled from the normal labelings list for Ks. Therefore the program modifies the line drawing, assuming that the K is really an obscured L, and now the line drawing can be labeled.

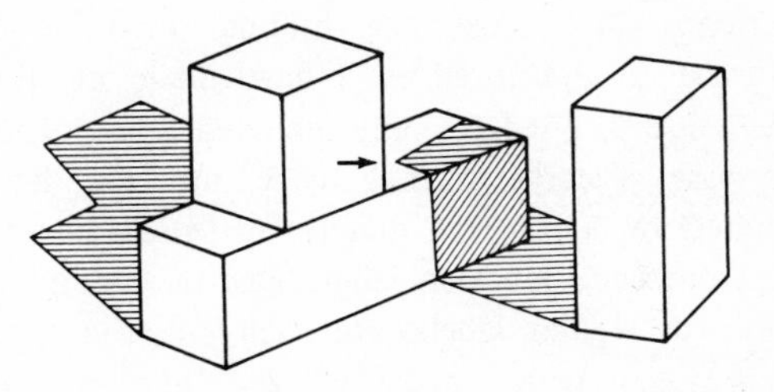

Fig. 2.41

required a much smaller program than would have been needed if I had included separate machinery for each type of junction. The program tries the possibilities for a K in the following order:

1. Try to label the K from the normal label lists.
2. Try to label the K as an obscured L vertex.
3. Try to label the K as an obscured ARROW vertex.
4. If all these fail, label the K as two T junctions. (See Fig. 2.42.)

The default condition represents the exact opposite of the previous conditions. The two Ts result if, instead of moving the eye (by imagination) to see what vertex is behind the obscuring edge, the program moves its eye (by imagination) to completely cover the vertex and eliminate the accidental

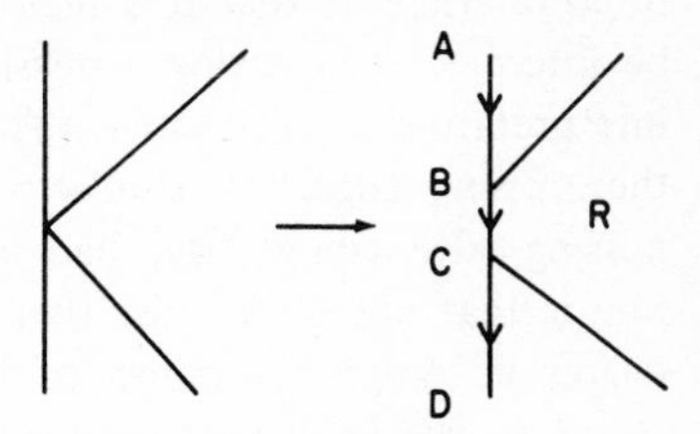

Default condition

alignment. Notice that the default condition gives much weaker constraints than could be obtained by trying all the rest of the junction types explicitly. The only relation that must hold for the two T uprights is that the region between them (marked R in Fig. 2.42) have an illumination value which matches both uprights. Nontheless this is a much stronger condition than is imposed by leaving the junction totally unlabeled and, in addition, the collinear segments (L-A-B, L-B-C, L-C-D in Fig. 2.42) can all be labeled unambiguously as occluding edges. The information I throw away requires that the two uprights be adjacent segments of the same vertex, where this vertex can presumably be labeled from the normal label lists.

2.6.6 Missing Edges

Missing edges usually occur when the brightness of adjacent regions is nearly the same, since most line finding programs depend heavily on steps in brightness to define edges. I have made no attempt to treat missing edges systematically, but have only included a few of the most common cases in the data base. Clearly missing edge junction labels could be systematically generated by a program merely by listing all possibilities for eliminating one edge from each junction label. This procedure would generate $(n-1) \times$ (old number of regular labels) for each junction type (where n is the number of line segments which make up the junction), and clearly this would be a rather unmanageable number of new labels. The number of new labels could be lessened somewhat by noting that certain types of edges such as cracks are likely to be missed, whereas certain other edges such as shadows are relatively unlikely to be missed.

Even if a program such as mine can recognize that a junction must be labeled as having a missing edge, problems still remain about exactly how the line drawing should be completed. This difficulty is illustrated in Fig. 2.43. Depending on the line segment directions and lengths, the missing edge junction D can be connected to vertex A, vertex B or vertex C, even though the topology of all the line drawings is identical.

The missing edge junctions which are included in the program's data base are all L junctions which result from deleting one of the branches of a FORK junction with three convex edges.

A rule which can be helpful in removing impossible missing edge interpretations is that if a region is bounded by only one junction which can be interpreted as having a missing edge in that region, then that missing edge interpretation is impossible. (There must be another junction to connect with the missing edge.) A similar rule depends on including the label that the missing edge would have had in each missing edge labeling. In this case, the rule is that not only must there be a pair of missing edge junctions around a region in order for either of them to be possible, but this pair must also match in the label that each gives to the missing edge. One final rule is that the previous rules only hold if the pair of missing edge junctions are not

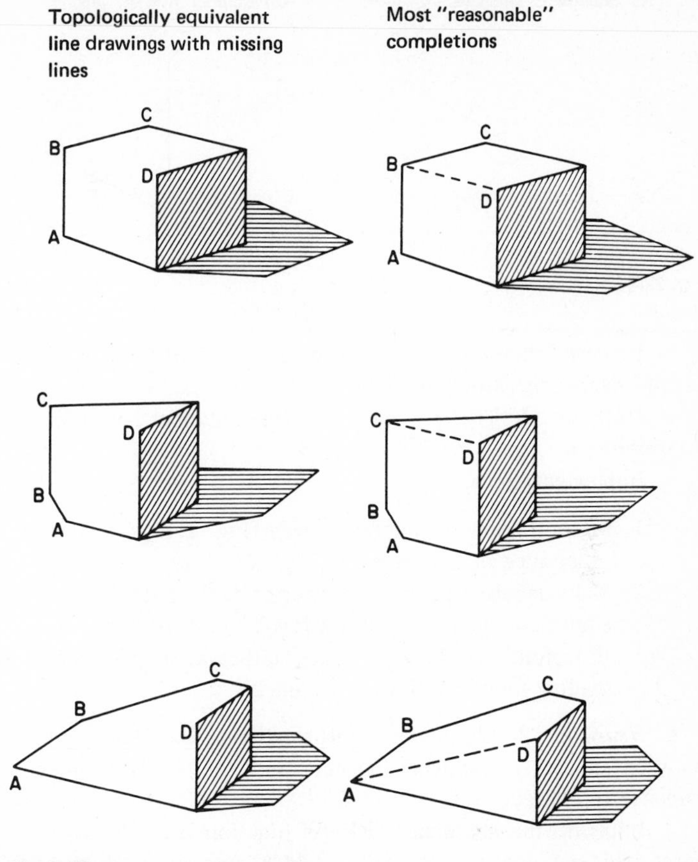

Fig. 2.43

adjacent to one another (i.e. each pair of junctions can be connected by only one straight line).

2.6.7 Heuristics

As I have mentioned earlier in several places, the program is able to remove junction labels selectively according to a crude probability measure of the relative likelihood of various individual feature interpretations. These heuristics are a poor substitute for foolproof rules; in essence I view the heuristics as an expedient method for handling problems I have not yet been able to solve properly. As I explained earlier, these heuristics may nonetheless be of considerable value in guiding programs which find sound solutions.

There is not much to say about the heuristics themselves. The ones I am using currently lump all the "unlikely" junction labels into one class, the "likely" ones into another, and simply eliminate all the "unlikely" labels as long as there are "likely" alternatives.

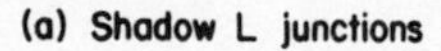

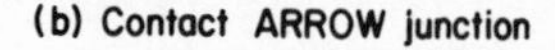

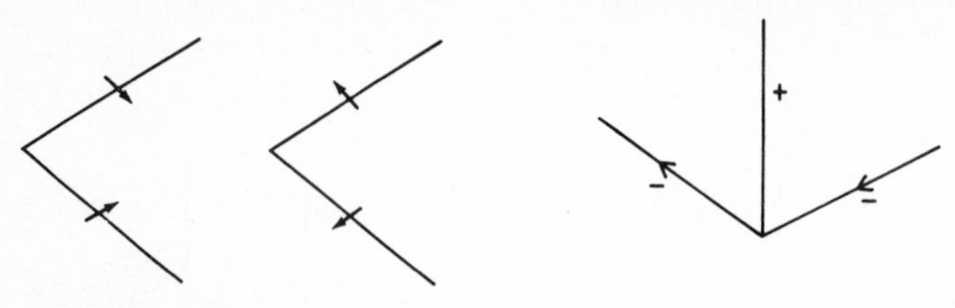

Fig. 2.44

However there are some interesting cases where I have found that I can usually handle the problem scenes.

Heuristic 1 Try to minimize the number of objects in a scene interpretation.

Implementations:

1. Make shadow L junction labels (Fig. 2.44[*a*]) more likely than any other type of L junction.
2. Make labels representing interior table regions more likely than the equivalent labels that do not involve table regions.
3. If regions can be interpreted either as shadows or as objects, make shadow interpretations more likely.

Heuristic 2 Eliminate interpretations that have points of contact between objects or between objects and the TABLE unless there is solid evidence of contact.

Implementation: Make ARROW junction labels which have two concave edges and one convex edge (Fig. 2.44(*b*) less likely than ARROW labels of other types.

These heuristics select interpretations (1), (2), and (7) from Fig. 2.33 and interpretations A(1) and B(1) from Fig. 2.35.

2.7 REGION ORIENTATIONS

What has obviously been missing from all that I have shown so far is a connection between line segment directions on the retina and possible labelings for these lines. Such a connection is extremely useful if the program is to understand gravity and support. In this section I describe approaches to this problem which I have not yet included in my program. There is probably as much work required to properly add the ability to handle direction information as I have already invested in my program. Nonetheless, I believe that this section provides a good idea of the work that needs to be done as well as the physical knowledge that these additions will allow one to include in the program.

2.7.1 General Region Orientations

In this section I define another scheme which assigns to each visible region one of 16 values. The regions are named in as sensible and simple a manner as I could devise, and are defined with respect to a coordinate system which is itself defined by the TABLE surface and the position of the eye viewing the scene. The region orientation values are each shown in Fig. 2.45. I assume that this figure will serve as an adequate specification for the meaning of the different orientation values. If the scene is moved with respect to the eye or vice versa, then the region values (except table and horizontal) may change, and regions previously invisible may become visible. Thus the region orientation values are not inherent properties of the surfaces, but are only defined with respect to a particular eye-table arrangement.

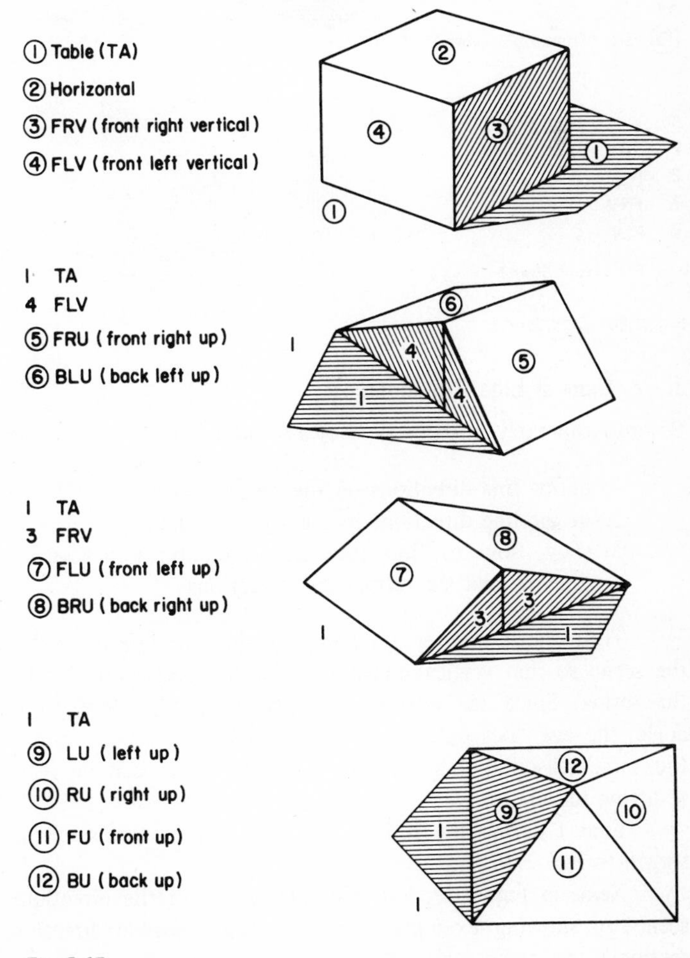

Fig. 2.45

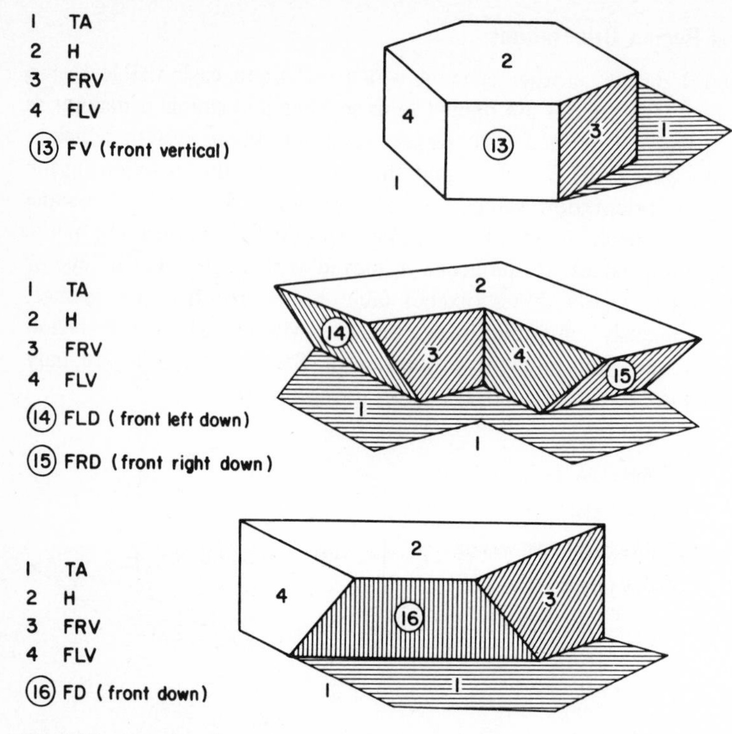

Fig. 2.45 *(continued)*

2.7.2 General Line Directions

Before I can carry out this type of association in general, I must

1. define line directions on the retina
2. define line directions in the scene domain
3. show how to find the scene direction values, given a labeled line drawing and the retinal line directions

Throughout this section I assume that the eye is far enough away from the scene so that vertical edges in the scene project into North/South lines on the retina. Since the definition of North/South edges includes a tolerance angle, the eye does not need to be at infinity for this condition to hold. By the same reasoning I assume that parallel edges can be recognized without resorting to perspective or vanishing point considerations.

First I define the retinal line directions in terms of compass points as shown in Fig. 2.46.

Next, in Fig. 2.47, I define the names for the directions of lines in the scene by showing examples for each type possible direction. These names resemble the names for region orientations, but I will always use lower case

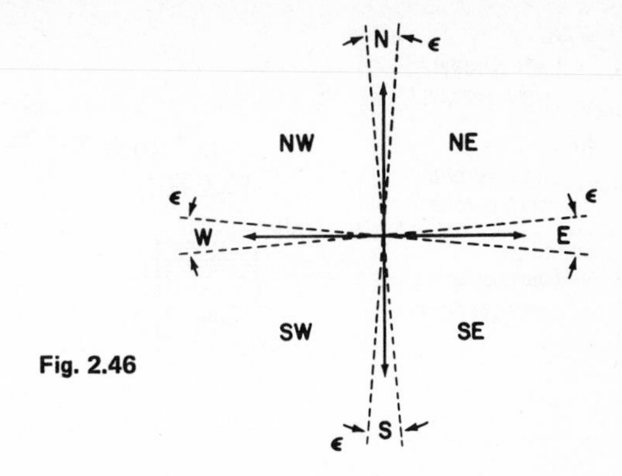

Fig. 2.46

letters in referring to the line names and will use upper case letters when I refer to the region names.

Now to make the connections between the retinal and scene line directions, note that I can catalog all the possible edge directions in the scene domain which can map into each of the direction values on the retina. As an example of how to do this, in Fig. 2.48 I show all the edge directions possible for an edge which bounds a type FRV region. The diagrams in this illustrate that an NE (Northeast) line on the retina which bounds a type FRV region can be an edge of types bru, brp, or brd, that an E (east) line on the retina

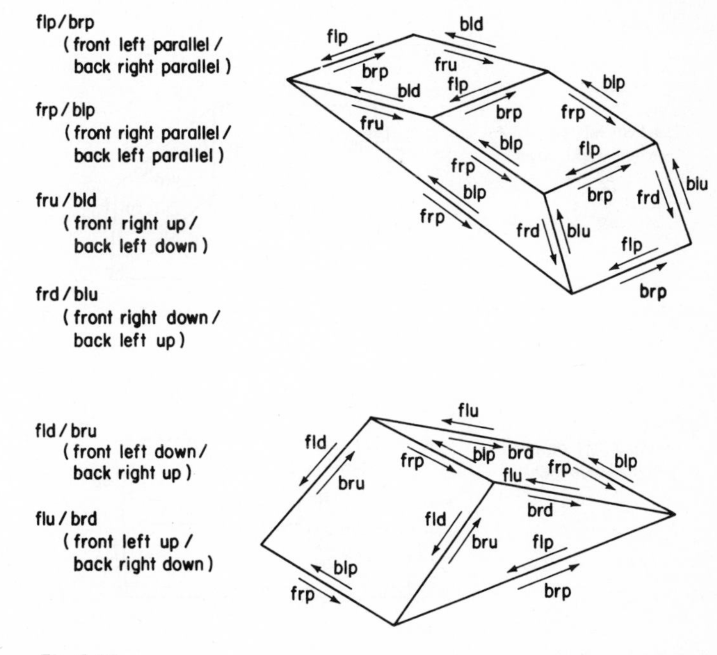

Fig. 2.47

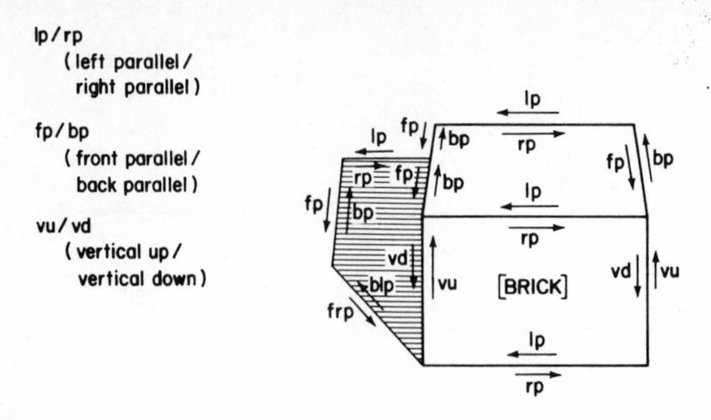

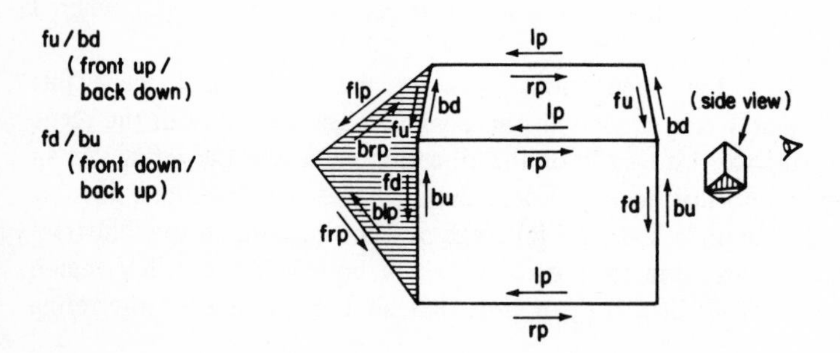

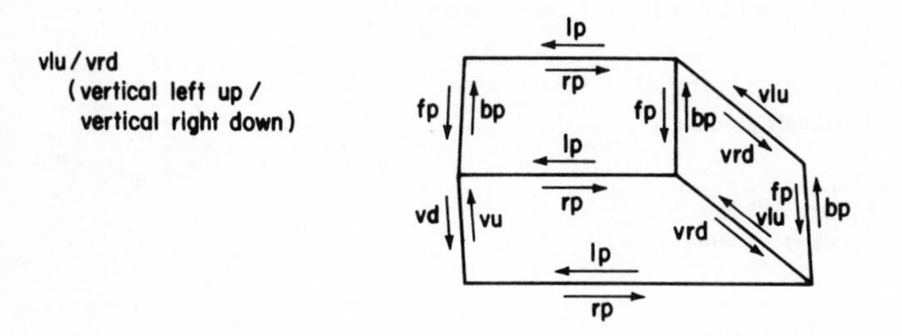

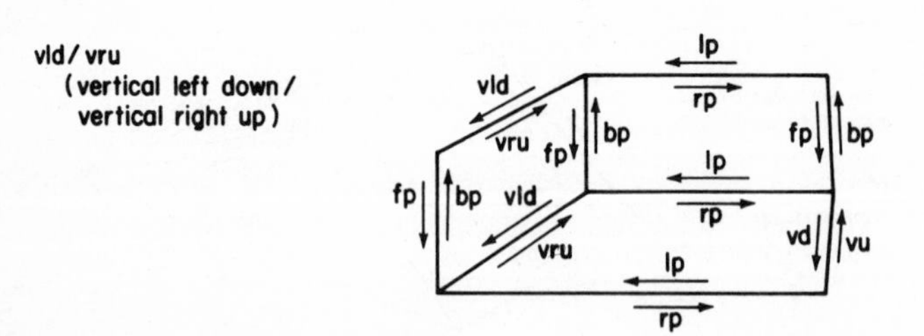

Fig. 2.47 *(continued)*

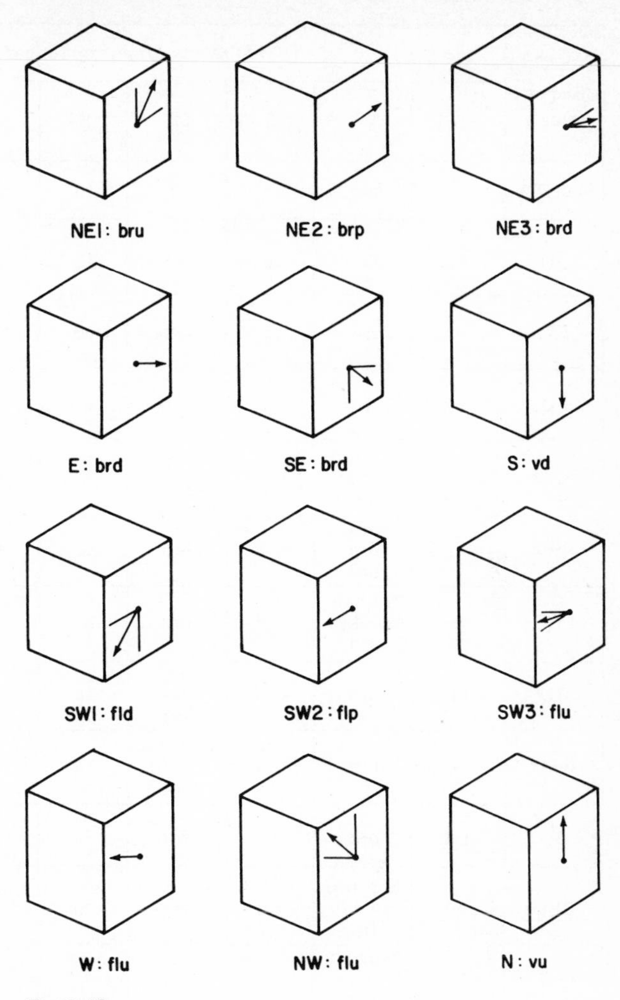

Fig. 2.48

which bounds a type FRV region can only be caused by a type brd edge, etc. Figure 2.49 is a summary of the types of scene edges which can cause lines of each type on the retina, arranged according to the types of regions that each edge can bound.

Now to tie everything together, notice that an edge can only separate two regions if the edge could have the same direction in both regions bounding the edge. Therefore, to find all the region pairs that an N (North) edge (as seen on the retina) could separate, look down the N column in Fig. 2.49 and find all the pairs of regions which can share an edge which points in a particular direction. A north pointing edge can thus separate any of the following pairs of region types (this is not a complete list):

Region type ↓	Direction of line on retina							
	N	NE	E	SE	S	SW	W	NW
H or TA	bp	brp	rp	frp	fp	flp	lp	blp
FU	bu	bru	rp	frd	fd	fld	lp	blu
FV	vu	vru	rp	vrd	vd	vld	lp	vlu
FD	fu	fru	rp	brd	bd	bld	lp	flu
FRU	bu	bru brp brd	brd	brd vrd frd	fd	fld flp flu	flu	flu vlu blu
FRV	vu	bru brp brd	brd	brd	vd	fld flp flu	flu	flu
FRD	fu	fru, vru brp, bru brd	brd	brd	bd	bld, vld fld, flp flu	flu	flu
RU	bp	brd	brd	brd vrd frd	fp	flu	flu	flu vlu blu
BRU	bd	brd	brd	brd, vrd frd, frp fru	fu	flu	flu	flu, vlu blu, blp bld
BU	bd	brd	rp	fru	fu	flu	lp	bld
BLU	bd	brd, brp bru, vru fru	fru	fru	fu	flu, flp fld,vld bld	bld	bld
LU	bp	bru vru fru	fru	fru	fp	fld vld bld	bld	bld
FLU	bu	bru vru fru	fru	fru frp frd	fd	fld vld bld	bld	bld blp blu
FLV	vu	fru	fru	fru frp frd	vd	bld	bld	bld blp blu
FLD	fu	fru	fru	fru, frp frd, vrd brd	bd	bld	bld	bld, blp blu, vlu flu

Fig. 2.49

((TA TA) (H H) (TA LU) (H LU) (H RU)
(RU TA) (RU H)
(FRV FRV) (FRV FLV) (FRV FV)
(FLV FRV) (FLV FV) (FLV FLV)
(FV FV) (FV FLV) (FV FRV)
(LU H) (LU RU) (LU LU)
(RU H) (RU LU) (RU RU)
(BLU BRU) (BRU BLU))

Not all these pairs can be separated by the same types of edges; shadows and cracks can only separate regions with the same orientation values, and convex edge pairs become concave edge pairs if the order of the pairs is reversed. For example, a North line separating regions with orientation values (FLV FRV) represents a convex edge (where the ordering of the regions is in a clockwise direction), but if the orientation values are (FRV FLV) for a North line, this must represent a concave edge.

A program can use this information in the following ways:

1. If there are ambiguities remaining after the regular labeling program has finished, pick a single labeling, assign region values and see whether this labeling can represent a possible interpretation; if the interpretation is not possible, then the program will be unable to assign orientation values to every region.
2. Region illumination values can be tied in with the region orientation values. For example, if a scene is lit from the left, and the light-eye angle is less than 90° (in Fig. 2.50, the light-eye angle is the angle

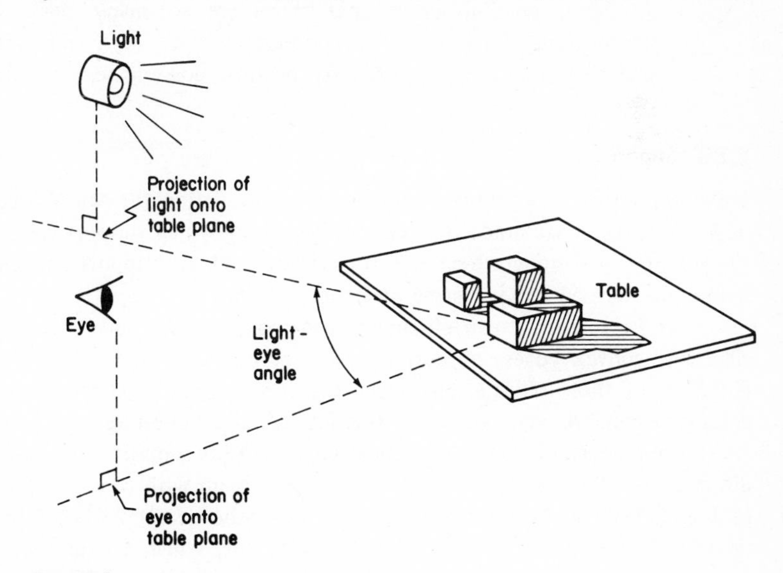

Fig. 2.50

between the projections of the eye and the light onto the plane of the TABLE, as measured from the center of the scene), then a region cannot be labeled simultaneously as orientation type FLV and illumination type SS (self-shadowed).

3. All these facts provide a neat way to integrate stereo information into a scene description. For example, if an edge is truly vertical (type vu) then it must appear as N (North) in any retinal projection of a stereo system. However an edge which is of type bp (back parallel) can appear to be N on the retina because of the particular placement of the eye with respect to the scene. If the eye is shifted slightly to the right, this edge will now appear to point NE (Northeast) and if the eye is shifted to the left, the edge will appear to point NW (Northwest). Clearly this knowledge would enable a program to much more severely restrict the region orientation pairs, and consequently the labelings, that can be assigned to a line drawing of a scene.
4. All the possibilities for region orientations can be generated by the function I use to build up sets of region illumination values. For each labeling which the program finds, region pairs can be selected according to the line directions and line labels, and a set of region orientation values can be built up. The difference is that there are far too many region orientation values in general to possibly include them in precompiled form; the values must be generated from the greatly reduced set of possibilities that remain after the regular labeling program has completed its work. The reason why there are so many possibilities is that there are so many possible region orientations. Each edge can potentially have $16 \times 16 = 256$ region orientation pairs as opposed to the nine possible region illumination pairs.

2.7.3 Support

Using the region orientation values, I can now define the set of edges along which support must hold, the set of edges along which support can hold, and the set of edges along which support cannot hold. By support I mean what is commonly termed either resting on or leaning on.

To start with, I can eliminate from consideration any edges which are shadows, convex edges, obscuring edges, or concave edges made up of one object or of three objects, and I can say for certain that support is exhibited along any concave edge which has the TABLE as a bounding region.

The important fact is that these edges exhibit support regardless of their directions on the retina, so that there is no problem with edges such as L-A-B in Fig. 2.51. The best previous rules to find where support holds in a scene (Winston[6]) are not able to handle cases like this; Winston's rules were biased toward finding ARROWs, Ks, and Xs which have vertical (or at least upward

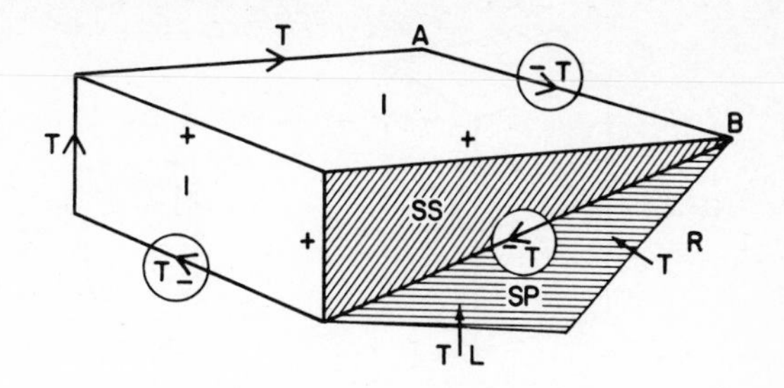

Support relations are circled.

Fig. 2.51

pointing) lines. In addition, Winston's rules failed to find support relations for leaning blocks; his rules assumed that objects would be supported by face contact only.

Although my program can find support in cases like Fig. 2.51, it is important to note that, in general, it is not possible to use my regular labelings and line directions alone to find which edges exhibit support and which do not. Suppose that on the basis of the frequency of crack edges like the ones shown in Fig. 2.52(*a*) I decided to label as supporting/crack edges ones in which the arrow of the crack label points SW, W, or NW, and to class all the others together as being crack edges without support relations. Then in Fig. 2.52(*b*) edges L-B-C and L-C-D would be correctly marked but L-A-B would not. I could patch up the rule by saying that if support holds for one noncollinear line in an X junction it must hold for the other noncollinear line of the X as well. Unfortunately this rule causes the program to assert that support holds between the two objects in Fig. 2.52(*c*) since support would be transferred by the rule from L-B-C to L-A-B.

Similarly, for concave edges I cannot use line directions and the direction of the arrow on the label to define support. As an example, observe that while L-A-B in Fig. 2.52(*d*) does not exhibit support, L-C-D in Fig. 2.52(*e*) does.

Region orientation values can help to avoid these problems, at least for some cases. (There are some cases, such as the one in Fig. 2.52[*f*], where I do not know whether to say that support holds along L-A-B and L-B-C or not.) Interestingly enough, with region orientations specified, I do not necessarily need line directions, although I certainly need line directions to find the region orientation values to begin with.

An example of an edge where support must hold is any concave edge which has a horizontal surface on its left when one looks along the edge in the direction of its "arrow", as does L-C-D in Fig. 2.52(*e*).

Some examples of edges where support cannot hold are concave edges which have vertical surfaces (FRV, FV, or FLV) or downward pointing

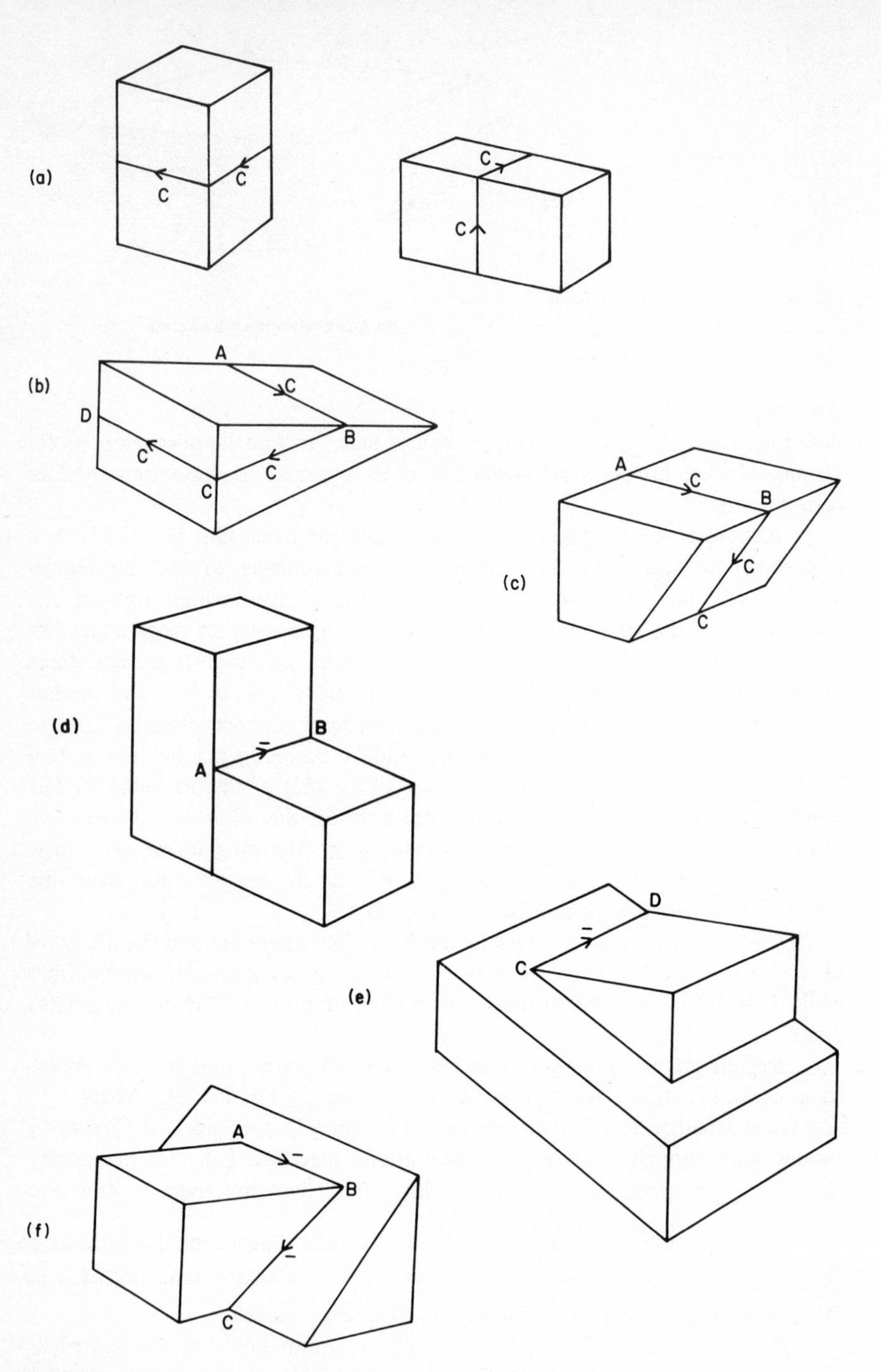

Fig. 2.52

surfaces (FRD, FD, or FLD) on the left of the edges when looking along the direction of the "arrow"; line L-A-B in Fig. 2.52(*d*) is an edge of this type.

REFERENCES

1. Huffman, David: Impossible Objects as Nonsense Sentences, in B. Meltzer and D. Michie (eds.), "Machine Intelligence 6," Edinburgh University Press, Edinburgh, Scotland, 1971.
2. Clowes, Maxwell: On Seeing Things, *Artif. Intel.*, **2**(1):79–116 (1971).
3. Sussman, G., T. Winograd, and D. McDermott: MICRO-PLANNER Reference Manual, *M.I.T. Artificial Intelligence Laboratory Memo* 203A, 1971.
4. Freuder, Eugene: The Object Partition Problem, *M.I.T. Artificial Intelligence Laboratory Working Paper* 4, 1971.
5. Mahabala, H. N. V.: Preprocessor for Programs which Recognize Scenes, *M.I.T. Artificial Intelligence Laboratory Memo* 177, 1969.
6. Winston, Patrick H.: "Learning Structural Descriptions from Examples," Ph.D. thesis, Massachusetts Institute of Technology, Cambridge, Mass., 1970 (included as Chap. 5 of this book).

3 ANALYZING INTENSITY ARRAYS USING KNOWLEDGE ABOUT SCENES

Yoshiaki Shirai

3.1 FROM PICTURE ARRAYS TO DRAWINGS

One of the shortcomings of many computer programs is their pass-oriented or hierarchical structure. This paper describes what Minsky and Papert call a heterarchical program, one organized more like a community of experts. The purpose of the program is to transform information from an image dissector camera into line drawings of polyhedra.

Most previous programs first find feature points in an entire scene and then make a complete line drawing using those feature points. But it has proved very difficult to work out a complete line drawing this way without using any knowledge about constraints that limit what can possibly be in the scene. If the line drawing has some errors, further analysis based on it is likely to lead to serious mistakes.

Our work is an attempt to recognize objects without a rigid ordering of steps and with fuller use of previous results as analysis proceeds. The program is

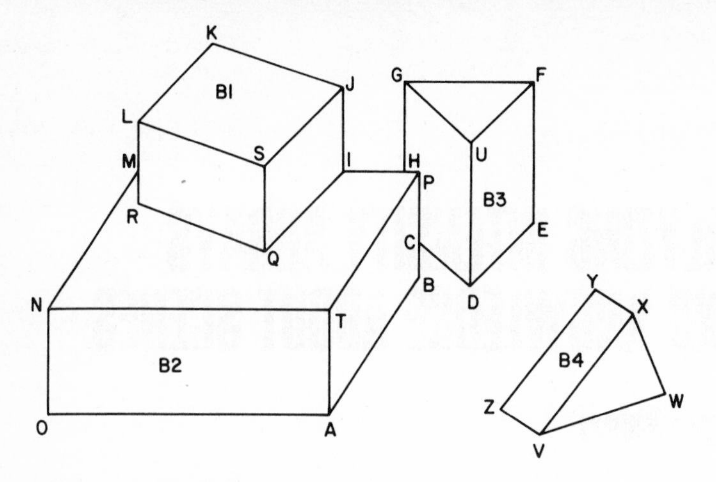

Fig. 3.1 A typical scene.

based upon the strategy of recognizing objects step by step, each time making use of previous results. The order of the lines to be detected is (1) contour lines which separate the bodies from the background, (2) other boundary lines which separate two bodies, and (3) internal lines which lie at the intersection of two faces of the same body.

We assume that the difference in brightness between the objects and the background is large enough to detect the background boundaries easily. Among other boundary lines and among internal lines, the most plausible lines are proposed at each stage and an attempt is made to find them. To find a line, the range where a line segment may exist is proposed, and it is detected in a way suitable for the proposed range. If a proper line segment is found, the end of the line is determined by tracking along the line. When the line is determined, the program tries to understand the scene taking this line into consideration. Because lines are mostly proposed instead of found by exhaustive search in the scene, the program is relatively efficient. At present, this program works well on moderately complicated configurations of blocks and wedges. Figure 3.1 shows an example.

3.2 STRATEGIES AND PROGRAMS

For convenience, we divide the edges of the objects in a scene into three classes. A contour line is formed at the boundary between the bodies and the outer background. In Fig. 3.1, lines AB, BC, CD, DE, EF, FG, GH, HI, IJ, JK, KL, LM, MN, NO, OA, VW, WX, XY, YZ, and ZV are contour lines. A boundary line is a line on the border of an object. Hence contour lines are boundary lines. In Fig. 3.1 the boundary lines are the contour lines plus the lines on the boundary between two bodies, CP, PH, IQ, QR, and RM. An internal line occurs at the intersection of two planes of the same body, such as AT.

The first action of the program is to find contour lines. If more than one contour is found, as in Fig. 3.1, where we have one contour for bodies B1, B2, and B3 and another for body B4, then processing proceeds independently on the separate groups.

Next the program searches for other boundary lines and internal lines within each contour.

Boundary lines are found before finding internal lines because boundary lines often give good clues for guessing internal lines. Note that to find boundary lines is to find bodies. In searching for lines, different situations require examination of larger or smaller areas. In this program, a smaller search area results in a higher priority for the search. In Fig. 3.1, for instance, to determine the existence of an extension of line BC, it is enough to search a small area whose center is on the extension of the line. To find line IQ, however, we should consider all possible directions of a line between IH and IJ. Thus the former search has priority over the latter.

3.2.1 Contour Finding

The picture data obtained with an image dissector usually consists of a large number of points (say about 100,000) each of which represents a light intensity level. To speed up the search for contour points, one point for every 8 X 8 points is sampled. This compressed picture data consists of 1/64 the number of points in the original picture. To find a contour, this data is scanned until a contour point is found. Discovery of a contour point is based upon the simple assumption that there is always enough contrast between the background and objects to distinguish them easily. Prospective points are separated into real countour points and noise points. Real points initiate tracking. In this manner, a set of contour points is found. Then, the remainder of the picture data is scanned until a new contour point is found. This process is repeated until the entire scene has been examined and all the sets of contour points are known.

Now, suppose a certain set of contour points is to be analyzed. The program returns to the original higher-resolution picture. It can approximate the position of a contour point in the original picture data by supposing it corresponds to the first point found in the sampled picture. The precise contour point is searched for near this approximation. A set of refined contour points is obtained by tracing from the precise point in the same way as in the sampled picture. A polygon is formed after we connect contour points one by one. To divide the points of this "curve" into segments, the "curvature" of the polygon is used. Figure 3.2 shows how we define curvature of a polygon. Each cell in the figure represents a contour point. The curvature at the point P is the difference in

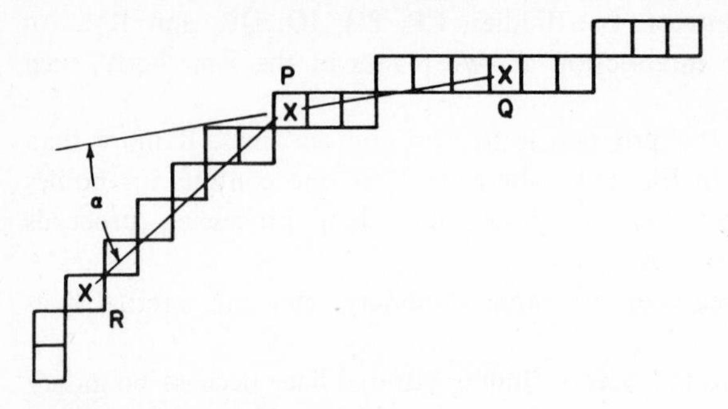

Fig. 3.2 The definition of curvature.

angle between PR and PQ, where Q and R are a constant number of points away from P (six points in this case).

Note that curvature is not very sensitive to noise or digitization error. If we integrate the curvature along a straight line, the result is nearly zero in spite of the effect of noise. If we sum up the curvatures of consecutive points and find the absolute value is greater than some threshold, we can determine the existence of a vertex. (See Fig. 3.3.) Thus every contour point is classified to be either in the straight part of a line or near a vertex. Using points which belong to the straight part of a line, the equation of the line is calculated.

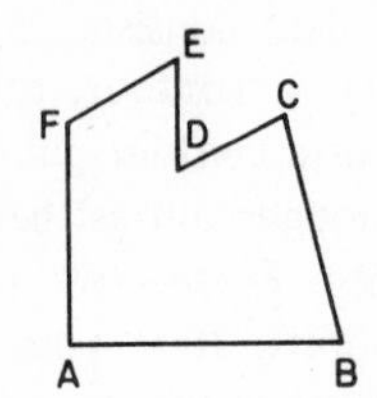

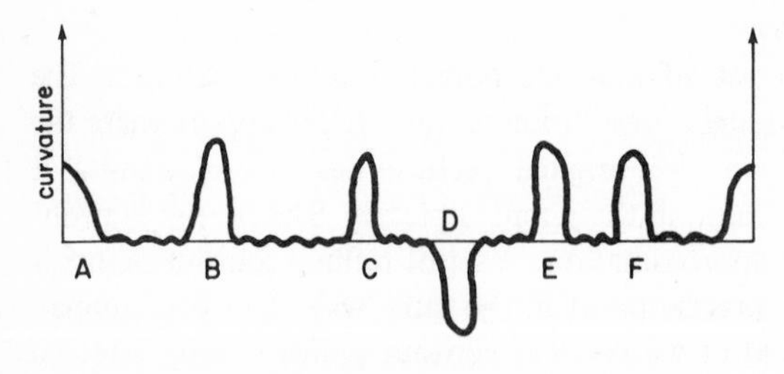

Fig. 3.3 Example of segment determination.

3.2.2 Hypothesizing Lines

Extracting the most obvious information first dictates the following order for the ten heuristic line proposing steps:

1. If two boundary lines make a concave point (such as the B points in Fig. 3.4), try to find collinear extensions of them. If only one extension is found, track along this line. Most of such cases are like the one in Fig. 3.4(*b*) where one body hides the other. It is easy to see to which body this line belongs.
2. If no extensions of two concave lines are found, try to find another line which starts from the concave point. If only one line is found, track along this line. Most of these cases are as in Fig. 3.4(*c*) where it is not clear locally to which body this line belongs.

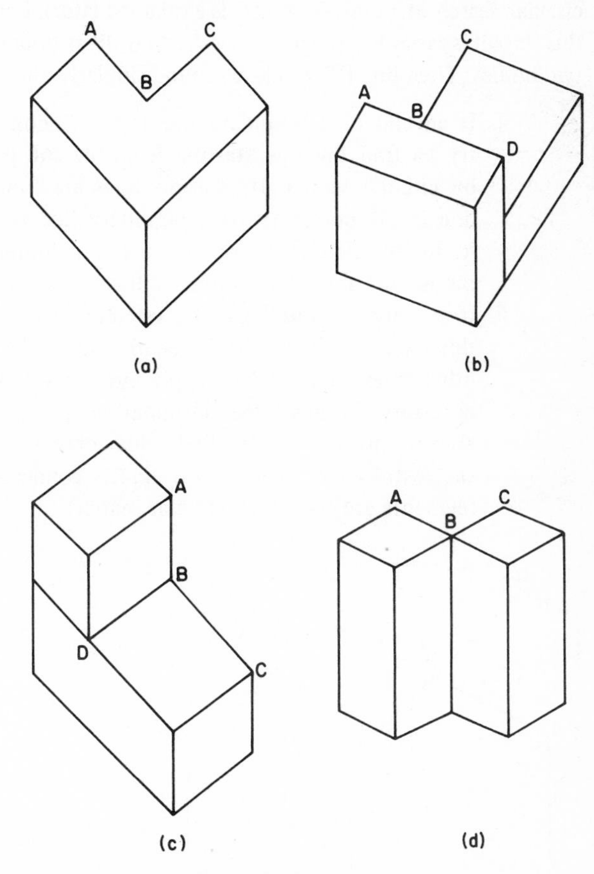

Fig. 3.4 Concave boundary lines.

In Fig. 3.4(*c*) line BD belongs to the upper body, but this is not always true. That is, the lines AB, BC, BD are not sufficient to decide.

3. If both extensions of the two lines are found at a concave point as in Fig. 3.4(*d*), try to find a third one. If only one new line is found, track along this line.

Whenever tracking terminates, an attempt is always made to connect the new line to the other lines already found. If more than one line segment is found in (1), (2) or (3), the tracking of all those lines is put off, hopefully to be clarified by the results obtained in simpler cases. Figure 3.5 illustrates two extensions found at concave point P. The interpretation of the two lines is put off to treat simpler cases first. That is, one would continue examining the contour and lines AB and CD might be found next; then, by a circular search at point B (which is explained later), line BP would be found. At this stage it is easier to interpret lines AB and BP as boundary lines which separate two bodies. Then line DP would be found similarly and interpreted correctly.

4. If an end of a boundary line is left unconnected as PQ in Fig. 3.6, try to find the line starting from the end point (Q in this example) by circular search. If multiple lines are found, try to decide which line is the boundary. If a boundary line is determined, track along it. In this figure, the dotted lines are found by circular search and the arrows show the boundary lines to be tracked.
5. If no line is found by the circular search, extend the line (PQ in this example) by a certain length and test if the line is connected to other lines. If not, then apply circular search again as in (4). This is necessary because the termination point of the tracking is not always precise. Note that this process can be repeated until successful (that is either the line is connected to other lines or line segments are found by circular search).

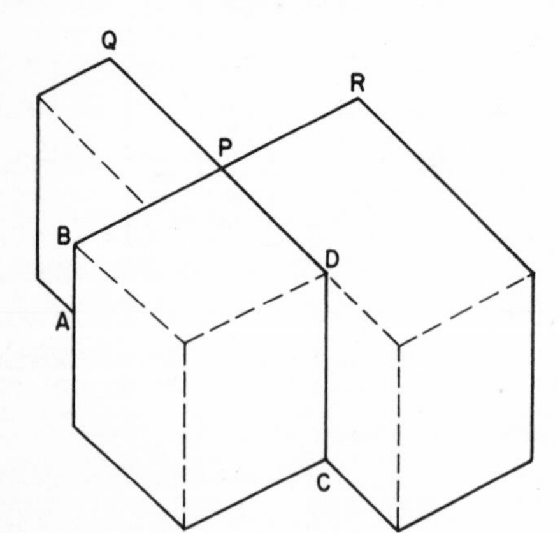

Fig. 3.5 Two extension lines are proposed at concave point P.

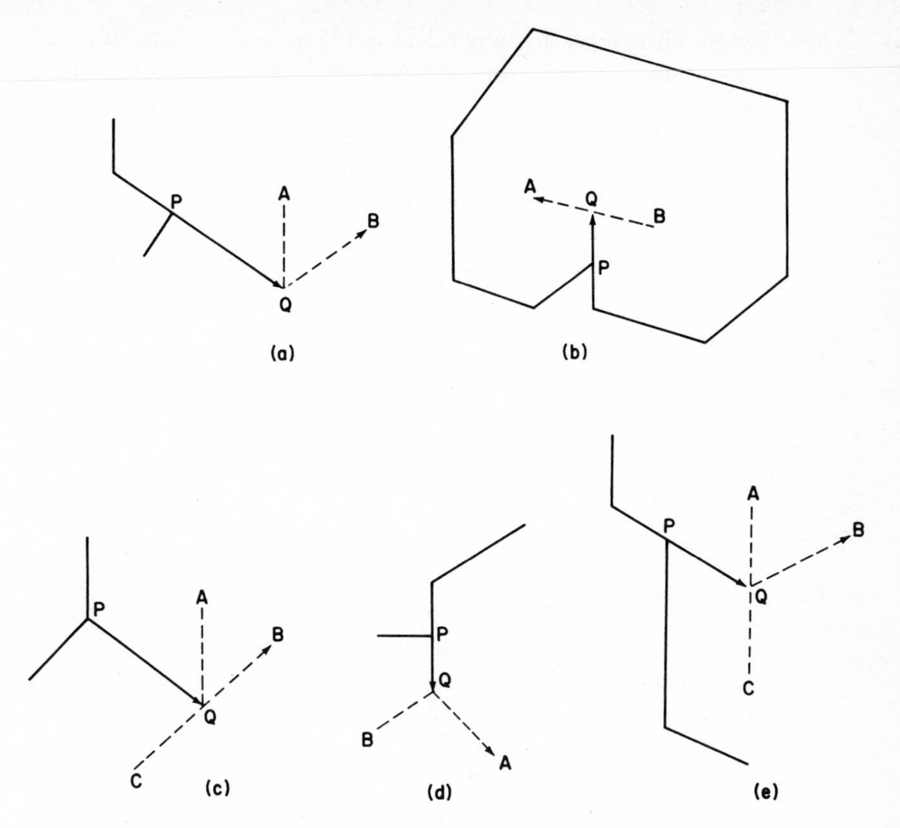

Fig. 3.6 Lines found by circular search.

6. If the boundary lines of a body are known, select the vertexes of the boundary that might have internal lines starting from them. The selection of vertexes is based on heuristics such as selecting upper right vertex rather than lower right vertex. At each vertex, try to find an internal line which is nearly parallel to other boundary lines. If one line is found, track along it. In Fig. 3.1, internal line JS is parallel to the boundary lines KL and IQ, and QS is parallel to RL and IJ. Line FU is parallel to ED and XV is parallel to YZ. Thus it is often useful to search for internal lines parallel to boundary lines of the same body. Note that this search for parallels covers only a small area.
7. If no line is found in (6), try to find one by circular search between adjacent boundary lines. When one line is found, track along it. In Fig. 3.7 circular search between BA and BC is necessary to find the internal line BE.
8. If two internal lines meet at a vertex, try to find another internal line starting at the vertex. This process is useful in two cases. One is

where no internal line was found in (7) because of little difference in brightness between adjacent faces. Suppose in Fig. 3.1, that the internal line SJ was not found at vertex J, but that LS and QS were found. Then try to find an internal line starting at S toward J. If there is enough contrast near S, a line segment is found. The other case is where a body is partly hidden by other bodies. In Fig. 3.7, the triangular prism is partly hidden. After BE and CE are found, EF is searched for. Sometimes the direction of the line is predictable and sometimes it is not. If it is predictable, then try that direction. If it is unpredictable or if the predicted direction failed, then apply circular search between the two internal lines. If one line is found, track along it.

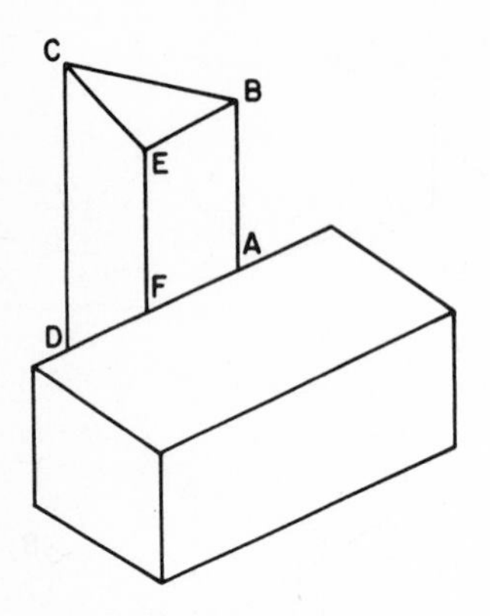

Fig. 3.7 Circular search for internal lines.

9. If an end of an internal line is not connected to any line, try to find lines starting from the end by circular search. If lines are found, track along them one by one.
10. If no line is found in (9), extend the line by a certain length as in (5) and test if it is connected to other lines. If not connected, try circular search again as in (9). This process can also be repeated until successful. Figure 3.8 illustrates this process. In Fig. 3.8(*a*) line MN′ is not connected to others at N′, thus step (9) is tried at N′ and fails. The line is extended to P1 and step (9) is again applied. This process is repeated until the line is connected to line KL at N. Figure 3.8(*b*) shows that line HI is extended by this process to P2 where a new line is found by circular search. Similarly line CG is

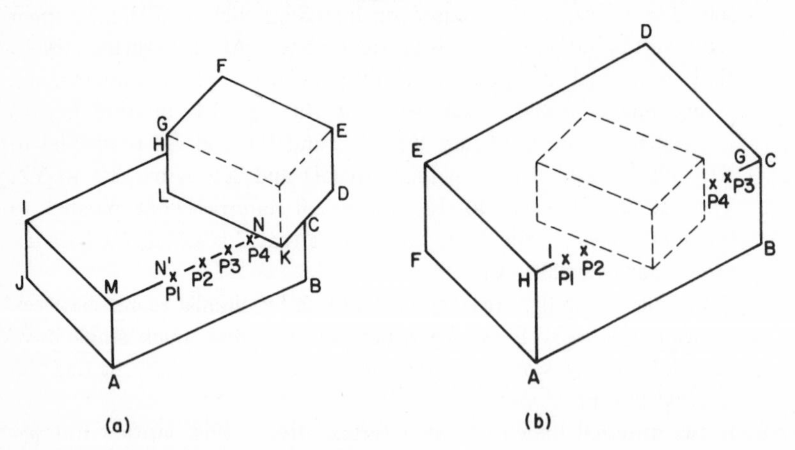

Fig. 3.8 Continuation by circular search.

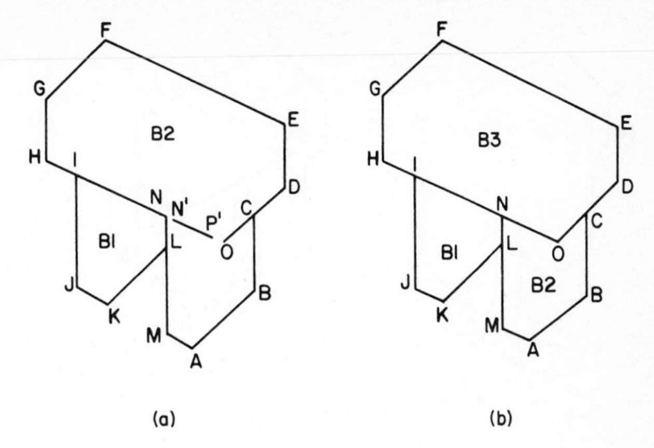

Fig. 3.9 Splitting a body into two new bodies.

extended to P4. This helps to find bodies sitting on obscured edges.

Whenever one of the above steps is finished, considerable information is stored. It is then available to help guide further search. For instance, if tracking along a line terminates, a test is made to see if the line is an extension of other known lines or if the line is connected to a known vertex. If a new boundary line connects two known boundary lines, the body is split into two. In Fig. 3.9, line N′P′ is obtained by tracking from point N. This line is interpreted as an extension of HN, and HN and N′P′ are merged into one straight line using the equations of these two lines. It is then connected to CO and Fig. 3.9(*b*) is obtained. Before the line was connected to CO, there were two bodies B1 and B2 as in Fig. 3.9(*a*). Now body B2 is split into two bodies, B2 and B3. We can interpret line NO as the boundary of B3 which hides a part of B2. Other properties of lines and vertexes are obtained similarly at this stage.

3.2.3 Examples of Line Hypothesizing

Figure 3.10 illustrates the entire line-finding procedure. At first, the contour lines AB, BC, CD, DE, EF, FG, GH, HI, IJ, JK and KA are obtained as shown in Fig. 3.10(*a*). Step (1) described in the previous section is tried for the concave points G and J. In this example, the position of G is not precise enough to find the extension of FG. On the other hand, a line segment is found as an extension of the line KJ. KJ is extended by tracking as far as L. Because there is no other point to which step (1) is applicable, step (2) is tried for point G. One line segment is found and extended until tracking terminates. Thus a line G′M′ is obtained as in Fig. 3.10(*b*). This line is interpreted as an extension of FG and connected to JL. Then the positions of points F, G, L are adjusted as shown in Fig. 3.10(*c*). Now two bodies B1

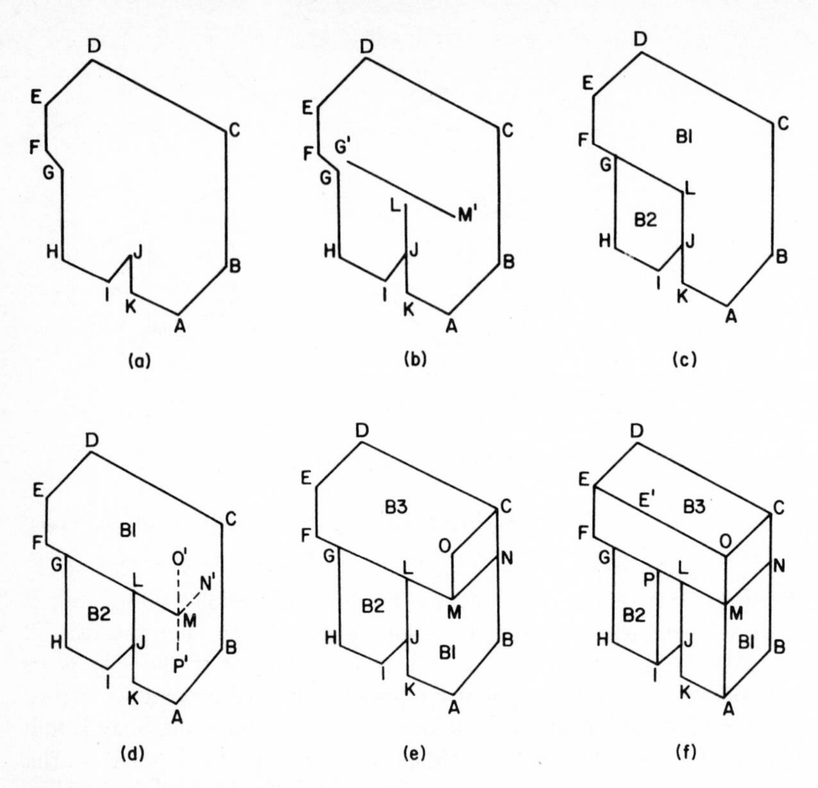

Fig. 3.10 Steps in analysis.

and B2 are created by the boundary lines GL and JL. It is important to notice this, for it means that step (1) is again applicable at this stage to point L. Thus line FL is extended as far as M in Fig. 3.10(*d*) (Note that line MN′ has not yet been found). LM is interpreted as an extension of FL but the end point M is not connected to any other lines. Thus vertexes F, G, L and end point M are adjusted considering the new line LM. Here neither step (1), (2), nor (3) is applicable, so that (4) is now applied to M. Three lines are found by circular search as Fig. 3.10(*d*). MN′ is determined as a boundary line and extended by tracking. When it terminates, the line is connected to boundary line BC at vertex N as in Fig. 3.10(*e*). Body B1 splits into bodies B1 and B3. It is known at this stage that B1 is hidden by B3, and B2 is hidden partly by B3 and partly by B1. Next, step (6) is applied to each body sequentially, selecting first the body for which it is easiest to propose the internal lines. In this example, the order is B3, B1, B2 because B3 hides B1 which hides B2. Internal lines CO and MO are found and connected at vertex O, but no line segment is found using step (6) and (7) applied to vertex E–this stage is shown in Fig. 3.10(*e*). Step (8) is applied to vertex O and a line segment toward E is found. This is extended by tracking as far as E′ as in Fig. 3.10(*f*).

Line OE′ fails to be connected to any other lines; this failure activates step (10). After a few trials, OE′ is extended to connect to vertex E. Similarly, internal line AM is obtained for body B1 and line IP is obtained for B2. When every step has finished, the three bodies and the relationships between them have been discovered.

We now describe the details of the algorithms that are used in finding contours and in the steps stated in Sec. 3.2.2. Some of them, such as tracking and circular search are used in more than one step. An algorithm used in more than one step may appear in slightly different forms but its essential part is not changed.

3.2.4 Verifying Hypothesized Initial Segments

Testing for a new line usually begins with a given hypothesis about starting point and direction. The procedure described in this section takes the given information and explores a small area in order to confirm or deny the presence of the proposed line. Confirmation of an initial start leads to tracking activity described later.

This verifying procedure is used in most of the steps cited earlier. The procedure consists of two parts: One is to detect the possible feature points which are to be regarded as elements of the line. The other is to test whether or not the possible feature points do indeed constitute a line segment.

In detecting feature points, we should consider various types of edges. Herskovits and Binford noted that the light intensity profiles across an edge divide nicely into three types–step, roof, and spike–and proposed three types of boundary detectors. In this paper, a roof type detector is not considered because roof type edges can be detected by a step detector or a spike detector. In addition, most roof type effects are accompanied by step or spike effects.

Imagine Cartesian coordinates U-V such that U is the direction of the line segment to be detected as shown in Fig. 3.11. Let I(u, v) denote the light intensity at point (u, v).

Now both step edges and spike edges are signaled by pronounced changes in intensity level. The temptation is therefore to search for them with a sort of derivative taking difference operation, $I(u, v + 1) - I(u, v)$. As is well known however, simple-minded differencing exaggerates noise. We therefore smooth the differencing. The measure of edge likelihood at some point v, the contrast function, is the average of a field of points to the right minus the average of a symmetric field to the left.

More precisely, we define the contrast function F(u, v) at (u, v) as

$$F(u, v) = \sum_{i,j} I(u + i, v + j) - I(u + i, v - j)$$

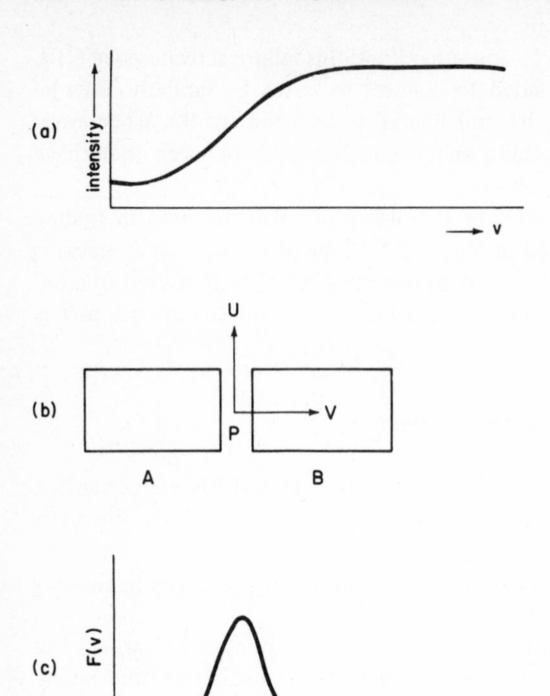

Fig. 3.11 Computation of F(u, v). (*a*) Light intensity level profile; (*b*) areas to compute F at P; (*c*) F(u, v) for (*a*).

Suppose we have an intensity profile as shown in Fig. 3.11(*a*). F(u, v) at P in Fig. 3.11(*b*) is the difference of summed intensity between areas A and B. F(u, v) for a typical step-type profile is shown in Fig. 3.11(*c*) in which the edge is detected as the peak. The typical profiles of F(u, v) for other types are shown in Fig. 3.12 where the edges are detected at the middle point between positive and negative peaks.

We are now interested in how F(u, v) varies with v. To avoid confusion, we drop the u parameter and write F(u, v) as F(v).

The basic procedure, therefore, is to detect the peak of F(v) and its position. But some care must be taken to find good peaks and to pinpoint their location. To be good a peak must be sufficiently high in an absolute sense and must be sufficiently high relative to the nearby troughs. These necessary properties are insured by the following points (See Fig. 3.13):

1. If v ranges from L to R, there must exist a maximum of F(v) at v = M where M is other than L or R.
2. It must be the case that F(M) > Ta where Ta is a threshold on absolute height.

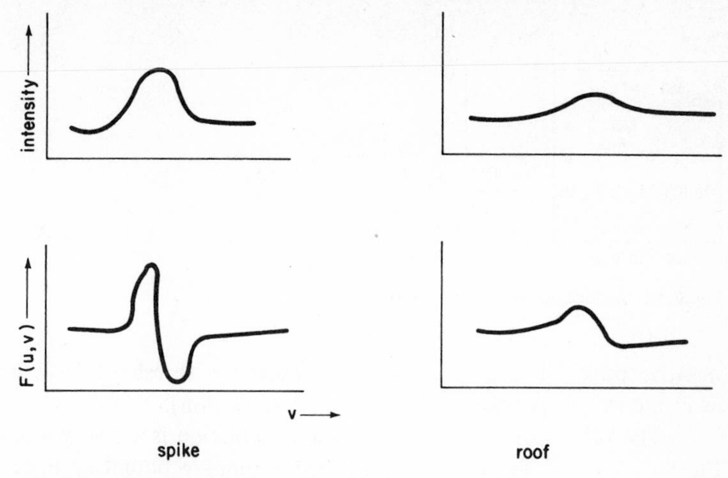

Fig. 3.12 Typical profile of F(u, v).

3. There must exist a minimum of F(v) at v = X between L and M and a minimum of F(v) at v = Y between M and R such that

$$F(M) - F(X) > Tr$$

$$F(M) - F(Y) > Tr$$

where Tr is a threshold on relative height.

A peak that passes these tests often has a broad flat top. Small amounts of noise can therefore move the maximum point widely between the peak's shoulders. Consequently, the location of the peak is not recorded as the point where the contrast function tops out but rather as the midpoint between the sharply defined shoulders. After the peak at M is found, the left shoulder of the peak S1 and the right shoulder of the peak S2 are determined as the intersection of F(v) with the line $G(v) = c1\,F(M) + c0$ as shown in Fig. 3.13. The position of the peak P is obtained as the middle of S1 and S2. If more than one peak is found between L and R, the point P which is nearest to the middle of L and R is adopted. A negative peak is similarly detected. A feature point for a spike or roof is obtained as the middle of the positive and

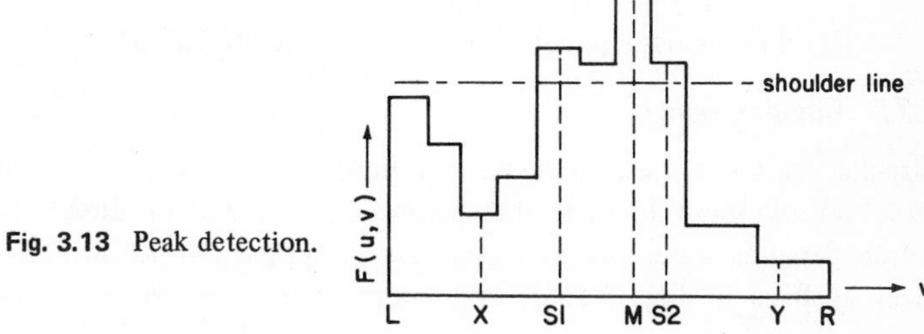

Fig. 3.13 Peak detection.

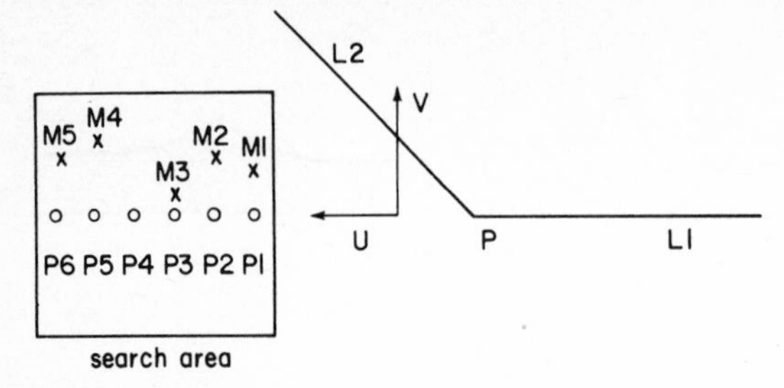

Fig. 3.14 Detection of feature point colinearity.

negative peaks, if both are found (although the threshold Ta is not the same as in the simple positive or negative peak detection).

The other part of the line segment detection is a test of the collinearity for the detected feature points. Suppose concave boundary lines L1 and L2 meet at P and suppose the line segment extending L1 is tested as shown in Fig. 3.14. Feature points are detected in a rectangular search area with given length and width in the direction of L1 at an appropriate place where the detection of feature points is not affected by the edge corresponding to L2. Feature points are looked for near the center points P1, P2, . . . , Pn sequentially. If positive peaks M1, M2, . . . , Mn are found, the collinearity of those points is determined as follows:

1. The number of the feature points must exceed a threshold number Tn.
2. The deviation σ^2 of the points in line fitting with the least square method must be less than a threshold Ts.
3. Let U′ denote the direction of line segment obtained by line fitting. U is the direction of L1. Then [U′ − U] must be less than Tu, where [U′ − U] denotes the difference in directions U′ and U.

Similar tests are made for each of the different types of feature points. If more than one type of line segment is found, the selection depends on the following criteria.

1. If a spike type is found, then it is selected.
2. For the line segment with σ^2 and U′, let the criterion function be $D = \sigma^2 + c[U' - U]$ where c is a constant.

The line segment selected is the one with smallest D.

3.2.5 Circular Search

Circular search is used to search for lines starting at a given point when the direction of these lines is not known. The range of directions in circular search depends upon the particular case. Suppose two known lines L1 and L2 meet at P as in Fig. 3.15(*a*) and suppose we wish to search for lines lying

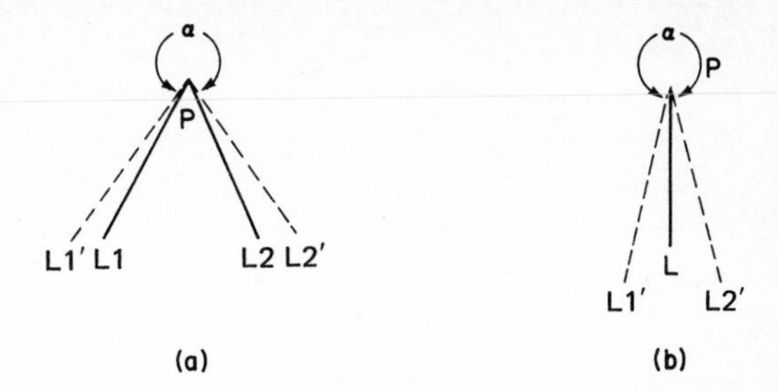

Fig. 3.15 Range of circular search.

between them. The search range alpha is between two lines L1′ and L2′ whose directions are slightly inside of L1 and L2 respectively. If lines starting at the end of an unconnected line L are searched for, as in Fig. 3.15(*b*), L1′ and L2′ are similarly set off from L. The center point P of the circular search is not always precisely determined, especially when tracking along a line has terminated at point P as shown in Fig. 3.15(*b*).

It might be natural to try to detect feature points based upon F(v) along arcs around the center. The difficulty with this search is the classification of feature points into line segments if there is more than one as shown in Fig. 3.16. To side step this difficulty, a simple algorithm is used in this system. Its basic method is to apply line segment detection successively in various directions. This is illustrated in Fig. 3.17, where successive line segment detections toward several directions are applied. The step of direction change and the search area are determined so that line segments of any direction near the center point can be found. Thus successive circular search along a line as shown back in Fig. 3.8 can find lines starting at points between two adjacent center points (e.g., line L in Fig. 3.18 starting between P1 and P2).

Fig. 3.16 Finding lines determined by feature points on circular arcs is difficult.

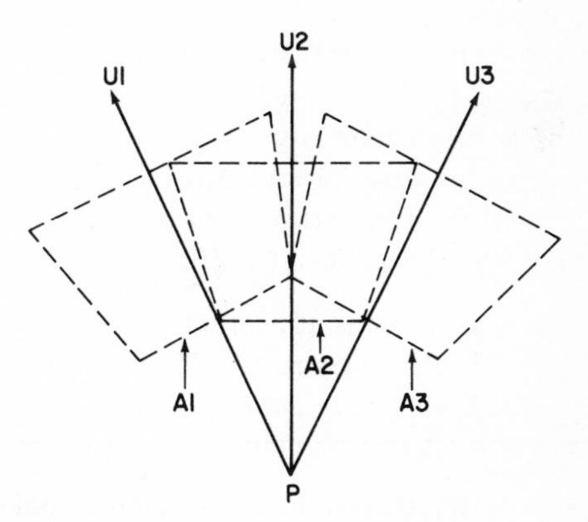

Fig. 3.17 Successive line detection in circular search.

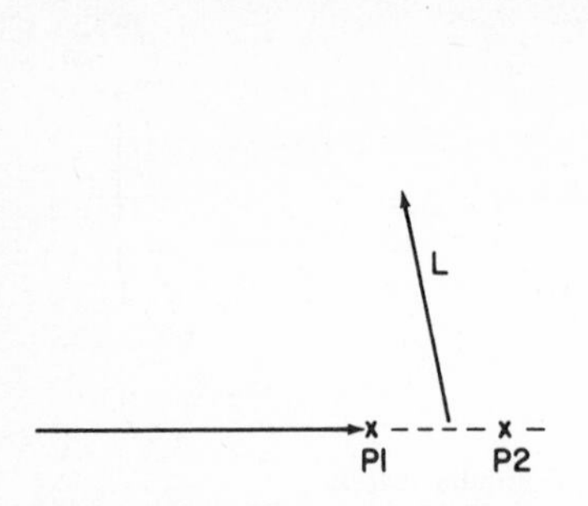

Fig. 3.18 Successive circular search.

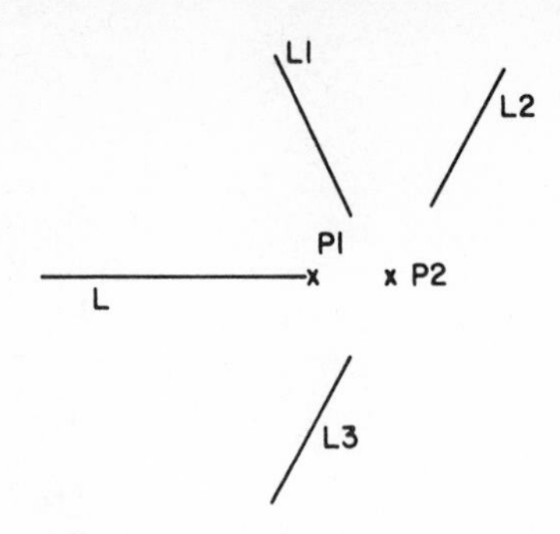

Fig. 3.19 Repeated circular search.

The algorithm for line segment detection is the same as that previously described for verifying initial line segments, differing only with respect to thresholds and search area. Because the search areas for different directions overlap each other, the same line segment may be found in different searches. Each time a line segment is found by line segment detection, a check is made to determine if it is the same as one obtained by the previous detection.

If the center point of circular search has not been determined precisely, it is not always possible to find all the lines starting at the given point. In Fig. 3.19, for example, line L2 might be missed in circular search at P1. To avoid this inconvenience, when any other lines segments are found (such as L1 and L3 in the figure), a new center point P2 is calculated based on the known line and the newly obtained line segments (L1 and L3).

3.2.6 Tracking Lines

Tracking is the process which crawls forward from a given initial line segment searching for the end of the line. The requirements for a tracking procedure are that the line should not be lost because of the effect of other lines or noise and that the procedure should terminate as precisely as possible at the end of the line. These requirements force a trade off because insensitivity to noise forces some insensitivity to line termination.

The basic procedure is to predict the location of a feature point and to search for it near that point using the line segment feature point detector. The result of the search is classified into the following four cases:

1. There is no feature point.
2. A feature point is on the line.
3. A feature point is not on the line.
4. A feature point may or may not be on the line.

The detection of a feature point is similar to line segment detection except that the type of edge is already known so that the thresholds can be adjusted based on the average peak of F(v). The decision among the other three cases is made straightforwardly, using the distance D between the point and the projection of the line as tracked so far.

If $D < D1$, then case (2)
If $D > D2$, then case (3)
If $D1 < D < D2$, then case (4)

As the procedure moves along, its confidence in continuing is determined by two numbers m and n. Roughly speaking, m is a nervousness parameter: it goes up when a scan yields no feature point and it goes down when a feature point is found within the distance D1 of the progressing line. Recall that D1 is the threshold which decides if a feature point is in fact on the line. D1 depends linearly on n. They move up together when a string of slightly off-line feature points suggest that the line has taken a jog. Thus off-line feature points move toward acceptance if there are enough of them. Both n and D1 go down as soon as a feature point falls with the broadening scope of the D1 threshold for a string of feature points. Both m and n start out at zero. Tracking stops when m gets too high indicating a lack of feature points or when the sum of m and n gets too high, indicating a combined insecurity stimulated both by a lack of feature points and by the poor position of those that are present.

The value of m and n are changed for all cases as follows:

1. *No feature point*

$$m \leftarrow m + 1$$

2. *Feature point on the line*

If $m > Tm$, then $m \leftarrow m - 1$, where Tm is a constant

Otherwise, $m \leftarrow 0$, $n \leftarrow 0$, and reclassify those feature points which have previously been classified in the doubtful category 4 into the on-the-line category 2. Adjust the equation of the line with these points and the present feature point.

3. *Feature point off the line*

If $D < Td$ and $m > Tm$, then $m \leftarrow m - 1$, where Td is a constant

Otherwise, no change

4. *Feature point position ambiguous*

$n \leftarrow n + 1$, and if $m > Tm$, then $m \leftarrow m - 1$

The threshold D1 is represented as $D1 = c1 + c2\,n$, where c1 and c2 are constants. This procedure is repeated and tracking proceeds step by step, extending the line until the termination condition is satisfied.

Tracking terminates when either $m > T1$ or $m + n > T2$, where T1 and T2 are constants. The terminal point is defined as the last point classified into

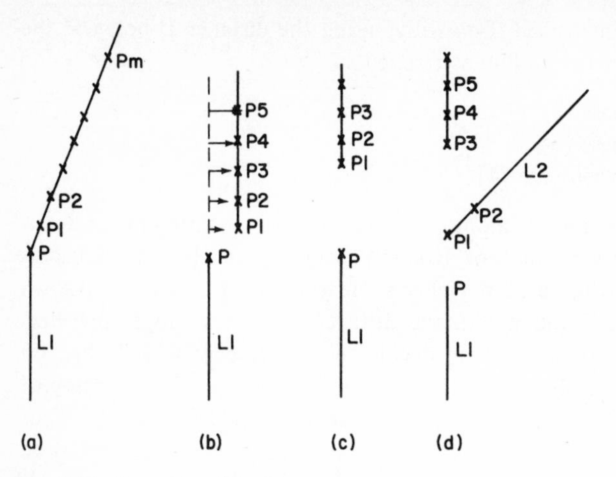

Fig. 3.20 Examples of tracking.

case 2. Figure 3.20 illustrates how this algorithm works. In Fig. 3.20(*a*) two lines cross at P. Tracking might finish at some point beyond P (Pm in the figure) which satisfies the termination condition. The terminal point of tracking is, however determined more precisely near P (P1 or P2). In Fig. 3.20(*b*), P1, P2, P3, and P4 are classified into case 4, increasing the value of n which classifies P5 into case 2. Then the line is adjusted with these points which are now classified into case 2 and tracking proceeds.

Figure 3.20(*c*) and (*d*) illustrate that even if a part of the intensity profile is disturbed by noise or other lines, tracking does not terminate there. In Fig. 3.20(*d*), however, if the light intensity of the right side of L1 changes across L2, the type of feature points might change after crossing L2. Thus feature points P3, P4, . . . might not be obtained and tracking might terminate at P1. When tracking terminates, the line segment detection is applied at the extension of the line to see if another type of line segment is found. If found, we adjust the line equation and tracking proceeds. If not found, tracking finally terminates at point P1 and the position of P1 is adjusted with the line equation.

3.3 EXPERIMENTAL RESULTS AND COMMENTS

To test the program, experiments were made with cubes and wedges having relatively uniform white surfaces placed on a black background. The image dissector camera, used as the input device, returns intensity information from points on a 1024 X 1024 grid. Objects occupy only a part of the scene. In a typical experimental scene, the rectangular area which includes the objects of interest may consist of only about 400 X 400 points.

Sound experimental practice requires that the pictures be stored to ease debugging and facilitate method comparisons. Consequently pictures are stored in mass memory in blocks which contain intensities from square patches each of which is made of 64 X 64 points giving fast access for these programs which know a lot about where to look. When a light intensity at some point is required, a block containing the point and adjacent points are brought into core memory.

In these experiments the light intensity is represented by a little less than 100 levels, spanning a range in intensity of about three to one. The input data for a clear bright edge in the dark background is blurred due to some optical and electo-optical limitations. If the real intensity change is a step function, there is a transient area in the input data about 10 points wide. Thus the resolution of the picture can be regarded as 10 points. The parameters used in line segment detection and tracking are based upon this resolution.

Some results are shown in Fig. 3.21. The difficulty or processing time of the recognition depends not only on the complexity of the object but also on the information known at each stage. In Fig. 3.21(*a*), for example, boundary

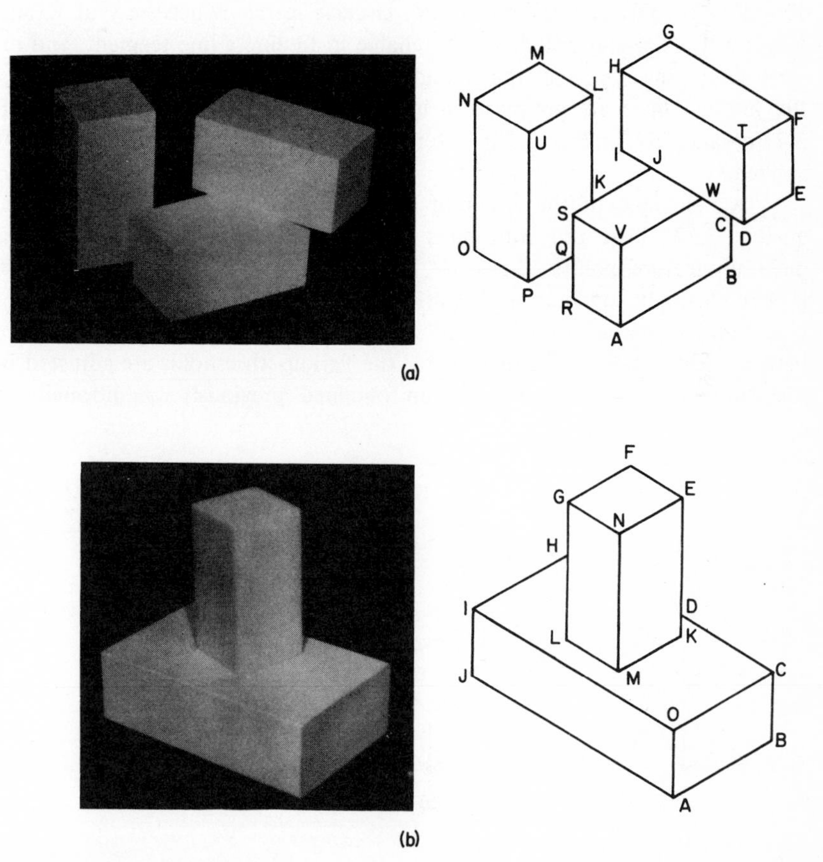

Fig. 3.21 Experimental results.

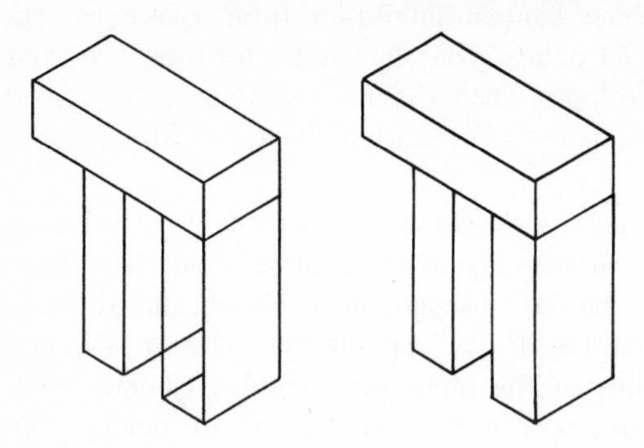

Fig. 3.22 Comparison between hierarchical and heterarchical program.

lines KS and QS are easily proposed as the extension of contour lines. On the other hand, it is not easy to find boundary lines KM or LM in Fig. 3.21(*b*). That is, after DK and HL are found, circular search is necessary at K and L respectively. Circular search is less reliable in finding a line segment, and more time consuming. Once all the boundary lines of an object are determined, all the internal lines are proposed in both cases. But tracking along VW in Fig. 3.21(*a*) and EN in Fig. 3.21(*b*) terminates in the middle. Then step (10) is applied.

An example of the result of an earlier pass-oriented program is shown in Fig. 3.22. That program looks at the whole scene homogeneously and picks up feature points. Lines are found using those feature points. But it is very difficult to determine a priori the various thresholds appropriate for detection of feature points, line fitting, and connection of lines. In the heterarchical program described here, the various thresholds are adjusted with the context of all the information obtained previously. Additionally, the

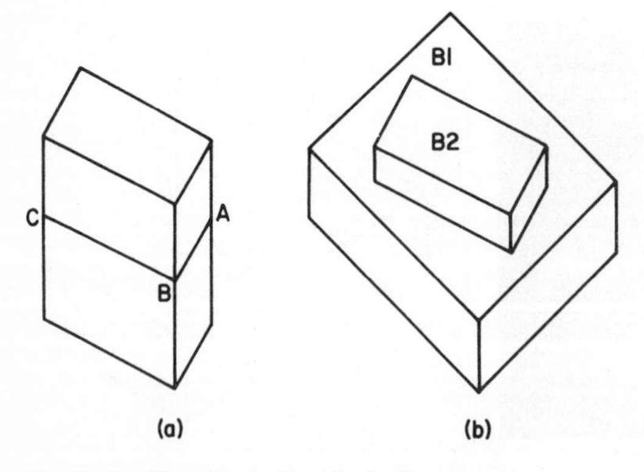

Fig. 3.23 Situations with a lack of cues.

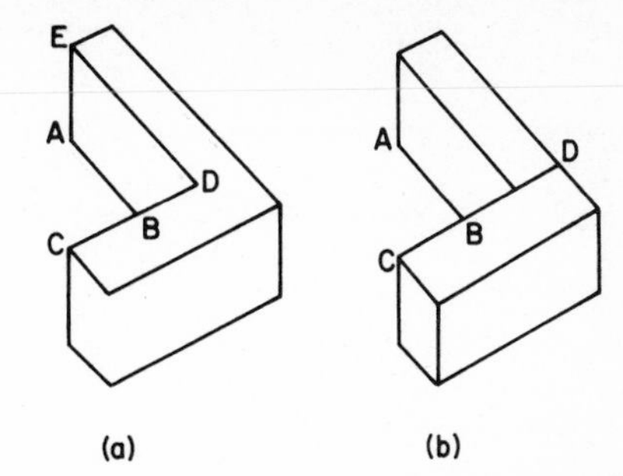

Fig. 3.24 Concave body difficulties.

particular tracking algorithm itself is changed from case to case depending on whether the line is a boundary or internal type.

The results of experiments with moderately complex scenes are mostly satisfactory. However, there are some limitations of this program at present. One of them is that bodies may be missed in some cases. A simple example is shown in Fig. 3.23. The boundary lines AB and BC in Fig. 3.23(*a*) are not proposed, though the other contour lines and internal lines are found, because the resulting regions are such that no concave vertexes activate step 1. In such a case when bodies are neatly stacked, it is necessary to search for boundary lines which start from some points on the contour line. In Fig. 3.23(*b*) body B2 is not found. To find a body that is included in a face of another body, it is necessary to search for line segments inside the region. Though these two kinds of search (search along the boundary line and search in the region) are required to find all the bodies in the scenes as shown in Fig. 3.23, they are still more effective than the exhaustive search in the entire scene.

A more serious limitation of the present program is that it is not always applicable to concave objects. Figure 3.24(*a*) shows a simple example. Line BD is found as an extension of line CB. If all the bodies are convex, line BD is interpreted like a boundary line as shown in Fig. 3.24(*b*). This does not hold for concave bodies. In this program, line BD is regarded as a boundary line, and then line DE is found by circular search at D. At this stage, however, DE should be interpreted as an internal line of the same body instead of as a boundary line which separates the body into two. If DE were interpreted correctly, then line BD could be determined to be an internal line.

4 OBTAINING SHAPE FROM SHADING INFORMATION

Berthold Horn

4.1 INTRODUCTION

4.1.1 Shading as a Monocular Depth Cue

An image of a smooth object known to have a uniform surface will exhibit gradations of reflected light intensity which can be used to determine its shape. This is not obvious since at each point in the image we know only the reflectivity at the corresponding object point. For some points (called singular points here) the reflectivity does uniquely determine the local normal, but for almost all points it does not. Consequently, the shape of the surface cannot be found by local operations alone.

For many surfaces the fraction of the incident light which is scattered in a given direction is a smooth function of the angles involved. It is convenient to think of the situation as depending on the three angles shown in Fig. 4.1: the incident angle between the local normal and the incident ray, the emittance angle between the local normal and the emitted ray, and the phase angle between the incident and the emitted rays.

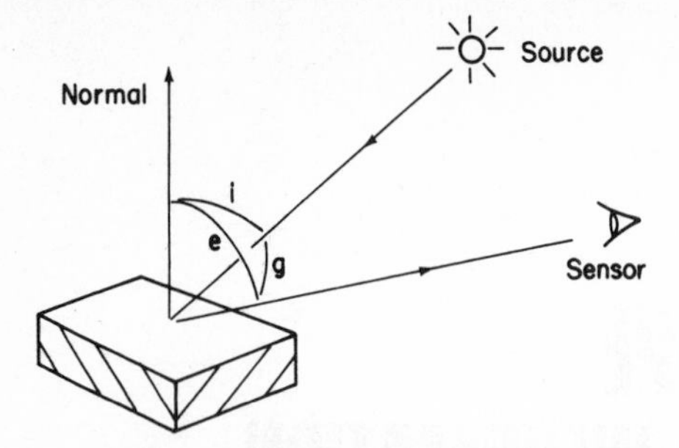

Fig. 4.1 Definition of the incident (i), emittance (e), and phase angle (g).

We will show that the shape can be obtained from the shading if we know the reflectivity function and the position of the light sources. The reflectivity and the gradient of the surface are related by a nonlinear first-order partial differential equation in two unknowns. The recipe for solving this equation involves setting up an equivalent set of five ordinary differential equations, three for the coordinates and two for the components of the gradient. These five equations can then be integrated numerically along certain curved paths. For while we cannot determine the gradient locally, we can, roughly speaking, determine its component in one special direction. Then taking a small step in this direction, we can repeat the process. The curve traced out on the object in this manner is called a characteristic. Figure 4.2 shows the characteristics determined for an experimental sphere. Their projections on the image plane will be referred to as the base characteristics. The shape of the visible surface of the object is thus given as a sequence of coordinates on characteristics along its surface.

Figures 4.3 and 4.4 show stereo pairs for three test cases. Figure 4.5 gives contour maps for the same three objects.

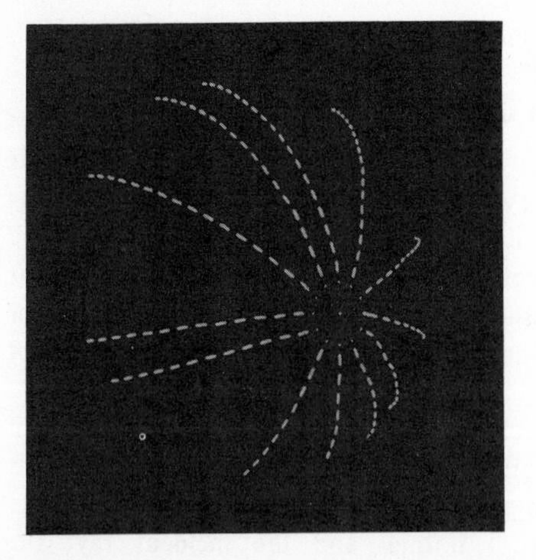

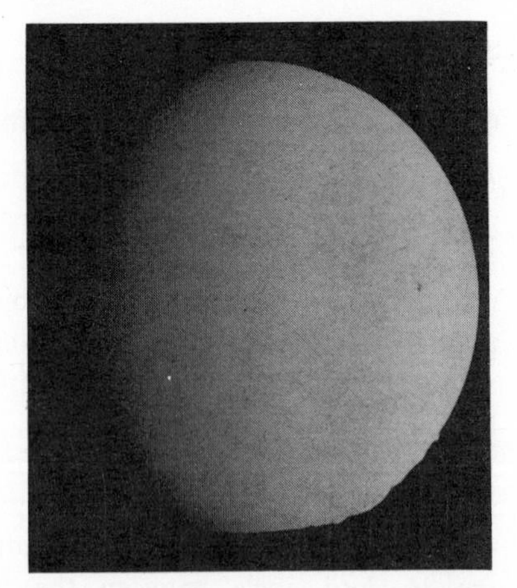

Fig. 4.2 Image of a sphere and a stereo pair of the characteristic curves obtained from the shading.

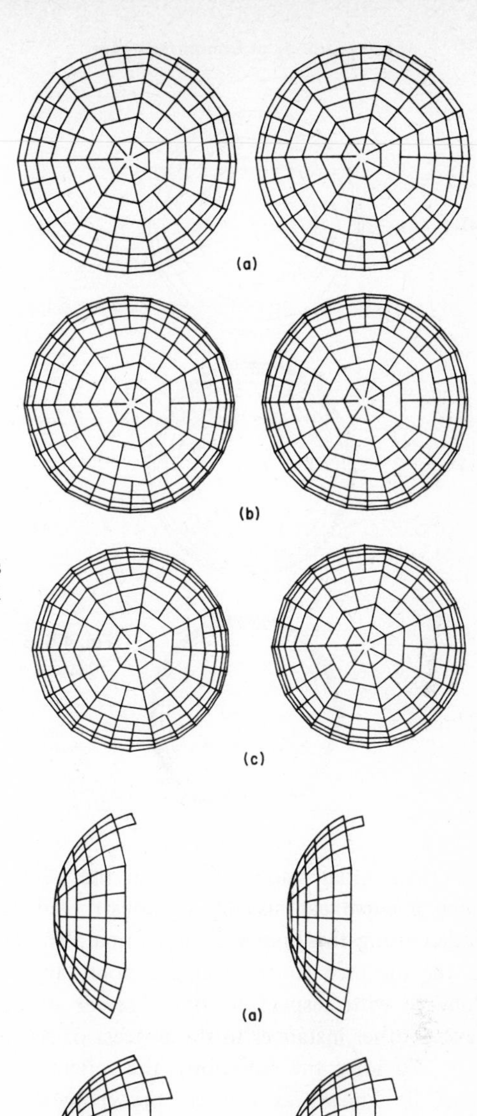

Fig. 4.3 Stereo pairs of solutions for dish-shaped, spherical, and bullet-shaped objects.

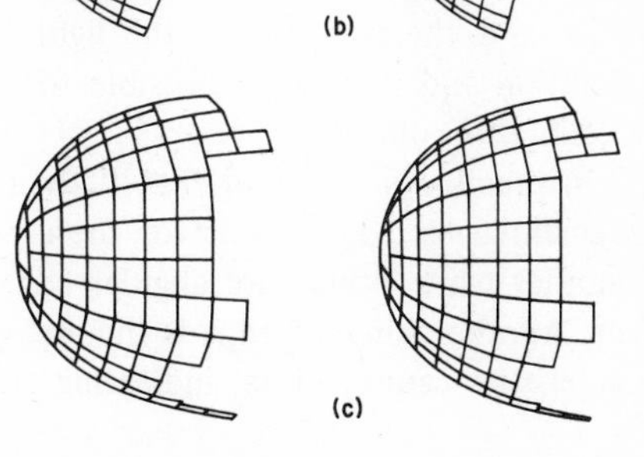

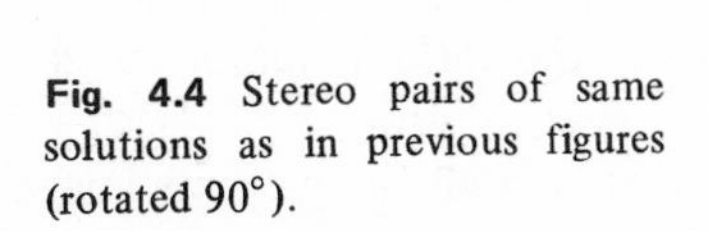

Fig. 4.4 Stereo pairs of same solutions as in previous figures (rotated 90°).

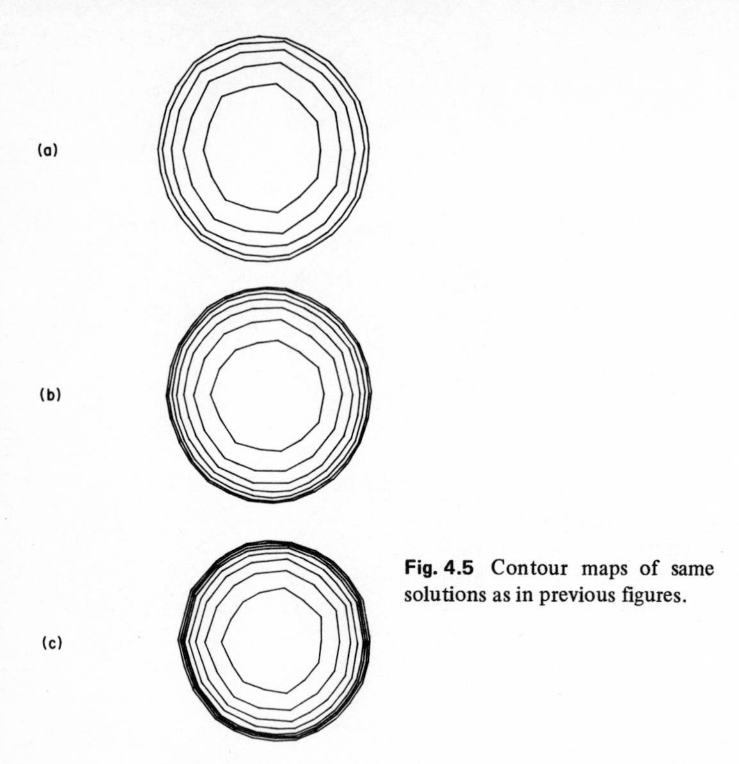

Fig. 4.5 Contour maps of same solutions as in previous figures.

An initial known curve on the object is needed to start the solution. Such a curve can usually be constructed near the singular points mentioned earlier using the known local normal. The only additional information needed is the distance to the singular point and whether the surface is convex or concave with respect to the observer at this point—such ambiguities arise in several other instances in the process of solution as will be seen.

To solve the equations, the reflectivity as a function of the three angles must be known as well as the geometry relating light source, object, and observer. Multiple or extended light sources increase the complexity of the solution algorithm presented. But all of this initially needed information can be deduced from the image if a calibration object of known shape is present in the same image. Furthermore, incorrect assumptions about the reflectivity function and the position of the light sources can lead to inconsistencies in the solution and it may be possible to utilize this information in the absence of a calibration object.

In practice it is found that if the object is at all complex, its image will be segmented by edges. Some of these represent the occlusion of one surface by another while others are angular edges (also called joints here) on a single object. Another kind of edge is the ambiguity edge. This is an edge which the characteristics cannot cross, indicating an ambiguity which cannot be resolved locally. One can solve inside each region bounded by these various edges, but some global or external knowledge is needed to match up the regions. In the case of an angular edge on an object one can integrate up to the edge and then use the known location of the edge as an initial curve for another region.

A very similar situation obtains when one bridges a shadow. Since one edge of the shadow and the position of the light source is known, we can trace along the rays grazing the edge until the corresponding image points fall on an illuminated region. Since we know the path of each ray, we can calculate the coordinates of the point where it impinges on the object by triangulation. The edge of the shadow (which need not be on the same object) can then serve as an initial curve from which to continue the solution.

4.1.2 Applications

A number of interesting applications of this method can be mentioned. The first of these concerns the scanning electron microscope which produces images which are particularly easy to interpret because the intensity recorded is a function of the slope of the object at that point and is thus a form of shading. In optical and transmission electron microscopes, intensities depend instead on thickness and optical or electron density. The geometry of the scanning electron microscope allows several simplifications in the algorithm for determining shape from shading. Because of the random access capability of the microscope beam, it should be easy and useful to combine it with a small computer to obtain three-dimensional information directly.

Another interesting demonstration lies in the determination of lunar topography. Here the special reflectivity function of the material in the maria of the moon allows a very great simplification of the equations used in the shape-from-shading algorithm. The equations in fact reduce to one integral which must be evaluated along each of a family of predetermined straight lines in the image.

So far we have assumed that the surface is uniform in its photometric properties. Any nonuniformity will cause this algorithm to determine an incorrect shape. This is one of the uses of facial makeup, because by darkening certain slopes those slopes can be made to appear steeper. In some cases surface-markings can be detected if they lead to discontinuities of the calculated shape.

Judging by our wide use of monocular pictures (photographs or even paintings and woodcuts) of people and other smooth objects, humans are good at interpreting shading information. The shortcomings of our method which are related to the shading information available can be expected to be found in human visual perception too. It will of course be difficult to decide whether the visual system actually determines the shape quantitatively or whether it uses the shading information in a very qualitative way only.

4.1.3 History of the Problem

The literature on perception has only a few conjectures on the possibility of determining shape from the monocular depth-cue of shading. One relevant paper is on lunar topography[1] which gives complete details of a solution obtained in the form of an integral in the special case of the reflectivity function of the moon. It can be shown that the result is in fact a special case of the general solution derived here.

Various defects of image-dissector sensing devices affect the accuracy of shape measurements. Since very little was known about the characteristics of this device on other than theoretical grounds, a program was developed to measure properties such as resolution, signal-to-noise ratio, drift, settling time, scatter, and pinholes in the photocathode.[2] Software now compensates for some defects such as geometric distortion and nonuniform sensitivity using measurements from test patterns.

In parallel with the programming work, theoretical efforts were made to define and get around some of the difficulties of the method. Of particular interest were applications where the equations simplify greatly. Unfortunately the massive simplification found in the case of lunar topography seems unique.

4.2 THEORY

4.2.1 Reflectivity Functions

Consider a surface element of size dS inclined i with respect to the incident ray and e with respect to the emitted ray. The angles are measured with respect to the normal as was shown in Fig. 4.1. Let the incident light intensity be I_1 per unit area perpendicular to the incident ray. The amount of light falling on the surface element is then $I_1 \cos(i)\, dS$.

Let the emitted ray have intensity I_2 per unit solid angle per unit area perpendicular to the emitted ray. Therefore the amount of light intercepted by an area subtending a solid angle dw at the surface element will be $I_2 \cos(e)\, dS\, dw$. The reflectivity function $\phi(i, e, g)$ is then defined to be I_2/I_1.

If we want to be more precise about what units the intensity is measured in, we have to take into account the spectral distribution of the light emitted by the source, as well as the spectral sensitivity of the sensor. With this proviso we can speak of watts per unit area and watts per unit solid angle per unit area. We need not be too concerned with this if we either use white paint, or measure the reflectivity function with the same equipment later used in the shape-from-shading algorithm. It should be noted that for most surfaces the reflectivity function is dependent on the color of the light used. Typically the specular component of the reflected light, being reflected before it has penetrated far into the surface, will be unchanged, while the mat component will be colored by pigments in the surface coating.

Several other definitions of the reflectivity function are in use which are multiples of the one defined here by π, 2, cos(e) and/or cos(i). The specific formulation chosen here makes the equation relating the incident light intensity to the image illumination very simple.

Surfaces where the three parameters i, e, and g are not sufficient to fully determine the reflectivity are unsuitable for this analysis. Examples are translucent objects and those with nonisotropic surface properties like hair and the mineral commonly called tigereye.

Perhaps the most important determinant of the reflectivity function is the microstructure of the surface. Different reflectivity functions may apply at different magnifications. At high magnification many objects become increasingly translucent. It is best therefore to determine the reflectivity function under conditions similar to those later used in the determination of the shape of the object.

One way to measure the reflectivity function is to employ a goniophotometer fitted with a small flat sample of the surface to be investigated. The device can be set for any combination of incident, emittance and phase angles.

To avoid having to move the source and the sensor into all possible positions with respect to a flat sample of the surface when measuring the reflectivity function, it is convenient to have a test-object which presents all possible values of i and e for a given g. The constraints are $i + e \leqslant g$, $e + g \leqslant i$ and $g + i \leqslant e$. Use of such an object is greatly simplified by using a telephoto lens and a distant source, giving almost constant g. It is convenient to tabulate the reflectivity versus i and e for each of a series of values of g. A sphere is the easiest test-object to use if one is willing to live with the decreasing accuracy in determining e as one approaches the edge.

One could also have an object of known shape in the same scene as the object to be analyzed. This solves the problem of having to know the source location and the transfer properties of the image forming system. In some cases objects of known shape and surface characteristics differing from those of the object under study are useful—for example a sphere with specular reflectivity can pinpoint the location of the light sources.

Alternately, one might hope to predict reflectivity functions on a theoretical basis starting with some assumed microstructure of the surface. White mat surfaces are usually finely divided grains of transparent material such as snow or crushed glass. White paint consists of transparent 'pigment' particles (e.g., SiO_2 or TiO_2) of high refractive index and small size (optimally about the wavelength of visible light) suspended in a transparent medium of low refractive index. If one chooses to model a regular arrangement of suspended particles of uniform size and makes restrictive assumptions, one can derive a reflectivity function and study its dependence on various parameters.

Another type of surface is that of a highly reflective material (such as a metal) where the light rays do not penetrate into the material. Choosing a particular type of surface depression and a statistical distribution of the size of these, one can again derive a reflectivity function.

Only a few such models have been studied and little hope exists for modelling real surfaces well enough without having to abandon closed expressions for the reflectivity function.

4.2.2 The Differential Equation of Image Illumination

This section contains the derivation of the image illumination equation and the analytical formulation of the shape-from-shading problem.

At a known point on the object we can calculate g. We should like to find the gradient (or at least its component in one direction) at this point so as to be able to continue the solution to a neighboring point. Measurement of the light reflected tells us something about i and e. Since only one measurement is involved, we cannot generally hope to determine both i and e locally, but only a relation between the two. There are exceptional points where the normal is locally fully determined and this is useful in finding initial conditions as explained later.

Suppose we collapse the two principal planes of the image-forming system together, forming the x–y plane as shown in Fig. 4.6. Let the z-axis coincide with the optical axis and extend toward the object. Let f be image-plane distance from the exit pupil and assume that the image and object space refractive indexes are equal.

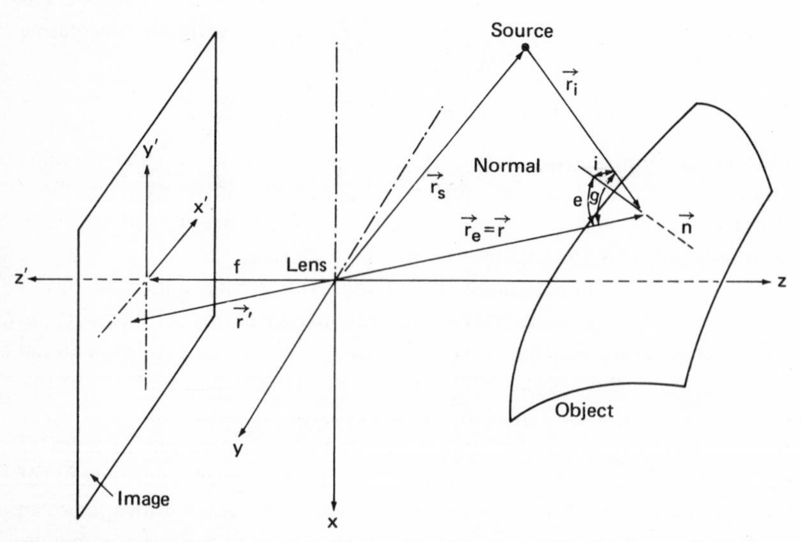

Fig. 4.6 Details of the geometry of image illumination and projection in the imaging system.

Let t be the ratio of image illumination to object luminescence.

Let $a(x, y, z)$ be the incident light intensity (usually constant or obeys some inverse square law).

Let $A(x, y, z) = t \cdot a(x, y, z)$.

Let $\mathbf{r} = (x, y, z)$ be a point on the object and $\mathbf{r}' = (x', y', f)$ the corresponding point in the image.

Let $b(x', y')$ be the intensity measured at the image point (x', y').

Let p and q be the partial derivatives of z with respect to x and y.

Let $I = \cos(i)$, $E = \cos(e)$ and $G = \cos(g)$.

We have $A(\mathbf{r})\,\phi(I, E, G) = b(\mathbf{r}')$.

We would like to show that this equation must be a first-order partial differential equation. This will be true if it contains only x, y, z, and the first partial derivatives p and q. We emphasize that this image illumination equation is the main equation studied here.

When finding a solution we assume $A(\mathbf{r})$ and $\phi(I, E, G)$ are known and $b(\mathbf{r}')$ is obtained from the image. We want to show that the equation is a first-order, nonlinear partial differential equation in two independent variables of the form:

$$F(x, y, z, p, q) = 0$$

From the simple projection geometry we have

$$\mathbf{r}' = \left(\frac{f}{z}\right) \cdot \mathbf{r}$$

where f is the image plane distance from the exit pupil. We took care of image reversal by orienting the x' and y' axes appropriately. It remains to show that I, E and G are functions of x, y, z, p and q. An inward normal to the surface at the point $\mathbf{r}$ is $\mathbf{n} = (-p, -q, 1)$.

Let the light source be at $\mathbf{r}_s = (x_s, y_s, z_s)$. Then the incident ray will be $\mathbf{r}_i = \mathbf{r} - \mathbf{r}_s$, and the emergent ray $-\mathbf{r}_e = -\mathbf{r}$. Clearly then

$$I = \hat{\mathbf{n}} \cdot \hat{\mathbf{r}}_i, \qquad E = \hat{\mathbf{n}} \cdot \hat{\mathbf{r}}_e \qquad \text{and} \qquad G = \hat{\mathbf{r}}_i \cdot \hat{\mathbf{r}}_e$$

where the ^'s denote unit vectors. All the terms thus involve only x, y, z, p and q. On substituting into the image illumination equation, it follows that we are dealing with a first-order nonlinear partial differential equation in the two unknowns x and y:

$$F(x, y, z, p, q) = A(\mathbf{r})\ \phi(I, E, G) - b(\mathbf{r}') = 0$$

4.2.3 Equivalent Ordinary Differential Equations

The usual method of dealing with a first-order nonlinear partial differential equation is to solve an equivalent set of five ordinary differential equations:

$$\dot{x} = F_p, \quad \dot{y} = F_q, \quad \dot{z} = pF_p + qF_q$$

$$\dot{p} = -F_x - pF_z \quad \text{and} \quad \dot{q} = -F_y - qF_z$$

The dot denotes differentiation with respect to s, a parameter which varies with distance along a so-called characteristic strip. The subscripts denote partial derivatives. These equations are solved along the characteristic strips. See, for example, Garabedian.[3] The characteristic strips are the characteristic curves described earlier (values of x, y, and z) plus the values of p and q on them.

It can be shown that these equations are equivalent to the image illumination equation. The demonstration is tedious and is omitted here. Interested readers may find the mathematics in books on partial differential equations.

Since we can multiply the equation $F = 0$ by any nonzero smooth function $\lambda(x, y, z, p, q)$ without altering the solution surface, we can obtain a different set of equations:

$$\dot{x} = \lambda F_p, \quad \dot{y} = \lambda F_q, \quad \dot{z} = \lambda(pF_p + qF_q)$$

$$\dot{p} = \lambda(-F_x - pF_z) \quad \text{and} \quad \dot{q} = \lambda(-F_q - qF_z)$$

The solution to this new set of equations will differ only in the values of the parameter s at any given point. For example if we let

$$\lambda = \frac{1}{\sqrt{F_p^2 + F_q^2 + (pF_p + qF_q)^2}}$$

the parameter s gives us arc-length along the characteristics. This is used in the programs to be described later. Of course we can only do this if the denominator is not zero.

At singular points and ambiguity edges the denominator will be zero since $F_p = F_q = 0$. A different choice for λ will be used later in the discussion of the scanning electron microscope.

4.2.4 Simplifying Situations

Since the general equations are fairly complex it is of great interest to find simplifying conditions. Some of these are presented in this section. But first we will need some partial derivatives, which it is convenient to introduce here.

The development of these partial derivatives requires some further simple notation. Let $\mathbf{A}$ be a vector (3-tuple) and $A = |\mathbf{A}|$ be the magnitude of A. Also let $\hat{\mathbf{A}} = \mathbf{A}/|\mathbf{A}|$ be the corresponding unit vector. Consider the dot-product $\mathbf{A} \cdot \mathbf{B}$ to be matrix multiplication of the 1 by 3 matrix $\mathbf{A}$ by the 3×1 matrix $\mathbf{B}^T$ (the transpose of B). Consider partial differentiation with respect to a vector to be the 3-tuple whose components are found by differentiating with respect to each component in turn. We denote this differentiation by a subscript. Then for example

$$A_A = \hat{A}$$

At times we will also need the partial derivatives of vectors with respect to vectors. These are defined as 3 X 3 matrices, the first row being the result of differentiating with respect to the first component and so on. Then for example

$$A_A = \begin{pmatrix} 1 & 0 & 0 \\ 0 & 1 & 0 \\ 0 & 0 & 1 \end{pmatrix}$$

We will also use partial derivatives of dot-produces of unit vectors with respect to vectors. For example

$$X = \hat{A} \cdot \hat{B} \qquad \text{and we want } X_A$$

To avoid finding $\hat{A}_A$ we write $A\,X = A \cdot \hat{B}$ and then

$$A_A\,X + A\,X_A = A_A \cdot \hat{B}$$

Extending the definition of dot-product in the appropriate way we find

$$A_A \cdot \hat{B} = \begin{pmatrix} 1 & 0 & 0 \\ 0 & 1 & 0 \\ 0 & 0 & 1 \end{pmatrix} \hat{B}^T = \hat{B}$$

$$A\,X_A = \hat{B} - X\,\hat{A}$$

$$X_A = \left(\frac{1}{A}\right)(\hat{B} - X\,\hat{A})$$

Given these results, we get the important relations, i.e.,

$$I_r = I_{r_i} = \left(\frac{1}{r_i}\right)(\hat{n} - I\,\hat{r}_i)$$

$$I_n = \left(\frac{1}{n}\right)(\hat{r}_i - I\,\hat{n})$$

$$E_r = E_{r_e} = \left(\frac{1}{r_e}\right)(\hat{n} - E\,\hat{r}_e)$$

$$E_n = \left(\frac{1}{n}\right)(\hat{r}_e - E\,\hat{n})$$

$$G_r = G_{r_i} + G_{r_e} = \left(\frac{1}{r_e}\right)(\hat{r}_i - G\,\hat{r}_e) + \left(\frac{1}{r_i}\right)(\hat{r}_e - G\,\hat{r}_i)$$

$$G_n = 0$$

We will now proceed to list some simplifying situations:

1. *Distant source*: Collimated source or the object subtends a small angle at the source.

   $A_r \cdot r_i = 0$ and for a truly distant source:

   $$A_r = 0$$

   Replace $\mathbf{r}_i$ by $k\mathbf{r}_i$ and let $k \to \infty$. Then

   $$I_r = 0, \; I_n \text{ unchanged}$$

   $$E_r \text{ and } E_n \text{ unchanged}$$

   $$G_r = \left(\frac{1}{r_e}\right)(\hat{r}_i - G\,\hat{r}_e), \; G_n = 0$$

   In addition choosing the z-axis along $\mathbf{r}_i$ removes further terms.

2. *Distant camera*: Telephoto lens or the object subtends a small angle at the camera.

   Replace $\mathbf{r}_e$ by $k\mathbf{r}_e$ and let $k \to \infty$. Then

   $$I_r \text{ and } I_n \text{ unchanged}$$

   $$E_r = 0, \; E_n \text{ unchanged}$$

   $$G_r = \left(\frac{1}{r_i}\right)(\hat{r}_e - G\,\hat{r}_i), \; G_n = 0$$

   In addition choosing the z-axis along $\mathbf{r}_e$ removes further terms.

3. *Distant source and distant camera*:

   $$I_r = 0, I_n \text{ unchanged}$$

   $$E_r = 0, E_n \text{ unchanged}$$

   $$G_r = 0, G_n = 0$$

   Most practical situations are an approximation of this case.

4. *Source at the camera*:

   $$\mathbf{r}_i = \mathbf{r}_e \qquad I = E \text{ and } G = 1$$

   $$I_r = E_r \text{ unchanged}$$

   $$I_n = E_n \text{ unchanged}$$

   $$G_r = 0 \text{ and } G_n = 0$$

5. *Distant source at distant camera*:

   $$I_r = E_r = G_r = 0$$

   $$I_n = E_n \text{ unchanged}, G_n = 0$$

Choosing the object to be on the z-axis removes further terms. This is the simplest possible case.

6. *Uniform illumination*: Uniform illumination (or an approximation thereof) is fairly common and might at first sight appear not to fit into our framework. It can be shown however that uniform illumination is equivalent to a point source at the camera and an altered reflectivity function.

4.2.5 The Five Differential Equations of Shading

We will now make further use of the notation and results of the last section. Recall the image illumination equation:

$$F(x, y, z, p, q) = A(\mathbf{r}) \quad \phi(I, E, G) - b(\mathbf{r}') = 0$$

We know $A(\mathbf{r})$ and $\phi(I, E, G)$, and obtain $b(\mathbf{r}')$ from the image. We need F_x, F_y, F_z, F_p and F_q. Since $\mathbf{r} = (x, y, z)$ and $\mathbf{n} = (-p, -q, 1)$ we can get all of these derivatives from $F_{\mathbf{r}}$ and $F_{\mathbf{n}}$.

$$F_{\mathbf{r}} = A(\mathbf{r}) \quad \phi_{\mathbf{r}}(I, E, G) + A_{\mathbf{r}}(\mathbf{r}) \quad \phi(I, E, G) - b_{\mathbf{r}}(\mathbf{r}')$$

$$F_{\mathbf{n}} = A(\mathbf{r}) \quad \phi_{\mathbf{n}}(I, E, G)$$

Let $\mathbf{a} = (I, E, G)$. Then

$$\phi_{\mathbf{r}} = \phi_{\mathbf{a}}\, \mathbf{a}_{\mathbf{r}} \qquad \text{and} \qquad \phi_{\mathbf{n}} = \phi_{\mathbf{a}}\, \mathbf{a}_{\mathbf{n}}$$

Note that $\mathbf{a}_{\mathbf{r}}$ and $\mathbf{a}_{\mathbf{n}}$ are 3×3 matrices, the rows of which we computed in the previous section.

$$\mathbf{a}_{\mathbf{r}} = \begin{bmatrix} \left(\frac{1}{r_i}\right)(\hat{\mathbf{n}} - I\,\hat{\mathbf{r}}_i) \\ \left(\frac{1}{r_e}\right)(\hat{\mathbf{n}} - E\,\hat{\mathbf{r}}_e) \\ \left(\frac{1}{r_e}\right)(\hat{\mathbf{r}}_i - G\,\hat{\mathbf{r}}_e) + \left(\frac{1}{r_i}\right)(\hat{\mathbf{r}}_e - G\,\hat{\mathbf{r}}_i) \end{bmatrix}$$

$$= \begin{bmatrix} \frac{1}{r_i} & -\frac{I}{r_i} & 0 \\ \frac{1}{r_e} & 0 & -\frac{E}{r_e} \\ 0 & \left(\frac{1}{r_e} - \frac{G}{r_i}\right) & \left(\frac{1}{r_i} - \frac{G}{r_e}\right) \end{bmatrix} \begin{bmatrix} \hat{\mathbf{n}} \\ \hat{\mathbf{r}}_i \\ \hat{\mathbf{r}}_e \end{bmatrix}$$

Note that this is the product of two 3×3 matrices. Similarly

$$a_n = \begin{bmatrix} \left(\frac{1}{n}\right)(\hat{r}_i - I\,\hat{n}) \\ \left(\frac{1}{n}\right)(\hat{r}_e - E\,\hat{n}) \\ \mathbf{0} \end{bmatrix}$$

$$= \begin{bmatrix} -\frac{I}{n} & \frac{1}{n} & 0 \\ -\frac{E}{n} & 0 & \frac{1}{n} \\ 0 & 0 & 0 \end{bmatrix} \begin{bmatrix} \hat{n} \\ \hat{r}_i \\ \hat{r}_e \end{bmatrix}$$

To evaluate the derivative F_r we need $b_r(r')$.

$$b_r(r') = b_{r'} \cdot r'_r$$

Written out in full we have

$$(b_x, b_y, b_z) = \left(\frac{f}{z}\right)\left\{b_{x'}, b_{y'}, -\left[\left(\frac{x}{z}\right)b_{x'} + \left(\frac{y}{z}\right)b_{y'}\right]\right\}$$

where $b_{x'}$ and $b_{y'}$ are measured directly from the image.

Since the intensities measured from the image do not locally determine the normal, one might well ask what, roughly, such measurements do determine. The components of the gradient of the intensity are related to the second derivatives of the distance to the surface, while the intensity itself is related to the magnitude of the first derivatives. This relationship becomes exact for the case of a distant source at a distant camera.

It should be noted that the equation for F_r also involves A_r. Usually A is fairly constant over the area of the object recorded in the image, or at least satisfies a simple inverse-square equation.

If $A = (r_l/r_i)^2$, then $A_r = -2(r_l^2/r_i^4)r_i$

where r_i is the incident vector, and r_l is the length of the incident vector to the singular point.

4.2.6 Initial Conditions and Singular Points

To select a particular solution surface among all possible solution surfaces one needs to specify an initial curve through which the solution surface must pass:

$$x = x(t), \quad y = y(t) \quad \text{and} \quad z = z(t)$$

Along this curve we must satisfy

$$z'(t) = p\,x'(t) + q\,y'(t)$$

$$F[x(t),\; y(t),\; z(t),\; p(t),\; q(t)] = 0$$

Here the dash represents differentiation with respect to t. This pair of nonlinear equations allows one to find p(t) and q(t) along the initial curve. There may be more than one solution, in which case there will be more than one solution surface. The characteristic strips sprout from the initial curve as for example in Fig. 4.7. The solution surface can be described parametrically:

$$x = x(s, t),\;\; y = y(s, t),\;\; z = z(s, t), \text{ and}$$

$$p = p(s, t),\;\; q = q(s, t)$$

Now it would be a great disadvantage if one always required an initial curve to start the solution from. Fortunately it is usually possible to calculate some initial curve if one makes some assumptions about the surface and uses the special singular points where the reflectivity uniquely determines the local normal.

The singular points are the brightest or the darkest points (depending on the reflectivity function). At all other points the normal cannot be locally determined. The singular points correspond to values of i and e for which the reflectivity is a unique global maximum or minimum. These may be either extrema or at the limiting values of the angles.

This method cannot be used if the surface does not contain a surface element oriented in this special direction. The points are found by looking for the brightest (or darkest) points in the image.

All we still need to know then is the distance of this point from the camera, but since one is usually only interested in relative distances this is not a serious restriction.

Unfortunately it will be found that the solution will not move from these singular points because $\dot{x} = \dot{y} = 0$. This is an indication that the algorithm needs to be informed about which way the surface is curved, convex or concave.

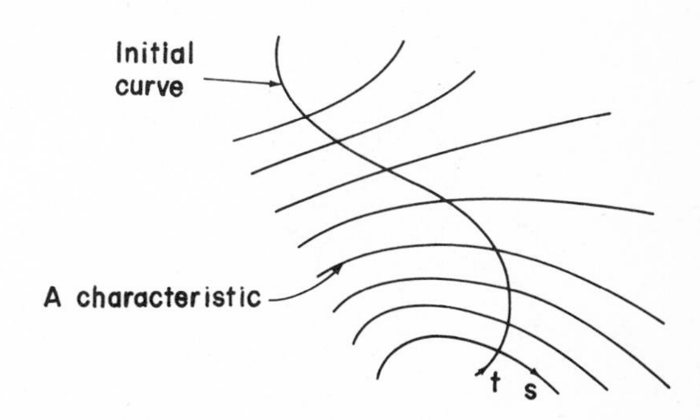

Fig. 4.7 Characteristic strips sprouting from an initial curve.

If the surface is convex (or concave) at the singular point and we have a guess at the radius of curvature (from the overall size of the object for example), we can get around the problem of singular points by constructing small spherical caps on them. Difficulties will be encountered if this point happens to be a saddle point, but the presence of a saddle point usually indicates that other singular points exist where the surface is either convex or concave.

Consider Fig. 4.8. Let **S** be the vector from the camera to the singular point (found from its known image coordinates and its distance from the camera). R is the estimated radius of curvature and ρ the distance we decide to step away from the singular point, determined in practice by considerations of uncertainty in the position of the singular point and the desired detail in the solution. The known normal at the singular point is $\hat{\mathbf{N}}_0$. We construct a spherical cap with center $\mathbf{S} - \mathrm{R}\hat{\mathbf{N}}_0$.

Let

$$R_1^2 = R^2 - r^2$$

$$\mathbf{S}_1 = \mathbf{S} + (R_1 - R)\hat{\mathbf{N}}_0$$

$$\mathbf{X} = \hat{\mathbf{y}} \times \hat{\mathbf{N}}_0 \text{ where } \hat{\mathbf{y}} = (0, 1, 0)$$

$$\mathbf{Y} = \hat{\mathbf{N}}_0 \times \hat{\mathbf{X}}$$

$$\mathbf{T}(t) = \rho(\hat{\mathbf{X}} \cos(2\pi\, t) + \hat{\mathbf{Y}} \sin(2\pi\, t)) \qquad 0 \leqslant t < 1$$

Points on the initial circle are then given by

$$\mathbf{S}_1 + \mathbf{T}(t)$$

We also need an initial guess at p and q, so we construct $\mathbf{N}_1$, (an outward normal):

$$\mathbf{N}_1(t) = R_1\hat{\mathbf{N}}_0 + \mathbf{T}(t)$$

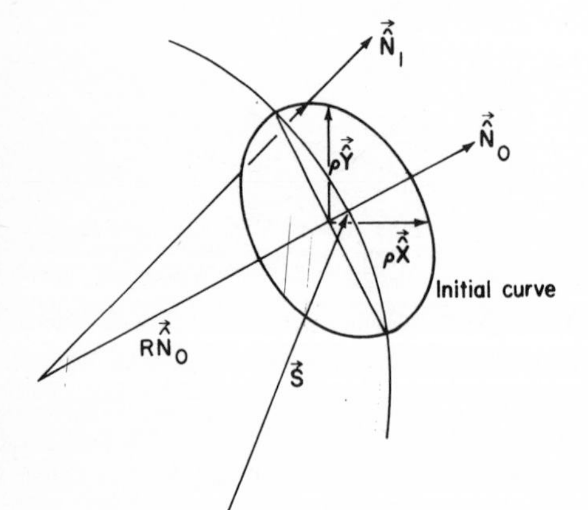

Fig. 4.8 Construction of the initial curve near a singular point.

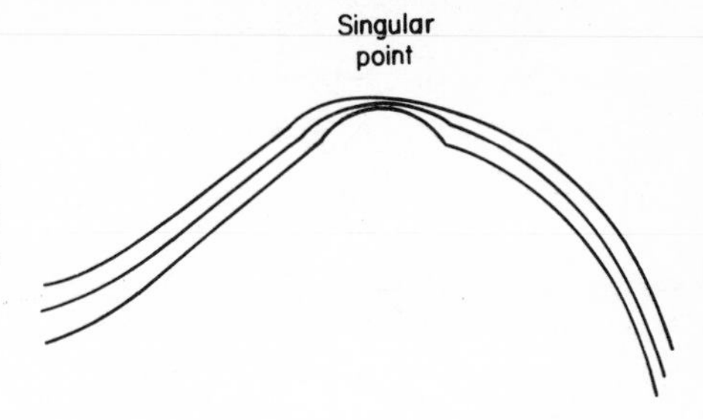

Fig. 4.9 Three solutions obtained for varying initial radius of curvature and the small effect which errors in the initial curve have on the solution.

The requirement for an initial guess at the radius of curvature is not as restrictive as it might seem, since the required accuracy is extremely low. This is because ρ is usually very much smaller than R, and hence a change in R affects the position of the initial curve very little. Even more importantly, the values derived for p and q need not be accurate since they are only used as a first guess in an iterative method of finding p and q on the initial curve before starting the solution. Figure 4.9 shows graphically how different radii might influence the solution in a typical case.

4.2.7 Nonpoint Sources

Uniform sources have already been dealt with. Perhaps the easiest other case is a circularly symmetric source at a distance large compared to the dimensions of the object.

Distant circularly symmetric sources can be replaced by a point source after modifying the reflectivity function. One merely convolves the reflectivity function with the spread function of the source (a bit of spherical trigonometry is involved). Strictly speaking, one should perform the same operation with the entrance pupil of the camera since it too subtends a finite angle at the object and accepts a bundle of light rays. Since ϕ is smooth (except at $I = 0$ and $I = 1$) it will be changed very little except at these points. The main change will be that ϕ does not tend to 0 as I tends to 0, but rather for some negative value of I. Also the specular component will be more smeared out.

Let the source intensity be I(a) per unit solid angle at the angle a from its center when viewed from the object. See Fig. 4.10. Then the new reflectivity function $\phi'(I, E, G)$ is

$$\phi'(I, E, G) = \frac{\int_0^{2\pi} \int_0^{a_0} I(a)\phi(I', E, G')a \, da \, dv}{\int_0^{2\pi} \int_0^{a_0} I(a) \, a \, da \, dv}$$

where a_0 = total angular diameter of the source

$\cos(A) = (\cos(g) - \cos(i)\cos(e))/(\sin(i)\sin(e))$

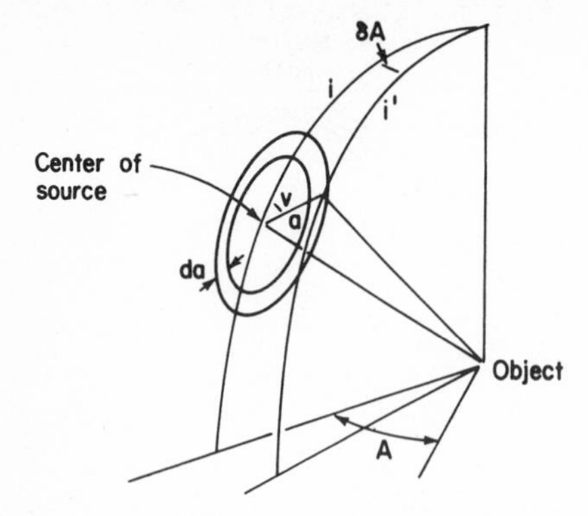

Fig. 4.10 Circularly symmetric source and quantities used in the convolution.

$$\cos(i') = \cos(i)\cos(a) + \sin(i)\sin(a)\cos(v)$$
$$\sin(\delta A) = \sin(i')\sin(a)/\sin(v)$$
$$\cos(g') = \cos(A + \delta A)\sin(i')\sin(e) + \cos(i')\cos(e)$$

When the source distribution is not easily treated as above one can introduce a different A_k for each source and replace the main equation by

$$\sum_k A_k(\mathbf{r}) \quad \phi(I_k, E, G_k) = b(\mathbf{r}')$$

Difficulties in finding initial conditions will be encountered with multiple sources unless they are of special kinds (e.g., a point source plus a uniform source).

4.2.8 Shadows and Other Edges

Several kinds of edges appear in an image, each with its own properties and problems for our algorithm:

1. Overlap–special case of occlusion of one object by another in which the line of occlusion corresponds to an angular edge on the occluding object. There is a discontinuity in z. The program must detect this or it will erroneously continue a solution across such an edge.
2. View edges–special case of occlusion where no angular edge is involved. The surface is smooth and E tends to 0 as we approach it. This is easily detected by the program during the calculation of the solution.
3. Joints–angular edges on an object. There are discontinuities in the derivatives of z. One cannot continue p and q across such an edge. It is possible however to use the position of the edge as a new initial curve. This and the previous condition can be detected as a step in the intensity distribution or from a highlight on the edge.

4. Shadow edges–here I tends to 0 as we approach the edge and again the program can easily detect this.
5. Projected shadow edges–if the shadow is bridged this edge may serve as a new initial curve as described below.
6. Ambiguity edges–some are lines of aggregation of singular points (on which $\lambda \to \infty$). The characteristics will not cross an ambiguity edge.

If the single source is not at the camera, shadows will appear. Solutions can be carried across shadows since the position of the source is known and one can construct a ray through the last illuminated point and trace it until it meets another illuminated region. The place where a glancing ray first strikes the surface on the other side of the shadow can be determined by triangulation on the source-surface ray and the surface-eye ray. Only the coordinates and not the local gradient of this new point will be known. It is necessary to carry this operation out for all characteristics entering the shadow, producing a new initial curve at the other edge of the shadow where we can restart the solution. In practice care has to be taken because of noise.

4.3 SPECIAL APPLICATIONS

4.3.1 The Scanning Electron Microscope

This section deals with two applications in which the equations simplify considerably. The first is scanning electron microscopy.

The scanning electron microscope device uses an electron beam which is focused and deflected much like the beam of a cathode ray tube and impinges on a specimen in an evacuated chamber. As shown in Fig. 4.11 the narrow ray penetrates into the specimen for some small distance, creating secondary

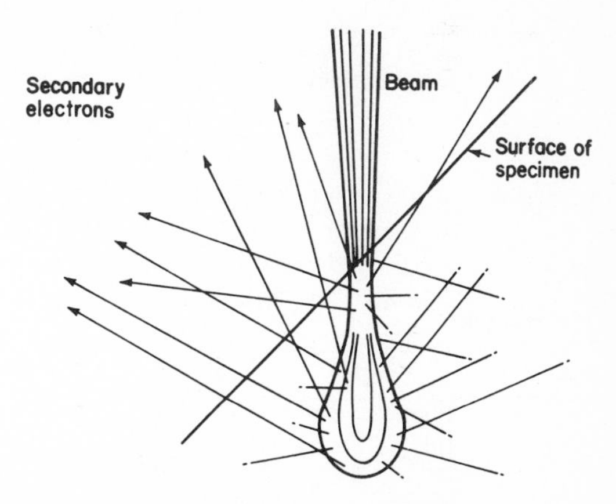

Fig. 4.11 Detail of electron beam impinging on specimen.

electrons along its path. The depth of penetration, the spread, and the number of secondary electrons are all functions of the material of that portion of the specimen. The number of secondary electrons which emerge from the specimen back into the vacuum through the surface will depend strongly on the inclination of the surface with respect to the beam.

These relatively slow secondary electrons are then attracted by a positively charged grid and impinge on a phosphor-coated photomultiplier. (See Fig. 4.12.) In this way a current is generated proportional to the number of secondary electrons escaping the specimen. The emerging electrons are analogous to photons reflected at a surface but in direct contrast to optical surfaces the intensity is least when the incident beam is perpendicular. Thus the steep edges are outlined more brightly. Strangely, people find this effect appealing.

The output is used to modulate the intensity of the beam in a cathode ray tube while both beams are scanned synchronously in a television-like raster. The image created exhibits shading and is remarkably easy to interpret topographically. This is quite unlike the normal use of optical or transmission electron microscopes which portray density and thickness.

The magnification is easily increased by decreasing the deflection in the microscope. The resolution is poor compared to the transmission electron microscope because of the spread of the beam as it enters the specimen, but the depth of field is much better than that of an optical microscope because of the very narrow beam (extremely high f-number).

There are important cases where the shape must be determined and stereoscopic methods are not applicable. This may be because at the magnification used the specimen appears smooth without significant surface detail or because it is difficult to line up the second image. Since the

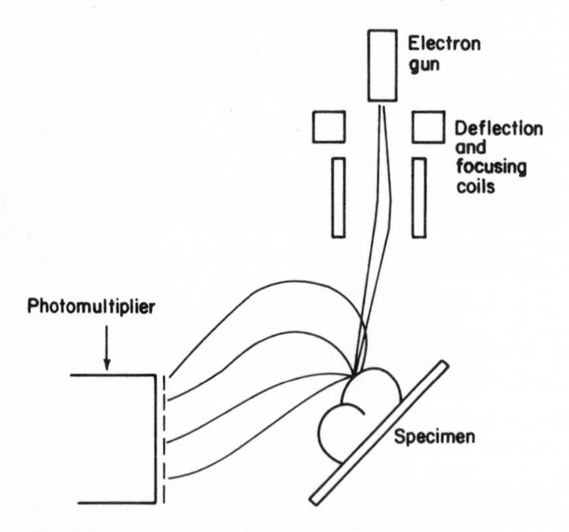

Fig. 4.12 A scanning electron microscope.

equations for this case turn out to be so simple, it should be rewarding to tie a scanning electron microscope directly into a small computer.

A little thought shows that this electron microscope situation is analogous to the case where a source is at the camera (or equivalently, the case where we have uniform illumination). Note that no shadows appear. Moreover the projection is ordinarily near-orthogonal. Because of these two effects the five ordinary differential equations simplify considerably:

$$\dot{x} = F_p, \quad \dot{y} = F_q, \quad \dot{z} = pF_p + qF_q$$

$$\dot{p} = -F_x - pF_z \quad \text{and} \quad \dot{q} = -F_y - qF_z$$

Now

$$\mathbf{F_n} = A\,\phi_I \mathbf{I_n} \quad \text{and} \quad \mathbf{F_r} = -\mathbf{b_r}$$

$$I = \frac{\mathbf{n} \cdot \hat{\mathbf{z}}}{n} = \frac{1}{n} \quad \text{where } \mathbf{n} = (-p, -q, 1)$$

$$\mathbf{I_n} = \left(\frac{1}{n}\right)(\hat{\mathbf{z}} - I\,\hat{\mathbf{n}}) = \left(\frac{\hat{\mathbf{z}}}{n}\right) - \left(\frac{1}{n^3}\right)\hat{\mathbf{n}}$$

$$I_p = \left(\frac{1}{n^3}\right)p \quad \text{and} \quad I_q = \left(\frac{1}{n^3}\right)q$$

Hence

$$\dot{x} = F_p = \left(\frac{A\,\phi_I}{n^3}\right)p, \quad \dot{y} = F_q = \left(\frac{A\,\phi_I}{n^3}\right)q$$

$$\dot{z} = \left(\frac{A\,\phi_I}{n^3}\right)(p^2 + q^2)$$

$$\dot{p} = -b_x \quad \text{and} \quad \dot{q} = -b_y$$

If $\phi_I \neq 0$ everywhere, we can change to a new measure s along the characteristic by multiplying all equations by $\lambda = n^3/(A\,\phi_I)$ and we get

$$\dot{x} = p, \quad \dot{y} = q, \quad \dot{z} = p^2 + q^2$$

$$\dot{p} = b_x \frac{n^3}{A\,\phi_I}, \quad q = b_y \frac{n^3}{A\,\phi_I}$$

Notice that the changes in x and y along the characteristics are given in this case by the partial derivatives of z with respect to x and y. This constrains the characteristics therefore to grow in the direction of the surface's gradient at each point. Thus this extremely simple case has characteristics which are curves of steepest descent. Also note that the equation for z does not couple back into the system of equations because of the orthogonal projection. This increases accuracy. The equations happen to be very similar to the Eikonel equations for the paths of light rays in refractive media. It may be possible to find ready-made solutions to some special cases by using this analogy.

We assumed that $\phi_I \neq 0$; this is equivalent to assuming that an inverse exists which allows us to find I from a measurement of the image intensity:

$$\psi[\phi(I, I, 1)] = I$$

Let

$$\xi(x) = \frac{1 - \psi^2(x)}{2\psi(x)}$$

Then

$$\xi[\phi(I, I, 1)] = \left(\frac{1}{2}\right)(p^2 + q^2)$$

So we can find at each point the magnitude, but not the direction of the local gradient.

Let us turn to the question of ambiguities since the subject is easy enough in the electron microscope case. Assume the camera and light source are at the same position and consider the two surfaces:

$$z = z + x^3, \qquad z = z + |x|^3$$

Clearly they cannot be distinguished in monocular views since they produce identical intensity distributions in the image. This manifests itself in a slowing down of the characteristics as they approach the line $x = 0$ (alternatively $\lambda \to \infty$). They cannot cross this line aggregation of singular points. Note that the characteristics approach this line at right angles and that the edge is determined locally, since in general each point on an ambiguity edge is a singular point.

A second kind of ambiguity edge can occur parallel to characteristics, separating those which can be reached from one singular point from those

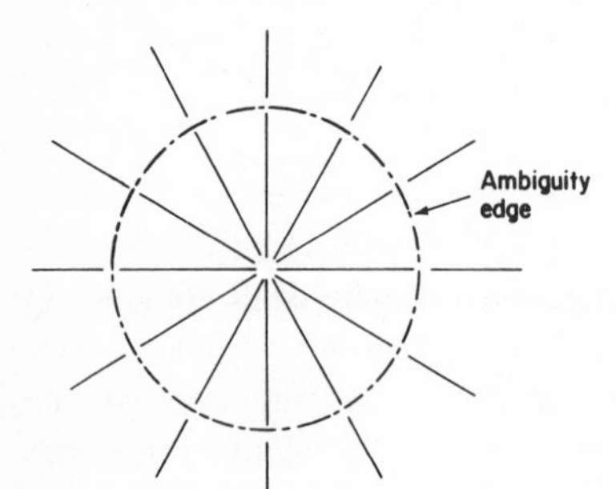

Fig. 4.13 A locally determined ambiguity edge: $f = 1/(x^2 + y^2 - 1)^2$.

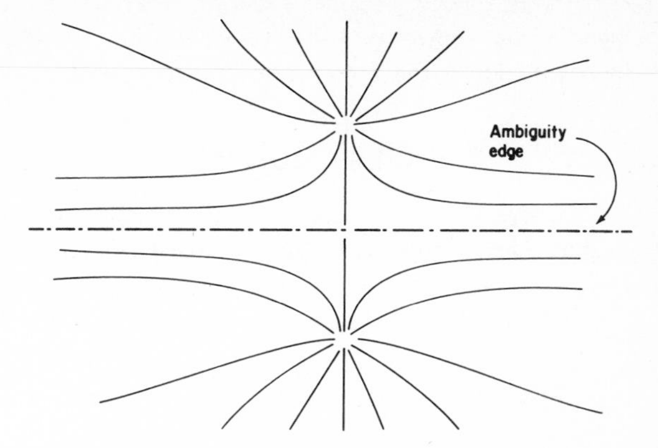

Fig. 4.14 A globally determined ambiguity edge: $f = 1/[1 + x^2 + (y-1)^2] + 1/[1 + x^2 + (y+1)^2]$.

reachable only from another. This kind of edge is not locally determined, since a change in the surface is possible which removes one of the singular points and makes all the characteristics accessible from the other. This can be done without altering an area near the two given points previously separated by an ambiguity edge. Figure 4.13 shows a locally defined ambiguity edge and Fig. 4.14 shows a globally defined one.

Both types of ambiguity edge occur in the general case but are not so easily studied there. They divide the image into regions within each of which a solution can be obtained. Typically most such regions will have one singular point from which one may obtain initial conditions (provided one makes a decision about whether the surface is concave or convex and knows the distance to the singular point).

4.3.2 Lunar Topography

The other very interesting simplification to the general shape from shading equations occurs when we introduce the special reflectivity function which applies to the material in the maria of the moon. This in fact was the first shape from shading problem solved both theoretically and in an operating algorithm.[1] Using the special reflectivity function and the fact that the sun is a distant source, it is possible (but very tedious) to show that the equations simplify so that the base characteristics (i.e., the projection of the characteristics on the image plane) become straight lines radiating from the zero-phase point, the point corresponding to $g = 0$. The camera lies directly between this point and the sun. Actually this is true only when the sun is located at negative z; for positive z (i.e., in front of the camera), the relevant point is the π-phase point, directly in the sun.

The variation of light reflected from the surface of the moon with phase and inclination of the surface has been studied for a long time. At a given lunar phase g, all possible combinations of incident angle i and emittance angle e are represented by some portion of the surface. A fairly good approximation is the Lommel-Seeliger formula:[4]

$$\phi(I, E, G) = \frac{\Gamma_0(I/E)}{(I/E) + \lambda(G)}$$

Where Γ_0 is a constant and the function $\lambda(G)$ is defined numerically by a table. This formula can also be derived from a simplified model of the lunar surface. A slight gain in accuracy is possible if Γ_0 is allowed to vary with G as well. In particular Fesenkov finds the more accurate formula

$$\phi(I, E, G) = \frac{\Gamma_0 (I/E)[1 + \cos^2(\alpha/2)]}{(I/E) + \lambda_0 [1 + \tan^2(\alpha/2)]}$$

where

$$\tan(\alpha) = \frac{G - (I/E)}{\sqrt{1 - G^2}}$$

A recent theoretical model is that of Hapke[5] which corresponds fairly closely to the measured reflectivity function. In most of these formulas we find that for a given G, ϕ is a constant for constant I/E. The lines of constant I/E are meridians.

At full moon, when $G = 1$ we find that the whole face has constant luminosity. This is quite unlike the effect on a sphere coated with a typical mat paint where the image intensity would vary as

$$\sqrt{1 - \left(\frac{r}{R}\right)^2}$$

Where R is the radius of the image and r the distance from the center of the image. The full moon thus has the same appearance as a flat disc if one is used to objects with normal mat surfaces. This may explain the flat appearance of the full moon.

In the case of pictures taken of the lunar surface from nearby (e.g., from orbit) we have the following:

1. Distant source (the moon subtends an angle of about .03 milliradians at the sun).
2. Near point source (the sun subtends an angle of about 10 milliradians at the moon).
3. Camera at the origin.
4. The reflectivity function is constant for constant I/E.

It can be demonstrated that the solution to the lunar topography problem is a special case of the more general formulation given in this paper. But since the details are tedious, we only note that the ordinary differential equation that constrains r has the simple solution:

$$\frac{r(s)}{r(0)} = e^{-P\int_0^s [\tan(\alpha)/Q^2]\, ds}$$

where

$$L = \frac{x_0}{z_0}\cos(t) + \frac{y_0}{z_0}\sin(t)$$

and

$$Q = \sqrt{s^2 + 2sL + \left(\frac{r_0}{z_0}\right)^2} \qquad P = \operatorname{sgn}(z_0)\sqrt{\left(\frac{r_0}{z_0}\right)^2 - L^2}$$

Note that r(0) is the distance to the point from where the integration was started, t is a parameter which varies from characteristic to characteristic, s is a parameter that varies along a given characteristic and $\hat{r}_0 = (x_0, y_0, z_0)$ is a unit vector parallel to the direction from the sun to the moon.

To sum up, as one advances along each characteristic in turn, one calculates G, measures b/A and uses ψ to obtain $\tan(\alpha)$, which is then used in the evaluation of the above integral. Here $\psi(b/A, G) = I/E$, that is to say, ψ is a kind of inverse function for $\phi(I, E, G)$. The process is much simpler than the general shape from shading algorithm.

Let us list some of the major points of interest.

1. The base characteristics are predetermined straight lines (independent of the image). This makes for high accuracy and ease in planning a picture-taking mission.
2. Only a single integral needs to be evaluated, not five differential equations.
3. The primary input is the intensity, not its gradients, again making for high accuracy.
4. Although, as usual, the reflected light-intensity does not give a unique normal, it does determine the slope component in the direction of the characteristic. J. van Diggelen[6] first noted a special case of this when he solved the lunar topography problem for the special case of an area near the terminator (line separating sunlit from dark areas). The characteristics are such that the slope along them can be determined locally. The slope at right angles to the characteristics cannot be determined locally.
5. Although T. Rindfleisch did not mention it in his paper[1] it is very easy to bridge shadows since each light ray lies in a sun-camera-characteristic plane. Its image can thus be traced on the base characteristic until we again meet a lighted area. One need not even make special provisions for this, but just use $\tan(\alpha)$ for grazing incidence (intensity = 0) in the shaded section.

4.4 IMPLEMENTATION

4.4.1 Measuring the Reflectivity Function

The reflectivity functions of some paints were measured using large rubber spheres as calibration objects. Both camera and source were moved as far away as possible to achieve almost constant phase angle g. The image of a convex object is especially useful because it contains two points for all possible combinations of the incident and emittance angles (i and e) for a given phase (angle g). The position of the light source is measured, as well as the distance from the front of the sphere to the entrance pupil. The image dissector is focused on the edge of the sphere.

With the sphere temporarily illuminated from several sources, a program finds its exact position and size, as well as the difference in horizontal and vertical deflection sensitivity of the image dissector. It is now possible to calculate the points in the image which correspond to given incident and emittance angles. For a number of choices of both of these angles one then reads the intensity at a small raster of points near these positions and averages them to reduce noise and the effect of pinholes in the photocathode. Since there are usually two places in the image with the same incident and emittance angle, a check on the data is possible. The resultant table of values (usually normalized with respect to the brightest intensity) can be printed and the whole process repeated after moving the light source to a new position for a new phase angle. The program accounts for such things as change in incident light intensity as the light source gets moved around.

Clearly the points for given incident angle lie on a circle on the surface of the sphere. Similarly for points with a given emittance angle. These two circles may intersect in two, one, or no points. One can find this intersection by first finding the line along which the planes containing these circles intersect. Examine Fig. 4.15. Applying the sine and cosine laws,

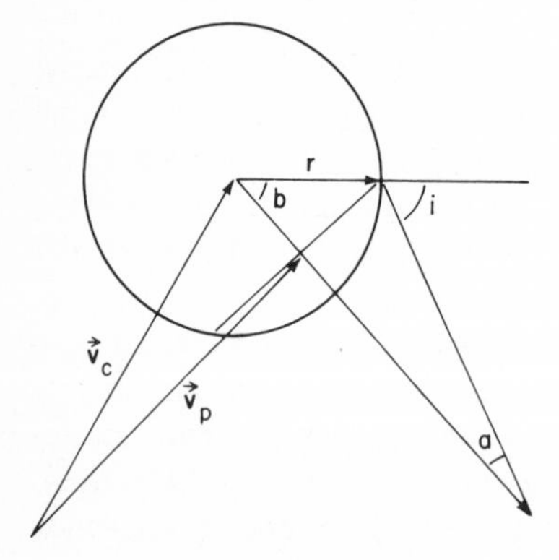

Fig. 4.15 Finding points for given incident and emittance angles.

$$I = \cos(i) \quad \text{as usual and} \quad D = |\mathbf{v}_s|$$

$$\frac{D}{\sin(\pi - i)} = \frac{r}{\sin(a)} \qquad b = i - a$$

$$r \cos(b) = r\,[\cos(i)\cos(a) + \sin(i)\sin(a)]$$

$$= \left(\frac{r}{D}\right)[I\sqrt{D^2 - r^2(1 - I^2)} + r(1 - I^2)]$$

$$d = r\cos(b)$$

$$\mathbf{v}_p = \mathbf{v}_c + d\,\hat{\mathbf{v}}_s$$

The equation of the plane in which the circle of points with given incident angle i lies is

$$\mathbf{v} \cdot \hat{\mathbf{v}}_s = \mathbf{v}_p \cdot \hat{\mathbf{v}}_s \qquad \text{where } \mathbf{v} = (x, y, z)$$

One can find a similar equation for the plane in which the circle of points with given emittance angle e lies. The introduction of an arbitrary third plane allows us to find one point $\mathbf{v}$ on the intersection of the first two. The line of intersection of the first two planes must be parallel to the cross product of their normals (let them be $\mathbf{v}_{s1}$ and $\mathbf{v}_{s2}$). So the equation of the line we are looking for is

$$(\mathbf{v} - \mathbf{v}_a) = k\,\mathbf{v}_1 \qquad \text{where } \mathbf{v}_1 = \mathbf{v}_{s1} \times \mathbf{v}_{s2}$$

The points we are trying to find must also lie on the sphere, that is,

$$(\mathbf{v} - \mathbf{v}_c)^2 = r^2$$

$$(\mathbf{v}_a + k\,\mathbf{v}_1 - \mathbf{v}_c) = r^2$$

$$k^2\mathbf{v}_1 \cdot \mathbf{v}_1 + 2\,k\,\mathbf{v}_1 \cdot (\mathbf{v}_a - \mathbf{v}_c) + (\mathbf{v}_a - \mathbf{v}_c)^2 - r^2 = 0$$

The above equation may have no solution for k, in which case no point exists for the given incident and emittance angle. Otherwise we can use the two solutions and substitute back to obtain the desired coordinates which are then transformed into image coordinates. Figure 4.16 shows the sort of table that results for a given phase angle g.

The first paint investigated was a mat white paint consisting of particles of SiO_2 and TiO_2 suspended in a transparent base. Very roughly one finds that the reflectivity function behaves like cos(i) for a given g. After playing with polynomial fits for a while, the following fairly accurate formula was found by a process of little interest here:

E ↓ \ I →	1.00	0.97	0.93	0.87	0.78	0.68	0.56	0.43	0.29	0.15
1.00					0.77					
0.97				0.87	0.78	0.66				
0.93			0.93	0.88	0.78	0.67	0.57			
0.87		0.97	9.94	0.89	0.79	0.67	0.57	0.45		
0.78	0.99	0.98	0.95	0.90	0.81	0.68	0.59	0.46	0.32	
0.68		0.98	0.95	0.91	0.82	0.71	0.59	0.47	0.33	0.18
0.56			0.94	0.90	0.83	0.74	0.61	0.48	0.34	0.17
0.43				0.88	0.79	0.74	0.62	0.50	0.34	0.18
0.29					0.79	0.70	0.58	0.42	0.30	0.15
0.15						0.65	0.50	0.38	0.26	0.13

Fig. 4.16 Table of reflectivity (for a white mat paint) vs. I = cos i and E = cos e for G = cos g = 0.81. The intervals chosen correspond to constant size steps in the angles. Note the blank areas for combinations of angles which cannot form a spherical triangle.

$$\phi(\mathrm{I}, \mathrm{E}, \mathrm{G}) = \frac{(1 + \mathrm{G})(2 + \mathrm{G})}{6}\left[\mathrm{I} + \frac{1 + 2\,\mathrm{IEG} - (\mathrm{I}^2 + \mathrm{E}^2 + \mathrm{G}^2)}{16(1 - \mathrm{G})}\right]$$

For reasonable angles the above formula is about 5 percent accurate, becoming worse for extreme angles. The repeatability of this measurement was disappointingly low, depending on the depth of the paint coat and the details of its application. Much of the investigation of the behavior of the image dissector was the result of efforts to trace the remaining causes of inaccuracy.

Some other paints and an eggshell showed a mat component similar to the above, plus a very strong specular component (which is small except near the point for which i = e and i + e = g). This component is very sensitive to small changes in the surface properties such as can be brought about by handling the object.

The image of a convex object with such a surface will usually have two local maxima in intensity. One of these will be broad (corresponding to the mat component), the other narrow and bright (corresponding to the specular component). These may be distinguished by a computer program on the basis of just these properties. It would then be possible to start a solution from the mat maximum (which is not a global maximum) rather than the specular maximum. This might be a good idea because of the increased accuracy (for one thing the normalization of image intensities would be more accurate).

In an attempt to track down poor results in the first try at finding reflectivity functions accurately, the image dissector was investigated in some detail[2]. Among problems found were:

1. Unequal deflection sensitivity in horizontal and vertical directions (differed by 12 percent).

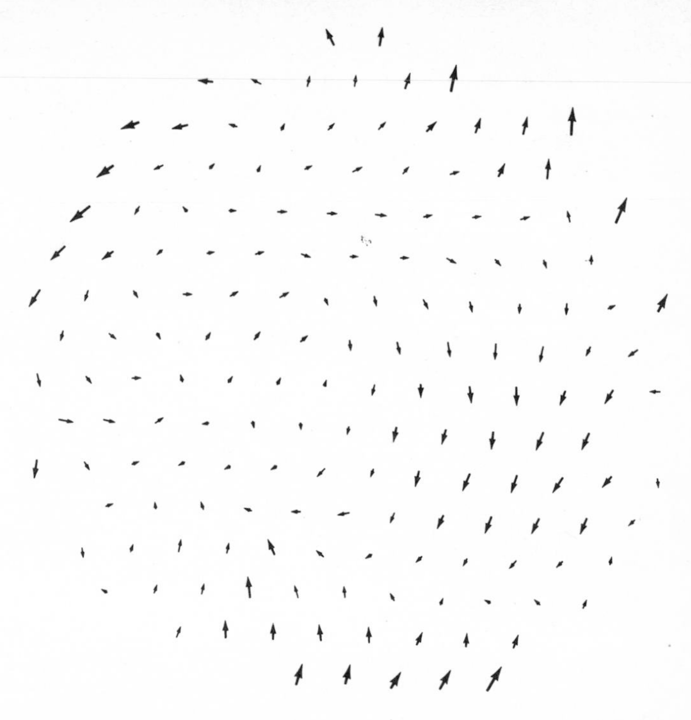

Fig. 4.17 Geometric distortion in image dissector for a triangular raster of points covering the photo-cathode. (The arrows are exaggerated three times.)

2. Twist of image varying with distance from center of field of view. (See Fig. 4.17.)
3. Poor resolution (3 line-pairs/mm — radius of tube 38 mm).
4. Pinholes in the photocathode (about 20 of up to 0.5 mm in size).
5. Nonuniform sensitivity of the photocathode (varies more than 30 percent).
6. Fairly long settling time of the deflection coils (on the order of 300 microseconds).
7. A large amount of scatter, which reduces the contrast by almost one-third and causes intensities measured on the image of a uniform square on a dark background to vary by 20 percent, depending on how close to the edge the measurement is taken.

4.4.2 Numerical Methods for Solving the Equations

The five ordinary differential equations were at first solved using a well-known Runge-Kutta method. The idea is to average together several estimates of the derivatives of the five variables (x, y, z, p, and q) with respect to the parameter s. The first estimates are the actual derivatives at s. These are used to take a half step forward and calculate new values for x , y , z, p , and q as though derivatives higher than the first were zero. We then calculate the derivatives at this new point to get a second set. Next we start over from s, probing out again by a half step but now using the second set of derivatives. We then get a third set of derivatives at $s + h/2$. The third set is used in the final probe from s which now extends fully to $s + h$ where we get a fourth set of derivatives. The official full step is taken using a weighted average of the four sets of derivatives found in this way. Written out in symbols this becomes:

Let h be the step-size (for the parameter s).
Let $\mathbf{Y} = (x, y, z, p, q)$.
And let the equations for the derivatives be

$$\mathbf{Y}' = F(s, \mathbf{Y})$$

(In our case, F is actually independent of s.)
Denote $\mathbf{Y}(s_n)$ by $\mathbf{Y}_n$ then at the nth step

$$\mathbf{K}_1 = h\,F(s_n, \mathbf{Y}_n)$$

$$\mathbf{K}_2 = h\,F\left(s_n + \frac{h}{2}, \mathbf{Y}_n + \frac{\mathbf{K}_1}{2}\right)$$

$$\mathbf{K}_3 = h\,F\left(s_n + \frac{h}{2}, \mathbf{Y}_n + \frac{\mathbf{K}_2}{2}\right)$$

$$\mathbf{K}_4 = h\,F(s_n + h, \mathbf{Y}_n + \mathbf{K}_3)$$

$$\mathbf{Y}_{n+1} = \mathbf{Y}_n + \left(\frac{1}{6}\right)(\mathbf{K}_1 + 2\mathbf{K}_2 + 2\mathbf{K}_3 + \mathbf{K}_4)$$

This method is easy to start (requires no previous values of **Y**) and stable, but requires four time-consuming evaluations of the derivatives per step. For this reason various predictor-modifier-corrector methods were tried and the simplest was found to give adequate accuracy

$$\mathbf{P}_{n+1} = \mathbf{Y}_n + 2\,h\,F(s_n, \mathbf{Y}_n)$$

$$\mathbf{M}_{n+1} = \mathbf{P}_{n+1} - \left(\frac{4}{5}\right)(\mathbf{P}_n - \mathbf{C}_n)$$

$$\mathbf{C}_{n+1} = \mathbf{Y}_n + \left(\frac{h}{2}\right)[F(s_n, \mathbf{M}_{n+1}) + F(s_n, \mathbf{Y}_n)]$$

$$\mathbf{Y}_{n+1} = \mathbf{C}_{n+1} + \left(\frac{1}{5}\right)(\mathbf{P}_{n+1} - \mathbf{C}_{n+1})$$

P, **M**, and **C** are the predictor, modifier and corrector respectively. This method is stable and requires only two derivative evaluations per step, but is not self-starting. The Runge-Kutta method was retained for the first step in the integration. Stability and accuracy were not serious concerns since the noise in the data input contributes far more to errors in the solution.

Under optimal conditions (using methods to cancel out most of the distortion and nonuniformity of photocathode sensitivity) the program was allowed to scan a sphere of 100 mm radius. A sphere was then fitted by an iterative least-square method to the data points found. The data points nowhere deviated from the fitted sphere by more than 10 mm, and by less than 5 mm except near the very edge of the image. Such accuracy will not usually be obtained because of nonuniformity in the paint, shortcomings of the sensing device, etc. For many purposes, however, less accuracy is quite acceptable and for object recognition in particular a more important criterion is that similar objects are distorted in similar ways.

4.4.3 A Program Solving the Characteristics in Parallel

It soon became apparent that integrating along each characteristic independently has many disadvantages in the general case, even though it works well for lunar topography. The first reason is that characteristics spreading out from the singular point begin to separate and leave large portions of the image unexplored. One obtains only a very uneven sampling of the surface of the object. With a more parallel approach new characteristics can be created as one goes along and some others can be deleted in areas where characteristics approach each other too closely.

Next we find that the base characteristics (projections of the characteristics onto the image) may sometimes cross! This would not be possible if the solution were exact, since it indicates that the surface is double-valued or at least that its gradient is double-valued. Solution of this problem is easy if the integrations are carried along in parallel, but involves lengthy comparison tests otherwise.

Once it had been demonstrated that the equations were correct and a numerical solution possible, it was decided to write a program which would explore the surface of the object by moving along all the characteristics in parallel and by interpolating new characteristics when needed. Accuracy in the solution was traded for more noise immunity. The solution is achieved by taking all characteristics one step forward at the same time. An effort to find a convenient coordinate system for this approach produced the notation and resultant equations given here. The solution was previously worked out in a different coordinate system requiring manipulation of extreme complexity.

The values stored for each point (x, y, z, intensity, p, q and pointers to the previous point on the same characteristic) are here arranged not by characteristic but by "ring." A ring is a curve of constant arc-distance from the singular point. That is, the nth points on all the characteristics form one ring. The complete data structure is made up of a number of rings, the first of which is the initial curve. As before, individual characteristics may stop for a variety of reasons and this causes breaks to appear in the current ring. Some rings thus represent closed curves and others more distant from the singular point are broken into sections, the final ring having no active point on it.

As we have seen, one of the main inducements for using the parallel solution method is to allow interpolation of new characteristics. This is one of the reasons why the number of points in a ring may change from one to the next and why each point has to have a pointer into the previous ring indicating which element is its predecessor in the same characteristic.

It should be noted that the use of constant size steps along the characteristics may produce difficulties on complex objects. For even with smooth surfaces the curves of constant arc-distance from the singular point may have cusps. An alternative, which would circumvent this problem, would be the use of steps traversing a constant increment in intensity. This would turn the rings into contours of constant intensity.

We have already described how one can obtain p(t) and q(t) on the initial curve by solving the set of nonlinear equations:

$$p(t)\, x_t(t) + q(t)\, y_t(t) - z_t(t) = 0$$

$$A(\mathbf{r})\, \phi(I, E, G) - b(\mathbf{r}') = 0$$

When solving a difference equation approximation from noisy data we can expect the solution for p and q to become progressively more inaccurate. Yet the above pair of equations must hold on any path along the surface of the object. In particular one can use them on the curve defined by one ring to determine values of p and q.

For the initial curve we had the additional difficulty that the two equations might have more than one solution and we selected one on the basis of some external knowledge (e.g., that the object is convex near the singular point). We have assumed that the object is smooth and therefore we will have fairly good values for p and q and cannot get into this difficulty at nonsingular points. Even a simple Newton-Raphsen method will suffice to get us more accurate values of p and q.

Let

$$g(p, q) = p\, x_t + q\, y_t - z_t$$

$$h(p, q) = \phi(I, E, G) - \frac{b}{A}$$

and suppose: $g(p + \delta p, q + \delta q) = h(p + \delta p, q + \delta q) = 0$.

Then ignoring other than first-order terms we have

$$\begin{pmatrix} g_p & g_q \\ h_p & h_q \end{pmatrix} \begin{pmatrix} \delta p \\ \delta q \end{pmatrix} = \begin{pmatrix} g(p, q) \\ h(p, q) \end{pmatrix}$$

That is,

$$\begin{pmatrix} x_t & y_t \\ p & q \end{pmatrix} \begin{pmatrix} \delta p \\ \delta q \end{pmatrix} = \begin{pmatrix} g(p, q) \\ h(p, q) \end{pmatrix}$$

Here x_t, y_t and z_t have to be estimated from difference approximations. One may not want to apply the full correction $(\delta p, \delta q)$. More than one iteration will not be required since after the first iteration p and q are very close to the correct values. We will call this process the sharpening of p and q.

When the separation between two neighboring points in a ring becomes greater than 1.5 times the step size along the characteristic, a new characteristic is interpolated. Its x, y, z, p, and q values are set to the average of its neighbors. A more complicated interpolation method can also be used which constructs the line of intersection of the tangent planes at the two neighboring points. It then finds the point on this line closest to the two neighbors and finally uses a point half-way between the point determined previously by the simpler method and this new point. This method does not, however, add significantly to the accuracy of the solution.

If two neighboring points in a section of a ring come closer than 0.7 times the step-size, one is deleted (it is important that this factor be less than 0.75, that is, one half of the factor used in the interpolation decision, or succesive rings on a flat region will have points interpolated on one step, only to be removed on the next, with consequent loss of accuracy).

Finally one wants to stop neighboring characteristics from crossing over each other. Consider the two points a and b on one ring and their successors c and d on the next as in Fig. 4.18. The test consists of checking whether c is to the left of the directed line through bd and whether d is to the right of the directed line through ac. Both tests are needed. If either fails, the corresponding characteristic is terminated, causing a break to appear in the ring at that point. The test is equivalent to checking whether the line segment cd falls in front of the line segment ab (and does not cross it). This test is applied across short breaks in rings as well to stop neighboring sections of the ring from crossing over each other.

Care has to be taken if the remaining sections of a ring all fall on one side of the singular point, since the break then actually encompasses an arc of

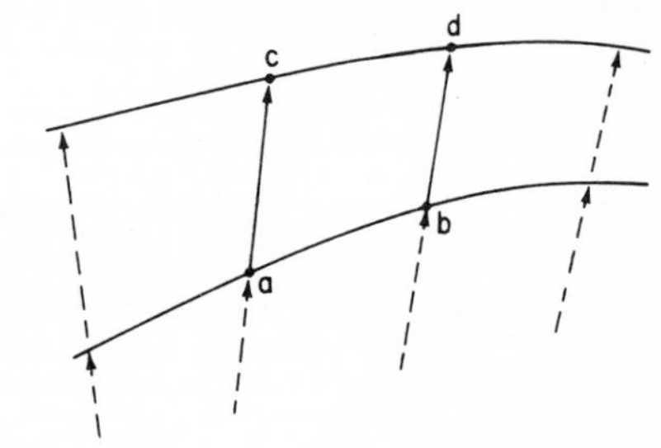

Fig. 4.18 The four points used in the crossing test.

more than π and crossing tests applied across it will invariable terminate more characteristics on either side of it. This can be avoided if the crossing test is not applied to points whose images fall too far apart in terms of the projection of the current step size.

Rather than use the intensities at a small raster of points to estimate the local gradient, it was decided to use a difference approximation from intensities measured at neighboring points. Using as many as possible of the intensities of the point itself and its five immediate neighbors, we can apply a simple least-squares method to estimate the gradient. (See Fig. 4.19.) Some of the points may not exist as explained previously and the characteristic is terminated if less than three points are available or only three which are nearly collinear. Suppose the coordinates of the points are (x'_k, y'_k) (image coordinate system) and the intensities are b_k. We wish to find b_0, $b_{x'}$ and $b_{y'}$, to minimize the following expression:

$$\sum_k (b_{x'} x'_k + b_{y'} y'_k + b_0 - b_k)^2$$

This happens when

$$\begin{bmatrix} \sum x'^2_k & \sum x'_k y'_k & \sum x'_k \\ \sum x'_k y'_k & \sum y'^2_k & \sum y'_k \\ \sum x'_k & \sum y'_k & \sum 1 \end{bmatrix} \begin{bmatrix} b_{x'} \\ b_{y'} \\ b_0 \end{bmatrix} = \begin{bmatrix} \sum b_k x'_k \\ \sum b_k y'_k \\ \sum b_k \end{bmatrix}$$

From $b_{x'}$ and $b_{y'}$ we can find b_x, b_y, and b_z by using the camera projection equations of an earlier section.

For good noise immunity and some ability to detect surface detail indicating that the solution is invalid, the intensity for each solution point is not read from only one image point. Small tilted rectangular rasters of points are established around each point of the solution as shown in Fig. 4.20. One axis of the rectangle is parallel to the base characteristic at that point, and the size is adjusted to correspond to the projection on the image of a square on the object of side-length equal to the step size. The intensity recorded for a solution point is the average of the intensities read for the points in this raster and the rms/average is used to make the edge-crossing decision. The rasters of all the points in the data structure almost but not quite touch and taken together almost cover the total area of the image explored. This insures that the data is not much affected by pinholes in the photocathode of the image

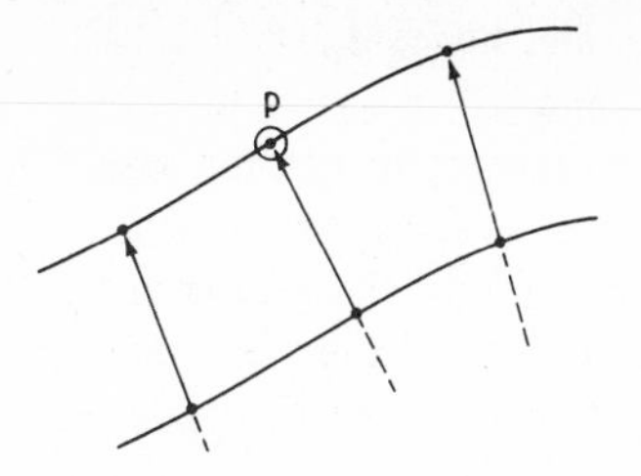

Fig. 4.19 The five neighbors used in determining the intensity gradient at p.

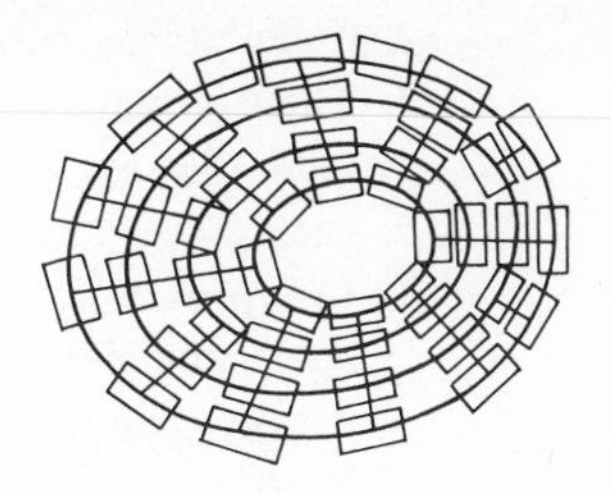

Fig. 4.20 Covering the image with the rasters of points read for each solution point.

dissector and that edge crossing can easily be detected without reducing the resolution.

This program spends more than half its time accessing the image dissector. Between 20 and 100 intensities are read for each point in the solution, and each access takes about 0.2 to 1.0 milliseconds. A complete solution requires from 1 to 5 minutes of real time.

4.4.4 Operation of the Program

First the program needs to be given such parameters as the position of the light source, the distance to the object, focal length of the lens and the step size to be used in the integration. It then proceeds to find a point of maximum intensity (for some reflectivity functions one needs to search for a minimum). This search can be directed to allow a choice of one of several possible maxima. The program then assumes that this point of maximum intensity is a singular point and that the object is convex at this point (in some cases we would like to assume it to be concave). After constructing an initial curve (a small circle) around the singular point, it proceeds to read the intensities at the corresponding image points. The nonlinear equations for p and q on this curve are than solved iteratively.

All intensities are normalized with respect to the intensity at the singular point unless the surface has a specular component. In the latter case, the intensities on the initial curve are used to establish a normalization value (the specular reflectivity is too variable for use in normalization). It is assumed that the initial curve has been chosen large enough to fall outside the region of strong specular reflection.

For each step in the parameter s, the following procedure is then carried out:

1. For each point calculate the normal ($\mathbf{n}$), the incident vector ($\mathbf{r}_i$) and the emittance vector ($\mathbf{r}_e$). From these obtain the derivatives $I_\mathbf{n}$, $E_\mathbf{n}$ and $G_\mathbf{n}$.

2. Calculate ϕ_I, ϕ_E, ϕ_G and hence $\phi_\mathbf{n}$.
3. Then obtain F_p, F_q and λ.
4. Add $(\delta x, \delta y, \delta z)$ to (x, y, z) to get the point on the next ring for each characteristic. Here $(\delta x, \delta y, \delta z) = \lambda(F_p, F_q, pF_p + qF_q)$.
5. Interpolate new points where the points in the new ring are too far apart and delete points where they are too close together. Produce breaks where characteristics have crossed over adjacent characteristics.
6. Now read the intensities for all the points. Terminate those characteristics with points of very low intensity or high rms/average.
7. Calculate $b_{x'}$, $b_{y'}$ for all those points for which enough neighbors exist. From these values obtain b_x, b_y and b_z by the projection equations.
8. Now use $\mathbf{n}$, $\mathbf{r}_i$ and $\mathbf{r}_e$ to calculate $I_\mathbf{r}$, $E_\mathbf{r}$ and $G_\mathbf{r}$.
9. Next use ϕ_I, ϕ_E and ϕ_G to calculate $\phi_\mathbf{r}$.
10. Then obtain F_x, F_y and F_z.
11. Add $(\delta p, \delta q)$ to (p, q) to obtain p and q for the uninterpolated points on the new ring. Here $(\delta p, \delta q) = [\lambda(-F_x - pF_z), \lambda(-F_y - qF_z)]$.
12. Interpolate p and q for the new points.
13. Sharpen up the values for p and q on all points in the new ring.
14. Garbage-collect various items.

The simpler Euler method for solving the differential equations could be replaced by a Runge-Kutta method with increases in running time of a factor of two, but little improvement in accuracy. Distortions in the imaging device produce distortions in x and y, while nonuniformities in the sensitivity will affect p and q and hence z. The only effect of low resolution will be that some edges will not be noticed and the solution erroneously continued across them.

It should be apparent where the various tests for terminating the characteristics fit into the above schema. The program terminates characteristics in the following situations:

1. The characteristic has moved out of the field of view of the image dissector.
2. The rms/average for the intensities read in the raster has become too great, indicating overlap of two objects or an angular joint on one object or some surface detail that is being missed.
3. The intensity has become too low, indicating a shadow region.
4. λ is too large, indicating approach to either another singular point or an ambiguity edge.
5. There are too few neighbors to construct a good estimate of the local intensity gradient.
6. I too small–indicating approach to a shadow edge.

7. E too small–indicating approach to an edge of the object.
8. The characteristic crossed over a neighboring one.
9. The intensity is equal to or greater than that measured at the singular point, indicating another singular point or ambiguity edge.

Note that several of these conditions are redundant to ensure that even with an inexact solution at least one will fail at the right place.

4.4.5 Summary and Conclusions

After defining the reflectivity function, an equation was found relating the intensity measured in the image of a smooth opaque object to the shape of the object. This equation was then shown to be a first-order nonlinear partial differential equation in two unknowns and the equivalent set of five ordinary differential equations was derived. Two especially simple cases were discussed, namely applications to lunar topography and the scanning electron microscope. Methods were described for obtaining the auxiliary information required (e.g., the reflectivity function) and how to avoid the need for an initial known curve on the object. Of importance too is the method demonstrated for continuously updating p and q (sharpening) as the solution progresses.

The analytical approach to the problem of determining shape from shading was developed to demonstrate that an exact solution is possible and to determine just what the limitations of this approach are. This is not to say that a more heuristic, approximate approach does not have its merits too for certain types of objects. It was decided to produce a program to allow experimentation with the solution method because many ideas in the field of artificial intelligence and visual perception are of little value until they can be tried on real data. Fortunately an image dissector was available to provide input of image intensities to the computer.

4.5 RELATED QUESTIONS

4.5.1 Likely Source Distributions

Since the complexity of the algorithms presented here increase with the complexity of the light source distribution and since we only know how to bridge shadows cast by one source, it is important to know which light source distributions occur in practice. First one notes that the situations found difficult by humans are almost certainly going to give difficulties to our algorithm. For example, when two sources cast shadows (such as on a road lighted by widely spaced streetlamps) the shape of unfamiliar objects becomes difficult to ascertain because of the crossed shadows. If the incident intensity varies greatly from one image area to another (such as in a lightly wooded forest) the tangle of lighted and dark areas makes perception more difficult.

On the other hand one would expect natural conditions to be particularly easy, as in the case of one point source somewhat above the observer (the sun) combined with a very diffuse (almost uniform) source (the sky). The diffuse source will not throw sharp shadows of its own. The absence of either of the two sources makes vision only slightly more difficult.

One would expect photographers to have something to contribute to this subject and introductory booklets on artificial light photography confirm the above conclusions. The beginner is advised to use a number of lights with different characteristics as follows:

1. The main light–The ideal main light is a large spot light approximating the effect of the sun. It is usually placed 45 degrees above and 45 degrees to the side of the subject. Its purpose is to establish the 'form of the subject' and fix the ratio of lighted to dark areas. The exact ratio is not important but the position of the source should result in good shading (which increases as the source is moved further from the camera) without too much shadow area (in which detail is more difficult to perceive).
2. The fill-in light (or axial light)–Its purpose is to lighten slightly the shadows cast by the main light and approximates the effect of the sky. This light is placed near the camera to prevent it from casting new shadows of its own and to simulate the effect of uniform lighting. The appearance of shadows within shadows is considered extremely "ugly" and should be avoided since it makes the picture more difficult to interpret. The ratio of fill-in light intensity to main light intensity is usually chosen to be about 1 to 3.
3. The accent light–Its purpose is to enliven the rendering by adding highlights and 'sparkle'. It should be a small collimated source which can be directed to illuminate small sections of the subject. It is placed behind and to the side of the subject so that it cannot cast shadows of its own. This light can add catchlights (specular reflections such as on eyes or metal objects) and bright outlines (particularly on hair).
4. The background light–Its purpose is to 'separate' the subject from the background. It illuminates the background only, such that the intensity reflected by the subject will nowhere match that of the background. This ensures that the two can be easily 'separated' because the edge between them will be visible.

Other hints are that too many lights spoil the effect, having the main light at the camera creates a "flat" image, shadows crossing edges on the subject are to be avoided and that light parts of the image draw the attention of the viewer. It is interesting to note how much of what is vaguely formulated in these introductions to photography can be understood from the point of view of shading.

4.5.2 Human Performance and the Science of Cosmetics

Judging by the popularity of monocular pictures of people and other smooth objects, humans are good at interpreting shading information. Since they use the same basic information as our shape-from-shading algorithm we expect to find similar shortcomings. Supposing the human visual system does not use the shading information in simple heuristic ways only, one might expect that the perception system 'solves' the equations or a much simplified form of them. Since this cannot be done locally (the way some portions of an edge-finding process might work) it is difficult to suggest an elegant and simple physiological mechanism and a place to look for it.

When a surface whose photometric properties are taken to be uniform is treated so as to change these properties in some areas, the apparent shape is changed. This of course is one of the uses of makeup. The shape of a face for example can be made to conform more closely to what a person thinks is currently considered ideal. This is achieved by making some areas darker (causing them to appear steeper) and others lighter. Areas lightened usually include singular points and cause a change in the apparent skin darkness (a normalization effect) and will change the apparent shape in areas other than the singular points.

These modifications can change the shape perceived when viewed under the right lighting conditions. The effect will change somewhat with orientation and may at times disappear when no reasonable shape would give rise to the shading observed. Because of a number of surface oils the skin has a specular component in its reflectivity. It is also fairly translucent. Both of these effects are sometimes controlled with talcum powder. The removal of the specular components makes the surface appear more rounded and soft.

4.5.3 Generating Shaded Images

The inverse problem of producing images of a specified scene with shading and shadows is vastly different from the method of shape-from-shading. Most programs written for this purpose can be used for objects bounded by planes only. The main issues of optimization of the calculation of which surfaces are visible to the source and camera respectively have been dealt with in some detail. Although the two problems are inverses of one another, the methods used are quite different.

An interesting problem of a mathematical nature (and incidentally with application to cutting woodcuts) is that of producing curved lines in a plane such that the density of lines is proportional to the shading in the image of some real or imagined object. Preferrably one would like as small a number of 'unnecessary' breaks in the lines as possible, i.e., the lines should either close on themselves or leave the image. Another restriction one might apply is that the lines should not cross (when producing woodcuts one would most likely also reflect some of the surface texture in the choice of lines).

For a special case, a solution is immediately at hand. This is the case where we have a distant camera at a distant source and a reflectivity function ϕ such that

$$\phi(I, I, 1) = I = \frac{1}{\sqrt{1 + p^2 + q^2}}$$

Here the contour lines give a solution, with no crossing lines and no "unnecessary" breaks. One of the most attractive features of contour maps is perhaps just this fact that they provide some shading information.

4.5.4 Determining Shape from Texture Gradients

A problem related to that of determining shape using shading is that of determining shape from the depth-cue of texture gradients. A textured surface will produce an image in which the texture is distorted in a way reflecting both the direction and the amount of the inclination of the surface. An image of a tilted surface with a random dot pattern for example will be compressed in one direction (the average distance between dots is decreased) by an amount proportional to the inclination of the surface. Both direction and magnitude of the gradient can thus be determined—except for a two-way ambiguity.

In practice it may not always be easy to determine such texture gradients reliably because of low resolution of the imaging device and scatter, causing a reduction in constrast. Some simple textures may be handled by simple counting or distance measurements as suggested above, while more complicated textures like a plastered wall will need more sophisticated techniques, such as two-dimensional correlation. Some experimentation with this technique showed promise, but did not supply very reliable gradients and the method was slow.

The next problem is how to obtain the shape from the texture gradients. Starting at some point (whose distance from the camera we assume known), we use some external knowledge to resolve the two-way ambiguity. We can now take a small step in any direction and find the gradient at this new point. Continuing in this way we trace out some curve on the surface of the object (somewhat analogous to the characteristics in the shape-from-shading method, except that here the curve is quite arbitrary).

Let s be the arc-distance along the curve, z the distance to the initial point, and p and q the components of the gradient. Then

$$z(s) = z_0 + \int_0^s (p, q) \cdot ds$$

If one takes small enough steps, one can continue to resolve the ambiguity at each step by using the assumption of smoothness. This can be done until we meet a point where the gradient is zero. To continue past such a point would require some external knowledge to again resolve the two-way ambiguity. An aggregation of points with zero inclination can form an ambiguity edge which cannot be crossed.

Clearly we can reach a given point through many paths from the initial point. This allows us some error checking, but there certainly are better ways of making use of the excess information. For that is what we have, since we know from the solution to the shape-from-shading problem that only one value is required at each point for the determination of the shape, while we here have two (the components of the gradient). Most commonly when faced with such an excess of information one can make use of some least-squares technique to improve the accuracy. Perhaps a relaxation method on a grid would be useful.

REFERENCES

1. Rindfleisch, T.: Photometric Method for Lunar Topography, *Photometric Eng.*, **32**(2):262–276 (1966).
2. Horn, Berthold K. P.: The Image Dissector Eyes, *M.I.T. Artificial Intelligence Laboratory Memo* 178, 1969.
3. Garabedian, D. R.: "Partial Differential Equations," John Wiley & Sons, New York, 1964.
4. Fesenkov, V. P.: Photometric Investigations of the Lunar Surface, *Astronomochheskii Zh.*, **5**:219–234 (1929).
5. Willingham, D. E.: The Lunar Reflectivity Model for Ranger Block III Analysis, *Jet Prop. Lab. Tech. Rept.* 32-664, Pasadena, Calif., November, 1964.
6. Van Diggelen, J.: A Photometric Investigation of the Slopes and Heights of the Ranges of Hills in the Maria of the Moon, *Bull. Astron. Inst. Netherlands,* **11**(423):283–289 (1951).

5 LEARNING STRUCTURAL DESCRIPTIONS FROM EXAMPLES

Patrick Henry Winston

5.1 KEY IDEAS

How do we recognize examples of various concepts?
How do we learn to make such recognitions?
How can machines do these things?
How important is careful teaching?

In this paper I describe a set of working computer programs that sheds some light on these questions by demonstrating how a machine can be taught to see and learn new visual concepts. The programs work in the domain of three-dimensional structures made of bricks, wedges, and other simple objects.

Centrally important is the notion of the near miss. By near miss I mean a sample in a training sequence quite like the concept to be learned but which differs from that concept in only a small number of significant points. These near misses prove to convey the essentials much more directly than repetitive exposure to ordinary examples.

Good descriptions are equally important. I believe learning from examples, learning by imitation, and learning by being told uniformly depend on good descriptions. My system therefore necessarily has good methods for scene description and description comparison.

I also argue the importance of good training sequences prepared by good teachers. I think it is reasonable to believe that neither machines nor children can be expected to learn much without them.

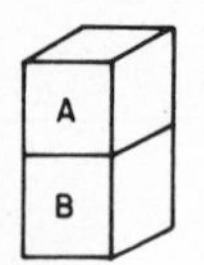

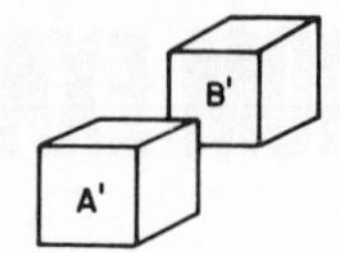

Fig. 5.1

5.1.1 Scene Description and Comparison

Much of the system to be described focuses on the problem of analyzing toy block scenes. There are two very simple examples of such scenes in Fig. 5.1.

From such visual images, the system builds a very coarse description as in Fig. 5.2. Then analysis proceeds, inserting more detail as shown in Fig. 5.3. And finally there is the very fine detail about the surfaces, lines, vertexes, and their relationships.

Such descriptions permit one to match, compare, and contrast scenes through programs that compare and contrast descriptions. After two scenes are described and corresponding parts related by the matching program, differences in the descriptions can be found, categorized, and themselves described. Of course, one hopes that the descriptions will be similar or dissimilar to the same degree that the scenes they represent seem similar or dissimilar to human intuition.

The program that does this must be able to examine the descriptions of Fig. 5.3 with the help of a matching program and deduce that the difference between the scenes is that there is a supported-by relation in one case, while there is an in-front-of relation in the other. Of course the matcher must be much more powerful than this simple example indicates in order to face more complex pairs of scenes exhibiting the entire spectrum between the nearly identical and the completely different.

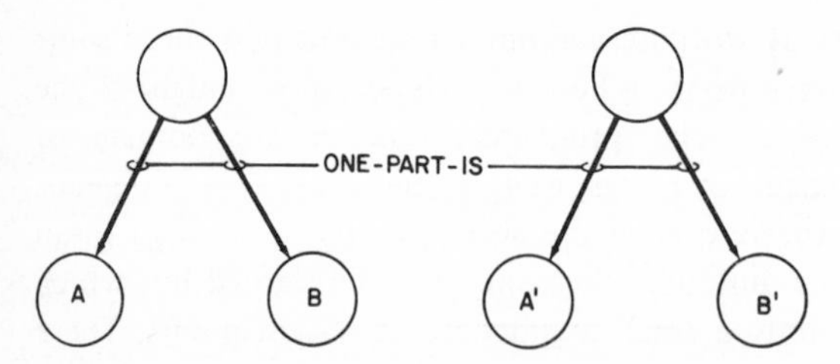

Fig. 5.2

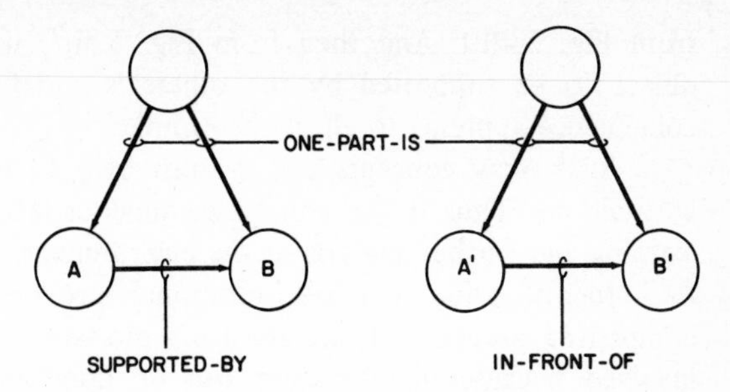

Fig. 5.3

5.1.2 Learning and Identification

To build a machine that can analyze line drawings and build descriptions relevant to some comparison procedure is interesting in itself. But this is just a step toward the more ambitious goal of creating a running program that can learn to recognize structures. I will describe a program that can use samples of simple concepts to generate models.

Figure 5.4 and the next few following it show a sequence of samples that enables the machine to learn what an arch is. First it gets the general idea by studying the first sample in Fig. 5.4(*a*). Then it learns refinements to its original conception by comparing its current impression of what an arch is with successive samples. It learns that the supports of an arch cannot touch from Fig. 5.4(*b*). It learns that it does not matter much what the top object is

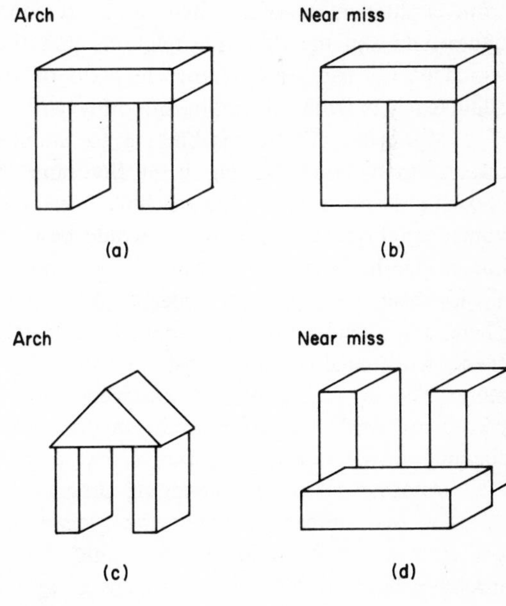

Fig. 5.4

from Fig. 5.4(*c*). And then from Fig. 5.4(*d*) it learns the fact that for one object to be supported by the others is a definite requirement, not just a coincidence applying to all of the samples.

Such new concepts can in turn help in making other, more complex abstractions. Thus the machine uses previous learning as an aid toward further learning and further analysis of the environment.

Identification requires additional programs that use the results of comparison programs. There are many problems and many alternative methods involved because identification can be done in a variety of ways. In one simple form of identification, the machine compares the description of some scene to be identified with a repertoire of models, or stored concepts. Then there is a method of evaluating the comparisons between the unknown and the models so that some match can be defined as best. But many sophistications lie beyond this skeletal scheme. For one thing, the identification can be either sensitive to context or prejudiced toward locating a particular type of object. Elementary algorithms for both of these kinds of identifications are discussed later.

5.1.3 Psychological Modeling

Simulation of human intelligence is not a primary goal of this work. Yet for the most part I have designed programs that see the world in terms conforming to human usage and taste. These programs produce descriptions that use notions such as left-of, on-top-of, behind, big, and part-of.

There are several reasons for this. One is that if a machine is to learn from a human teacher, then it is reasonable that the machine should understand and use the same relations that the human does. Otherwise there would be the sort of difference in point of view that prevents inexperienced adult teachers from interacting smoothly with small children.

Moreover, if the machine is to understand its environment for any reason, then understanding it in the same terms humans do helps us to understand and improve the machine's operation. Little is known about how human intelligence works, but it would be foolish to ignore conjectures about human methods and abilities if those things can help machines. Much has already been learned from programs that use what seem like human methods. There are already programs that prove mathematical theorems, play good chess, work analogy problems, understand restricted forms of English, and more. Yet in contrast, little knowledge about intelligence has come from perceptron work and other approaches to intelligence that do not exploit the planning and hierarchical organization that seems characteristic of human thought.

Another reason for designing programs that describe scenes in human terms is that human judgment then serves as a standard. There will be no contentment with machines that only do as well as humans. But until machines become better than humans at seeing, doing as well is a reasonable goal, and comparing the performance of the machine with that of the human is a convenient way to measure success.

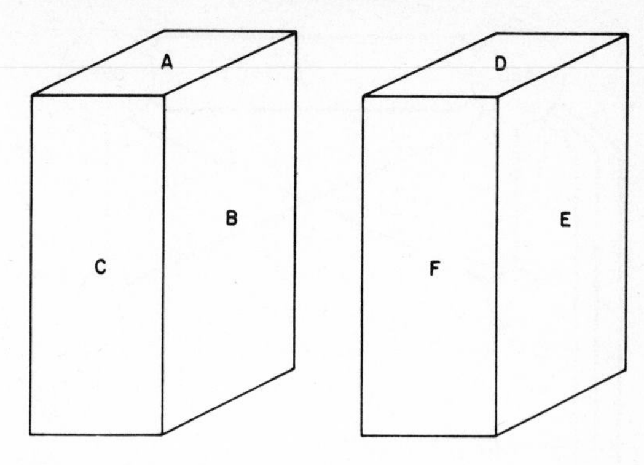

Fig. 5.5

5.2 BUILDING DESCRIPTIONS

The network seems to have the appropriate blend of flexibility and simplicity needed to deal straightforwardly with scenes. It is the natural format. Like words in a dictionary, each object is naturally thought of in terms of relationships to other objects and to descriptive concepts. In Fig. 5.5, for example, one has concepts such as OBJECT-ABC and OBJECT-DEF. These are represented diagrammatically as circles in Fig. 5.6. Labelled arrows or pointers define the relationships between the concepts. Other pointers indicate membership in general classes or specify particular properties. And pointers to circles representing the sides extend the depth of the description and allow more detail as shown in Fig. 5.7.

Now notice that notions like SUPPORTED-BY, ABOVE, LEFT-OF, BENEATH, and A-KIND-OF may be used not only as relations, but also as concepts. Consider SUPPORTED-BY. The statement, "The WEDGE is

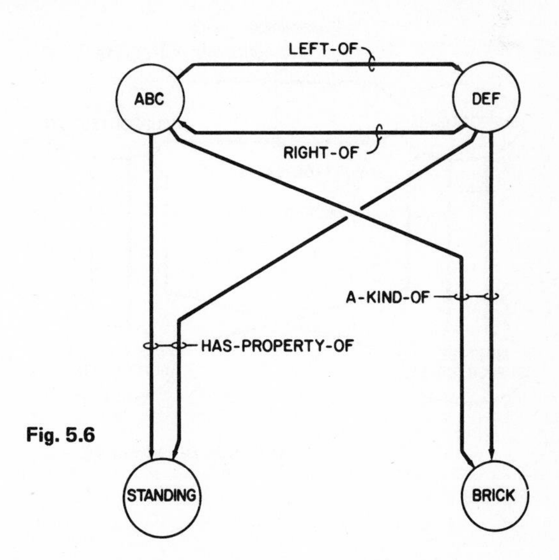

Fig. 5.6

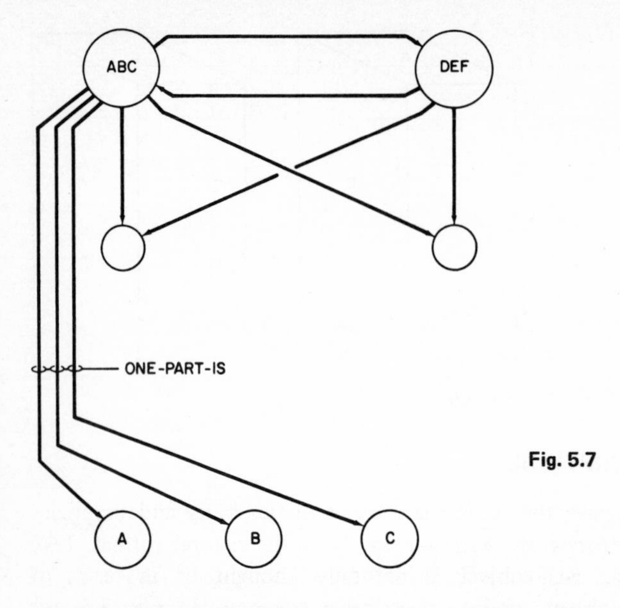

Fig. 5.7

SUPPORTED-BY the BLOCK," uses SUPPORTED-BY as a relation. But the statement, "SUPPORTED-BY is the opposite of NOT-SUPPORTED-BY," uses SUPPORTED-BY as a concept undergoing explication. Consequently, SUPPORTED-BY is a node in the network as well as a pointer label, and SUPPORTED-BY itself is defined in terms of relations to other nodes. Figure 5.8 shows some of the surrounding nodes of SUPPORTED-BY. I will generally call such related nodes satellites.

Thus, descriptions of relationships can be stored in a homogeneous network along with the descriptions of scenes that use those relationships.

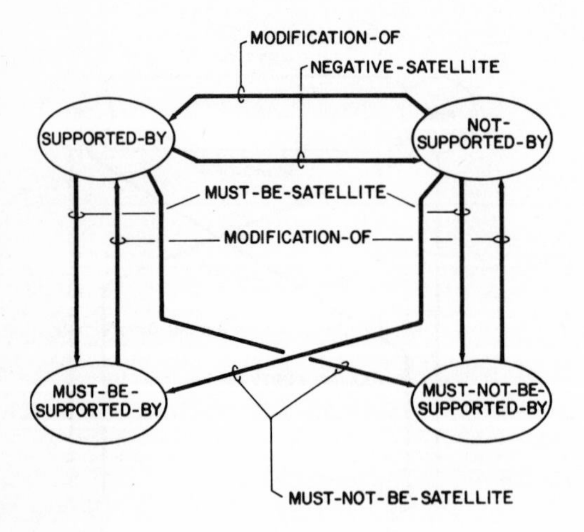

Fig. 5.8

This permits big steps toward program generality. A program to find negatives need only know about the relation NEGATIVE-SATELLITE and have access to the general memory net. There is no need for the program itself to contain a distended table. This way programs can operate in many environments, both anticipated and not anticipated. Algorithms designed to manipulate networks at the level of scene description can work as easily with descriptions of objects, sides, or even of functions of objects, given the appropriate network.

5.2.1 Preliminary Scene Analysis

Consider now the generation of a scene description. The starting point is a line drawing, with or without perspective distortion, and the result is to be a network relating and describing the various objects with pointers such as IN-FRONT-OF, ABOVE, SUPPORTED-BY, A-KIND-OF, and HAS-PROPERTY-OF.

My system's first step in processing a scene is the application of a program written by H. N. Mahabala[1] which classifies and labels the vertexes of a scene according to the number of converging lines and the angles between them. Figure 5.9 displays the available categories. Notice that Mahabala's program finds pairs of Ts where the crossbars lie between collinear uprights.

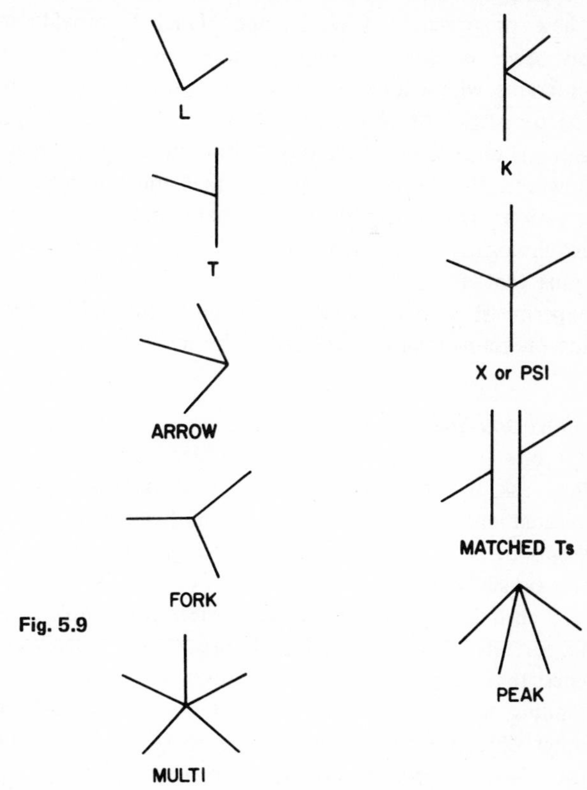

Fig. 5.9

These are called matched Ts. Such pairs occur frequently when one object partially occludes another.

Mahabala's program creates names for all of the regions in the scene. Various properties are calculated and stored for these regions. Among these are a list of the vertexes surrounding each region and a list of the neighboring regions.

These results are then supplied to descendants of a program developed by Adolfo Guzman.[2] This program conjectures about which regions belong to the same objects. Surprisingly it contains no explicit models for the objects it expects to see. It simply examines the vertexes and uses the vertex classifications to determine which of the neighboring regions are likely to be part of the same object. Arrows, for example, strongly suggest that the two regions bordering the shaft belong to the same body. This sort of evidence, together with a moderately sophisticated executive, can sort out the regions in most simple scenes.

5.2.2 Selected Relation and Property Algorithms

These programs by Guzman and Mahabala provide information required by my own description-building programs now to be described. There are programs which look for relations between objects and programs which look for properties of objects. Generally these programs produce descriptions that are in remarkable harmony with those of human observers. Sometimes, however, they make conjectures that most humans disagree with. On these occasions one should remember that there is no intention to precisely mimic psychological phenomena. The goal is simply to produce reasonable descriptions that are easy to work with. Right now it is important to design and experiment with a capable set of programs and postpone the question of how the programs might be refined to be more completely lifelike, if desired.

Above and Support

T joints are strong clues that one object partly obscures another, but then one may ask if the obscuring occurs because one object is above the other or because one is in front of the other. Even in the simple two brick case there seems to be an enormous number of configurations. Figure 5.10 shows just a few possibilities.

But in spite of this variety, there is a simple procedure that often seems to correctly decide the ABOVE versus IN-FRONT-OF question. Consider the lines that form the bottom border of the obscuring objects in Fig. 5.10. Finding these lines is the first job of the program. Next the program finds other objects whose regions share these lines. In general these other objects are below the original, obscuring object.

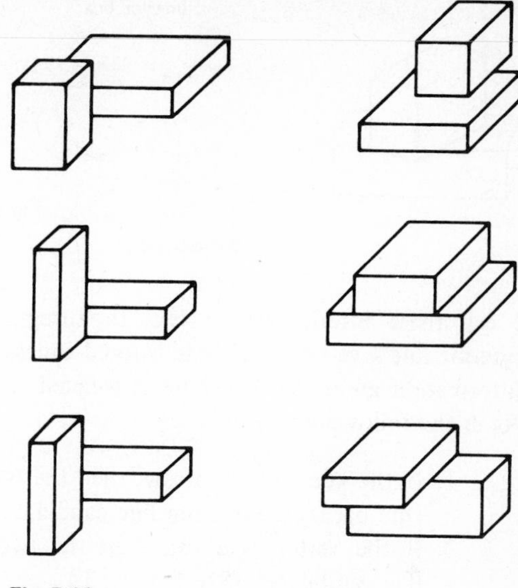

Fig. 5.10

This algorithm works on all the simple two-block situations depicted in Fig. 5.10. It even works correctly on the much more complicated, many-object scene in Fig. 5.11, shown with the bottom lines highlighted.

The difficult part is to find the so-called bottom lines, which correspond roughly to one's intuitive notion of bottom border. The process proceeds by first noting those lines that lie between two regions of the object in question.

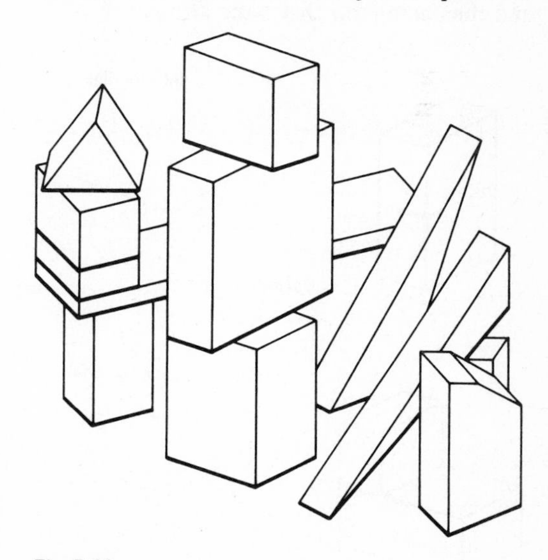

Fig. 5.11

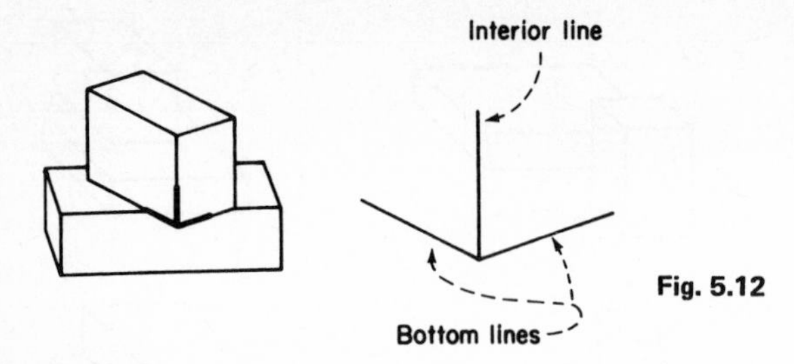

Fig. 5.12

I call these interior lines. Next the program examines the lower of each interior line's vertexes. This is ignored unless it is an arrow, psi, or a K. Then information about bottom lines is gleaned from each of the arrows, psis, and Ks in the following way:

1. If the vertex is an arrow, then the two lines forming the largest angle (the barbs) are bottom line candidates. (See Fig. 5.12.)
2. If the vertex is a psi, then the two non-collinear lines are bottom line candidates. (See Fig. 5.13.)
3. If the vertex is a K, then the two adjacent lines, those forming the smallest clockwise and the smallest counter-clockwise angles with the interior line are bottom line candidates. (See Fig. 5.14.)

This is really a rule and two corollaries, rather than three separate rules. Psis and Ks result primarily when arrows appear incognito, camouflaged by an alignment of objects as illustrated by Figs. 5.13 and 14. Consequently, the corresponding rules amount to locating the arrow-forming parts of the vertex and then acting on that basic arrow.

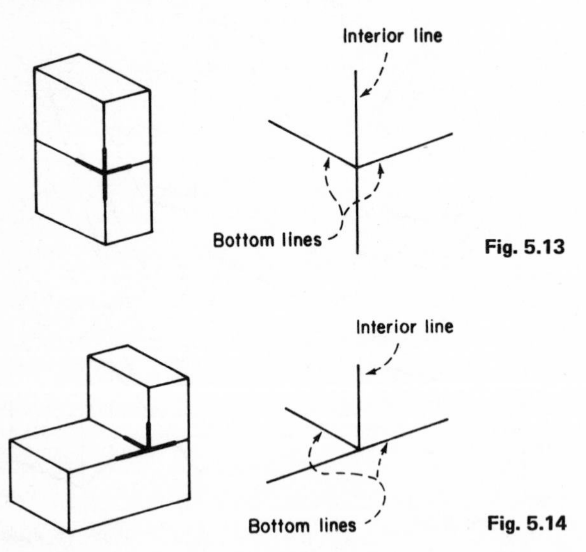

Fig. 5.13

Fig. 5.14

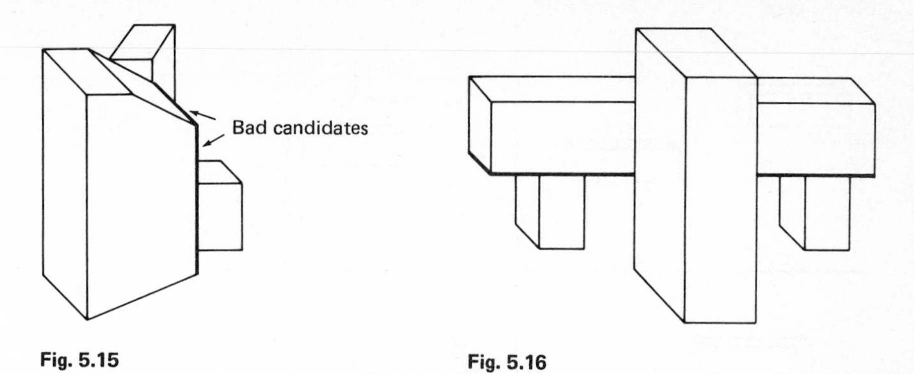

Fig. 5.15

Fig. 5.16

One further step is necessary before a line can become an approved bottom line. As shown by Fig. 5.15, some of the lines which qualify so far must be eliminated. They fail because they are too vertical, or more precisely, because they are too vertical with respect to the arrow's shaft. The effective way to weed out bad lines is to eliminate any bottom-line candidate which is more vertical than the shaft of the arrow suggesting that candidate.

Of course the program extends rudimentary bottom lines through certain vertexes. Figure 5.16 shows the obvious situations in which the bottom line property is extended through the crossbar of a T or the shafts of a pair of matched Ts.

Left and Right

Consider the spectrum of situations in Fig. 5.17. For the first pair of objects, the relations LEFT-OF and RIGHT-OF are clearly appropriate. For the last, they are clearly not appropriate. To me, the crossover point seems to be between the situations expressed by pairs 4 and 5.

Now notice that the center of area of one object is to the left of the left-most point of the other object in those cases where LEFT-OF seems to hold. It is not so positioned if LEFT-OF does not hold. Such a criterion seems in reasonable agreement with intuitive pronouncements for many of the cases I have studied. It also yields reasonable answers in Fig. 5.18 where in one case A is to the left of B and in the other case it is not. Notice that the relation is not symmetric, however, as the center of area of the much longer brick, brick B, indicates B is to the right of A in both cases.

Extra consideration is needed if one object extends beyond the other in both directions. No matter what the center of mass relationships, humans are reluctant to use either LEFT-OF or RIGHT-OF in such a situation. One must additionally specify a rule against this, leaving the following for LEFT-OF:

Say A is left of B $\Leftarrow\Rightarrow$

1. The center of area of A is left of the leftmost point of B.
2. The rightmost point of A is left of the rightmost point of B.

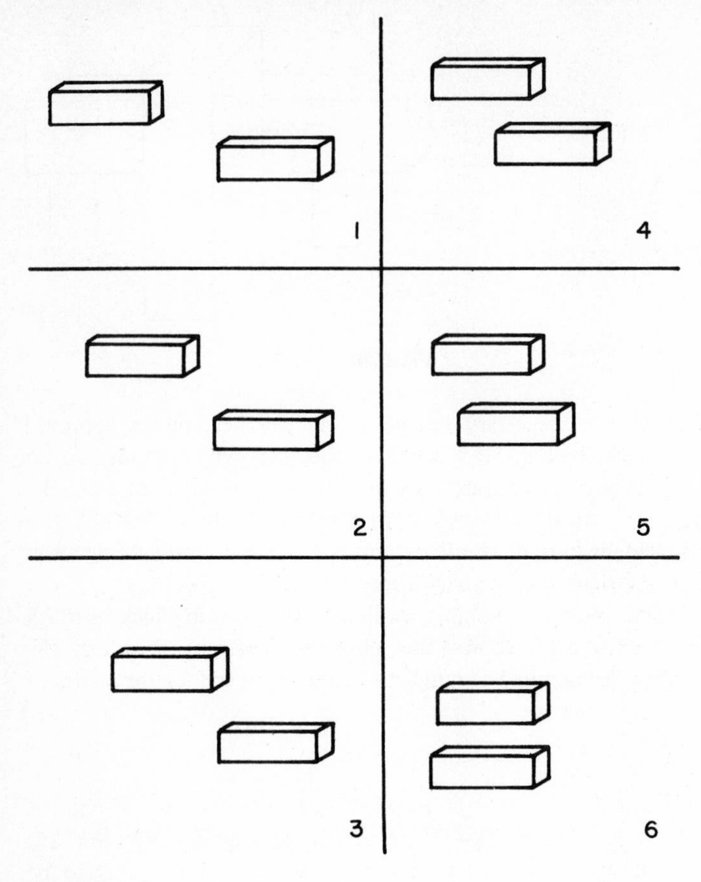

Fig. 5.17

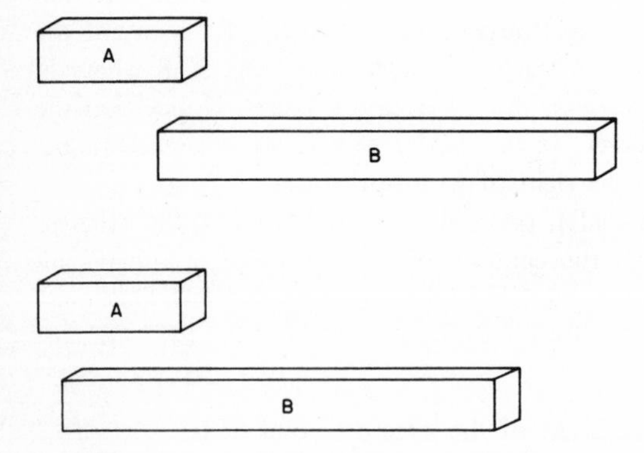

Fig. 5.18

The rule for RIGHT-OF is of course parallel in form.

Deciding if one object is to the left of another stimulates far more argument than do questions involving relations like IN-FRONT-OF and SUPPORTED-BY. People have difficulty verbalizing how they perceive LEFT-OF and tend to waver in their methods, but implications are that criteria change depending on whether the objects involved are also related by IN-FRONT-OF, ON-TOP-OF, BIGGER-THAN, and so on. The orientations of objects involved are also a strong influence, and my procedure could probably do better by asking basically the same questions as before, but about lines through the left-most, right-most, and center-of-area points in the direction of orientation instead of what amounts to vertical projection of the points to the x axis.

Marries

The abuts and aligned-with relations arise frequently, perhaps because of human predilection to order. As intuitively used, however, neither of these words corresponds to the notion I want the machine to deal with. To avoid confusion, I therefore prefer to use the term marry, which I define as follows:

> An object marries another if those objects have faces that touch each other and have at least one common edge.

Thus the objects in Fig. 5.19 are said to marry one another. Those in Fig. 5.20 do not because they have no common edge. Similarly those in Fig. 5.21 do not because they have no touching faces. The MARRIES relation is sensed by methods resembling those previously described.

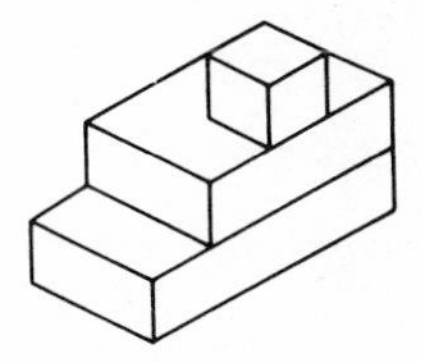

Fig. 5.19

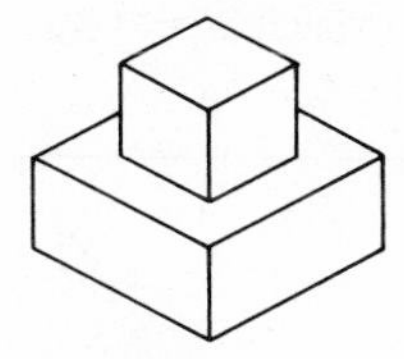

Fig. 5.20

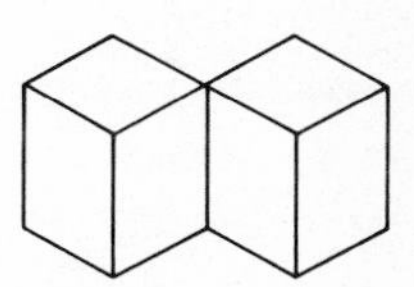

Fig. 5.21

Size

Piaget has shown that at a certain age children generally associate physical size with greatest dimension. They will, for example, adamantly maintain that a tall thin beaker has more water in it than a short fat one even though they have seen them filled from other beakers of equal size.

Adults do not develop as far beyond this as might be expected. I do not think we really use the notion of volume naturally. Apparent area seems much more closely related to adult size judgment. Notice that beaker A in Fig. 5.22 appears to have about the same amount of water in it as does beaker B, even though it must contain twice as much. Unless a subject consciously exercises a formula for volume, he is likely to report that object B in Fig. 5.23 is approximately ten times larger than object A, even if told both objects are cubes. The true factor of 27 times seems large when the trouble is taken to calculate it.

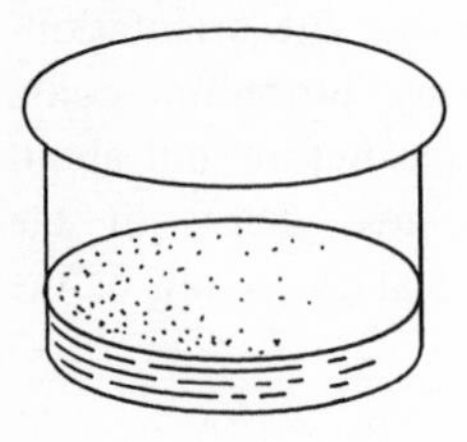

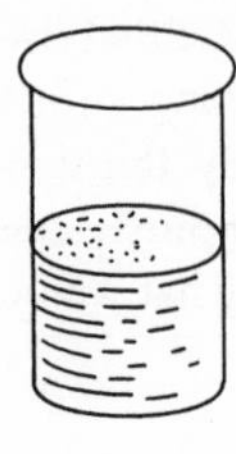

Fig. 5.22

Consequently, the size-generating program does not use volume. Instead it calculates the area of each shape produced by the shape detecting algorithm. Next it adds together the areas of all shapes belonging to an object to get its total area. Then using these areas it can compare two objects in size or consult the following table for a reasonably believable discrete partitioning of the area scale:

0.0% to 0.5% of the visual area → tiny

0.5 to 1.5 of the visual area → small

1.5 to 15 of the visual area → medium

15 to 35 of the visual area → large

35 to 100 of the visual area → huge

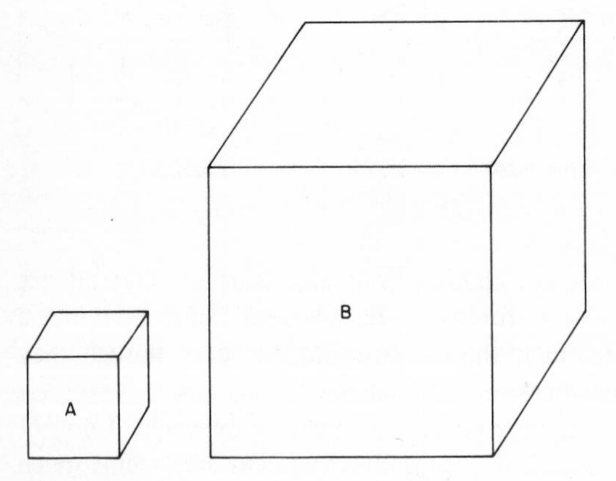

Fig. 5.23

5.3 DISCOVERING GROUPS OF OBJECTS

When a scene has more than a few objects, it is usually useful to deepen the hierarchy of the description by dividing the objects into smaller groups which can be described and thought of as individual concepts. Figure 5.24 seems to divide naturally into two groups of objects, one being three objects tied together by SUPPORTED-BY pointers, and one being three objects on top of a fourth.

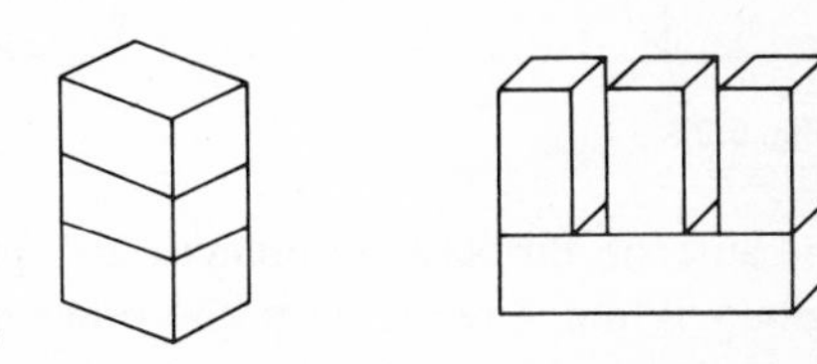

Fig. 5.24

Recognition of such groups seems to be a two part process of conjecture followed by criticism and revision. Conjectures follow from searches for objects linked by pointer chains or for objects bearing the same relation to some grouping object that binds the potential group members together. Criticism and revision is then needed to exclude from membership those objects that are weak compared with the average for the group.

5.3.1 Sequences

A simple kind of group consists of chains of SUPPORTED-BY or IN-FRONT-OF pointers. The first act of the grouping program is to find sets of objects that are chained together in this way. All such sets with three or more elements qualify as groups.

Using chains to define groups requires a rule for handling the situation illustrated by the scenes in Fig. 5.25. On the left a chain of SUPPORTED-BY pointers splits into two branches at the point where object C is supported by two objects, D and E. On the right two chains of SUPPORTED-BY pointers join at M which supports both I and L. The current version of the grouping program terminates chains at junction points without further fuss. This seems reasonable for it is natural to think of the scenes in Fig. 5.25 as a set of groups consisting of A-B-C, G-H-I, and J-K-L.

Another problem arises when objects tied together by a simple chain of relations should not constitute a group because of other factors. Here a need for the criticism part of the grouping process becomes clear. Figure 5.26 shows one kind of situation that can occur. In this scene the machine first conjectures a single object conglomerate, grouped together by virtue of an unbroken chain of SUPPORTED-BY pointers. But most humans see a short tower on top of a board on top of another tower. This must be partly

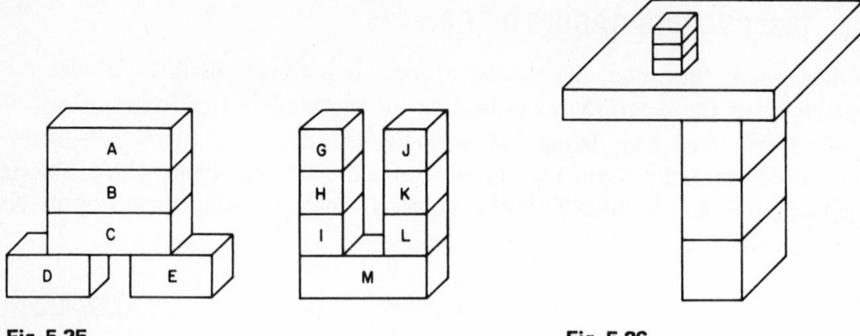

Fig. 5.25

Fig. 5.26

because of the size differences and partly because of the fact that the top group is not directly over the other objects. My system uses either of these radical changes as grounds for breaking the chain.

5.3.2 Common Relations and Properties

For this kind of grouping, the basic idea is again to make a generous hypothesis as to what objects may be in a group and then to eliminate objects which seem atypical until a fairly homogeneous set remains. When several objects relate to some other object in the same way, they are immediately solid candidates for a group. The legs on the table in Fig. 5.27 are typical. They form a convincing group partly because they have the same relation to the table top and partly because all are bricks and all are standing.

All candidates for group membership must be related to one or more particular objects in the same way. For the table, all four objects are related to the board by SUPPORTED-BY. This restriction is a useful heuristic because uniform relationship to a single object seems to have strong binding power. The bricks in Fig. 5.28 naturally constitute two groups, not one.

Now it is necessary to criticize the group with a view toward finishing with a group whose members all have about the same right to group membership. Said another way, established groups where the members are very much alike should have high standards for entry while weaker groups should be more penetrable. The somewhat involved criticism algorithm now

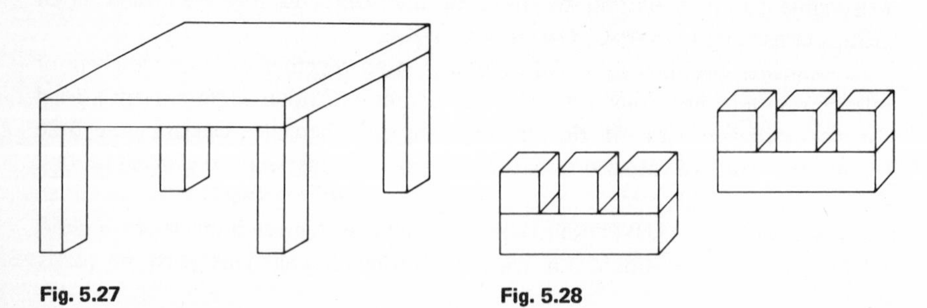

Fig. 5.27

Fig. 5.28

presented helps insure this characteristic in a group by iteratively casting out the clear losers from those proposed.

The flow chart in Fig. 5.29 and the example in Fig. 5.30 help explain. The program first forms a common-relationships-lists, a list of all relationships exhibited by more than half of the candidates in the set. Objects A through F are immediately perceived to be a possible group because they all have a SUPPORTED-BY relationship with a single object G. The relationships exhibited by the candidates are:

A, B, and C:
1 SUPPORTED-BY pointer to G
2 MARRIES pointer to G
3 A-KIND-OF pointer to BRICK
4 HAS-PROPERTY-OF pointer to MEDIUM-SIZE

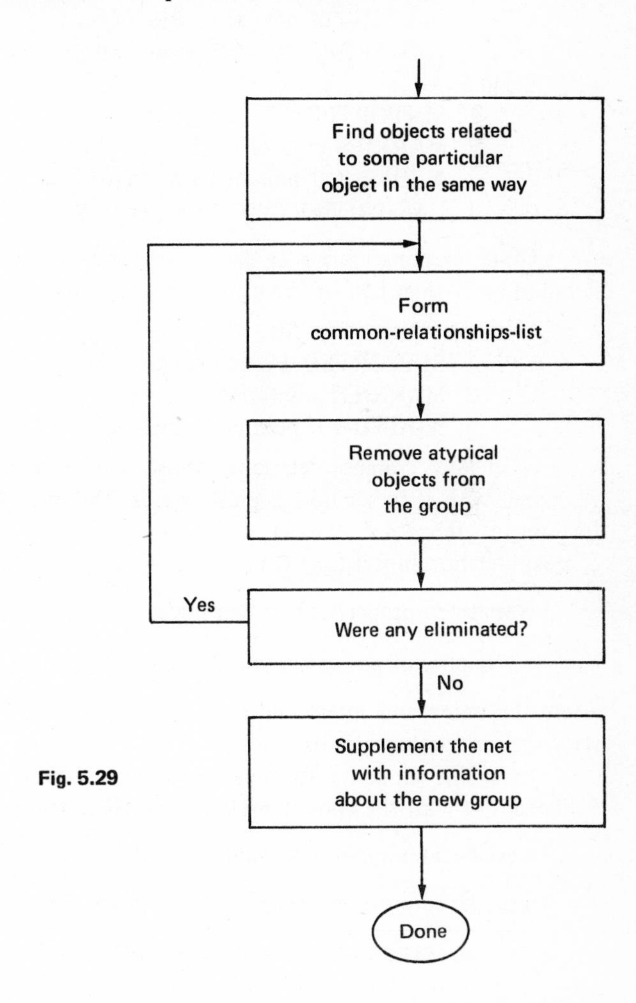

Fig. 5.29

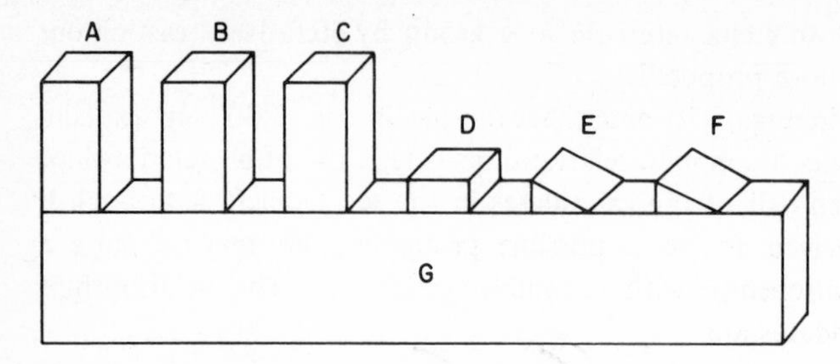

Fig. 5.30

D:

1 SUPPORTED-BY pointer to G
2 MARRIES pointer to G
3 A-KIND-OF pointer to BRICK
4 HAS-PROPERTY-OF pointer to SMALL

E and F:

1 SUPPORTED-BY pointer to G
2 MARRIES pointer to G
3 A-KIND-OF pointer to WEDGE
4 HAS-PROPERTY-OF pointer to SMALL

Three relations appear in the common-relationships-list because they are found in more than half of the candidates' relationships lists:

Common-relationships-list:

1 SUPPORTED-BY pointer to G
2 MARRIES pointer to G
3 A-KIND-OF pointer to BRICK

After this common-relationships-list is formed, all candidates are next compared with it to see how typical each is. The measure is simply the shared fraction of the total number of properties in the candidate list and the common-relationships-list. Said in a more formal way, the measure is

$$\frac{\text{Number of properties in intersection}}{\text{Number of properties in union}}$$

where the union and intersection are of the candidate's relationships list and the common-relationships-list.

Using this similarity formula to compare the various objects of the Fig. 5.30 example with the common-relationships-list, one has:

A vs. the common-relationships-list → 3/4 = .75

B vs. the common-relationships-list → 3/4 = .75

C vs. the common-relationships-list → 3/4 = .75

D vs. the common-relationships-list → 3/4 = .75

E vs. the common-relationships-list → 2/5 = .20

F vs. the common-relationships-list → 2/5 = .20

A, B, C, and D do not have scores of 1 only because the common-relationships-list does not yet have a property indicating size. The reason is that there is no size common to more than half of the currently possible group members, A, B, C, D, E, and F.

The much lower scores of E and F reflect the additional fact that as wedges they are different from the standard type. They are immediately eliminated according to the following general rule:

Eliminate all candidate objects whose similarity scores are less than 80 percent of the best score any object attains. This insures that the group will have members all with a nearly equal right to belong.

Next the process is repeated because those properties common to the remaining candidates may differ from those properties common to the original group enough that one or more changes should be made to the common-relationships-list. This repetition continues until the elimination process fails to oust a candidate or until fewer than three candidates remain.

After the first elimination of objects leaves A, B, C, and D, there is a new common-relationships-list:

Common-relationships-list:
1 SUPPORTED-BY pointer to G
2 MARRIES pointer to G
3 A-KIND-OF pointer to BRICK
4 HAS-PROPERTY-OF pointer to MEDIUM-SIZE

Notice that there is now a size property since three of the four remaining objects have a pointer to medium size. The new comparison scores are:

A vs. the common-relationships-list → 4/4 = 1

B vs. the common-relationships-list → 4/4 = 1

C vs. the common-relationships-list → 4/4 = 1

D vs. the common-relationships-list → 3/5 = .6

This time D is rejected because its uncommon size causes a low score, leaving a stable group in which the objects are all quite alike.

5.3.3 Other Kinds of Grouping

There obviously cannot be a single universal grouping procedure because attention must be paid not only to the scene involved, but also to the needs of the various programs that may request the grouping activity. I have

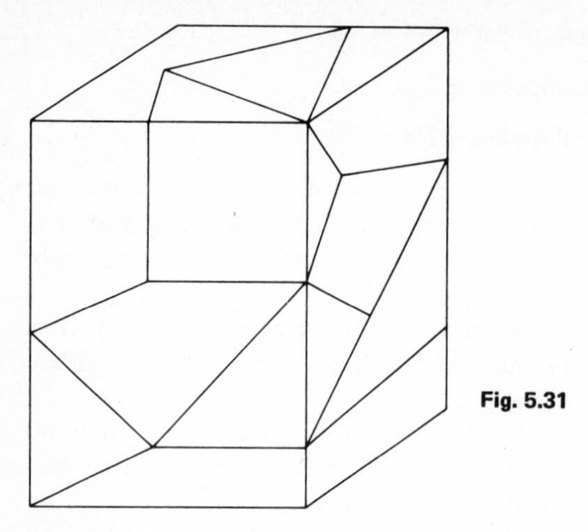

Fig. 5.31

discussed two grouping modes that programs can now do in response to various demands. There remain many others to be explored.

One of these involves looking for things that fit together. Children frequently do this at play without prompting, and adults do it extensively in solving jigsaw puzzles.

Another kind of grouping, one particularly sensitive to the goals of the request, is grouping on the basis of some specified property. The idea is to pick out all things satisfying some criteria, such as all the big standing bricks. The result could be a focusing of attention.

Still another way to group involves overall properties that are not obvious from purely local observations. Techniques in this area are again largely unexplored, but it seems that overall shape can sometimes impose unity on a complete hodge-podge. Figure 5.31 illustrates this point. All of the objects fit together to form a brick-shaped group. This is clearly not inherited from any consistency in how the parts are shaped or how they interact with their immediate neighbors.

5.3.4 Describing a Group Using the Typical Member

The machine needs some means of describing groups. The method it uses seems to work, but there is room for improvement.

First, the parts of the group are gathered together under a node created specifically to represent the group as a conceptual unit. Figure 5.32 illustrates this step for a group of three objects, A, B, and C, all arranged in a tower.

Next comes a concise statement of what membership in the group means. This is done through the use of a typical-member node. Properties and relations that most of the group members share contribute to this node's description. For our A B C case, the typical member is described as a kind of

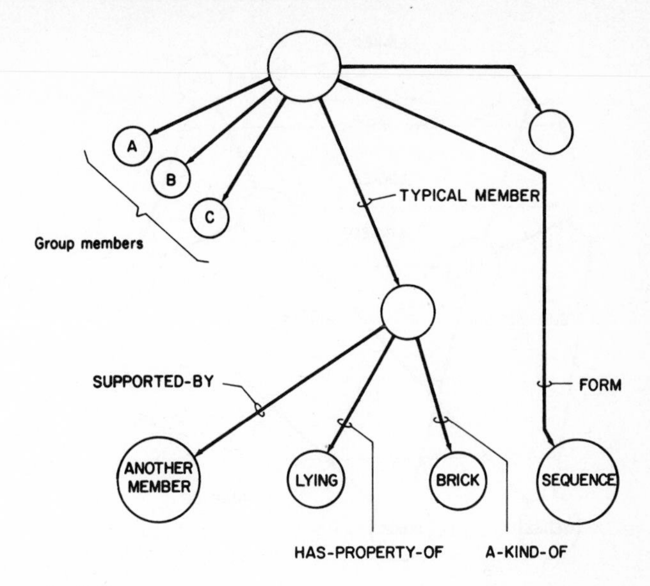

Fig. 5.32

brick, as lying, and as on top of another member of the group. Notice also the FORM pointer to SEQUENCE which indicates the kind of group formed.

5.4 NETWORK SIMILARITIES AND DIFFERENCES

Powerful scene description programs are essential to scene comparison and identification. Matching is equally important since the machine must know which parts of two descriptions correspond before it can compute similarities and differences. Figure 5.33 briefly illustrates. A process explores the two descriptive networks and decides which nodes of the two best correspond in the sense that they have the same function in their respective networks. The nodes in a pair that so correspond are said to be linked to each other. The job of the matching program is simply to find the linked pairs. Node LC and node RC in Fig. 5.33 both have only A-KIND-OF pointers to BRICK. Since no other nodes have similar descriptions, it is clear that LC and RC should be a linked pair. Similarly, LB and RB should be a linked pair since both have A-KIND-OF pointers to WEDGE and both have SUPPORTED-BY pointers to parts of a pair of nodes already known to be linked.

Of course the job of the matching program is not so easy when the two scenes and the resulting two networks are not identical. In this case the process forms linked pairs involving nodes that may not have identical descriptions, but seem similar nevertheless.

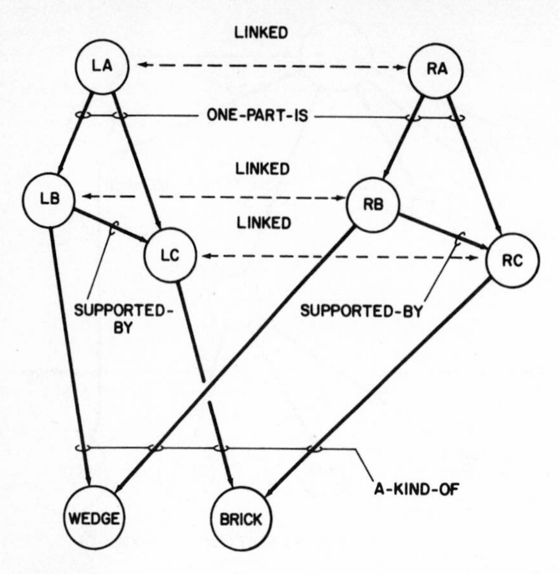

Fig. 5.33

5.4.1 The Skeleton and Comparison Notes

Once the matching process has examined two networks and has established the linked pairs of nodes, then description of network similarities proceeds. The result is simply a new chunk of network that describes those parts of the compared networks that correspond. This chunk is called the skeleton because it is a framework for the rest of the comparison description. As Fig. 5.34 suggests, each linked pair contributes a node to the skeleton. Certain pointers connect the new nodes together. These occur precisely where the compared networks both have the same pointer from one member of some linked pair to a member of some other linked pair. Notice that the skeleton is basically a copy of the structure that the compared networks duplicate.

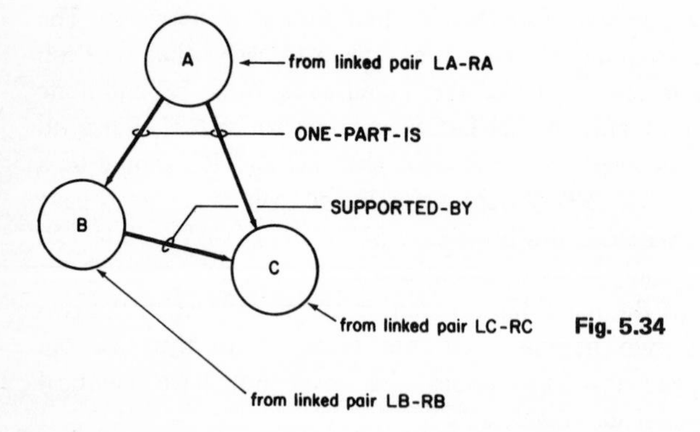

Fig. 5.34

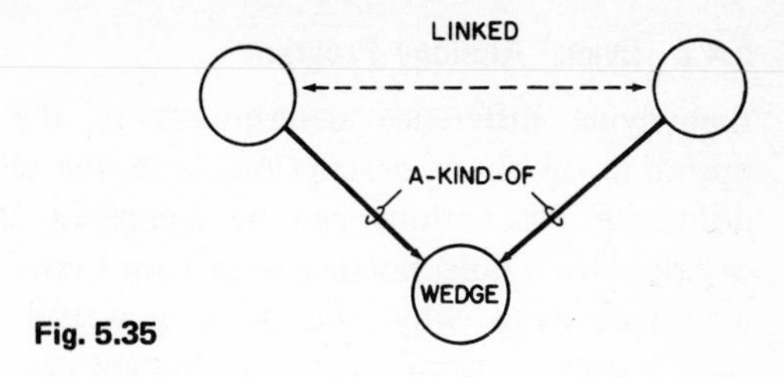

Fig. 5.35

Complete comparison descriptions consist of the skeleton together with a second group of nodes attached to the skeleton like grapes on a grape cluster. Each of the nodes in this second category is called a comparison note or C-NOTE for short. The most common type of comparison note is the intersection comparison note which describes the situation in which both members of a linked pair point to the same concept with the same pointer. Suppose, for example, that a pair of corresponding objects from two scenes are both wedges. Then both concepts exhibit an A-KIND-OF pointer to the concept WEDGE as shown by Fig. 5.35. In English one can say:

1. There is something to be said about a certain linked pair.
2. There is an intersection involved.
3. The associated pointer is A-KIND-OF.
4. The intersection occurs at the concept WEDGE.

Figure 5.36 shows how each of these simple facts translates to a network entry. First, a pointer named C-NOTE extends from the skeleton concept corresponding to the linked pair to a new concept that anchors the intersection description. The A-KIND-OF pointer identifies this concept as a kind of intersection. Finally other pointers identify the pointer, A-KIND-OF, and the concept, WEDGE, associated with the intersection.

All of the comparison notes look like this intersection paradigm.

C-NOTE
A-KIND-OF
POINTER
INTERSECTION
WEDGE
A-KIND-OF
POINTER-DESTINATION

Fig. 5.36

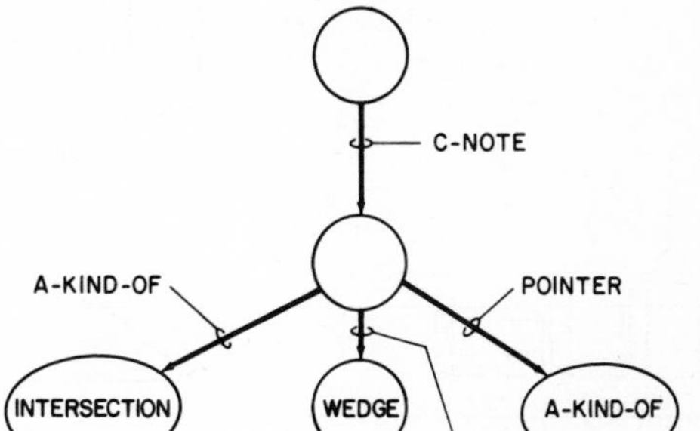

5.4.2 Evans' Analogy Program

Embodying difference descriptions in the same network format permits operation on those descriptions with the same network programs. Thus two difference descriptions can be compared as handily as any other pair of descriptions. Those familiar with Tom Evans' vanguard program, ANALOGY,[3] can understand why this is a powerful feature, rather than simply a contribution toward memory homogeneity. Evans' program worked on two-dimensional geometric figures rather than drawings of three dimensional configurations. Nevertheless his ideas generalize easily and fit nicely into the vocabulary used here.

Figure 5.37 suggests the standard sort of intelligence test problem involved. The machine must select the scene X which best completes the statement: A is to B as C is to X. In human terms one must discover how B relates to A and find an X that relates to C in the same way.

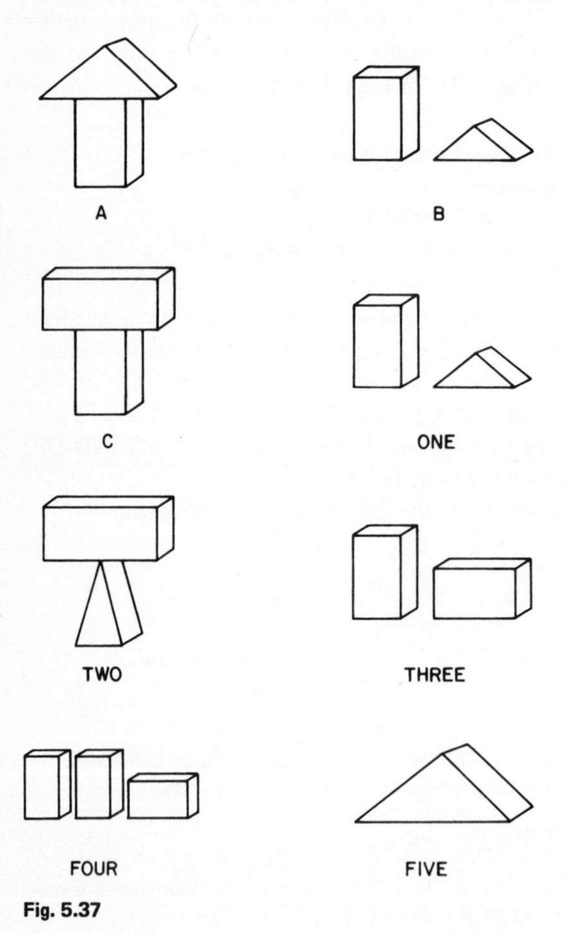

Fig. 5.37

Using the terminology of nets and descriptions, one solution process can be formalized in the following way: First compare A with B and denote the resulting comparison-describing network by

d{A:B}

Similarly compare C with the answer generating descriptions of the form d{C:X}. The result is a complete set of comparisons describing the transformations that carry one figure into another. Next one should compare the description of the transformation from A to B, d{A:B}, with the others to see which is most like it. The best match is associated with the best answer to the problem. If M is a metric on comparison networks that measures the difference between the compared networks, one can say

choose X such that

M(d{d{A:B}:d{C:X}})

is minimum

The metric I use is not fancy. It is the one discussed later that serves to identify some scene with some member of a group of models. It works because the identification problem entirely parallels the problem of identifying a given A to B transformation description with some member of the group of answer connected C to X transformations. The identification program, together with a short executive routine, handles the problem of Fig. 5.37 easily, correctly reporting scene three as the best answer. Reasonably enough, the machine thinks scene one is the second best answer.

Of course if the machine's answers are to be those of the problem's formulator, then the machine's describing, comparing, and comparison measuring processes should all give results that resemble his. Moreover, a really good analogy program should have available alternatives to these basic describing, comparing, and comparison measuring processes. Then in the event no single answer is much better than the others, the program can try some of its alternatives as one or more of its basic functions must not be operating according to what the problem maker intended. Evans' program is superior to mine in this respect because it can often compare two drawings in more than one way. It can visualize some changes as either reflections or any of several rotations.

Given my formulation of the analogy problem, it is easy to see how certain interesting generalizations can be made. After all, once an X is selected, the network symbolized by d{d{A:B}:d{C:X}} describes the problem, and as a descripiton, it can be compared with the descriptions of other problems. By thus applying the comparison programs for the third time, one can deal with the question: Analogy problem alpha is most like which other analogy problem? Alternatively, one can apply the analogy solving program to problem descriptions instead of scenes and answer the question: Analogy problem alpha is to analogy problem beta as analogy problem gamma is to which other analogy problem? This involves four levels of comparison. But of course there is no limit, and with time and memory machines could happily think about extended analogy problems involving an arbitrary number of comparison levels.

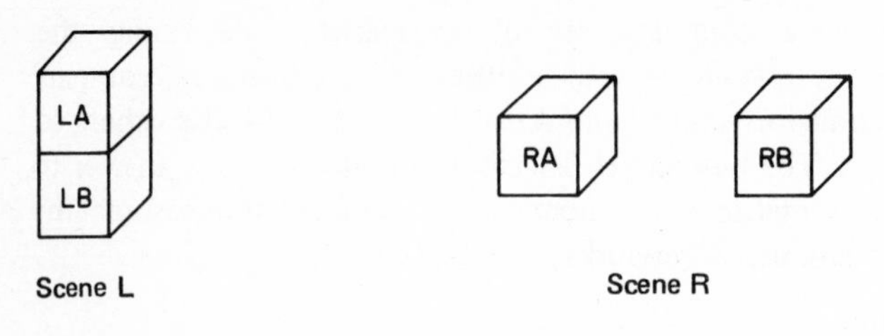

Fig. 5.38

5.4.3 A Catalog of Comparison-Note Types

The Supplementary-Pointer and the Exit

Consider the scenes in Fig. 5.38 and their descriptions in Fig. 5.39. Scene L has the pointer SUPPORTED-BY between LA and LB, but scene R does not have a pointer between the objects linked to LA and LB. The note describing this situation is called a supplementary-pointer comparison note and has the form shown in Fig. 5.40.

Suppose now we consider a standing brick and compare it with a cube. Here the linked concepts would differ only in that the brick has an additional pointer identifying it as standing. This differs from the supplementary-pointer case in that STANDING is a node outside the scene description. A pointer to the concept EXIT signals this situation. Exits involve concepts generated by the scene description program as well as concepts like STANDING that reside in the net permanently. If one scene contains more objects than another, the concepts left over and not matched end up in exit packages.

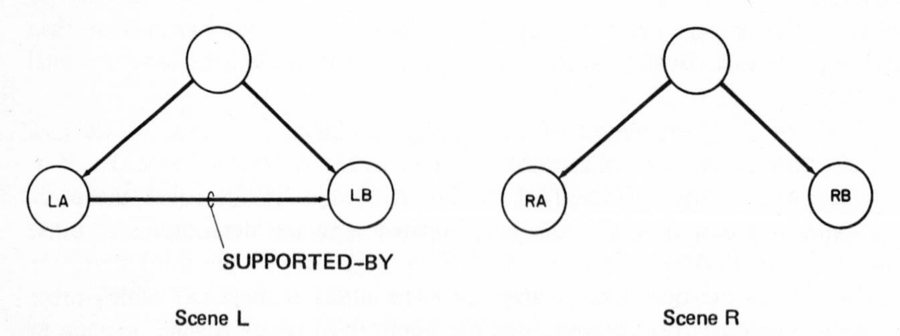

Fig. 5.39

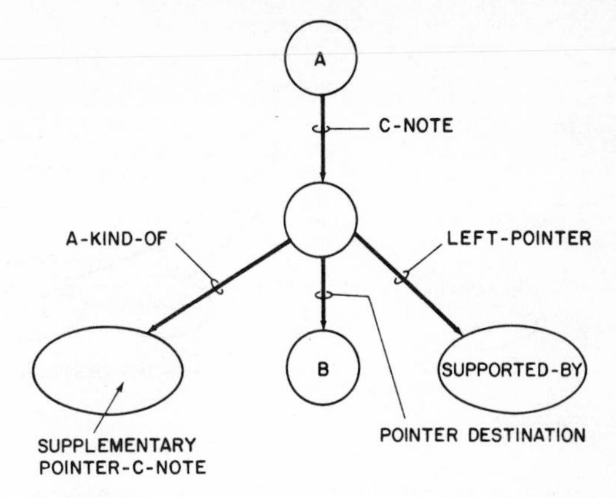

Fig. 5.40

Pointer Modifications

Suppose the left and right networks in Fig. 5.41 are compared. Notice the MARRIES pointer between LA and LB and the DOES-NOT-MARRY pointer between RA and RB. These could be handled individually as unrelated supplementary-pointer comparison notes, but this would ignore the close relationship between MARRIES and DOES-NOT-MARRY. Consequently a different type of comparison note is used that recognizes the relationship. It is the negative-satellite-pair comparison note. With it, the comparison looks as shown in Fig. 5.42. To find such negative-satellite-pair comparison notes, the comparison programs peruse the descriptions of unmatched pointers between linked pairs for evidence of relationship. For example, MARRIES is described in part by a NEGATIVE-SATELLITE pointer to DOES-NOT-MARRY. Now of course there are other pointers that are also just one step removed from a basic relation. All such pointers that are modifications of the basic relation are called satellites because they cluster around the basic relation to which they are attached by the pointer MODIFICATION-OF. Uncertainty, for example, is expressed by PROBABLY satellites or MAYBE satellites. The MUST satellites

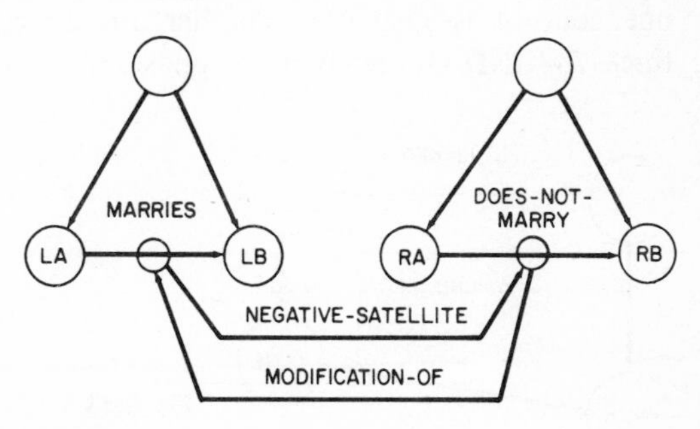

Fig. 5.41

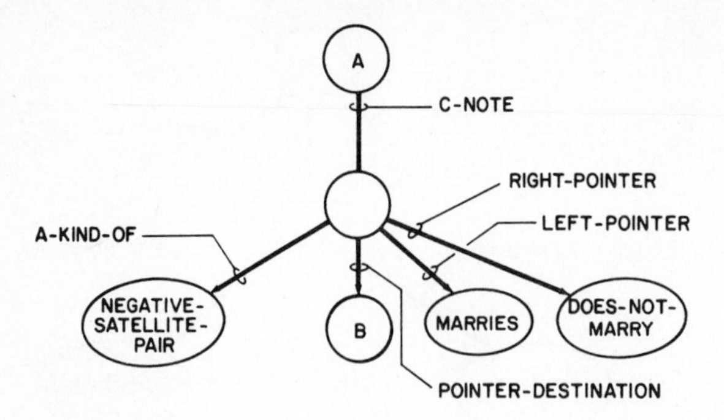

Fig. 5.42

and the MUST-NOT satellites are others of particular importance in model construction. These inform the model matching programs that the presence or absence of some pointer is vital if some unidentified network is to be associated with a particular model network containing such a pointer.

Each type of satellite is associated with a type of comparison note forming an open-ended family. Thus in addition to negative-satellite-pair comparison notes, there are probably-satellite-pair comparison notes, maybe-satellite-pair comparison notes, must-satellite-pair comparison notes, must-not-satellite-pair comparison notes, and so on.

Concept Modifications

Frequently the members of a linked pair both have pointers to closely related concepts. For example, if a brick in one scene is linked to a cube in another, the situation is as shown in Fig. 5.43. This is very much like the pointer-satellite idea with A-KIND-OF replacing MODIFICATION-OF. In any case, the description generator recognizes this and similar situations and again generates a group of comparison note types. The first of these is the A-KIND-OF chain illustrated by the above situation. This causes the comparison note of Fig. 5.44.

The a-kind-of-chain comparison note also includes situations in which one concept is related to another not directly, but rather through two or three A-KIND-OF relations. Suppose, for example, a cube is linked with an

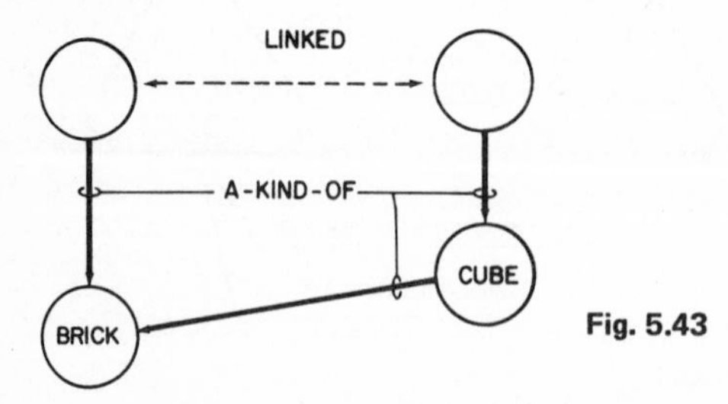

Fig. 5.43

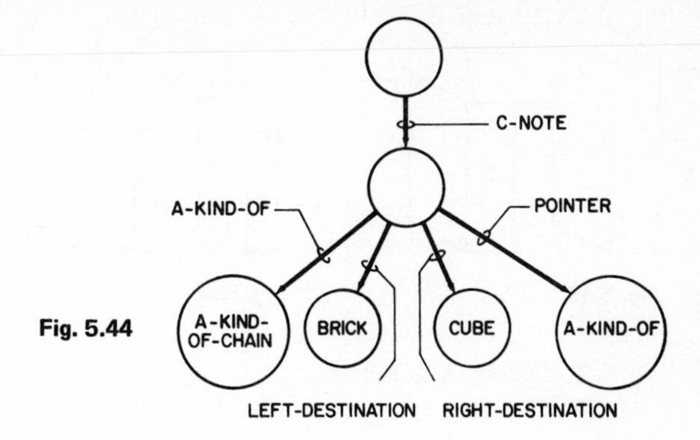

Fig. 5.44

object for which no identification can be made. There is still an a-kind-of-chain comparison note because CUBE is linked to the general concept OBJECT by a sequence of A-KIND-OF relations.

Another kind of popular concept modification is the a-kind-of-merge comparison note. These a-kind-of-merge comparison notes occur if there is no A-KIND-OF chain as described above, but each concept has a chain of A-KIND-OF pointers to some third concept. For example, WEDGE and BRICK are both connected to the concept OBJECT by A-KIND-OF.

5.5 LEARNING AND THE NEAR MISS

I can now discuss the problem of learning to recognize simple block configurations. Although this may seem like a very special kind of learning, I think the implications are far ranging, because I believe that learning by examples, learning by being told, learning by imitation, learning by reinforcement and other forms are much like one another.

In the literature of learning there is frequently an unstated assumption that these various forms are fundamentally different. But I think the classical boundaries between the various kinds of learning will disappear once superficially different kinds of learning are understood in terms of processes that construct and manipulate descriptions. No kind of learning need be desperately complicated once the descriptive machinery is available, but all constitute opaque, intractable processes without it.

To begin with I want to make clear a distinction between a description of a particular scene and a model of a concept. A model is like an ordinary description in that it carries information about the various parts of a configuration, but a model is more in that it exhibits and indicates those relations and properties that must and must not be in evidence in any example of the concept involved.

Suppose, for example, the description generating programs report the following facts in connection with the arch in Fig. 5.45.

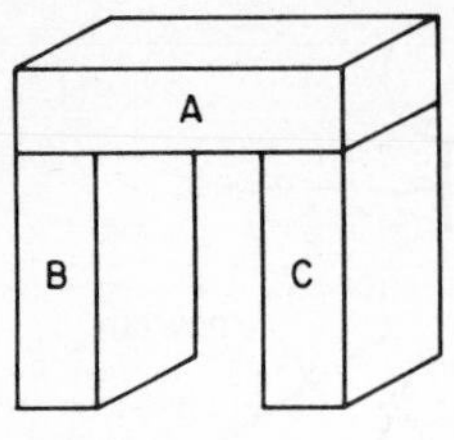

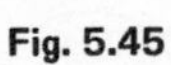
Fig. 5.45

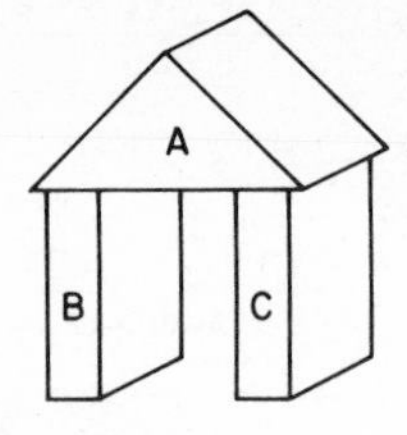

Fig. 5.46

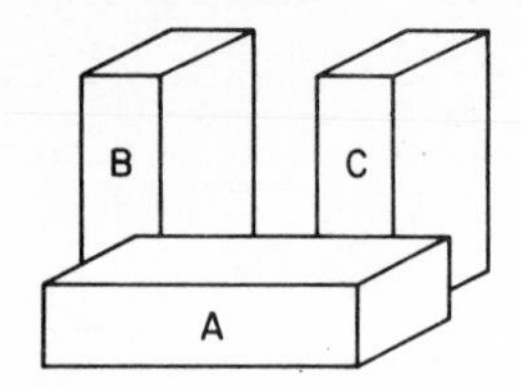

Fig. 5.47

1. Object A is a brick.
2. Object A is supported by B and C.

Now suppose the description containing these facts are compared with the scene in Fig. 5.46, where object A is a wedge, and with the scene in Fig. 5.47, where object A lies on the table. In both cases comparison could be made and differences appropriately noted, but the identification of one or the other of these new scenes as arches would be equally likely if the machine knows only what one arch looks like without knowing what in that description is important!

Humans, however, have no trouble identifying the scene in Fig. 5.46 as an arch because they know that the exact shape of the top object in an arch is unimportant. On the other hand, no one fails to reject the scene in Fig. 5.47 because the support relations of the arch are crucial. Consequently, it seems that a description must indicate which relations are mandatory and which are inconsequential before that description qualifies as a model. This does not require any descriptive apparatus not already on hand. One need only substitute emphatic forms like MUST-BE-SUPPORTED-BY for basic pointers like SUPPORTED-BY or, in some cases, add new pointers.

In the learning of such models, near misses are the really important learning samples. In conveying the idea of an arch, an arch certainly should be shown first. But then there should be some samples that are not arches, but do not miss being arches by much. Small differences permit the machine to localize some part of its current opinion about a concept for improvement. If one wants the machine to learn that the uprights of an arch cannot marry, one should show it a scene that fails to be an arch only in this respect. Such carefully selected near misses can suggest to the machine the important qualities of a concept, can indicate what properties are never found, and permit the teacher to convey particular ideas quite directly.

It is curious how little there is in the literature of machine learning about mechanisms that depend on good training sequences. This may be partly because previous schemes have been too inadequate to bear or even invite extensive exploration of this centrally important topic. Perhaps there is also a feeling that creating a training sequence is too much like direct programming of the machine to involve real learning. This is probably an exaggerated fear. I agree with those who believe that the learning of children is better described by theories using the notions of programming and self-programming, rather than by theories advocating the idea of self-organization. It is doubtful, for example, that a child could develop much intelligence without the programming implicit in his instruction, guidance, closely supervised activity, and general interaction with other humans.

5.5.1 Elementary Model Building Operations

The machine's model building program starts with a description of some example of the concept to be learned. This description is itself the first model of the concept. Subsequent samples are either examples of the concept or near misses. One has a sequence of more and more sophisticated models.

Frequently, several responses may appropriately address the comparison between the current model and a new sample. When this happens, branches occur in the model development sequence and it is convenient to talk about a tree of models. Later I discuss in more detail how the alternative branches occur in the model development sequence. This section considers the case in which the matching program finds only one difference between the current model and a new example or near miss. The tables at the end of this section summarize the results.

The A-Kind-of-Merge: Example Case

Suppose the initial model consists of a plain brick while the example is a wedge. Figure 5.48 shows the resulting comparison description. Only one difference is found: the object of the model is related to BRICK while the object of the example is related to WEDGE. But since both BRICK and WEDGE relate by A-KIND-OF to OBJECT, the a-kind-of-merge comparison note occurs. Several explanations and companion responses are possible. One is that the source of the comparison note may in general point to either of the things pointed to by the A-KIND-OF pointer in the two scenes. Thus the object could be either a WEDGE or a BRICK. Another possibility is that the A-KIND-OF pointers from the object do not matter at all and can be dropped from the model. Still another option and the one preferred by the program is that the object may be any member of some class in which both WEDGE and BRICK are represented. In the example two such classes are simply the concepts OBJECT and RIGHT-PRISM. These are both located as the intersection of A-KIND-OF paths. The program responds by replacing the pointer in the comparison network that points to the a-kind-of-merge comparison note by an A-KIND-OF pointer to one of the intersection or merge concepts. In this case an A-KIND-OF pointer is installed between the comparison note origin and the concept OBJECT. Here the altered comparison network is the new model shown in Fig. 5.49. Note that this primary response I have selected for the machine represents a moderate stand with respect to a rather serious induction problem. I have avoided the extremes of pointing to

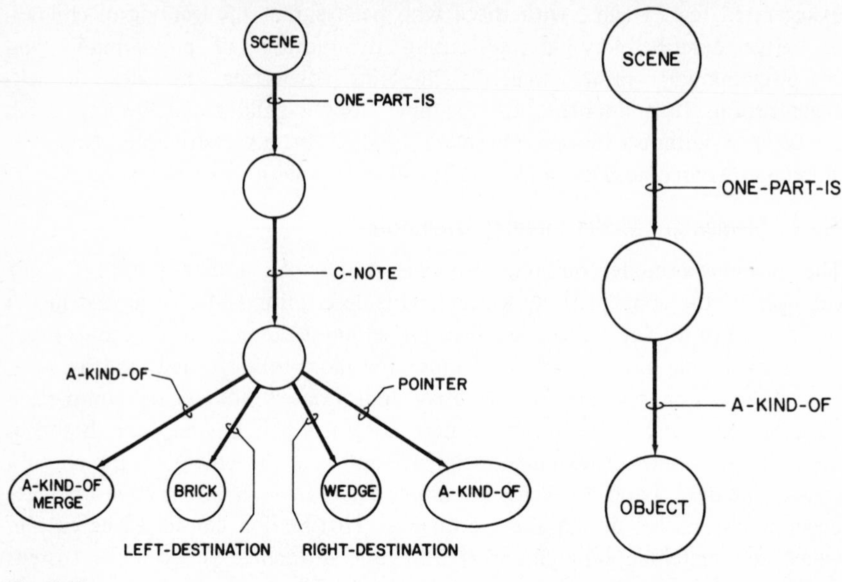

Fig. 5.48

Fig. 5.49

THING or the OR of brick and wedge, but just where in the spectrum to settle on is a difficult question. Another reasonable position would be to choose RIGHT-PRISM, for example.

The Supplementary-Pointer: Near Miss Case

Now suppose Scene 1 in Fig. 5.50 represents the current model while Scene 2 contributes as a near miss. The matching routine soon discovers that Scene 1 produces a SUPPORTED-BY relation between the two objects whereas Scene 2 does not. A supplementary-pointer comparison note results. Of course the implication is that the concept studied requires the two objects to stand together under the support relation. Consequently, when such a supple-

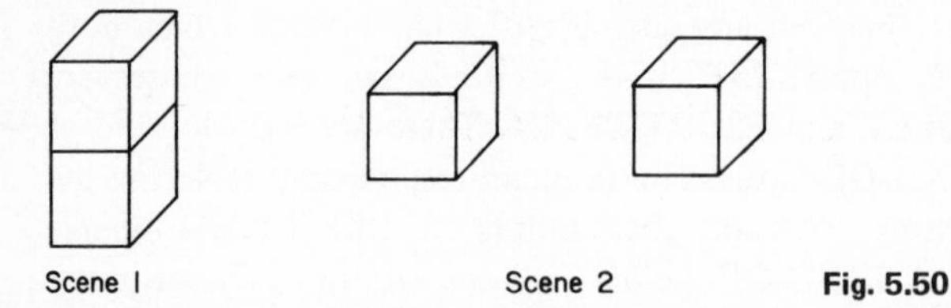

Fig. 5.50

mentary-pointer comparison note turns up, it transforms to the emphatic MUST version of the pointer involved. Thus the new model is the one in Fig. 5.51.

Of course the supplementary pointer can turn up in the near miss as well as in the current model. Suppose Scene 1 in Fig. 5.50 is the near miss

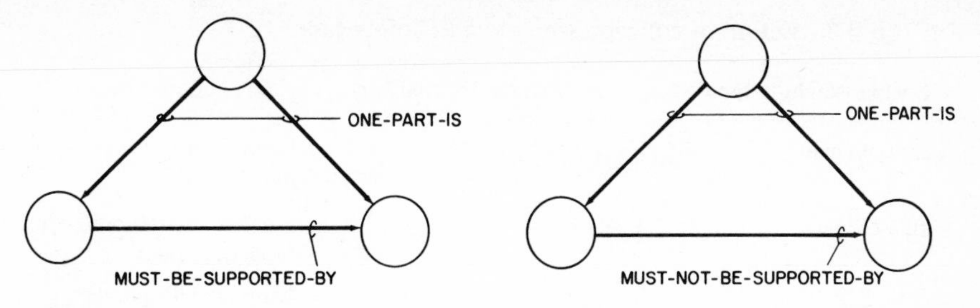

Fig. 5.51

Fig. 5.52

instead of the current model. One concludes A cannot be on B. The supplementary-pointer comparison note now indicates a relation that apparently cannot hold. Appropriately, the MUST-NOT version of the supplementary pointer is substituted in and the new net appears as in Fig. 5.52.

The Must-Satellite-Pair

Frequently comparison between the current model and a new sample displays comparison notes that do not reveal any new feature, but rather result from previous refinements in the model. Suppose, for example, that the current model has a MUST-MARRY pointer in a given location, while the sample has a MARRIES pointer. Now clearly the MARRIES pointer is appropriate in the description and the must-satellite-pair comparison note consequent to matching it with MUST-MARRY should be replaced again by MUST-MARRY. Thus the emphatic form in a must-satellite-pair situation is retained and not interfered with by refinement operations attempted subsequent to its formation.

The A-Kind-of-Merge: Near Miss Case

Sometimes a comparison note offers two or more nearly equal explanations. Consider the very simple current model and near miss in Fig. 5.53. The comparison note is an a-kind-of-merge announcing that the current model points with HAS-PROPERTY-OF to STANDING, the near miss to LYING, and both LYING and STANDING have A-KIND-OF paths to ORIENTATIONS. Now the near miss may fail either because it is lying or because it is

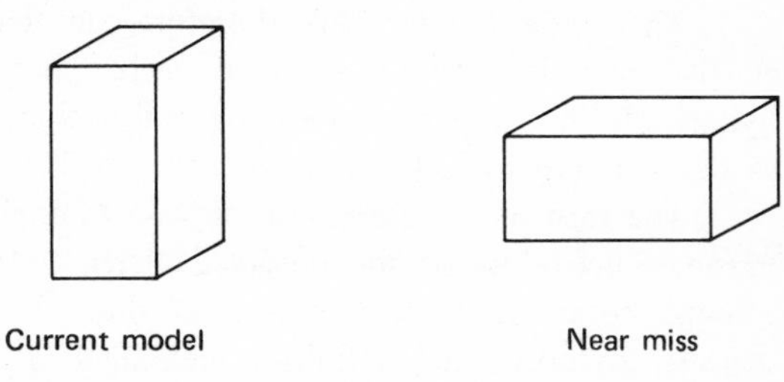

Fig. 5.53

TABLE 5.1 Action of concept generator: Example case

Comparison note type	Pointer involved	Response
A-kind-of-chain	–	Point to intersection with model's pointer
A-kind-of-merge	–	Point to intersection with model's pointer Drop model's pointer
Negative-satellite pair	–	Drop model's pointer
Must-be-satellite pair	–	Retain model's pointer
Must-not-be-satellite pair	–	Contradiction
Supplementary-pointer or exit	Negative-satellite or fundamental pointer in the model	Drop model's pointer
	Negative-satellite or fundamental pointer in the example	Ignore
	Must-be-satellite	Contradiction
	Must-not-be-satellite	Retain model's pointer

not standing. Responding to these explanations, the model builder might replace the a-kind-of-merge comparison note by a MUST-NOT-HAVE-PROPERTY-OF pointer to LYING or by a MUST-HAVE-PROPERTY-OF pointer to STANDING. Since most concepts humans discuss are defined in terms of properties rather than antiproperties, the MUST version is considered more likely. (Tables 5.1 and 5.2 summarize the points made in this section.)

5.5.2 Coping with Multiple Differences

Comparisons yielding single comparison notes are rare. More often, the model builder must make sense out of a whole group of comparison notes. If the comparison involves a near miss, any one of the comparison notes might be the key to proper model refinement. Moreover, many of the comparison notes have alternative interpretations that make further demands on executive expertise.

The model builder must therefore consider all the comparison notes and all the possible interpretations of each. Then it must produce the set of hypotheses that form the model tree's branches. These in turn must be ranked so that the best hypothesis may be pursued first.

The case of refinement through an example is simpler than through near misses. Since none of the observed differences are sufficient to remove the example from the class, it is assumed that all of the differences found act in concert to loosen the definition embodied in the model. Consequently each

TABLE 5.2 Action of concept generator: Near miss case

Comparison note type	Pointer involved	Response
A-kind-of-chain	–	If model's node is at the end of the chain add must-not-be satellite to near miss' node
		If near miss' node is at the end of the chain, use must-be satellite to model's node
A-kind-of-merge	–	Replace model's pointer by its must-be satellite
		Replace model's pointer by must-not-be satellite of near miss' pointer
Negative-satellite pair	–	Replace model's pointer by its must-be satellite
Must-not-be-satellite pair	–	Retain model's pointer
Supplementary-pointer or exit	Fundamental pointer in the model	Replace pointer with its must-be satellite
	Fundamental pointer in the near miss	Insert pointer into the model using must-not-be satellite
	Negative-satellite in the model	Replace pointer with its must-not-be satellite
	Negative-satellite in the near miss	Insert pointer into model using must-be satellite

comparison note can be transformed independently and a new model generated by their combined action. There is no problem of deciding if one difference is more important than another.

Consequently, if all the comparison notes had but one interpretation, only one new branch would be generated. The a-kind-of-merge comparison note has two possible interpretations, however, and if one such comparison note occurs, it is only reasonable to create two branches instead of one. The action on the other comparison notes is the same for both branches.

Near misses cause more severe problems. If two differences are found, either of them may be sufficient to cause the sample to be a near miss, while the other difference may be equally sufficient or merely irrelevant. If the differences have multiple interpretations or more than two differences occur, the number of possibilities explodes and the machine cannot work by simply generating an alternative for each possibility. The model builder clearly must decide which interpretation of which differences are most likely to cause the near miss.

The most obvious way to search for key differences is by level. This assumes only that the differences nearer the origin of the comparison description are the more important. This certainly is a reasonable heuristic since a missing group of blocks generally impresses a human as being more important than a shape change, which in turn dwarfs a minor blemish. Consequently, the program determines the depth of the comparison notes which are nearest to the origin of the comparison description. All those candidates found at greater depth are considered secondary.

The highest level differences allow quick formation of little hypotheses about why the near miss misses and what to do as a consequence. A complete hypothesis specifies one comparison note as the sole cause of the miss and it further specifies which interpretation of that comparison note is assumed. Consequently there is a hypothesis for each interpretation of each potentially central comparison note.

The comparison note specified as crucial by a hypothesis is transformed as if it were the only comparison note. The other comparison notes are assumed by the hypothesis to be insufficient cause for the near miss. Consequently as a new model is formulated according to the hypothesis, all of the comparison notes but one are treated exactly as if the near miss were not a miss at all!

So far a single comparison note is assumed to be the exclusive cause of the miss. Were all possible combinations considered as well, not only would the branching increase enormously, but the ranking of those branches would be difficult. I have therefore decided that only one special combination of two comparison notes is ever permitted to form a hypothesis.

Hypotheses based on two contributing comparison notes are added to the hypothesis list only when two comparison notes with nearly identical descriptions occur.

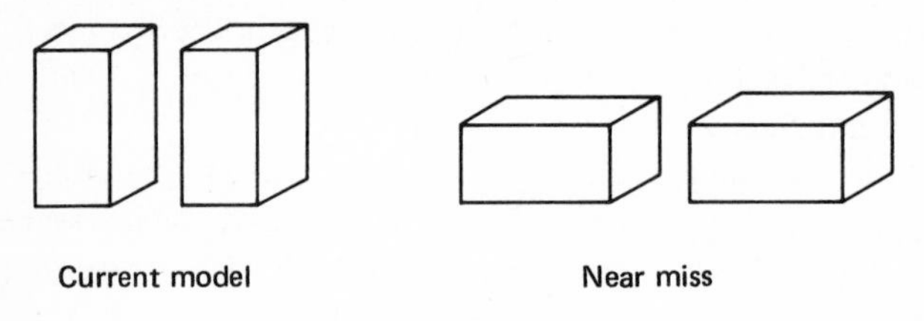

Fig. 5.54

Consider Fig. 5.54. Since exactly the same thing characterizes both blocks in the near miss, there is no particular reason to suppose that one difference should be singled out. Consequently a third hypothesis is formed, namely that both differences act cooperatively. This additional hypothesis takes precedence over the two hypotheses that consider the differences separately. It seems heuristically sound that coincidences are significant. The machine creates new models with such hypotheses by transforming both of the specified comparison notes in the miss-explanation mode.

5.5.3 Contradictions and Backing Up

By now one may wonder why the program should deal with alternatives to the main line of model development at all. To be sure, maximum likelihood assumptions may be wrong, but then how could the machine ever know when such a decision is an error? The answer is that the main line assumptions may lead to contradiction crises which in turn cause the model building program to retreat up the tree and attempt model development along other branches.

Consider the very simple situation already presented back in Fig. 5.53. Think again of the left side as the current model and the right side as the near miss. The current model and the near miss combination generate an a-kind-of-merge comparison note for which the priority interpretation is that examples of the concept must be standing. The alternative that examples must not be lying causes a side branch in the model development tree. But suppose one really wants the concept to exclude lying but not insist on standing. Showing the machine a tilted brick does the job. A tilted brick certainly is not standing and its description has no HAS-PROPERTY-OF pointer to STANDING. Yet the current model has a MUST-HAVE-PROPERTY-OF pointer to STANDING. This is a contradictory situation.

When contradictory situations occur, the program assumes it has made an incorrect choice somewhere, closes the branch to further exploration, and backs up to select another alternative.

In the case at hand, an alternative is found and the must-not-be-lying interpretation of the comparison between the scenes leads to a new intermediate model. This in turn is refined by the tilted brick scene which originally caused the contradiction on the former main line. No contradiction occurs on the new path because the MUST-NOT-HAVE-PROPERTY-OF/LYING combination of the intermediate model has nothing to clash with in the example. Indeed the new example lends no new information to model development along this path, the model being the same before and after comparison. The new example served solely to terminate development of an improper path in the model development.

5.6 SOME GENERATED CONCEPTS

In this section I explore some of the properties of the model generator through a series of examples. In the course of this discussion, words like house, arch, and tent occur frequently as they are convenient names for the ideas the machine assimilates. Be cautioned, however, to avoid thinking of these entities in terms of functional definitions. To a human, an arch may be something to walk through, as well as an appropriate alignment of bricks. And certainly, a flat rock serves as a table to a hungry person, although far removed from the image the word *table* usually calls to mind.

But the machine does not yet know anything of walking or eating, so the programs discussed here handle only some of the physical aspects of these human notions. There is no inherent obstacle forbidding the machine to enjoy functional understanding. It is a matter of generalizing the machine's descriptive ability to acts and properties required by those acts. Then chains of pointers can link TABLE to FOOD as well as to the physical image of a table, and the machine will be perfectly happy to draw up its chair to a flat rock with the human, given that there is something on that table which it wishes to eat.

5.6.1 The House

Figure 5.55(*a*) illustrates what house means here. Basically the scene is just one wedge on top of one brick. But lacking human experience, this one picture is insufficient to convey much of the notion to the machine. The model builder must be used, and it must be permitted to observe other samples.

Suppose the model builder starts with the scene in Fig. 5.55(*a*). Then its description generation apparatus contributes the network which serves as the first unrefined, unembellished model of Fig. 5.56. Now suppose the scene in Fig. 5.55(*b*), a near miss, is the next sample. Its net is that shown in Fig. 5.57. The only difference is the supplementary pointer SUPPORTED-BY. Glancing at Table 5.2, it is clear that the overall result is conversion of the

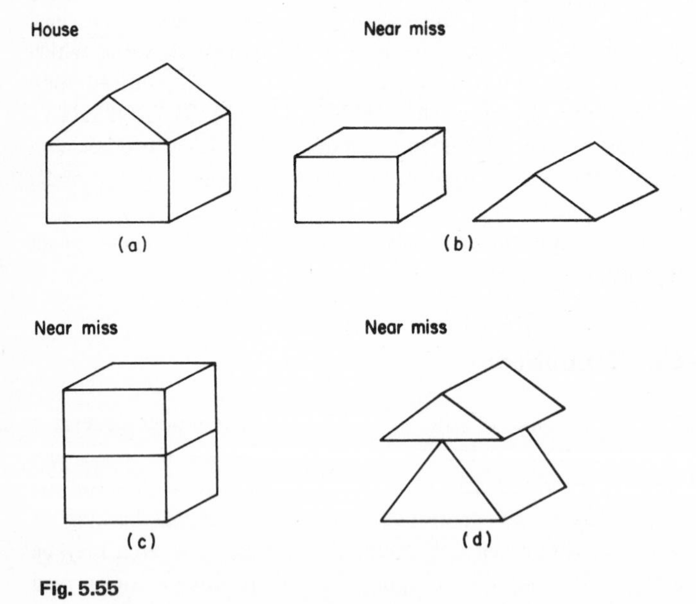

Fig. 5.55

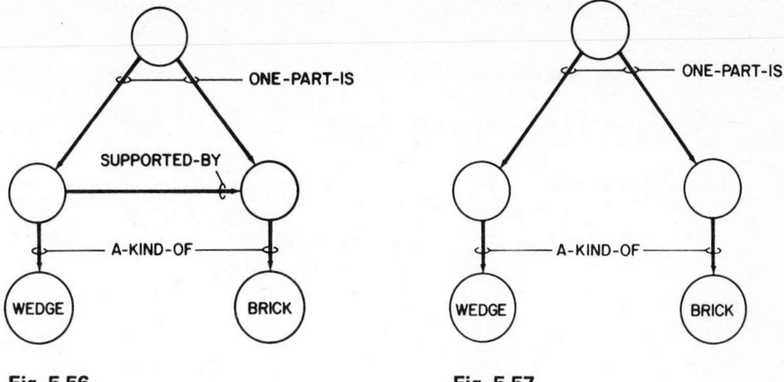

Fig. 5.56

Fig. 5.57

SUPPORTED-BY pointer in the old model to MUST-BE-SUPPORTED-BY in the new model. Thus the new model is that of Fig. 5.58.

Much is yet to be learned. For one thing, the top object certainly must be a wedge. Showing the machine the near miss of Fig. 5.55(*c*) conveys this point immediately. Similarly the near miss of Fig. 5.55(*d*) makes the brick property of the bottom object mandatory. But notice that both of these steps cause bifurcation of the model tree. The reason is that the machine cannot be completely sure the miss occurs because the old property is lost or because the new property is added. The program prefers the old-property-is-lost theory and moves down the corresponding branch unless contradicted. In both of these situations, the preferred theory is correct resulting in the final model shown in Fig. 5.59.

5.6.2 The Tent

Think of the tent as two wedges marrying each other. As such it illustrates the handling of two similar differences simultaneously.

The base model is the description of the scene in Fig. 5.60(*a*) and the first sample is the near miss in Fig. 5.60(*b*). Two a-kind-of-merge comparison

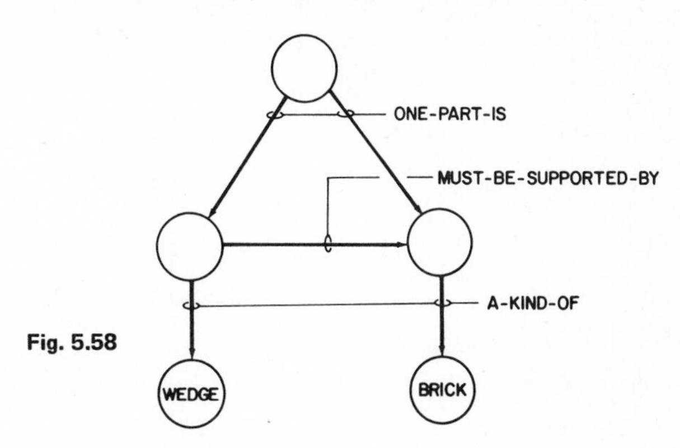

Fig. 5.58

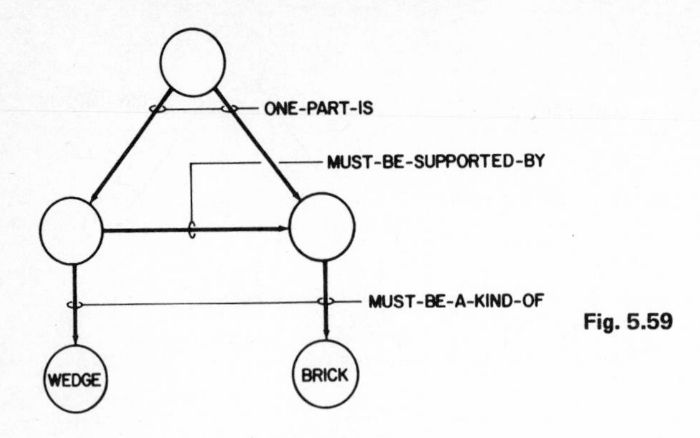

Fig. 5.59

notes result, one from each of the two objects because they are bricks, not wedges. Since they differ only in source, the hypothesis that both act together has priority. Now this result is complemented by the near miss in Fig. 5.60(*c*) which informs the machine of the importance of the MARRIES relation. Again dual comparison notes announce the loss of a pair of MARRIES pointers, and twin MUST-MARRY pointers are installed.

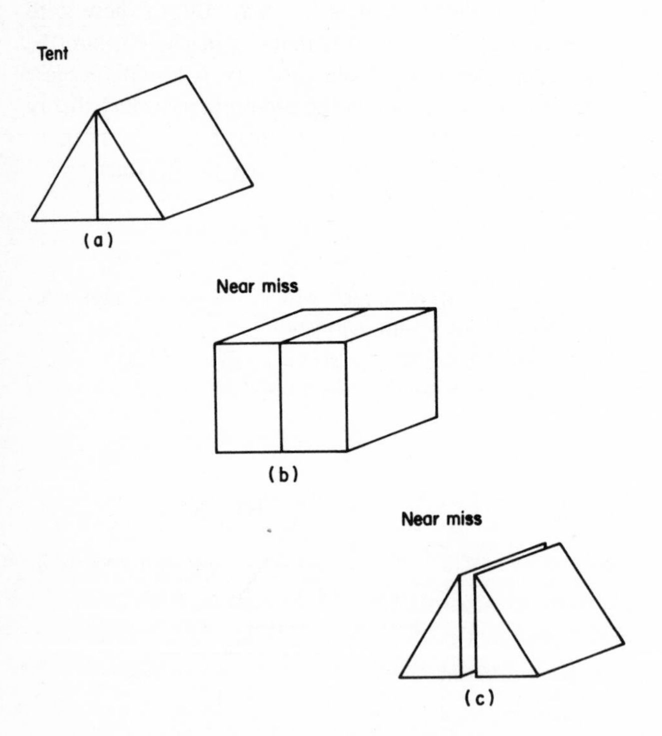

Fig. 5.60

5.6.3 The Arch

The arch involves a mixture of the elements seen in the previous examples. Because of the wider variety of differences encountered, it produces a bushy model tree and a challenge to routines that select priority hypotheses.

An arch with sides neatly aligned with the lintel forms the first model. Combining this with the scene in Fig. 5.61(*a*) the machine deduces that the MARRIES relations between the top and the supports are not crucial.

Next the near miss of Fig. 5.61(*b*) indicates that the support relations are crucial. Again, both new MUST-BE-SUPPORTED-BY pointers are handled jointly, and are installed at once.

The machine learns perhaps the most important fact from the near miss in Fig. 5.61(*c*). Here the two supports touch, supplying two MARRIES pointers to the description. This cannot be allowed. Responding, the machine inserts MUST-NOT-MARRY pointers between the two supports in the model. Some may think that in asserting the MUST-NOT-MARRY relations, the machine overlooks what they consider to be the real principle, that of a hole or passage. But for a child building with blocks, to have a hole and to have two non-touching supports are very nearly the same idea. Consequently the machine's opinion seems adequate for the moment.

Finally, the top object is not necessarily a brick. The sample in Fig. 5.61(*d*) teaches the machine that anything in the class OBJECT will do, since OBJECT lies but one step removed by an A-KIND-OF pointer from both WEDGE and BRICK.

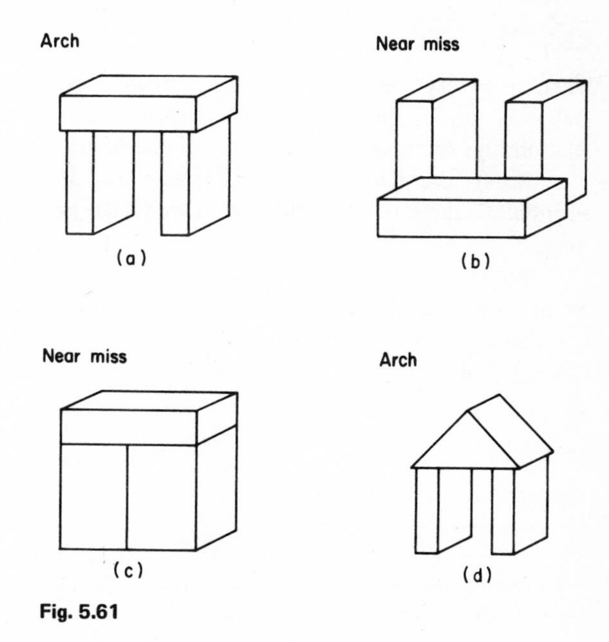

Fig. 5.61

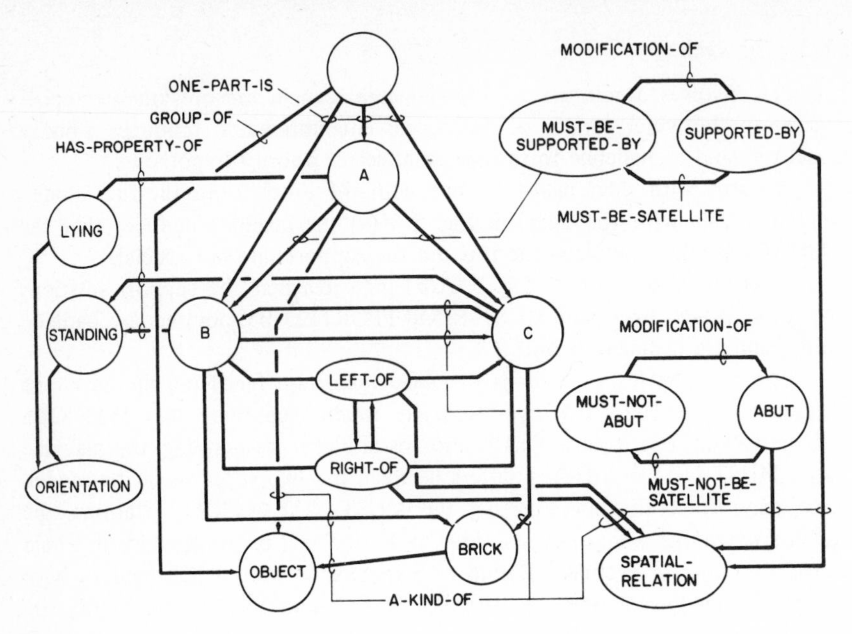

Fig. 5.62

Figure 5.62 shows the resulting model. I give it in somewhat more detail than usual to convey a feeling for the complexity the programs actually deal with.

5.6.4 The Table

When a concept involves groups of objects, the model generation problem really is no more difficult. It becomes a matter of concentrating on relationships of the typical members of the groups studied.

Study the table in Fig. 5.63 and the description in Fig. 5.64. The essential features of the table are introduced by the following sequence of steps:

First the table should have bricks for legs. This idea is easily conveyed by the near miss non-table of Fig. 5.65(*a*). Moreover, this conception of table excludes structures such as that in Fig. 5.65(*b*), a fact which is handily incorporated through a MUST-NOT-MARRY pointer. Next, since the non-

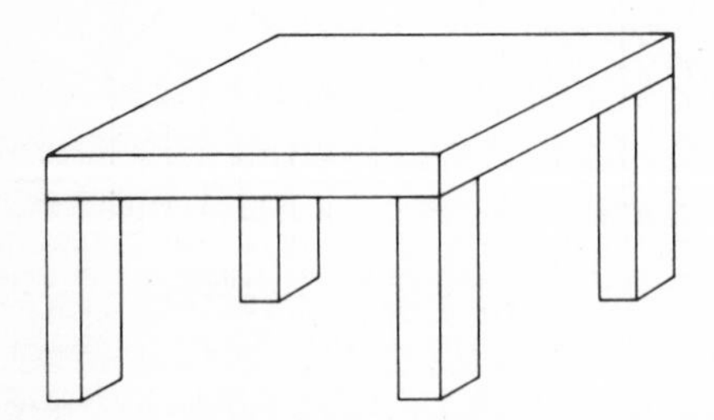

Fig. 5.63

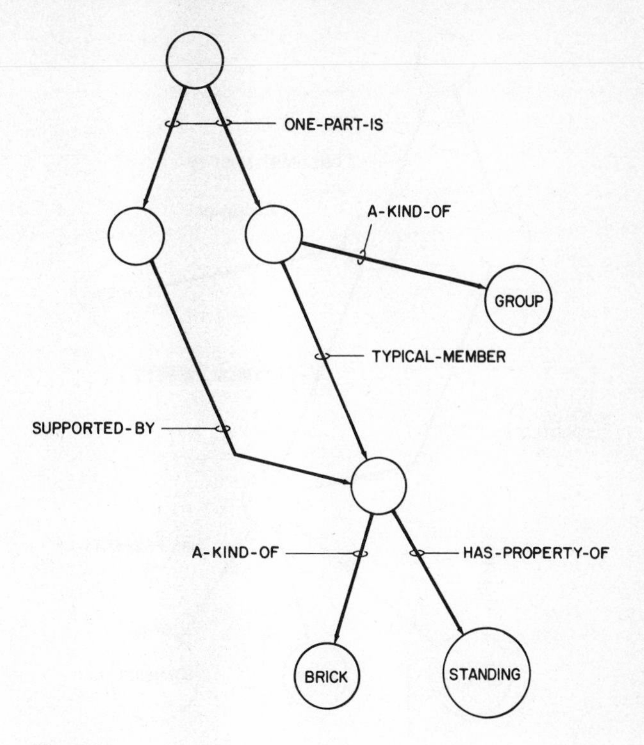

Fig. 5.64

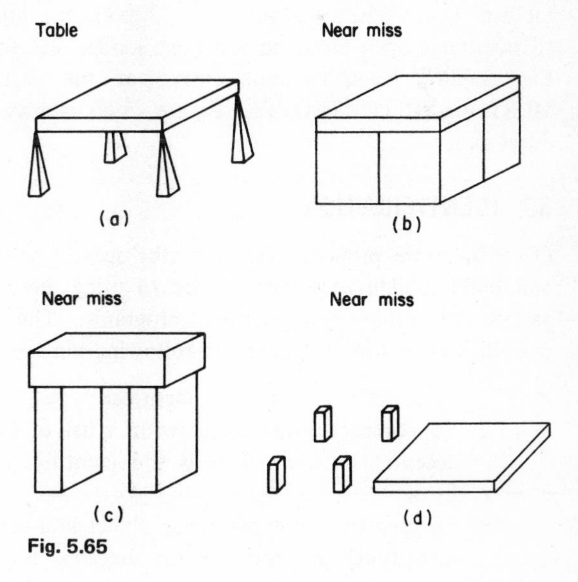

Fig. 5.65

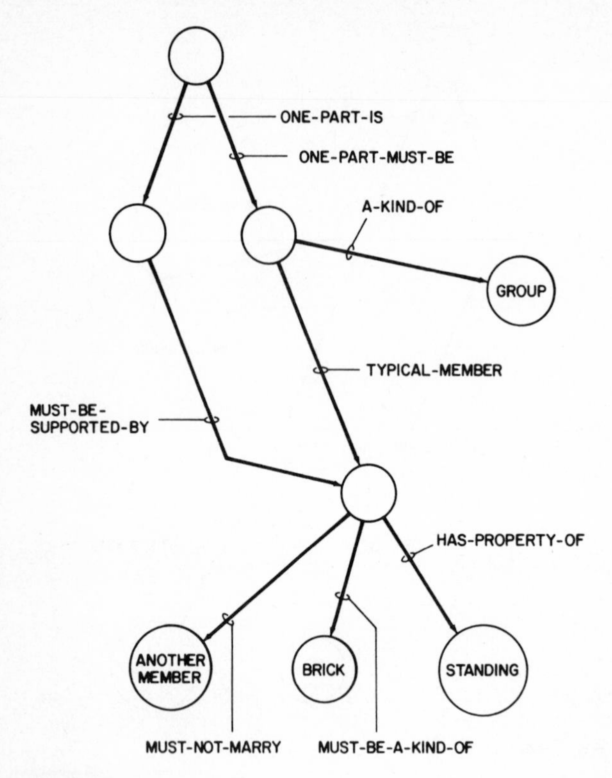

Fig. 5.66

table in Fig. 5.65(*c*) has only two supports, no grouping occurs, which leads to insistence on a group in the next model refinement. Finally, the scene in Fig. 5.65(*d*) leads to replacement of the SUPPORTED-BY pointer by MUST-BE-SUPPORTED-BY. Figure 5.66 shows the last model in this development.

5.7 IDENTIFICATION

Once there are programs that describe scenes, compare description networks, and build models, one may go on to using these programs as elements in a variety of other goal-oriented programs. The problem-solving programs described in this section have the following kind of responsibilities:

1. To see if two scenes are identical.
2. To compare some scene with a list of models and report the most acceptable match. This is the identification problem in its simplest form.
3. To identify some particular object in a scene. This is not the same as identifying an entire scene because important properties may be

hidden and because context may make some identifications more probable than others.

4. To find instances of some particular model in a scene. It is frequently the case that the presence of some configuration can be confirmed even though it would not be found in the ordinary course of scene description. This requires the ability to discern groups with the required properties in spite of a shroud of irrelevant and distracting information.

5.7.1 Exact Match and Discovering Symmetry

If two scenes are identical, then the networks describing those scenes must be isomorphic. The nodes of the two networks must relate with each other in the same ways, and the nodes must relate to general concepts such as BRICK and STANDING in the same ways. Consequently, comparing two such networks produces a simple kind of comparison description. There is a skeleton, which indicates how the parts of the scenes interrelate, and there is a group of intersection comparison notes that describe how the parts of the scene are anchored to the general store of concepts. None of the other types of comparison notes appear because identical scenes cannot produce two networks with the necessary aberrations of form.

Conversely, if comparison of two networks results in intersection comparison notes only, then the parent scenes must be identical in the sense that the description generating mechanisms employed produce exactly matching networks. There can be variation, but nothing so great as to vary the action of the description generator. The scenes in Fig. 5.67 are identical with respect to the descriptive power of my programs because in both cases the relations observed are LEFT-OF and RIGHT-OF. More capable programs might complain that FAR-TO-THE-LEFT-OF and FAR-TO-THE-RIGHT-OF hold in one scene, while only LEFT-OF and RIGHT-OF hold in the other. The scenes are clearly not identical with respect to a program with such a capability.

It is interesting to note in passing that the exact match detector is a major part of a curiously simple program that checks for a certain kind of left-right symmetry. The method is as follows:

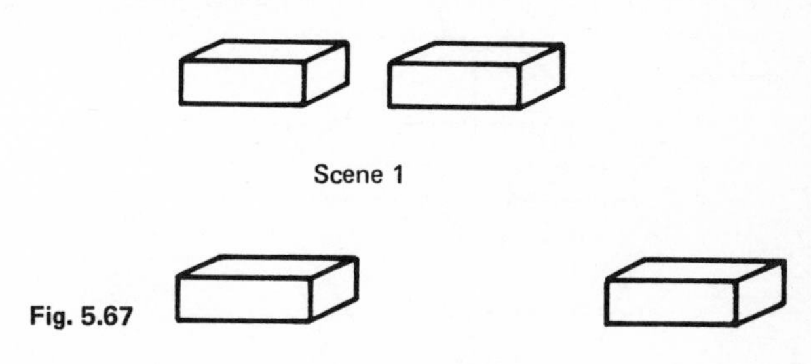

Fig. 5.67

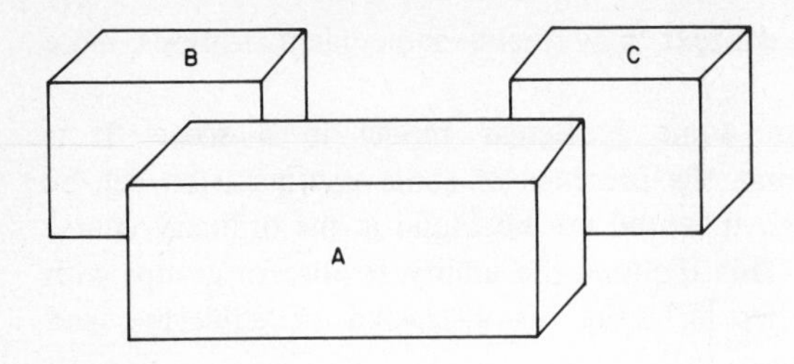

Fig. 5.68

1. Copy the description of the scene exactly.
2. Convert all LEFT-OF pointers in the copy to RIGHT-OF, and all RIGHT-OF pointers to LEFT-OF.
3. Compare the original description against the modified copy. If the match is exact, the scene is symmetric.

This is, of course, an abstraction of the familiar condition for y-axis symmetry in the mathematical sense, whereby symmetry is confirmed if and only if for every point in the scene, (x, y), the point (–x, y) is also in the scene. Switching LEFT-OF and RIGHT-OF pointers is the analog of x-coordinate negation and network matching corresponds to a check for invariance.

To see how this works, consider the scene in Fig. 5.68. The center object A is flanked by B on the left and by C on the right. Figure 5.69 shows the resulting description. There are nodes corresponding to objects A, B, and C, and there are LEFT-OF and RIGHT-OF pointers indicating their relationships.

Figure 5.70 shows the copy of the network with the LEFT-OF and RIGHT-OF pointers switched. Notice that the original network and the copy are identical. Node A matches with A′, B with C′, and C with B′. Since there are no differences, the machine concludes the scene is in fact symmetric.

The machine knows LEFT-OF and RIGHT-OF are opposites because they are linked together by OPPOSITE pointers. Consequently, it is

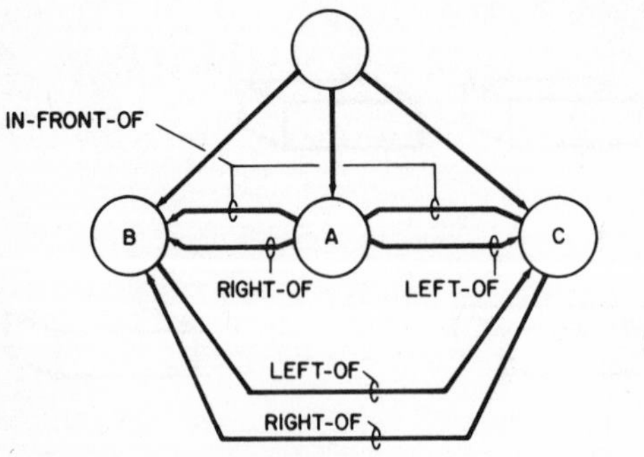

Fig. 5.69

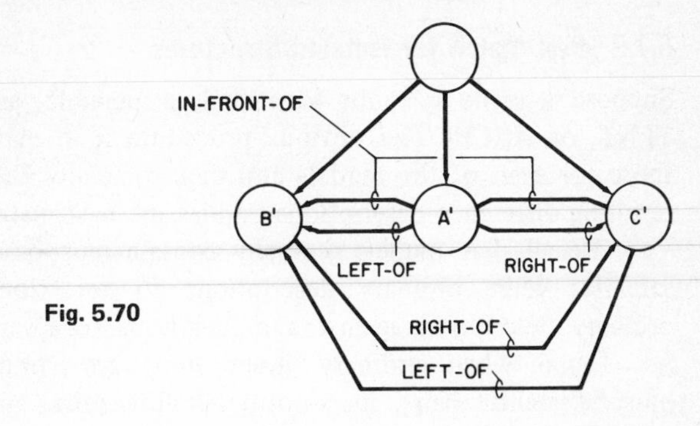

Fig. 5.70

unnecessary to tell the program explicitly to substitute RIGHT-OF for LEFT-OF and vice versa. One need only ask the symmetry program if there is symmetry with respect to either the pointer LEFT-OF or RIGHT-OF. The machine itself can conjure up the appropriate substitutions by working through the OPPOSITE pointer from whichever relation is supplied, be it LEFT-OF or RIGHT-OF. Similarly, if one asks for symmetry with respect to ABOVE, the program realizes that the proper substitutions are BELOW for ABOVE and ABOVE for BELOW.

An interesting combination is a simultaneous LEFT-RIGHT and an IN-FRONT-OF–BEHIND SWITCH. This one gives the machine a chance of realizing that two scenes are simply front and back views of the same configuration as are the scenes in Fig. 5.71.

Eventually I think the machine can come upon the symmetry notion in the same way it now learns about arches and houses. But at this point I do not think there is enough comparison describing capability. The needed step is the introduction of a program that generates global comparison notes from the local ones already at hand, thereby introducing the kind of hierarchy into the comparison descriptions that is already the standard in scene descriptions. One obvious ability of such a program would be that of noticing a preponderance of similar comparison notes. This and some of the double comparison ideas proven useful in doing analogy problems are the things the machine needs to learn about symmetry.

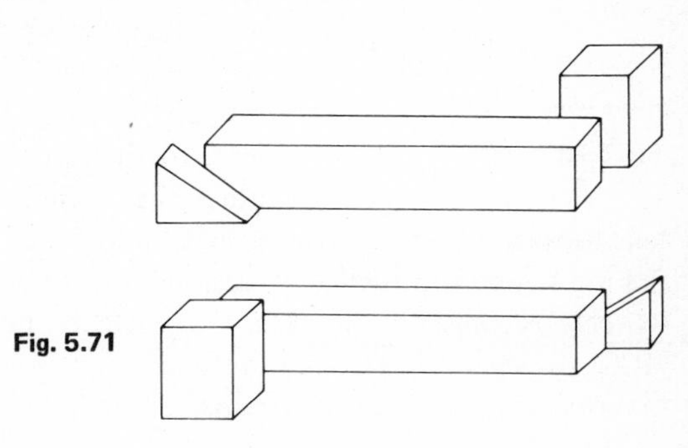

Fig. 5.71

5.7.2 Best Match for Isolated Structures

Suppose a scene is to be identified, if possible, as a HOUSE, PEDESTAL, TENT, or ARCH. The obvious procedure is to match its description against those for each of the models and then somehow determine which of the four resulting difference descriptions implies the best match.

Recall that models generally contain must-be satellites and must-not-be satellites while ordinary descriptions do not. Consequently, comparing an ordinary description against a model leads to a variety of comparison notes not found when ordinary descriptions are compared. Among these are must-be-satellite pairs, must-not-be-satellite pairs, and various flavors of exits and supplementary-pointers. Such comparison notes are decisive in the identification process.

Consider the case where some pointer in a scene's description corresponds to its must-not-be satellite in the model. This clearly means a relation is present that the model specifically forbids. The resulting must-not-be-satellite-pair comparison note in the difference network is such a serious association impediment that identification of the unknown with the model is rejected outright, without further consideration. This means that the near-arch in Fig. 5.72 cannot be identified as an arch because the network describing the near-arch has MARRIES pointers between the two supports while the model has MUST-NOT-MARRY pointers in the same place. The combination produces a comparison description with a must-not-be-satellite-pair comparison note that positively prevents a match.

Identification with a particular model is also rejected if the difference description contains exits or supplementary-pointer comparison notes which involve must-be satellites. Such comparison notes occur when essential relations or properties are missing in the unknown. Two bricks lying on a table do not form a pedestal because the model for the pedestal has a MUST-BE-SUPPORTED-BY pointer. The result is a supplementary-pointer comparison note involving the must-be satellite MUST-BE-SUPPORTED-BY. Again there is no match.

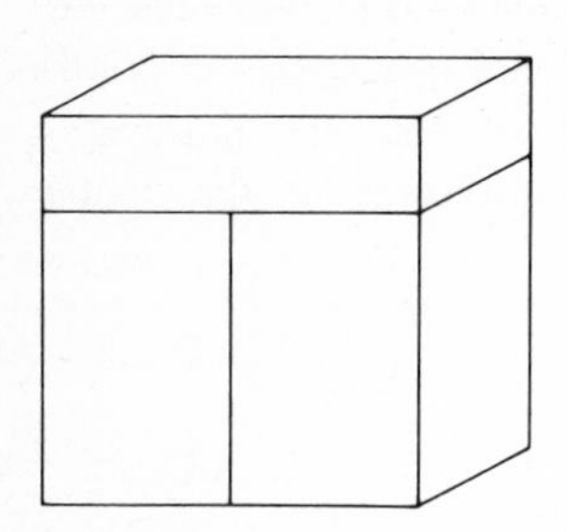

Fig. 5.72

Suppose we have a HOUSE but its identity is as yet unknown. Match of a HOUSE against the PEDESTAL, the TENT, and the ARCH all lead to difference descriptions with comparison notes that forbid identification. The PEDESTAL fails because a merge indicates that the required A-KIND-OF relation between the top object and BRICK is missing. The TENT similarly fails because both of its objects must be wedges. The ARCH fails because the model has a MUST-BE-SUPPORTED-BY pointer to an object missing in the HOUSE. This in turn causes a fatal exit comparison note in the difference description.

The next problem emerges because some unknown may acceptably match more than one model in a trail list. Given several possible identifications, there should be some way of ordering them such that one could be reported to be best in some sense. To do this I associate each kind of difference with a number and combine the results by forming a weighted sum for each comparison. This seems to work well enough for the moment, but I do not think it would pay to put much effort into tuning such a formula. Instead more knowledge about the priorities of differences should lead to far better programs that do not use such a primitive scoring mechanism.

5.7.3 Best Match for Structures in a Context

Examine Fig. 5.73. Notice that object B seems to be a brick while object D seems to be a wedge. This is curious because B and D show exactly the same arrangement of lines and faces. The result also seems at odds with the models and identification process of the system as described so far, because so far anything identified as a wedge must have a triangular face.

But of course context is the explanation. Different rules must be used when programs try to identify objects or groups of objects that are only parts of scenes, rather than the whole scene. In the case where the question is whether or not the whole scene can be identified as a particular model, it is reasonable to insist that all relations deemed essential by the model be present, while all those forbidden be absent. But when the question is whether or not a few parts of a scene can be identified as a particular model, then there is the possibility that some important part may be obscured by other objects. In these situations, my identification program uses two special heuristics:

First, the coincidence of objects lying in a line seems to suggest that each object is the same type as the one obscuring it unless there is good reason to reject this hypothesis. This is what suggests object D is a wedge in Fig. 5.73.

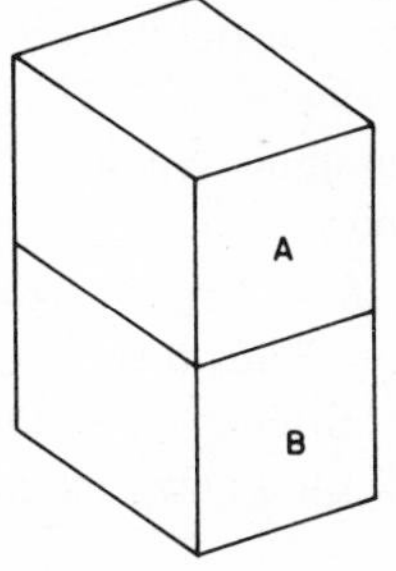

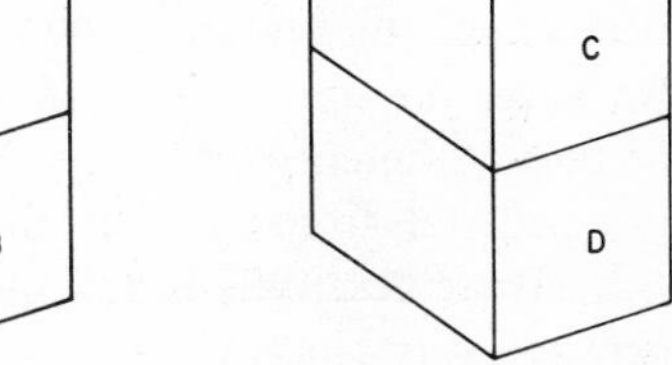

Fig. 5.73

Second, essential properties in the model may be absent in the unknown because the parts involved are hidden. This is why identification of object D with wedge works even though D lacks the otherwise essential triangular face. The requirement that forbidden properties do not occur remains in force, however.

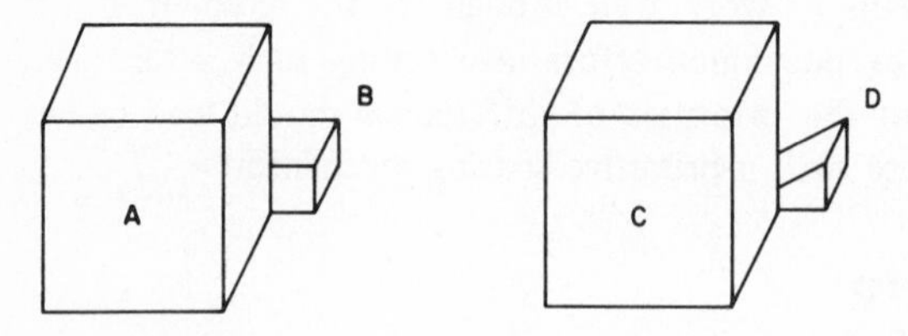

Fig. 5.74

Elaborate work can be done on the problem of deciding if the omission of a particular feature of some model is admissable in any particular situation. My program takes a singularly crude view and ignores all omissions. Rejection of the hypothesis that the obscured is like the obscuror happens only if the machine notices details specifically forbidden by relations in the model. Thus the effort is not to select the best matching model, but only to verify that a particular identification is not contradictory. This means that object B in Fig. 5.74 is confirmed to be brick-like while brick-ness is denied to D because of the ruinous apparent triangularity of the side face.

Of course if the propagation of a property like brick-ness or wedge-ness down a series of objects is interrupted, then the unknown must be compared with a battery of models with the program still forgiving omissions but now searching for the best of many possible identifications.

5.7.4 Learning from Mistakes

Suppose the program attempts to identify a house as a pedestal. Identification fails because the wedge will not match the top of the pedestal and the resulting type of a-kind-of-merge comparison note cannot be tolerated. Still it would be a pity to throw away the information about why the match failed. Instead the otherwise wasted matching effort can be used to suggest new identification candidates.

The way this works is quite simple. First the machine spends idle time comparing the various models in its armamentarium with each other. Whenever the number of differences observed are few, a simplified description of those differences is stored. Thus the machine knows that a house is similar to a pedestal, from which it differs only in the nature of the top object.

These descriptions link the known models together in a sort of similarity network.

This network and the difference descriptions noted in the course of identification failure help decide what model should be tried next. The description of the differences between an unknown and a particular model is compared with the descriptions of the similarity net. If the difference between the unknown and a particular model matches the difference between that model and some other model, then identification with that other model is likely.

For example, an unknown which happened to be a house relates to the model of a pedestal in roughly the same way that the model of a house relates to the model of a pedestal. HOUSE is consequently elevated to the top of the list of trial models. Notice that the process requires the same steps as do analogy problems as described earlier. Figure 5.75 clarifies the procedure.

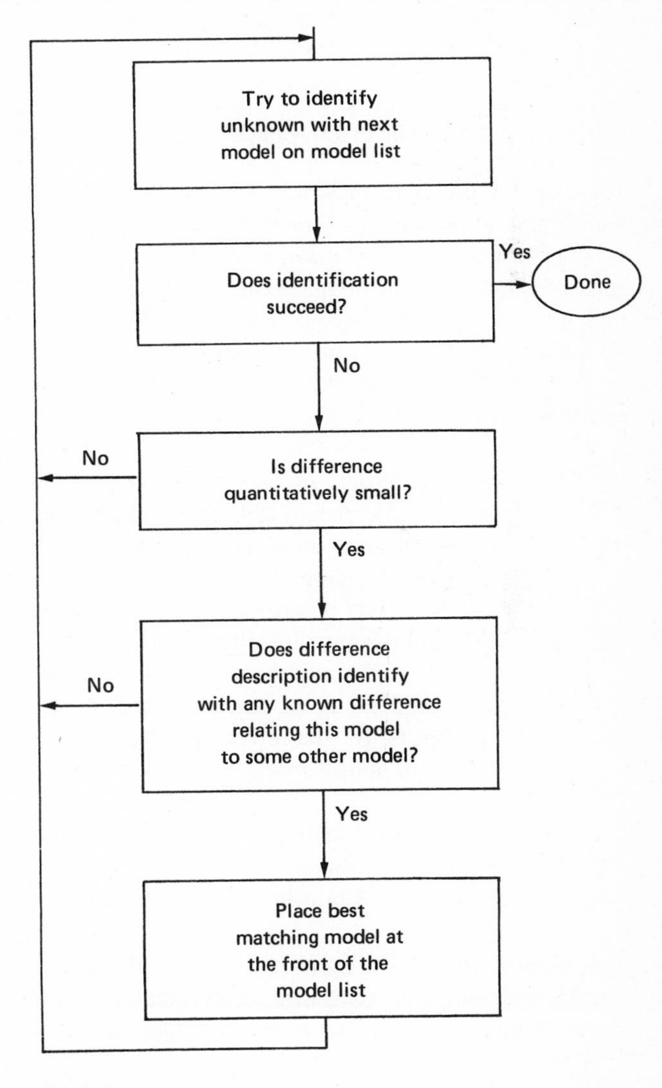

Fig. 5.75

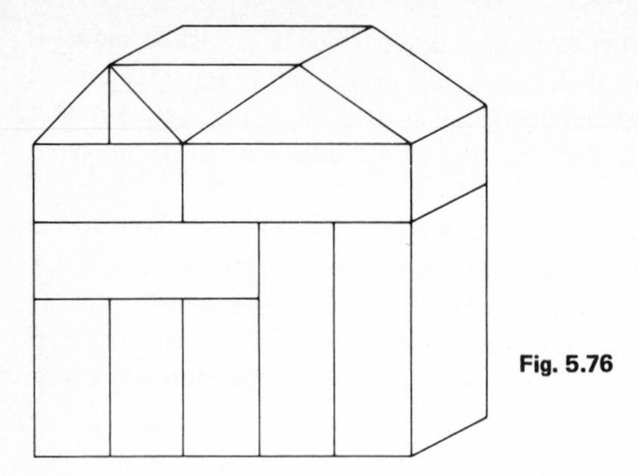

Fig. 5.76

5.7.5 Finding a Needle in a Haystack

The scene of Fig. 5.76 is curious in that one can find an arch, a pedestal, a house, and a tent in it if one is looking for them. But if they are not specifically searched for, mention of these particular models is unlikely to appear in a description of the scene. Although the configurations are present, they are hidden by extraneous objects so well that general grouping programs are unlikely to sort them out. Yet the question, "Does a certain model appear in the scene?" is certainly a reasonable one. One way to attack it divides nicely into three parts:

1. Find those objects in the scene that have the best chance of being identified with the model. If the model has unusual pointers or references unusual concepts, the program pays particular attention to them. Similarly, extra attention is paid to the emphasized parts of the model, for if mates cannot be established for them, solid identification cannot be affirmed. The result is a set of links between the objects of the model and their nearest analogues in the scene.
2. Once a good group of objects is picked, then the pointers relating these objects to the other objects in the scene are temporarily forgotten. In human terms, this is like painting the subgroup a special color.
3. Finally, with the best group of objects set into relief by the previous excision, the ordinary identification routines are applied with the expectation of reasonable performance.

The problem with direct application of the identification programs lies in the myriad irrelevant exit comparison notes that the extra objects in the scene would cause. Such clutter leaves the machine as bewildered as it does humans.

REFERENCES

1. Mahabala, H. N. V.: Preprocessor for Programs which Recognize Scenes, *M.I.T. Artificial Intelligence Laboratory Memo* 177, 1969.
2. Guzman, Adolfo: "Computer Recognition of Three-dimensional Objects in a Visual Scene," Ph.D. thesis, MAC-TR-59, Project MAC, Massachusetts Institute of Technology, Cambridge, Mass., 1968.
3. Evans, Thomas G.: "A Heuristic Program to Solve Geometric Analogy Problems," Ph.D. thesis, in Marvin Minsky (ed.), "Semantic Information Processing," The M.I.T. Press, Cambridge, Mass., 1963.

6 A FRAMEWORK FOR REPRESENTING KNOWLEDGE

Marvin Minsky

6.1 FRAMES

It seems to me that the ingredients of most theories both in artificial intelligence and in psychology have been on the whole too minute, local, and unstructured to account–either practically or phenomenologically–for the effectiveness of common sense thought. The "chunks" of reasoning, language, memory, and "perception" ought to be larger and more structured, and their factual and procedural contents must be more intimately connected in order to explain the apparent power and speed of mental activities.

Similar feelings seem to be emerging in several centers working on theories of intelligence. They take one form in the proposal of Papert and myself[1] to substructure knowledge into "microworlds"; another form in the "problem-spaces" of Newell and Simon;[2] and yet another in new, larger structures that theorists like Schank,[3] Abelson,[4] and Norman[5] assign to linguistic objects. I see all these as moving away from the traditional attempts both by behavioristic psychologists and by logic-oriented students of artificial intelligence in attempts to represent knowledge as collections of separate, simple fragments.

I try here to bring together several of these issues by pretending to have a unified, coherent theory. The paper raises more questions than it answers, and I have tried to note the deficiencies of the theory.

Here is the essence of the theory: When one encounters a new situation (or makes a substantial change in one's view of the present problem) one selects from memory a substantial structure called a frame. This is a remembered framework to be adapted to fit reality by changing details as necessary.

A *frame* is a data-structure for representing a stereotyped situation, like being in a certain kind of living room, or going to a child's birthday party. Attached to each frame are several kinds of information. Some of this information is about how to use the frame. Some is about what one can expect to happen next. Some is about what to do if these expectations are not confirmed.

We can think of a frame as a network of nodes and relations. The "top levels" of a frame are fixed, and represent things that are always true about the supposed situation. The lower levels have many *terminals*–"slots" that must be filled by specific instances or data. Each terminal can specify conditions its assignments must meet. (The assignments themselves are usually smaller "subframes.") Simple conditions are specified by markers that might require a terminal assignment to be a person, an object of sufficient value, or a pointer to a sub-frame of a certain type. More complex conditions can specify relations among the things assigned to several terminals.

Collections of related frames are linked together into *frame systems.* The effects of important actions are mirrored by transformations between the frames of a system. These are used to make certain kinds of calculations economical, to represent changes of emphasis and attention, and to account for the effectiveness of "imagery."

For visual scene analysis, the different frames of a system describe the scene from different viewpoints, and the transformations between one frame and another represent the effects of moving from place to place. For nonvisual kinds of frames, the differences between the frames of a system can represent actions, cause-effect relations, or changes in metaphorical viewpoint. Different frames of a system share the same terminals; this is the critical point that makes it possible to coordinate information gathered from different viewpoints.

Much of the phenomenological power of the theory hinges on the inclusion of expectations and other kinds of presumptions. A frame's terminals are normally already filled with "default" assignments. Thus, a frame may contain a great many details whose supposition is not specifically warranted by the situation. These have many uses in representing general information, most-likely cases, techniques for bypassing "logic," and ways to make useful generalizations.

The default assignments are attached loosely to their terminals, so that they can be easily displaced by new items that better fit the current situation. They thus can serve also as "variables" or as special cases for "reasoning by example," or as "textbook cases," and often make the use of logical quantifiers unnecessary.

The frame systems are linked, in turn, by an information retrieval network. When a proposed frame cannot be made to fit reality–when we cannot find terminal assignments that suitably match its terminal marker conditions–this network provides a replacement frame. These interframe structures make possible other ways to represent knowledge about facts, analogies, and other information useful in understanding.

Once a frame is proposed to represent a situation, a matching process tries to assign values to the terminals of each frame, consistent with the markers at each place. The matching process is partly controlled by information associated with the frame (which includes information about how to deal with surprises) and partly by knowledge about the system's current goals. There are important uses for the information obtained when a matching process fails. I will discuss how it can be used to select an alternative frame that better suits the situation.

Apology! The schemes proposed herein are incomplete in many respects. First, I often propose representations without specifying the processes that will use them. Sometimes I only describe properties the structures should exhibit. I talk about markers and assignments as though it were obvious how they are attached and linked; it is not.

Besides the technical gaps, I will talk as though unaware of many other important kinds of problems. I simplify many issues related to "understanding" that really need much deeper analysis. I often treat statically things that probably require procedural representations. I do not claim that the ideas proposed here are enough for a complete theory, but only that the frame-system scheme may help explain a number of phenomena of human intelligence. The frame idea itself is not particularly original–it is in the tradition of the "schema" of Bartlett and the "paradigms" of Kuhn; the idea of a frame system is probably more novel.

6.1.1 Local and Global Theories for Vision

> For there exists a great chasm between those, on the one side, who relate everything to a single central vision, one system more or less coherent or articulate, in terms of which they understand, think and feel–a single, universal, organizing principle in terms of which alone all that they are and say has significance–and, on the other side, those who pursue many ends, often unrelated and even contradictory, connected, if at all, only in some de facto way, for some psychological or physiological cause, related by no moral or esthetic principle. . . .
>
> –Berlin, I.: "The Hedgehog and the Fox," 1953

When we enter a room we seem to see the entire scene at a glance. But seeing is really an extended process. It takes time to fill in details, collect evidence, make conjectures, test, deduce, and interpret in ways that depend on our knowledge, expectations and goals. Wrong first impressions have to be revised. Nevertheless, all this proceeds so quickly and smoothly that it seems to demand a special explanation.

Some people dislike theories of vision that explain scene analysis largely in terms of discrete, serial, symbolic processes. They feel that although programs built on such theories may indeed seem to "see," they must be too slow and clumsy for a nervous system to use. But the alternative usually proposed is some extreme position of "holism" that never materializes into a technical proposal. I will argue that it is indeed possible for essentially serial symbolic mechanisms to explain much of the phenomenology of the apparent instantaneity and completeness of visual experience.

Some early Gestalt theorists tried to explain a variety of visual phenomena in terms of global properties of electrical fields in the brain. This idea did not come to much.[6] Its modern counterpart, a scattered collection of attempts to use ideas about integral transforms, holograms, and interference phenomena, has done no better. In spite of this, most thinkers outside (and some inside) the symbolic processing community still believe that only through some sort of field-like global parallel process could the required speed be attained.

While my theory is thus addressed to basic problems of Gestalt psychology, the method is fundamentally different. In both approaches, one wants to explain the structuring of sensory data into wholes and parts. Gestalt theorists hoped this could be based primarily on the operation of a few general and powerful principles; but these never crystallized effectively and the proposal lost popularity. In my theory the analysis is based on the interactions between sensations and a huge network of learned symbolic information. While ultimately those interactions must themselves be based also on a reasonable set of powerful principles, the performance theory is separate from the theory of how the system might originate and develop.

6.1.2 Parallelism

Would parallel processing help? This is a more technical question than it might seem. At the level of detecting elementary visual features, texture elements, stereoscopic and motion-parallax cues, it is obvious that parallel processing might be useful. At the level of grouping features into objects, it is harder to see exactly how to use parallelism, but one can at least conceive of the aggregation of connected "nuclei,"[7] or the application of boundary line constraint semantics,[8a] performed in a special parallel network.

At "higher" levels of cognitive processing, however, I suspect fundamental limitations in the usefulness of parallelism. Many "integral" schemes were proposed in the literature on "pattern recognition" for parallel operations on pictorial material—perceptrons, integral transforms, skeletonizers, and so forth. These mathematically and computationally interesting schemes might quite possibly serve as ingredients of perceptual processing theories. But as ingredients only! Basically, "integral" methods work only on isolated figures in two dimensions. They fail disastrously to cope with complicated, three-dimensional scenery. Why?

In complex scenes, the features belonging to different objects have to be correctly segregated to be meaningful; but solving this problem—which is equivalent to the traditional Gestalt "figure-ground" problem—presupposes solutions for so many visual problems that the possibility and perhaps even the desirability of a separate recognition technique falls into question, as noted by Minsky and Papert.[9] In three dimensions the problem is further confounded by the distortion of perspective and by the occlusions of parts of each figure by its own surfaces and those of other figures.

The new, more successful symbolic theories use hypothesis formation and confirmation methods that seem, on the surface at least, more inherently serial. It is hard to solve any very complicated problem without giving essentially full attention, at different times, to different subproblems. Fortunately, however, beyond the brute idea of doing many things in parallel, one can imagine a more serial process that deals with large, complex, symbolic structures as units! This opens a new theoretical "niche" for performing a rapid selection of large substructures; in this niche our theory hopes to find the secret of speed, both in vision and in ordinary thinking.

6.1.3 Artificial Intelligence and Human Problem Solving

In this essay I draw no boundary between a theory of human thinking and a scheme for making an intelligent machine; no purpose would be served by separating these today since neither domain has theories good enough to explain—or to produce—mental imagery. There is, however, a difference in professional attitudes. Workers from psychology inherit stronger desires to minimize the variety of assumed mechanisms. I believe this leads to attempts to extract more performance from fewer "basic mechanisms" than is reasonable. Such theories especially neglect mechanisms of procedure control and explicit representations of processes. On the other side, workers in artificial intelligence have perhaps focused too sharply on just such questions. Neither have given enough attention to the structure of knowledge, especially procedural knowledge.

It is understandable why psychologists are uncomfortable with complex proposals not based on well established mechanisms. But I believe that parsimony is still inappropriate at this stage, valuable as it may be in later phases of every science. There is room in the anatomy and genetics of the brain for much more mechanism than anyone today is prepared to propose, and we should concentrate for a while more on sufficiency and efficiency rather than on necessity.

Up to a few years ago, the primary goal of AI work on vision had to be sufficiency: to find any way at all to make a machine analyze scenes. Only recently have we seen the first signs of adequate capacity to aggregate features and cues correctly into parts and wholes. I cite especially the sequence of work of Roberts,[10] Guzman,[7] Winston,[8b] Huffman,[11] Clowes,[12] Shirai,[13] Waltz,[8a] Binford and Horn,[14] Nevatia and Binford,[15] and Binford and Agin[16] to indicate some steps toward adequate analyses of figure-ground, whole-part, and group-structuring issues.

Although this line of development is still primitive, I feel it is sound enough that we can ask it to explain not only the brute performance of vision but also some of its speed and smoothness. Some new issues confront our theory when we turn from sufficiency to efficiency: How can different kinds of "cues" lead so quickly to identifying and describing complex situations? How can one make changes in case of error or if new evidence is found? How does one resolve inconsistencies? How can position change without recomputing everything? What about moving objects? How does the vision process exploit knowledge associated with general, nonvisual activities? How does one synthesize the information obtained from different viewpoints? How can the system exploit generally correct expectations about effects of contemplated actions? Can the theory account for the phenomenological effects of imagery, the self-directed construction and manipulation of imaginary scenes?

Very little was learned about such matters in the main traditions of behavioral or of perceptual psychology; but the speculations of some earlier psychologists, particularly of Bartlett,[17] have surely found their way into this essay. In the more recent tradition of symbolic information processing theories, papers like those of Newell[18,19] and Pylyshyn[20] take larger technical steps to formulate these issues.

6.1.4 Tracking the Image of a Cube

> But in the common way of taking the view of any opake object, that part of its surface, which fronts the eye, is apt to occupy the mind alone, and the opposite, nay even every other part of it whatever, is left unthought of at that time: and the least motion we make to reconnoitre any other side of the object, confounds our first idea, for want of the connexion of the two ideas, which the complete knowledge of the whole world would naturally have given us, if we had considered it the other way before.
>
> –Hogarth, W.: The Analysis of Beauty, in "Hogarth Essays," 1955

I begin by developing a simplified frame system to represent the perspective appearances of a cube. Later I will adapt it to represent the insides of rooms and to acquiring, using, and revising the kinds of information one needs to move around within a house.

In the tradition of Guzman and Winston, I begin by assuming that the result of looking at a cube is a structure something like that in Fig. 6.1. The substructures A and B represent details or decorations on two faces of the

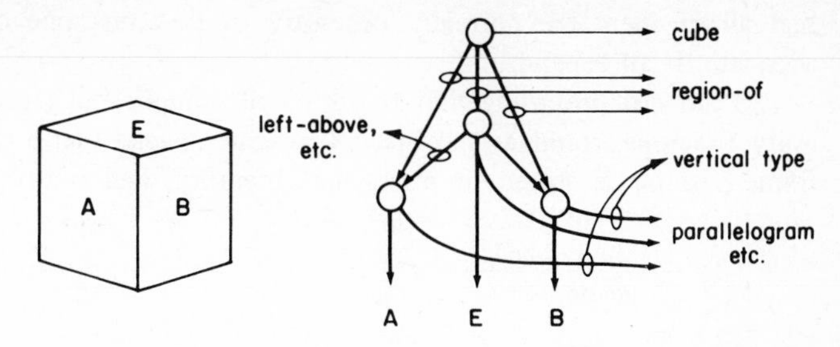

Fig. 6.1

cube. When we move to the right, face A disappears from view, while a new face decorated with C is now seen. If we had to reanalyze the scene from the start, we would have to

1. lose the knowledge about A
2. recompute B
3. compute the description of C

But since we know we moved to the right, we can save B by assigning it also to the "left face" terminal of a second cube frame. To save A–just in case!–we connect it also to an extra, invisible face-terminal of the new cube-schema as in Fig. 6.2.

If later we move back to the left, we can reconstruct the first scene without any perceptual computation at all: just restore the top-level pointers to the first cube frame. We now need a place to store C; we can add yet another invisible face to the right in the first cube frame! (See Fig. 6.3.) We could extend this to represent further excursions around the object. This would lead to a more comprehensive frame system, in which each frame represents a different "perspective" of a cube. In Fig. 6.4 there are three frames corresponding to 45-degree MOVE-RIGHT and MOVE-LEFT actions. If we pursue this analysis, the resulting system can become very large; more complex objects need even more different projections. It is not obvious either

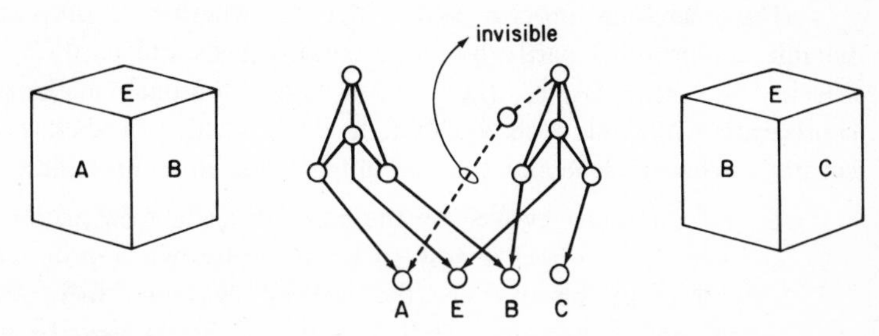

Fig. 6.2

that all of them are normally necessary or that just one of each variety is adequate. It all depends.

I am not proposing that this kind of complicated structure is recreated every time one examines an object. I imagine instead that a great collection of frame systems is stored in permanent memory, and one of them is evoked

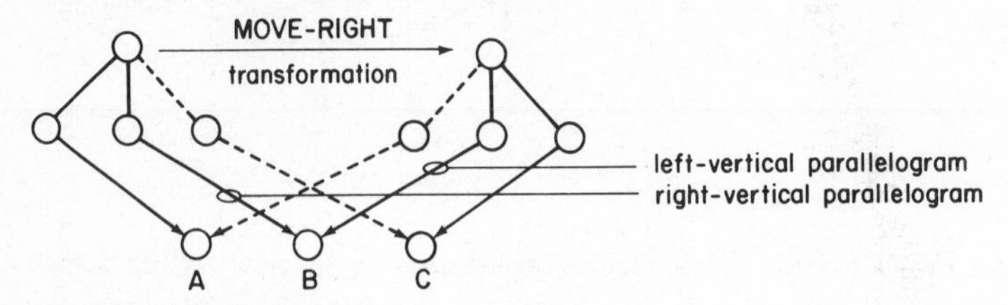

Fig. 6.3

when evidence and expectation make it plausible that the scene in view will fit it. How are they acquired? I will propose that if a chosen frame does not fit well enough, and if no better one is easily found, and if the matter is important enough, then an adaptation of the best one so far discovered will be constructed and remembered for future use.

Do we build such a system for every object we know? That would seem extravagant. More likely, I would think, one has special systems for important objects but also a variety of frames for generally useful "basic shapes"; these are composed to form frames for new cases.

The different frames of a system resemble the multiple "models" described in Guzman[21] and Winston.[8b] Different frames correspond to different views, and the names of pointers between frames correspond to the motions or actions that change the viewpoint. Later I discuss whether these views should be considered as two- or as three-dimensional.

Each frame has terminals for attaching pointers to substructures. Different frames can share the same terminal, which can thus correspond to the same physical feature as seen in different views. This permits us to represent, in a single place, view-independent information gathered at different times and places. This is important also in nonvisual applications.

The matching process which decides whether a proposed frame is suitable is controlled partly by one's current goals and partly by information attached to the frame; the frames carry terminal markers and other constraints, while the goals are used to decide which of these constraints are currently relevant. Generally, the matching process could have these components:

1. A frame, once evoked on the basis of partial evidence or expectation, would first direct a test to confirm its own appropriateness, using knowledge about recently noticed features, loci, relations, and plausible subframes. The current goal list is used to decide which terminals and conditions must be made to match reality.

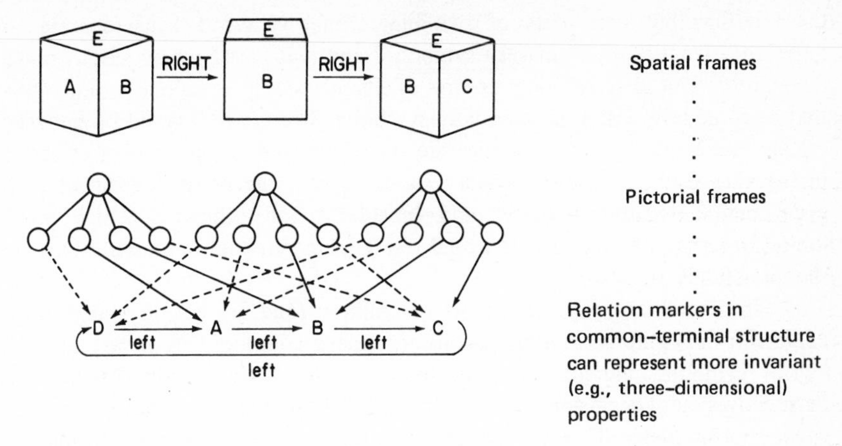

Fig. 6.4

2. Next it would request information needed to assign values to those terminals that cannot retain their default assignments. For example, it might request a description of face C, if this terminal is currently unassigned, but only if it is not marked "invisible." Such assignments must agree with the current markers at the terminal. For example, in assigning face C, one might already have markers for such constraints or expectations as:

   Right-middle visual field
   Must be assigned
   Should be visible; if not, consider moving right
   Should be a cube-face subframe
   Share left vertical boundary terminal with face B
   If failure, consider box-lying-on-side frame
   Same background color as face B

3. Finally, if informed about a transformation (e.g., an impending motion) it would transfer control to the appropriate other frame of that system.

Within the details of the control scheme are opportunities to embed many kinds of knowledge. When a terminal-assigning attempt fails, the resulting error message can be used to propose a second-guess alternative. Later I will suggest using these to organize memory into a similarity network as proposed by Winston.[8b]

6.1.5 Is Vision Symbolic?

Can one really believe that a person's appreciation of three-dimensional structure can be so fragmentary and atomic as to be representable in terms of the relations between parts of two-dimensional views? Let us separate, at once, the two issues: is imagery symbolic? and is it based on two-dimensional fragments? The first problem is one of degree; surely everyone would agree that at some level vision is essentially symbolic. The quarrel would be between certain naive conceptions on one side—in which one accepts seeing either as picture-like or as evoking imaginary solids—against the confrontation of such experimental results of Piaget and Inhelder[22] and others in which many limitations that one might fear would result from symbolic representations are shown actually to exist!

Thus we know that in the art of children (and, in fact, in that of most adult cultures) graphic representations are indeed composed from very limited, highly symbolic ingredients. See, for example, Chap. 2 of Gombrich.[23] Perspectives and occlusions are usually not represented "realistically" but by conventions. Metrical relations are grossly distorted; complex forms are replaced by signs for a few of their important features. Naive observers do not usually recognize these devices, and maintain that they do "see and manipulate pictorial images" in ways that, to them, could not conceivably be accounted for by discrete descriptions.

As for our second question, the issue of two vs. three dimensions evaporates at the symbolic level; the very concept of dimension becomes inappropriate. Each particular symbolic representation of an object serves some goals well and others poorly. If we attach the relation labels *left-of, right-of,* and *above* between parts of the structure, say, as markers on pairs of terminals, certain manipulations will work out smoothly; for example, some properties of these relations are "invariant" if we rotate the cube while keeping the same face on the table. Most objects have "permanent" tops and bottoms. But if we turn the cube on its side such predictions become harder to make; people have great difficulty keeping track of the faces of a six-colored cube if one makes them roll it around in their mind.

If one uses instead more "intrinsic" relations like *next-to* and *opposite-to,* then turning the object on its side disturbs the "image" much less. In Winston we see how systematic replacements (e.g., of "left" for "behind," and "right" for "in-front-of") can simulate the effect of spatial rotation.

Hogarth did not take a position on the symbolic issue, but he did consider good imagery to be an acquired skill and scolds artists who give too little time to perfecting the ideas they ought to have in their minds of the objects in nature. He recommends that

> [he who will undertake the acquisition of] perfect ideas of the distances, bearings, and oppositions of several material points and lines in even the most irregular figures, will gradually arrive at the knack of recalling them into his mind when the objects themselves are not before him—and will be of infinite service to those who invent and draw from fancy, as well as to enable those to be more correct who draw from the life.
>
> —Hogarth, W.: The Analysis of Beauty, in "Hogarth Essays," 1955

Thus, deliberate self-discipline in cataloguing relations between points on opposing surfaces is, he thinks, a key to understanding the invariant relations between the visible and invisible parts; they supply the information needed to imagine oneself within the interior of the object, or at other unexperienced locations; he thus rejects the naive image idea.

Some people believe that we solve spatial problems by maintaining in one's head, somehow, the analog of a three-dimensional structure. But even if one somehow could assemble such a model there would remain, for the "mind's eye," most of the old problems we had for the real eye as well as the new and very hard problem of assembling–from two-dimensional data–the hypothetical imaginary solid.

Although these arguments may seem to favor interconnected two-dimensional views for aggregation and recognition, I do not consider these satisfactory for planning or for manipulative activities. Another representation, still symbolic but in terms of basic solid forms, would seem more natural. Thus a telephone handset could be described in terms of two modified spherical forms connected by a curved, rectangular bar. The problem of connecting two or more qualitatively different ways to represent the same thing is discussed, but not solved, in a later section.

6.1.6 Seeing a Room

Visual experience seems continuous. One reason is that we move continuously. A deeper explanation is that our "expectations" usually interact smoothly with our perceptions. Suppose you were to leave a room, close the door, turn to reopen it, and find an entirely different room. You would be shocked. The sense of change would be almost as startling as if the world suddenly changed before your eyes.

A naive theory of phenomenological continuity is that we see so quickly that our image changes as fast as does the scene. Below I press an alternative theory: the changes in one's frame-structure representation proceed at their own pace; the system prefers to make small changes whenever possible; and the illusion of continuity is due to the persistence of assignments to terminals common to the different view frames. Thus, continuity depends on the confirmation of expectations which in turn depends on rapid access to remembered knowledge about the visual world.

Just before you enter a room, you usually know enough to "expect" a room rather than, say, a landscape. You can usually tell just by the character of the door. And you can often select in advance a frame for the new room. Very often, one expects a certain particular room. Then many assignments are already filled in.

The simplest sort of room-frame candidate is like the inside of a box. Following our cube-model, the room-frame might have the structure shown in Fig. 6.5 at its top level.

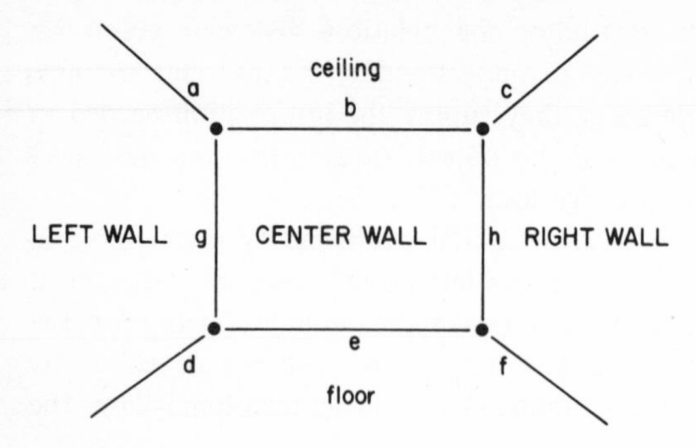

Fig. 6.5

One has to assign to the frame's terminals the things that are seen. If the room is familiar, some are already assigned. If no expectations are recorded already, the first priority might be locating the principal geometric landmarks. To fill in LEFT WALL one might first try to find edges **a** and **d** and then the associated corners **ag** and **gd**. Edge **g**, for example, is usually easy to find because it should intersect any eye-level horizontal scan from left to right. Eventually, **ag**, **gb**, and **ba** must not be too inconsistent with one another because they are the same physical vertex.

However the process is directed, there are some generally useful knowledge-based tactics. It is probably easier to find edge e than any other edge, because if we have just entered a normal rectangular room, then we may expect that

Edge e is a horizontal line.
It is below eye level.
It defines a floor-wall texture boundary.

Given an expectation about the size of a room, we can estimate the elevation of **e**, and vice versa. In outdoor scenes, **e** is the horizon and on flat ground we can expect to see it at eye level. If we fail quickly to locate and assign this horizon, we must consider rejecting the proposed frame: either the room is not normal or there is a large obstruction.

The room-analysis strategy might try next to establish some other landmarks. Given **e**, we next look for its left and right corners, and then for the verticals rising from them. Once such gross geometrical landmarks are located, we can guess the room's general shape and size. This might lead to selecting a new frame better matched to that shape and size, with additional markers confirming the choice and completing the structure with further details.

Of course a competent vision system has to analyze the scene not merely as a picture, but also in relation to some sort of external space-frame. For vision to proceed smoothly when one is moving around, one has to know where each feature "is," in the external world of mobility, to compensate for transformations induced by eye, head, and body motions, as well as for gross locomotion. I discuss this in Sec. 6.5.

6.1.7 Scene Analysis and Subframes

If the new room is unfamiliar, no preassembled frame can supply fine details; more scene analysis is needed. Even so, the complexity of the work can be reduced, given suitable subframes for constructing hypotheses about substructures in the scene. How useful these will be depends both on their inherent adequacy and on the quality of the expectation process that selects which one to use next. One can say a lot even about an unfamiliar room. Most rooms are like boxes, and they can be categorized into types: kitchen, hall, living room, theater, and so on. One knows dozens of kinds of rooms and hundreds of particular rooms; one no doubt has them structured into some sort of similarity network for effective access. This will be discussed later.

A typical room-frame has three or four visible walls, each perhaps of a different "kind." One knows many kinds of walls: walls with windows, shelves, pictures, and fireplaces. Each kind of room has its own kinds of walls.

A typical wall might have a 3 X 3 array of region-terminals given by combinations of (left-center-right) and (top-middle-bottom) so that wall objects can be assigned qualitative locations. One would further want to locate objects relative to geometric interrelations in order to represent such facts as "Y is a little above the center of the line between X and Z."

In three dimensions, the location of a visual feature of a subframe is ambiguous, given only eye direction. A feature in the middle of the visual field could belong either to a Center Front Wall object or to a High Middle Floor object; these attach to different subframes. The decision could depend on reasoned evidence for support, on more directly visual distance information derived from stereo disparity or motion-parallax, or on plausibility information derived from other frames. A clock would be plausible only on the wall-frame while a person is almost certainly standing on the floor.

I do not imagine the boundaries of spatial frame cells to be constrained by accurate metrical dimensions. Each cell terminal would specify the (approximate) location of a typically central place in that cell, and some comparative size range. We expect correct topological constraints; a left-wall-edge must agree to stay to the left of any object assigned to lie flat against that wall. The process of "matching" a scene to an acceptable subset of all such constraints may result in a certain degree of "strain," as a cell is expanded (against its size-range specification) to include the objects proposed for its interior. The tolerance of such strains should depend on constraint priorities that in turn should depend on one's current purpose, past experience, and so forth. I repeat: the richness of visual experience does not support, at this stage, a drive toward the most elegant and parsimonious theory.

6.1.8 Perspective and Viewpoint Transformations

> In sum, at Substage IIIB (age 8 or 9, typically) the operations required to coordinate perspectives are complete, and in the following quite independent forms. First, to each position of the observer there corresponds a particular set of left-right, before-behind relations between the objects. . . . These are governed by the projections and sections appropriate to the visual plane of the observer (perspective). During this final substage the point to point nature of the correspondence between position and perspective is discovered. Second, between each perspective viewpoint valid for a given position of the observer and each of the others, there is also a correspondence expressed by specific changes of left-right, before-behind relations, and consequently by changes of the appropriate projections and sections. It is this correspondence between all possible points of view which constitutes co-ordination of perspectives . . . though as yet only in a rudimentary form.
>
> –Piaget, J., and Inhelder, B.: "The Child's Conception of Space," 1956

When we move about a room, the shapes of things change. How can these changes be anticipated, or compensated, without complete reprocessing? The results of eye and head rotation are simple: things move in the visual field but keep their shapes; but changing place causes large shape changes that depend both on angle and on distance relations between the object and observer. The problem is particularly important for fast-moving animals because a model of the scene must be built up from different, partially analyzed views. Perhaps the need to do this, even in a relatively primitive fashion, was a major evolutionary stimulus to develop frame systems, and later, other symbolic mechanisms.

Given a box-shaped room, lateral motions induce orderly changes in the quadrilateral shapes of the walls as in Fig. 6.6. A picture-frame rectangle, lying

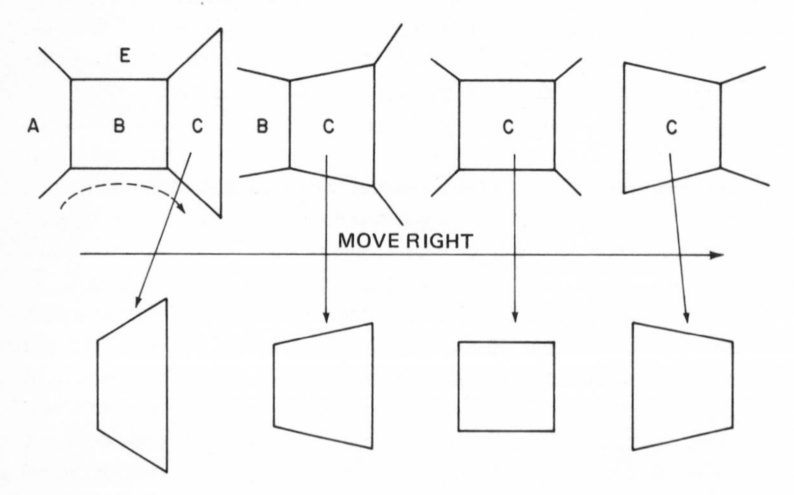

Fig. 6.6

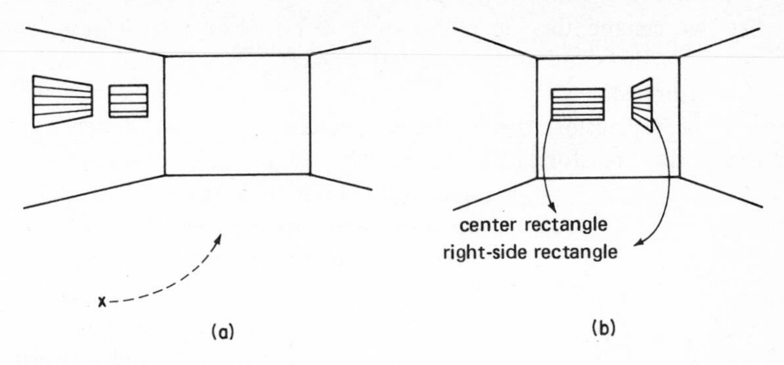

Fig. 6.7

flat against a wall, should transform in the same way as does its wall. If a "center rectangle" is drawn on a left wall it will appear to project out because one makes the default assumption that any such quadrilateral is actually a rectangle, and hence it must lie in a plane that would so project. In Fig. 6.7(*a*), both quadrilaterals could "look like" rectangles, but the one to the right does not match the markers for a "left rectangle" subframe (these require, e.g., that the left side be longer than the right side). That rectangle is therefore represented by a center-rectangle frame and seems to project out as though parallel to the center wall.

Thus we must not simply assign the label "rectangle" to a quadrilateral but to a particular frame of a rectangle system. When we move, we expect whatever space transformation is applied to the top-level system will be applied also to its subsystems as suggested in Fig. 6.7(*b*). Similarly the sequence of elliptical projections of a circle contains congruent pairs that are visually ambiguous as shown in Fig. 6.8. But because wall objects usually lie

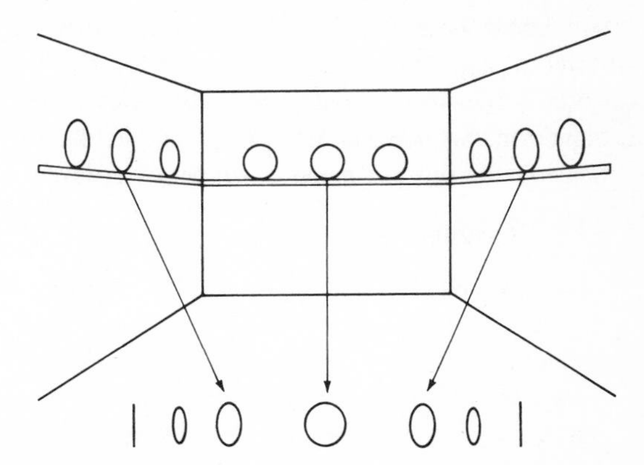

Two figures are congruent, but transform differently.

Fig. 6.8

flat, we assume that an ellipse on a left wall is a left-ellipse, expect it to transform the same way as the left wall, and are surprised if the prediction is not confirmed.

Is it plausible that a finite, qualitative symbolic system can represent perspective transformations adequately? People in our culture are chronically unrealistic about their visualization abilities, e.g., to visualize how spatial relations will appear from other viewpoints. We noted that people who claim to have clear images of such configurations often make qualitative errors in describing the rotations of a simple multicolored cube. And even where we are actually able to make accurate metrical judgements we do not always make them; few people are disturbed by Huffman's "impossible" pyramid, shown in Fig. 6.9. This is not a perspective of any actual truncated pyramid; if it were, the three edges when extended would all meet at one point. In well-developed skills, no doubt, people can routinely make more precise judgements, but this need not require a different mechanism. Where a layman uses 10 frames for some job, an expert might use 1000 and thus get the appearance of a different order of performance.

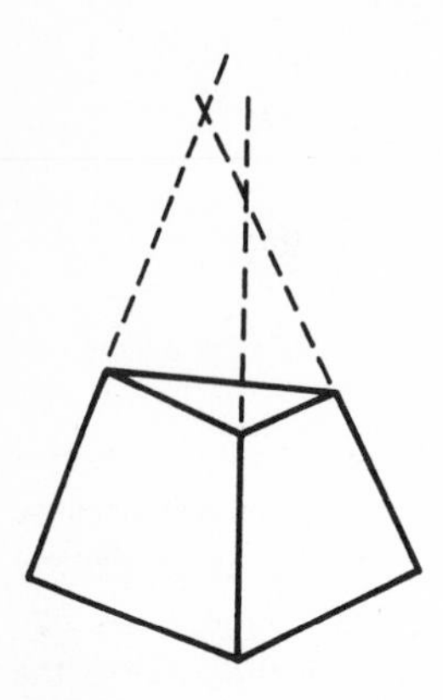

Fig. 6.9

In any case, to correctly anticipate perspective changes in our systems, the top-level transformation must induce appropriate transforms in the subframe systems. To a first approximation, this can be done simply by using the same transformation names. Then a "move-right" action on a room frame would induce a "move-right" action on objects attached to the wall subframes (and to their subframes).

I said "first approximation" because this scheme has a serious bug. If you stand near a left wall and walk forward, the nearby left-wall objects suffer a large "move-right" transform, the front wall experiences a "move closer" transform, and the right wall experiences a small "move left" transform. So matters are not so simple that it is always sufficient merely to transmit the motion name down to lower levels.

6.1.9 Occlusions

When we move to the right, a large object in the center foreground will probably occlude any further-away object to its visual left. When a motion is planned, one should be able to anticipate some of these changes. Some objects should become invisible and other objects should appear. Our prototype cube system has no occlusion problem because the scene is completely convex; the disappearance of an entire side and its contents is easily handled at the top level. But in a room, which is basically concave, the subobjects of different terminals can occlude one another. We consider two extreme strategies:

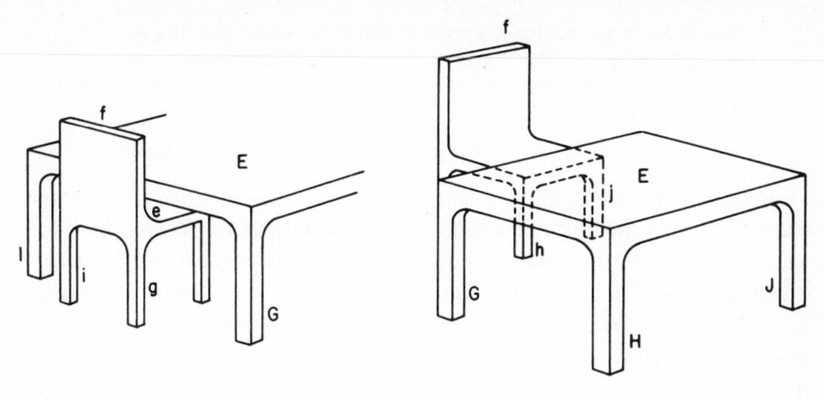

Fig. 6.10

Local assemblies: Just as for the different views of a single object, occlusions of a familiar assembly could be handled by a special frame system for that configuration; e.g., a chair and table as in Fig. 6.10. If we apply the same perspective transformations to such a "niche-frame" that we apply to its superiors, then to a first approximation, occlusions between the objects are handled automatically.

This works for compact, familiar subgroups of objects but cannot handle the details of occlusions between elements of the niche and other things in the room. For engineering applications the scheme's simplicity would not outweigh its frequent errors. As a theory of human performance, it might be good enough. A trained artist or draftsman can answer such questions better, but such activities proceed slowly and need not be explained by a first-order theory concerned mainly with speed.

Global occlusion system: A more radical scheme would make all perspective frames subsidiary to a central, common, space-frame system. The terminals of that system would correspond to cells of a gross subjective space, whose transformations represent, once-and-for-all, facts about which cells occlude others from different viewpoints.

If there were such a supersystem, would it be learned or innate? The context of the Piaget-Inhelder quotation presents evidence that complete coordination structures of this sort are not available to children in their first decade.

6.1.10 Imagery and Frame Systems

Everyone will readily allow that there is a considerable difference between the perceptions of the mind, when a man feels the pain of excessive heat, or the pleasure of moderate warmth, and when he afterwards recalls to his memory this

> sensation, or anticipates it by his imagination. These faculties may mimic or copy the perceptions of the senses; but they never can entirely reach the force and vivacity of the original sentiment. . . . The most lively thought is still inferior to the dullest sensation.
>
> –Hume, D.: An Enquiry Concerning Human Understanding

A theory of seeing should be also a theory of imagining. In our concept both have the same end results: assignments to terminals of frames. Everyone will agree with Hume that there are differences between vision and imagery. Hume theorizes that this is because vision is immediate and direct, whereas imagery is derived from recombinations of memories of direct "impressions" and that some of the force is lost, somehow, in the storage, retrieval, and computation. I propose instead that seeing seems more vivid than imagining because its assignments are less flexible: they more firmly resist the attempts of other processes to modify them. If you try to change the description of a scene actually projected on your retinae, your vision system is likely simply to change it right back. There is no correspondingly rigid constraint on phantasies.

However, even "seen" assignments are not completely inflexible; anyone can learn to mentally reverse the interpretation of a skeleton-cube drawing. So-called "ambiguous" figures are those that are easy to describe in different ways. Changing a frame for such a purpose amounts to a change in "descriptive viewpoint," one in which the action or transformation is symbolic rather than physical; in any case, we are told that there are mental states in which phantasies are more inflexible than "direct impressions" and even, sometimes, more "vivid."

6.1.11 Default Assignment

While both seeing and imagining result in assignments to frame terminals, imagination leaves us wider choices of detail and variety of such assignments. I conjecture that frames are never stored in long-term memory with unassigned terminal values. Instead, what really happens is that frames are stored with weakly bound default assignments at every terminal! These manifest themselves as often useful but sometimes counterproductive stereotypes.

Thus if I say, "John kicked the ball," you probably cannot think of a purely abstract ball, but must imagine characteristics of a vaguely particular ball; it probably has a certain default size, default color, default weight. Perhaps it is a descendant of one you first owned or were injured by. Perhaps it resembles your latest one. In any case your image lacks the sharpness of presence because the processes that inspect and operate upon the weakly bound default features are very likely to change, adapt, or detach them.

Such default assignments would have subtle, idiosyncratic influences on the paths an individual would tend to follow in making analogies, generalizations, and judgments, especially when the exterior influences on such choices are weak. Properly chosen, such stereotypes could serve as a storehouse of valuable heuristic plan-skeletons; badly selected, they could form paralyzing collections of irrational biases. Because of them one might expect, as reported by Freud, to detect evidences of early cognitive structures in "free association" thinking.

6.1.12 Frame-Systems and Piaget's Concrete Operations

> What, in effect, are the conditions for the construction of formal thought? The child must not only apply operations to objects–in other words, mentally execute possible actions on them–he must also "reflect" those operations in the absence of the objects which are replaced by pure propositions. This "reflection" is thought raised to the second power. Concrete thinking is the representation of a possible action, and formal thinking is the representation of a representation of possible action.
>
> It is not surprising, therefore, that the system of concrete operations must be completed during the last years of childhood before it can be "reflected" by formal operations. In terms of their function, formal operations do not differ from concrete operations except that they are applied to hypotheses or propositions [whose logic is] an abstract translation of the system of "inference" that governs concrete operations.
>
> –Piaget, J.: "Mental Imagery in the Child: A Study of the Development of Imaginal Representation," 1971

I think there is a similarity between Piaget's idea of a concrete operation and the effects of applying a transformation between frames of a system. What kinds of superficially "logical" operations are easy to perform with frames by using loosely attached default assignments? It should be easy, for example, to approximate logical transitivities; thus surface syllogisms of the form

All A's are B's and All B's are C's
⇒
All A's are C's

would occur in the natural course of substituting acceptable subframes into marked terminals of a frame. (I do not mean that the generalization itself is asserted, but only that its content is applied to particular cases because of the transitivity of instantiation of subframes.) One would expect, then, to also find the same belief in

Most A's are B's and Most B's are C's
⇒
Most A's are C's

even though this is sometimes false, as some adults have learned.

I do not understand the limitations of what can be done by simple processes working on frames. One could surely invent some "inference-frame technique" that culd be used to rearrange terminals of other frames so as to simulate deductive logic. As in other aspects of the theory of computation, we often find tricky encoding operations to transform these apparently limited formalisms into "universal" ones, but it might be hard to do this in ways easy to develop or practical to use.

It appears that only with the emergence of Piaget's "formal" stage (for perspective, not usually until the second decade) are children reliably able to reason *about,* rather than *with* transformations. Nor do such capacities appear at once, or synchronously in all mental activities. To get greater reasoning power—and to be released from the useful but unreliable pseudologic of manipulating default assignments—one must learn the equivalent of operating on the transformations themselves. (One needs to get at the transformations because they contain knowledge needed for more sophisticated reasoning.) In a computational model constructed for artificial intelligence, one might try to make the system read its own programs. An alternative is to represent (redundantly) information about processes some other way. Workers on recent "program-understanding" programs in our laboratory have usually decided, for one reason or another, that programs should carry "commentaries" that express more directly their intentions, prerequisites, and effects; these commentaries are (at present) usually written in specialized sublanguages.

This raises an important point about the purpose of our theory. "Schematic" thinking, based on matching complicated situations against stereotyped frame structures, must be inadequate for some aspects of mental activity. Obviously mature people can to some extent think about, as well as use their own representations. Let us speculatively interpret "formal operations" as processes that can examine and criticize our earlier representations (be they frame-like or whatever). With these we can begin to build up new structures to correspond to "representations of representations." I have no idea what role frame systems might play in these more complex activities.

The same strategy suggests that we identify (schematically, at least) the direct use of frames with Piaget's "concrete operations." If we do this then I find Piaget's explanation of the late occurrence of "formal thinking" paradoxically reassuring. In first trying to apply the frame-system paradigm to various problems, I was disturbed by how well it explained some things and how poorly others. But it was foolish to expect any single scheme to explain very much about thinking. Certainly one cannot expect to solve all the problems of sophisticated reasoning within a system confined to concrete operations—if that indeed amounts to the manipulation of stereotypes.

6.2 LANGUAGE, UNDERSTANDING, AND SCENARIOS

6.2.1 Words, Sentences, and Meanings

> The device of images has several defects that are the price of its peculiar excellences. Two of these are perhaps the most important: the image, and particularly the visual image, is apt to go farther in the direction of the individualization of situation than is biologically useful; and the principles of the

> combination of images have their own peculiarities and result in constructions which are relatively wild, jerky and irregular, compared with the straightforward unwinding of a habit, or with the somewhat orderly march of thought.
>
> –Bartlett, F. C.: "Remembering: A Study in Experimental and Social Psychology," 1932 (revised, 1961)

The concepts of frame and default assignment seem helpful in discussing the phenomenology of "meaning." Chomsky[24] points out that such a sentence as

a. "colorless green ideas sleep furiously"

is treated very differently than the nonsentence

b. "furiously sleep ideas green colorless"

and suggests that because both are "equally nonsensical," what is involved in the recognition of sentences must be quite different from what is involved in the appreciation of meanings.

There is no doubt that there are processes especially concerned with grammar. Since the meaning of an utterance is "encoded" as much in the positional and structural relations between the words as in the word choices themselves, there must be processes concerned with analyzing those relations in the course of building the structures that will more directly represent the meaning. What makes the words of (a) more effective and predictable than (b) in producing such a structure–putting aside the question of whether that structure should be called semantic or syntactic–is that the word-order relations in (a) exploit the (grammatical) conventions and rules people usually use to induce others to make assignments to terminals of structures. This is entirely consistent with grammar theories. A generative grammar would be a summary description of the exterior appearance of those frame rules–or their associated processes–while the operators of transformational grammars seem similar enough to some of our frame transformations.

But one must also ask: to what degree does grammar have a separate identity in the actual working of a human mind? Perhaps the rejection of an utterance (either as nongrammatical, as meaningless, or most important, as not understood) indicates a more complex failure of the semantic process to arrive at any usable representation; I will argue now that the grammar-meaning distinction may illuminate two extremes of a continuum, but obscures its all-important interior.

We certainly cannot assume that "logical" meaninglessness has a precise psychological counterpart. Sentence (a) can certainly generate an image! The dominant frame (in my case) is that of someone sleeping; the default system assigns a particular bed, and in it lies a mummy-like shape-frame with a translucent green color property. In this frame there is a terminal for the character of the sleep–restless, perhaps–and "furiously" seems somewhat inappropriate at that terminal, perhaps because the terminal does not like to accept anything so "intentional" for a sleeper. "Idea" is even more disturbing, because a person is expected, or at least something animate. I sense frustrated procedures trying to resolve these tensions and conflicts more properly, here or there, into the sleeping framework that has been evoked.

Utterance (b) does not get nearly so far because no subframe accepts any substantial fragment. As a result no larger frame finds anything to match its terminals, hence finally, no top level "meaning" or "sentence" frame can organize the utterance as either meaningful or grammatical. By combining this "soft" theory with gradations of assignment tolerances, I imagine one could develop systems that degrade properly for sentences with "poor" grammar rather than none; if the smaller fragments–phrases and subclauses–satisfy subframes well enough, an image adequate for certain kinds of comprehension could be constructed anyway, even though some parts of the top level structure are not entirely satisfied. Thus, we arrive at a qualitative theory of "grammatical:" if the top levels are satisfied but some lower terminals are not we have a meaningless sentence; if the top is weak but the bottom solid, we can have an ungrammatical but meaningful utterance.

I do not mean to suggest that sentences must evoke visual images. Some people do not admit to assigning a color to the ball in "he kicked the ball." But everyone admits (eventually) to having assumed, if not a size or color, at least some purpose, attitude, or other elements of an assumed scenario. When we go beyond vision, terminals and their default assignments can represent purposes and functions, not just colors, sizes and shapes.

6.2.2 Discourse

Linguistic activity involves larger structures than can be described in terms of sentential grammar, and these larger structures further blur the distinctness of the syntax-semantic dichotomy. Consider the following fable, as told by W. Chafe.[25]

> There was once a Wolf who saw a Lamb drinking at a river and wanted an excuse to eat it. For that purpose, even though he himself was upstream, he accused the Lamb of stirring up the water and keeping him from drinking . . .

To understand this, one must realize that the Wolf is lying! To understand the key conjunctive "even though" one must realize that contamination never flows upstream. This in turn requires us to understand (among other things) the word "upstream" itself. Within a declarative, predicate-based "logical" system, one might try to axiomatize "upstream" by some formula like:

A upstream B

[Event T, Stream muddy at A]

$\Rightarrow$

[Exists [Event U, Stream muddy at B]]

Later U, T

But an adequate definition would need a good deal more. What about the fact that the order of things being transported by water currents is not ordinarily changed? A logician might try to deduce this from a suitably intricate set of "local" axioms, together with appropriate "induction" axioms. I propose instead to represent this knowledge in a structure that automatically translocates spatial descriptions from the terminals of one frame to those of another frame of the same system. While this might be considered to be a form of logic, it uses some of the same mechanisms designed for spatial thinking.

In many instances we would handle a change over time, or a cause-effect relation, in the same way as we deal with a change in position. Thus, the concept *river-flow* could evoke a frame-system structure something like that below, where S1, S2, and S3 are abstract slices of the flowing river shown in Fig. 6.11. In my default system the Wolf is at the left, the Lamb at the right, and S1, S2, and S3 flow past them. In the diagram, presume that the S's cannot be seen unless they are directly next to either the wolf or the lamb. On reflection, my imaginary currents usually flow from left to right, and I find it some effort to use reversed versions. Perhaps they all descend from copies of the same protosystem.

The time (and not coincidentally, current) transformation represents part of our understanding of the effects of the flow of the river. If the terminal S3 is the mud effect produced by the Lamb, the frame system causes the mud effect to become invisible and not near the Wolf. Thus, he has no valid reason to complain. A more detailed system could have intermediate frames; in none of them is the Wolf contaminated.

There are many more nuances to fill in. What is "stirring up" and why would it keep the wolf from drinking? One might normally assign default floating objects to the S's, but here S3 interacts with "stirring up" to yield something that "drink" does not find acceptable. Was it "deduced" that

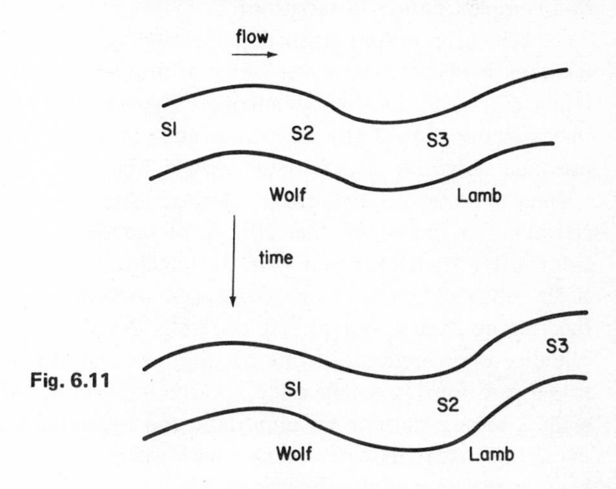

Fig. 6.11

stirring river-water means that S3 in the first frame should have "mud" assigned to it; or is this simply the default assignment for stirred water? The meaning of "eat" ought to be understood, too. In children's stories, being eaten is a bad way to disappear, but it is not always irreversible.

Almost any event, action, change, flow of material, or even flow of information can be represented to a first approximation by a two-frame generalized event. One can have slots for agents, tools, side-effects, preconditions, generalized trajectories, just as in the "trans" verbs of "case grammar" theories.

To see if one has understood an event or action, one can try to build an appropriate instantiated frame-pair. If one stores the important parts of the new construct so that it can be retrieved under similar conditions, one should understand it faster the next time. Thus the relation between understanding and learning should be very intimate.

But in representing changes by simple "before-after" frame-pairs, one may have to pay a price for the convenience of using implicit representation: it will not make it easy to do planning or abstract reasoning. The problem is that with implicit representation, there is no convenient place to attach properties of, or information about, the transformation. As a second approximation, we could label pairs of nodes that point to corresponding terminals, obtaining structure like the "comparison-notes" in Winston,[8] or we might place at the top of the frame system information describing the differences more abstractly. Something of this sort will be needed eventually.

This is perhaps a good point to mention the work of R. Schank on "conceptual dependency",[26] he attempts to construct representations of the meanings of such diverse assertions as "Sam believes that John is a fool" (in which the thing that Sam believes is not an object but requires a "conceptualization"), or "Q: Do you want a piece of chocolate? A: No. I just had an ice cream cone" (in which understanding requires representing details of a complex notion of satiation).

Schank proposes a small collection of "basic conceptualizations" and relations between them from which to build representations for any meaning. I find it hard to decide how adequate these are. How well, for example, could they describe flows? His schemes include an idea of "conceptual cases" which resemble some of our frame-terminals. (See Sec. 6.2.8.) His representation scheme is quite different from mine, at least on the surface, in that, e.g., he attempts to represent the effects of actions more abstractly than as a before-after transformation pair. It remains to be seen, for example, how a single abstract concept of cause (or even several) would be used in a functioning "belief system." It certainly would not be enough to characterize causality only in terms of one condition or action being necessary for another to happen. Putting details aside, what is important, I think, is that Schank has made a strong start on an important and neglected area of epistemology and, once this area develops some performance tests, it should yield good knowledge-representation methods.

The work of Y. Wilks[27] on "preference semantics" also seems rich in ideas about ways to build frame-like structures out of simpler ones, and his preference proposals embody specific ways one might represent default assignments and procedures for making them depend on larger aspects of a discourse than mere sentences. Wilks' system is interesting also in demonstrating, I think, ways in which one can get some useful informal reasoning or pseudodeduction as a product of the template building and instantiation processes without an elaborate formal logical system or undue concern with consistency.

R. P. Abelson[4] has worked toward representing even more extended activities. Beginning with elements like Schank's, he works out schemes in which the different concepts interact, arriving at intricate scripts–skeletonized scenarios of elaborate belief systems, attempting even to portray such interactions as one's image of the role he plays in another person's plans.

D. McDermott[28] discusses many issues related to knowledge representations. In his scheme for plausible inference, statements are not simply accepted, but are subjected to a process of "doubting" and "believing"; in effect, things assumed by default (or plausibility) are retained with mechanisms for revising those beliefs when later, dependent assumptions run into problems. McDermott is particularly attentive to the problems involved in recovery from the errors any such system is forced to make in the course of informal, common sense inference.

6.2.3 Meaning-Structure of a Discourse

> Words . . . can indicate the qualitative and relational features of a situation in their general aspect just as directly as, and perhaps even more satisfactorily than, they can describe its particular individuality. This is, in fact, what gives to language its intimate relation to thought processes. For thinking, in the proper psychological sense, is never the mere reinstatement of some suitable past situation produced by a crossing of interests, but is the utilization of the past in solution of difficulties set by the present. . . . Equally, nobody ever thinks who, being challenged, merely sets up an image from some more or less relevant situation, and then finds for himself a solution, without in any way formulating the relational principle involved.
>
> –Bartlett, F. C.: "Remembering: A Study in Experimental and Social Psychology," 1932 (revised, 1961)

"Case grammar" sentence-analysis theories such as those of Fillmore[29] and Celce-Murcia[30] involve structures somewhat like frames. Centered mainly around the verb, parts of a sentence are used to instantiate a sort of verb frame in accord with various uses of prepositions. I agree that this surely is a real phenomenon; sentences are built around verbs, so it makes sense to use verb-centered frame-like structures for analyzing sentences.

In more extended discourse, however, I think that verb-centered structures often become subordinate or even disappear. The topic or "theme" of a paragraph is as likely to be a scene as to be an action, as likely to be a characterization of a person as to be something he is doing. Thus in understanding a discourse, the synthesis of a verb-structure with its case assignments may be a necessary but transient phase. As sentences are understood, the resulting substructures must be transferred to a growing "scene frame" to build up the larger picture. An action that is the chief concern of one sentence might, for example, become subsidiary to a characterization of one of the actors in a larger story-frame.

I am not proposing anything like "verbs describe local (sentential) structures and nouns describe global (paragraphic) structures"—although that might be a conceptually useful first approximation. Any concept can be invoked by all sorts of linguistic representations. It is not a matter of nouns or verbs. The important point is that we must not assume that the transient semantic structure built during the syntactic analysis (what language theorists today call the "deep structure" of a sentence) is identical with the larger (and "deeper") structure built up incrementally as each fragment of a coherent linguistic communication operates upon it!

I do not want this emphasis on topical or thematic superframes to suggest a radical confrontation between linguistic vs. nonlinguistic representations. Introspectively, a substantial portion of common sense thinking and reasoning seem to resemble linguistic transformations and other manipulations. The frames associated with word senses, be they noun, verb or whatever, are surely centers for the concentrated representation of vital knowledge about how different things are related, how they are used, and how they transform one another. Practically, there would be large advantages in having mechanisms that could use these same structures both for thinking and for communicating.

Let us imagine a frame-oriented scenario for how coherent discourse might be represented. At the start of a story, we know little other than that it will be a story, but even this gives us a start. A conventional frame for "story" (in general) would arrive with slots for setting, protagonists, main event, moral, etc. Indeed, the first line of a properly told story usually helps with the setting; the wolf and lamb story immediately introduces two antagonists, places them by the river (setting), and provides the wolf with a motive. The word "excuse" somehow prepares us for the likelihood of the wolf making false statements.

Each sentential analysis need be maintained only until its contents can be used to instantiate a larger structure. The terminals of the growing meaning-structure thus accumulate indicators and descriptors, which expect and key further assignments. A terminal that has acquired a "female person" marker will reject "male" pronominal assignments using, I suppose, the same sorts of considerations that resist assignment of tables and chairs to terminals of wall frames. As the story proceeds, information is transferred to superframes whenever possible, instantiating or elaborating the scenario. In some cases we will be lucky enough to attach a whole subframe, for example, a description of the hero, to a single terminal in the superframe. This could happen if a terminal of the "story" superframe matches a top level indicator on the current sentence-frame. Other sentences might produce relations constraining pairs of already existing terminals. But what if no such transfer can be made because the listener expected a wrong kind of story and has no terminals to receive the new structure?

We go on to suppose that the listener actually has many story frames, linked by the kinds of retrieval structures discussed later on. First we try to fit the new information into the current story frame. If we fail, we construct an error comment like "there is no place here for an animal." This causes us to replace the current story frame by, say, an animal-story frame. The previous assignments to terminals may all survive, if the new story frame has the same kinds of terminals. But if many previous assignments do not so transfer, we must get another new story frame. If we fail, we must either construct a basically new story frame–a major intellectual event, perhaps–or just give up and forget the assignments. (Presumably that is the usual reaction to radically new narrative forms! One does not learn well if the required jumps are too large: one cannot really understand animal stories until one possesses the conventional personality frames for the wolf, pig, fox, etc.)

Thus a discourse assembles a network of instantiated frames and subframes. Attributive or descriptive information can often be represented by simple substructures, but actions, temporal successions, explanations and other complicated things surely need more elaborate attachments. We must recognize that profoundly hard questions, central to epistemology as well as to linguistics, are entrained in this problem of how to merge information from different sources and subframes. The next few sections raise more questions about these than they begin to answer.

6.2.4 Language Translation

Translation affords an opportunity to observe defaults at work. In translating the story about the wolf and the lamb from English to Japanese, according to Chafe, it is required to mention the place on the river where the actors stand, although it is not required in English. In English one must cite the time–if only by saying "Once. . . ." In Japanese, it is customary to characterize the place, as well as the time, even if only by a nonspecific "In a certain place. . . ."

I think both place and time are required, in the deeper meaning frames of people who think much as we do whatever natural language they speak! Hence, default assignments for both would be immediately available to the translator if he understood the sentence at all. Good simultaneous translators proceed so rapidly that one wonders how much they can really understand before speaking; our theory makes this less of an issue because if the proper frame is retrieved in the course of partial understanding, its default assignments are available instantly, before the more complex assignment negotiations are completed.

A translation of "The Wolf and Lamb" into Japanese with acceptable surface structure might be, according to Chafe,

> Once certain place in river at water drinking be child-sheep saw one animal wolf was and that wolf that child-sheep eat for excuse make-want-seeming was....

It is more natural, in Japanese, to say what the Lamb was drinking than just to say he was drinking. Here is one way that language affects thinking: each such linguistic convention focuses special attention on filling certain terminals. If water is the usual thing to drink in one's culture, then water is the default assignment for what is being drunk. When speech production requires such an assignment in a sentence-output frame, that default will normally be assumed. Of course, one should be even more certain of water if the drinking is done beside a river; this needs some machinery for relating drinking and river stereotypes. It seems clear that if there is a weakly bound drinkable-fluid slot in one frame, and a strongly bound drinkable fluid in the subframe to be attached, the latter should dislodge the former. Thus, even if our listener usually drinks wine, he should correctly imagine the lamb drinking water.

6.2.5 Active Vs. Passive

In our traditional "folk phenomenology," seeing and imagining are usually seen as "passive" and "active." It is tempting to exploit this viewpoint for vision:

> In seeing, one analyzes a scene by assembling and instantiating frames, generally without much choice because of the domination of the need to resolve "objective" visual evidence against the need for a consistent and plausible spatial scene-description.
>
> In imagining, we have much more choice, for we are trying to assemble and instantiate frames to represent a "scene" that satisfies internally chosen—hence changeable—goals.

In language, a similar contrast is tempting:

> In listening (which includes parsing) one has little choice because of the need to resolve the objective word string into a structure consistent with grammar, context, and the (assumed) intention.
>
> In speaking, we have much more choice, because there are so many ways to assemble sentence-making frames for our chosen purpose, be it to inform, convince, or mislead.

However, these are dangerous oversimplifications; things are often quite the other way around! Speaking is often a straightforward encoding from a semantic structure into a word sequence, while listening often involves extensive and difficult constructions—which involve the totality of complexities we call understanding.

Consider the analogy between a frame for a room in a visual scene and a frame for a noun phrase in a discourse. In each case, some assignments to terminals are mandatory, while others are optional. A wall need not be decorated, but every moveable object must be supported. A noun phrase need not contain a numerical determiner, but it must contain a noun or pronoun equivalent. One generally has little choice so far as surface structure is concerned: one must account for all the words in a sentence and for all the major features of a scene. However, surface structure is not everything in vision or in language. One has unlimited options about incorporating consequences of context and knowledge into semantic structure. An object has not only a visual form, but a history. Its presence has usually a cause and often some other significance—perhaps as a clue in a puzzle, or as a symbol of a changing relationship.

Any sentence can be understood in many ways. I emphasize that I am not talking of the accidental (and relatively unimportant) ambiguities of parsing, but of the purposeful variations of interpretation. Just as any room can be seen from different physical viewpoints, so any assertion can be "viewed" from different representational viewpoints as in the following, each of which suggests a different structure:

He kicked the ball.
The ball was kicked.

or even

There was some kicking today.

Because these variations formally resemble the results of the syntactic, active-passive operations of transformational grammars, one might overlook their semantic significance. We select one or the other in accord with thematic issues—on whether one is concerned with what "he" did, with finding a lost ball, with who damaged it, or whatever. One answers such questions most easily by bringing the appropriate entity or action into the focus of attention by evoking a frame primarily concerned with that topic.

In the traditional view of transformational linguistics, these alternate frames have no separate existence but are only potential derivatives from a single deep structure. There is an advantage to supposing their separate existence in long term memory: we could attach specific knowledge to each about how it should be used. However, as language theorists rightly point out, there are systematic regularities which suggest that such "transformations" are nearly as readily applied to unfamiliar verbs with the same redirections of concern; this makes separate existence less plausible. I have the impression that transformational theorists tend to believe in some special central mechanisms for management of such changes of "semantic perspective," even though, I should think, the variety of idiosyncracies attached to individual words makes this technically difficult. A theory more in the spirit of this essay would suggest that whenever one encounters an unfamiliar usage (or an unfamiliar word) he applies some matching process to guess—rightly or wrongly—which familiar usage it resembles, and then adapts the existing attention-transformation system for that word. I cannot see what kind of experiment might distinguish between these conjectures, but I still feel that the distinction is important.

Some readers might object that things should not be so complicated—that we need a simpler theory if only to explain how people understand sentences so quickly. One must not forget that it often takes minutes, hours, or forever, to understand something.

6.2.6 Scenarios

> Thinking . . . is biologically subsequent to the image-forming process. It is possible only when a way has been found of breaking up the "massed" influence of past stimuli and situations, only when a device has already been discovered for conquering the sequential tyranny of past reactions. But though it is a later and a higher development, it does not supercede the method of images. It has its own drawbacks. Contrasted with imaging it loses something of vivacity, of vividness, of variety. Its prevailing instruments are words, and, not only because these are social, but also because in use they are necessarily strung out in sequence, they drop into habit reactions even more readily than images do. [With thinking] we run greater and greater risk of being caught up in generalities that may have little to do with actual concrete experience. If we fail to maintain the methods of thinking, we run the risks of becoming tied to individual instances and of being made sport of by the accidental circumstances belonging to these.
>
> —Bartlett, F. C.: "Remembering: A Study in Experimental and Social Psychology," 1932, (revised, 1961)

We condense and conventionalize, in language and thought, complex situations and sequences into compact words and symbols. Some words can perhaps be "defined" in elegant, simple structures, but only a small part of the meaning of "trade" is captured by

first frame		→	second frame	
A has X	B has Y		B has X	A has Y

Trading normally occurs in a social context of law, trust, and convention. Unless we also represent these other facts, most trade transactions will be almost meaningless. It is usually essential to know that each party usually wants both things but has to compromise. It is a happy but unusual circumstance in which each trader is glad to get rid of what he has. To represent trading strategies, one could insert the basic maneuvers right into the above frame-pair scenario: in order for A to make B want X more (or want Y less) we expect him to select one of the familiar tactics:

Offer more for Y.
Explain why X is so good.
Create favorable side-effect of B having X.

Disparage the competition.
Make B think C wants X.

These only scratch the surface. Trades usually occur within a scenario tied together by more than a simple chain of events each linked to the next. No single such scenario will do; when a clue about trading appears it is essential to guess which of the different available scenarios is most likely to be useful.

Charniak's thesis[31] studies questions about transactions that seem easy for people to comprehend yet obviously need rich default structures. We find in elementary school reading books such stories as:

Jane was invited to Jack's birthday party.
She wondered if he would like a kite.
She went to her room and shook her piggy bank.
It made no sound.

Most young readers understand that Jane wants money to buy Jack a kite for a present but that there is no money to pay for it in her piggy bank. Charniak proposes a variety of ways to facilitate such inferences–a "demon" for *present* that looks for things concerned with *money*, a demon for "piggy bank" which knows that shaking without sound means the bank is empty, etc. But although *present* now activates *money*, the reader may be surprised to find that neither of those words (nor any of their synonyms) occurs in the story. "Present" is certainly associated with "party" and "money" with "bank," but how are the longer chains built up? Here is another problem raised in Charniak. A friend tells Jane:

He already has a kite.
He will make you take it back.

Take which kite back? We do not want Jane to return Jack's old kite. To determine the referent of the pronoun "it" requires understanding a lot about an assumed scenario. Clearly, "it" refers to the proposed new kite. How does one know this? (Note that we need not agree on any single explanation.) Generally, pronouns refer to recently mentioned things, but as this example shows, the referent depends on more than the local syntax.

Suppose for the moment we are already trying to instantiate a "buying a present" default subframe. Now, the word "it" alone is too small a fragment to deal with, but "take it back" could be a plausible unit to match a terminal of an appropriately elaborate buying scenario. Since that terminal would be constrained to agree with the assignment of "present" itself, we are assured of the correct meaning of it in "take X back." Automatically, the correct kite is selected. Of course, that terminal will have its own constraints as well; a subframe for the "take it back" idiom should know that "take X back" requires that:

X was recently purchased.
The return is to the place of purchase.
You must have your sales slip.
Etc.

If the current scenario does not contain a "take it back" terminal, then we have to find one that does and substitute it, maintaining as many prior assignments as possible. Notice that if things go well the question of it being the old kite never even arises. The sense of ambiguity arises only when a "near miss" mismatch is tried and rejected.

Charniak's proposed solution to this problem is in the same spirit but emphasizes understanding that because Jack already has a kite, he may not want another one. He proposes a mechanism associated with "present":

a. If we see that a person P might not like a present X, then look for X being returned to the store where it was bought.
b. If we see this happening, or even being suggested, assert that the reason why is that P does not like X.

This statement of "advice" is intended by Charniak to be realized as a production-like entity to be added to the currently active data-base whenever a certain kind of context is encountered. Later, if its antecedent condition is satisfied, its action adds enough information about Jack and about the new kite to lead to a correct decision about the pronoun.

Charniak in effect proposes that the system should watch for certain kinds of events or situations and inject proposed reasons, motives, and explanations for them. The additional interconnections between the story elements are expected to help bridge the gaps that logic might find it hard to cross, because the additions are only "plausible" default explanations, assumed without corroborative assertions. By assuming (tentatively) "does not like X" when X is taken back, Charniak hopes to simulate much of ordinary "comprehension" of what is happening. We do not yet know how complex and various such plausible inferences must be to get a given level of performance, and the thesis does not answer this because it did not include a large simulation. Usually he proposes terminating the process by asserting the allegedly plausible motive without further analysis unless necessary. To understand why Jack might return the additional kite it should usually be enough to assert that he does not like it. A deeper analysis might reveal that Jack would not really mind having two kites but he probably realizes that he will get only one present; his utility for two different presents is probably higher.

6.2.7 More Complex Scenarios

The meaning of a child's birthday party is very poorly approximated by any dictionary definition like "a party assembled to celebrate a birthday," where a party would be defined, in turn, as "people assembled for a celebration." This lacks all the flavor of the culturally required activities. Children know that the "definition" should include more specifications, the particulars of which can normally be assumed by way of default assignments:

DRESS . . . . SUNDAY BEST.
PRESENT . . . . . MUST PLEASE HOST.
MUST BE BOUGHT AND GIFT-WRAPPED.
GAMES . . . . . . HIDE AND SEEK. PIN TAIL ON DONKEY.
DECOR . . . . . . BALLOONS. FAVORS. CREPE-PAPER.
PARTY-MEAL . CAKE. ICE-CREAM. SODA. HOT DOGS.
CAKE . . . . CANDLES. BLOW-OUT. WISH. SING BIRTHDAY SONG.
ICE-CREAM . . . STANDARD THREE-FLAVOR.

These ingredients for a typical American birthday party must be set into a larger structure. Extended events take place in one or more days. A Party takes place in a Day, of course, and occupies a substantial part of it, so we locate it in an appropriate day frame. A typical day has main events such as

Get-up Dress Eat-1 Go-to-Work Eat-2 . . .

but a School-Day has more fixed detail:

Get-up Dress
Eat-1 Go-to-School Be-in-School
Home-Room Assembly English Math (arrgh)
Eat-2 Science Recess Sport
Go-Home Play
Eat-3 Homework Go-to-Bed

Birthday parties obviously do not fit well into school-day frames. Any parent knows that the Party-Meal is bound to Eat-2 of its Day. I remember a child who did not seem to realize this. Absolutely stuffed after the Party-Meal, he asked when he would get Lunch.

Returning to Jane's problem with the kite, we first hear that she is invited to Jack's Birthday Party. Without the party scenario, or at least an invitation scenario, the second line seems rather mysterious:

She wondered if he would like a kite.

To explain one's rapid comprehension of this, I will make a somewhat radical proposal: to represent explicitly, in the frame for the party scenario's structure, pointers to a collection of the most serious problems commonly associated with it:

Y must get P for X . . . . Choose P!
X must like P . . . . Will X like P?

Buy P . . . . Where to buy P?
Get money to buy P . . . Where to get money?
Y must dress up . . . . . . What should Y wear?

The reader is free to wonder, with the author, whether this solution is acceptable. The question, "Will X like P?" certainly matches "She wondered if he would like a kite?" and correctly assigns the kite to P. But is our world regular enough that such question sets could be precompiled to make this mechanism often work smoothly? I think the answer is mixed. We do indeed expect many such questions; we surely do not expect all of them. But surely "expertise" consists partly in not having to realize *ab initio,* what are the outstanding problems and interactions in situations. Notice, for example, that there is no default assignment for the present in our party-scenario frame. This mandates attention to that assignment problem (and prepares us for a possible thematic concern; at least it does for me). In any case, we probably need a more active mechanism for understanding *wondered* that can apply the information currently in the frame to produce an expectation of what Jane will think about.

The third line of our story, about shaking the bank, should also eventually match one of the present-frame questions, but the unstated connection between Money and Piggy-Bank is presumably represented in the piggy-bank frame, not the party frame, although once it is found it will match our Get-Money question terminal. The primary functions and actions associated with piggy banks are Saving and Getting-Money-Out, and the latter has three principal methods:

1. Using a key. Most piggy banks don't offer this option.
2. Breaking it. Children hate this.
3. Shaking the money out or using a thin slider.

In the fourth line does one know specifically that a silent Piggy Bank is empty, and hence out of money (I think, yes) or does one use general knowledge that a hard container which makes no noise when shaken is empty? I have found quite a number of people to prefer the latter. Logically the "general principle" would suffice, but I feel that this misses the important point that a specific scenario of this character is engraved in every child's memory. The story is instantly intelligible to most readers. If more complex reasoning from general principles were required this would not be so, and more readers would surely go astray.

It is all too easy to find even more complex problems:

> A goat wandered into the yard where Jack was painting. The goat got the paint all over himself. When Mother saw the goat she asked, "Jack, did you do that?"

There is no one word or line, which is the referent of "that." It seems to refer, as Charniak notes, to "cause the goat to be covered with paint."

Charniak does not permit himself to make a specific proposal to handle this kind of problem, remarking only that his "demon" model would need a substantial extension to deal with such a poorly localized "thematic subject." Consider how much one has to know about our culture to realize that *that* is not the goat-in-the-yard but the goat-covered-with-paint. Charniak's thesis—basically a study rather than a debugged system—discusses issues about the activation, operation, and dismissal of expectation and default-knowledge demons. Many of his ideas have been absorbed into this essay.

I wish I could present a working hierarchy of how these different kinds of frameworks could be classified and organized into a system. In order of "scale," among the ingredients of such a structure there might be these kinds of levels:

Surface syntactic frames: Mainly verb cases. Prepositional and word-order indicator conventions.

Surface semantic frames: Deep syntactic frames perhaps. Action-centered meanings of words. Qualifiers and relations concerning participants, instruments, trajectories and strategies, goals, consequences and side-effects.

Thematic frames: Topics, activities, portraits, setting. Outstanding problems and strategies commonly connected with topic.

Narrative frames: Stories, explanations, and arguments. Conventions about foci, protagonists, plots, development, etc., with the purpose of causing the listener to construct a new Thematic Frame in his own mind.

In spite of this tentative character, I will try to summarize my image of language understanding, as somewhat parallel to seeing.

> The key words and ideas of a discourse evoke substantial thematic or scenario structures, drawn from memory with rich default assumptions. The individual statements of a discourse lead to temporary representations—which seem to correspond to what contemporary linguists call "deep structures"—which are then quickly rearranged or consumed in elaborating the growing scenario representation.
>
> A single sentence can assign terminals, attach subframes, apply a transformation, or cause a gross replacement of a high level frame (because a proposed assignment no longer fits well enough). A pronoun is comprehensible (only) when general linguistic conventions, interacting with defaults and specific indicators, determine a terminal or subframe of the current scenario.
>
> In vision the transformations usually have a simple group-like structure, in language we can expect more complex, less regular systems of frames. Nevertheless, because time, cause, and action are so important to us, we often use sequential transformation pairs that replace situations by their temporal or causal successors.
>
> Because syntactic structural rules direct the selection and assembly of the transient sentence frames, linguistic findings should help us understand how our frame systems are constructed. One might look for such structures specifically associated with assigning terminals, selecting emphasis or attention viewpoints (transformations), inserting sentential structures into thematic structures, and changing gross thematic representations.

Finally, just as there are familiar "basic plots" for stories, there must be basic superframes for discourses, arguments, narratives, and so forth. As with sentences, we should expect to find special linguistic indicators for operations concerning these larger structures; we should move beyond the grammar of sentences to try to find and systematize the linguistic conventions that, operating across wider spans, must be involved with assembling and transforming scenarios and plans.

6.2.8 Questions, Systems, and Cases

> Questions arise from a point of view—from something that helps to structure what is problematical, what is worth asking, and what constitutes an answer (or progress). It is not that the view determines reality, only what we accept from reality and how we structure it. I am realist enough to believe that in the long run reality gets its own chance to accept or reject our various views.
>
> —Newell, A.: Artificial Intelligence and the Concept of Mind, in R. C. Schank and K. M. Colby (eds.), "Computer Models of Thought and Language," 1973

Examination of linguistic discourse leads thus to a view of the frame concept in which the "terminals" serve to represent the questions most likely to arise in a situation. To make this important viewpoint more explicit, I will spell out this reinterpretation:

> A Frame is a collection of questions to be asked about a hypothetical situation; it specifies issues to be raised and methods to be used in dealing with them.

The terminals of a frame correspond perhaps to what Schank[32] calls "conceptual cases," although I do not think we should restrict them to so few types as Schank suggests. To understand a narrated or perceived action, one often feels compelled to ask such questions as

What caused it? (agent)
What was the purpose? (intention)
What are the consequences? (side effects)
Who does it affect? (recipient)
How is it done? (instrument)

The number of such "cases" or questions is problematical. While we would like to reduce meaning to a very few "primitive" concepts—perhaps in analogy to the situation in traditional linguistic analysis—I know of no reason to suppose that that goal can be achieved. My own inclination is to side with such workers as Martin,[33] who look toward very large collections of "primitives," annotated with comments about how they are related. Only time will tell which is better.

For entities other than actions one asks different questions; for thematic topics the questions may be much less localized, e.g.,

How can I find out more about this?
How will it help with the "real problem?"

In a "story" one asks what is the topic, what is the author's attitude, what is the main event, who are the protagonists and so on. As each question is given a tentative answer the corresponding subframes are attached and the questions they ask become active in turn.

The "markers" I proposed for vision frames become more complex in this view. If we adopt for the moment Newell's larger sense of "view", it is not enough simply to ask a question; one must indicate how it is to be answered. Thus a terminal should also contain (or point to) suggestions and recommendations about how to find an assignment. "Default" assignments then become the simplest special cases of such recommendations, and one certainly could have a hierarchy in which such proposals depend on features of the situation, perhaps along the lines of Wilks' "preference" structures.[27]

It is tempting to imagine varieties of frame systems that span from simple template-filling structures to implementations of the "views" of Newell—with all their implications about coherent generators of issues to be concerned with, ways to investigate them, and procedures for evaluating proposed solutions. But as I noted in Sec. 6.1.12, I feel uncomfortable about any superficially coherent synthesis in which one expects the same kind of theoretical framework to function well on many different levels of scale or concept. We should expect very different question-processing mechanisms to operate on our low-level stereotypes and on our most comprehensive strategic overviews.

6.3 LEARNING, MEMORY, AND PARADIGMS

> To the child, nature gives various means of rectifying any mistakes he may commit respecting the salutary or hurtful qualities of the objects which surround him. On every occasion his judgements are corrected by experience; want and pain are the necessary consequences arising from false judgement; gratification and pleasure are produced by judging aright. Under such masters, we cannot fail but to become well informed; and we soon learn to reason justly, when want and pain are the necessary consequences of a contrary conduct.
>
> In the study and practice of the sciences it is quite different; the false judgements we form neither affect our existence nor our welfare; and we are not forced by any physical necessity to correct them. Imagination, on the contrary, which is ever wandering beyond the bounds of truth, joined to self-love and that self-confidence we are so apt to indulge, prompt us to draw conclusions that are not immediately derived from facts. . . ."
>
> —Lavoisier, A.: "Elements of Chemistry," 1952

How does one locate a frame to represent a new situation? Obviously, we cannot begin any complete theory outside the context of some proposed global scheme for the organization of knowledge in general. But if we imagine working within some bounded domain we can discuss some important issues:

Expectation: How to select an initial frame to meet some given conditions?

Elaboration: How to select and assign subframes to represent additional details?

Alteration: How to find a frame to replace one that does not fit well enough?

Novelty: What to do if no acceptable frame can be found? Can we modify an old frame or must we build a new one?

Learning: What frames should be stored, or modified, as a result of the experience?

In popular culture, memory is seen as separate from the rest of thinking; but finding the right memory–it would be better to say: finding a *useful* memory–needs the same sorts of strategies used in other kinds of thinking! We say someone is "clever" who is unusually good at quickly locating highly appropriate frames. His information retrieval systems are better at making good hypotheses, formulating the conditions the new frame should meet, and exploiting knowledge gained in the "unsuccessful" part of the search. Finding the right memory is no less a problem than solving any other kind of puzzle!

Because of this, a good retrieval mechanism can be based only in part upon basic "innate" mechanisms. It must also depend largely on (learned) knowledge about the structure of one's own knowledge! Our proposal will combine several elements–a pattern matching process, a clustering theory, and a similarity network.

In seeing a room, or understanding a story, one assembles a network of frames and subframes. Everything noticed or guessed, rightly or wrongly, is represented in this network. We have already suggested that an active frame cannot be maintained unless its terminal conditions are satisfied. We now add the postulate that even the satisfied frames must be assigned to terminals of superior frames. This applies, as a special case, to any substantial fragments of "data" that have been observed and represented.

Of course, there must be an exception! We must allow a certain number of items to be attached to something like a set of "short term memory" registers. But the intention is that very little can be remembered unless embedded in a suitable frame. This, at any rate, is the conceptual scheme; in particular domains we would of course admit other kinds of memory "hooks" and special sensory buffers.

6.3.1 Requests to Memory

We can now imagine the memory system as driven by two complementary needs. On one side are items demanding to be properly represented by being embedded into larger frames; on the other side are incompletely-filled frames demanding terminal assignments. The rest of the system will try to placate these lobbyists, but not so much in accord with "general principles" as in accord with special knowledge and conditions imposed by the currently active goals.

When a frame encounters trouble–when an important condition cannot be satisfied–something must be done. We envision the following major kinds of accomodation to trouble.

Matching: When nothing more specific is found, we can attempt to use some "basic" associative memory mechanism. This will succeed by itself only in relatively simple situations, but should play a supporting role in the other tactics.

Excuse: An apparent misfit can often be excused or explained. A "chair" that meets all other conditions but is much too small could be a "toy."

Advice: The frame contains explicit knowledge about what to do about the trouble. Below, we describe an extensive learned "similarity network" in which to embed such knowledge.

Summary: If a frame cannot be completed or replaced, one must give it up. But first one must construct a well-formulated complaint or summary to help whatever process next becomes responsible for reassigning the subframes left in limbo.

In my view, all four of these are vitally important. I discuss them in the following sections.

6.3.2 Matching

When replacing a frame, we do not want to start all over again. How can we remember what was already "seen?" We consider here only the case in which the system has no specific knowledge about what to do and must resort to some "general" strategy. No completely general method can be very good, but if we could find a new frame that shares enough terminals with the old frame, then some of the common assignments can be retained, and we will probably do better than chance.

The problem can be formulated as follows: let E be the cost of losing a certain already assigned terminal and let F be the cost of being unable to assign some other terminal. If E is worse than F, then any new frame should retain the old subframe. Thus, given any sort of priority ordering on the terminals, a typical request for a new frame should include:

1. Find a frame with as many terminals in common with [a, b, . . . , z] as possible, where we list high priority terminals already assigned in the old frame.

But the frame being replaced is usually already a subframe of some other frame and must satisfy the markers of its attachment terminal, lest the entire structure be lost. This suggests another form of memory request, looking upward rather than downward:

2. Find or build a frame that has properties [a, b, . . . , z]

If we emphasize differences rather than absolute specifications, we can merge (1) and (2):

3. Find a frame that is like the old frame except for certain differences [a, b, . . . , z] between them.

One can imagine a parallel-search or hash-coded memory to handle (1) and (2) if the terminals or properties are simple atomic symbols. (There must be some such mechanism, in any case, to support a production-based program or some sort of pattern matcher.) Unfortunately, there are so many ways to do this that it implies no specific design requirements.

Although (1) and (2) are formally special cases of (3), they are different in practice because complicated cases of (3) require knowledge about differences. In fact (3) is too general to be useful as stated, and I will later propose to depend on specific, learned, knowledge about differences between pairs of frames rather than on broad, general principles.

It should be emphasized again that we must not expect magic. For difficult, novel problems a new representation structure will have to be constructed, and this will require application of both general and special knowledge. The paper of Freeman and Newell[34] discusses the problem of design of structures. That paper complements this one in an important dimension, for it discusses how to make a structure that satisfies a collection of functional requirements–conditions related to satisfying goals–in addition to conditions on containment of specified substructures and symbols.

6.3.3 Excuses

We can think of a frame as describing an "ideal." If an ideal does not match reality because it is "basically" wrong, it must be replaced. But it is in the nature of ideals that they are really elegant simplifications; their attractiveness derives from their simplicity, but their real power depends upon additional knowledge about interactions between them! Accordingly we need not abandon an ideal because of a failure to substantiate it, provided one can explain the discrepancy in terms of such an interaction. Here are some examples in which such an "excuse" can save a failing match:

Occlusion: A table, in a certain view, should have four legs, but a chair might occlude one of them. One can look for things like T-joints and shadows to support such an excuse.

Functional variant: A chair-leg is usually a stick, geometrically; but more important, it is functionally a support. Therefore, a strong center post, with an adequate base plate, should be an acceptable replacement for all the legs. Many objects are multiple purpose and need functional rather than physical descriptions.

Broken: A visually missing component could be explained as in fact physically missing, or it could be broken. Reality has a variety of ways to frustrate ideals.

Parasitic contexts: An object that is just like a chair, except in size, could be (and probably is) a toy chair. The complaint "too small" could often be so interpreted in contexts with other things too small, children playing, peculiarly large "grain," and so forth.

In most of those examples, the kinds of knowledge to make the repair—and thus salvage the current frame—are "general" enough usually to be attached to the thematic context of a superior frame. In the remainder of this essay, I will concentrate on types of more sharply localized knowledge that would naturally be attached to a frame itself for recommending its own replacement.

6.3.4 Advice and Similarity Networks

> The justification of Napoleon's statement—if, indeed he ever made it—that those who form a picture of everything are unfit to command, is to be found in the first of these defects. A commander who approaches a battle with a picture before him of how such and such a fight went on such and such an occasion, will find, two minutes after the forces have joined, that something has gone awry. Then his picture is destroyed. He has nothing in reserve except another individual picture and this also will not serve him for long. Or it may be that when his first pictured forecast is found to be inapplicable, he has so multifarious and pressing a collection of pictures that equally he is at a loss what practical adjustment to make. Too great individuality of past reference may be very nearly as embarrassing as no individuality of past reference at all. To serve adequately the demands of a constantly changing environment, we have not only to pick items out of their general setting, but we must know what parts of them may flow and alter without disturbing their general significance and functions.
>
> —Bartlett, F. C.: "Remembering: A study in Experimental and Social Psychology," 1932 (revised 1961)

In moving about a familiar house, we already know a dependable structure for "information retrieval" of room frames. When we move through Door D, in Room X, we expect to enter Room Y (assuming D is not the exit). We could represent this as an action transformation of the simplest kind, consisting of pointers between pairs of room frames of a particular house system.

When the house is not familiar, a "logical" strategy might be to move up a level of classification: when you leave one room, you may not know which room you are entering, but you usually know that it is some room. Thus, one can partially evade lack of specific information by dealing with classes—and one has to use some form of abstraction or generalization to escape the dilemma of Bartlett's commander.

In some sense the use of classes is inescapable; when specific information is unavailable, one turns to classes as a "first-order" theory underlying any more sophisticated model. Fortunately, it is not necessary to use classes explicitly; indeed, that leads to trouble! While "class," taken literally or mathematically, forces one into an inclusion-based hierarchy, "concepts" are interrelated in different ways when in different contexts, and no single hierarchical ordering is generally satisfactory for all goals. This observation holds also for procedures and for frames. We do not want to be committed to an inflexible, inclusion-oriented classification of knowledge.

Winston's thesis[8b] proposes a way to construct a retrieval system that can represent classes but has additional flexibility. His retrieval pointers can be made to represent goal requirements and action effects as well as class memberships. Because the idea is not well-known, I will explain it by elaborating an example sketched in his thesis:

> What does it mean to expect a chair? Typically, four legs, some assortment of rungs, a level seat, an upper back, One expects also certain relations between these "parts." The legs must be below the seat, the back above. The legs must be supported by the floor. The seat must be horizontal, the back vertical, and so forth.
>
> Now suppose that this description does not match; the vision system finds four legs, a level plane, but no back. The "difference" between what we expect and what we see is "too few backs." This suggests not a chair, but a table or a bench.

Winston proposes pointers from each description in memory to other descriptions, with each pointer labelled by a difference marker. Complaints about mismatch are matched to the difference pointers leaving the frame and thus may propose a better candidate frame. Winston calls the resulting structure a similarity network. (See Fig. 6.12.)

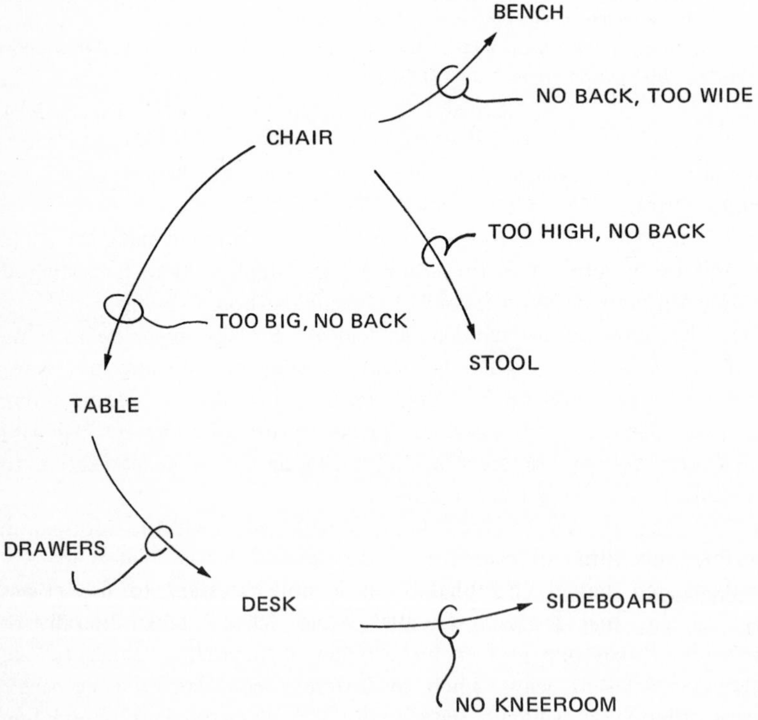

Fig. 6.12

Winston proposes, incidentally, that a machine might spend idle time in an orderly comparison of various models in memory with one another. Whenever it finds few important differences between a pair, it inserts difference pointers for them.

But difference information becomes available also in any attempt to match a situation with memory, as successive attempts yield models that are generally similar but have specific, describable differences. Thus, instead of wasting this information one can use it to make the similarity network structure grow in the course of normal use of memory. If this pointer-building procedure is sensible about recording differences "relevant" to achieving goals, the result will be so much the more useful, and we have a mechanism for learning from experience.

Is a similarity network practical? At first sight, there might seem to be a danger of unconstrained growth of memory. If there are N frames, and K kinds of differences, then there could be as many as $K \times N \times N$ interframe pointers. One might fear the following consequences:

1. If N is large, say 10^7, then $N \times N$ is very large–of the order of 10^{14}–which might be impractical, at least for human memory.
2. There might be so many pointers for a given difference and a given frame that the system will not be selective enough to be useful.
3. K itself might be very large if the system is sensitive to many different kinds of issues.

Actually, none of these problems seem really serious in connection with human memory. According to contemporary opinions (admittedly, not very conclusive) about the rate of storage into human long-term memory there are probably not enough seconds in a lifetime to cause a saturation problem.

In regard to (2), most pairs of frames that make up the $N \times N$ term should be so different that no plausible comparison mechanism should consider inserting any pointers at all between them. As Winston notes, only a "near miss" is likely to be of much value. Certainly, excessive reliance on undiscriminating differences will lead to confusion.

So the real problem, paradoxically, is that there will be too few connections! One cannot expect to have enough time to fill out the network to saturation. Given two frames that should be linked by a difference, we cannot count on that pointer being there; the problem may not have occurred before. However, in the next section we see how to partially escape this problem.

6.3.5 Clusters, Classes, and a Geographic Analogy

Though a discussion of some of the attributes shared by a number of games or chairs or leaves often helps us to learn how to employ the corresponding term, there is no set of characteristics that is simultaneously applicable to all members of

> the class and to them alone. Instead, confronted with a previously unobserved activity, we apply the term "game" because what we are seeing bears a close "family resemblance" to a number of the activities we have previously learned to call by that name. For Wittgenstein, in short, games, chairs, and leaves are natural families, each constituted by a network of overlapping and crisscross resemblances. The existence of such a network sufficiently accounts for our success in identifying the corresponding object or activity.
>
> –Kuhn, T.: "The Structure of Scientific Revolutions," 1970

To make the similarity network act more "complete," consider the following analogy. In a city, any person should be able to visit any other; but we do not build a special road between each pair of houses; we place a group of houses on a "block." We do not connect roads between each pair of blocks; but have them share streets. We do not connect each town to every other; but construct main routes, connecting the centers of larger groups. Within such an organization, each member has direct links to some other individuals at his own "level," mainly to nearby, highly similar ones; but each individual has also at least a few links to "distinguished" members of higher level groups. The result is that there is usually a rather short sequence between any two individuals, if one can but find it.

To locate something in such a structure, one uses a hierarchy like the one implicit in a mail address. Everyone knows something about the largest categories, in that he knows where the major cities are. An inhabitant of a city knows the nearby towns, and people in the towns know the nearby villages. No person knows all the individual routes between pairs of houses; but, for a particular friend, one may know a special route to his home in a nearby town that is better than going to the city and back. Directories factor the problem, basing paths on standard routes between major nodes in the network. Personal shortcuts can bypass major nodes and go straight between familiar locations. Although the standard routes are usually not quite the very best possible, our stratified transport and communication services connect everything together reasonably well, with comparatively few connections.

At each level, the aggregates usually have distinguished foci or capitols. These serve as elements for clustering at the next level of aggregation. There is no nonstop airplane service between New Haven and San Jose because it is more efficient overall to share the "trunk" route between New York and San Francisco, which are the capitols at that level of aggregation.

As our memory networks grow, we can expect similar aggregations of the destinations of our similarity pointers. Our decisions about what we consider to be primary or "trunk" difference features and which are considered subsidiary will have large effects on our abilities. Such decisions eventually accumulate to become epistemological commitments about the "conceptual" cities of our mental universe.

The nonrandom convergences and divergences of the similarity pointers, for each difference **d**, thus tend to structure our conceptual world around

1. the aggregation into **d**-clusters
2. the selection of **d**-capitols

Note that it is perfectly all right to have several capitols in a cluster, so that there need be no one attribute common to them all. The "crisscross resemblances" of Wittgenstein are then consequences of the local connections in our similarity network, which are surely adequate to explain how we can feel as though we know what is a chair or a game—yet cannot always define it in a "logical" way as an element in some class-hierarchy or by any other kind of compact, formal, declarative rule. The apparent coherence of the conceptual aggregates need not reflect explicit definitions, but can emerge from the success-directed sharpening of the difference-describing processes.

The selection of capitols corresponds to selecting stereotypes or typical elements whose default assignments are unusually useful. There are many forms of chairs, for example, and one should choose carefully the chair-description frames that are to be the major capitols of chair-land. These are used for rapid matching and assigning priorities to the various differences. The lower priority features of the cluster center then serve either as default properties of the chair types or, if more realism is required, as dispatch pointers to the local chair villages and towns. Difference pointers could be "functional" as well as geometric. Thus, after rejecting a first try at "chair" one might try the functional idea of "something one can sit on" to explain an unconventional form. This requires a deeper analysis in terms of forces and strengths. Of course, that analysis would fail to capture toy chairs, or chairs of such ornamental delicacy that their actual use would be unthinkable. These would be better handled by the method of excuses, in which one would bypass the usual geometrical or functional explanations in favor of responding to contexts involving art or play.

It is important to reemphasize that there is no reason to restrict the memory structure to a single hierarchy; the notions of "level" of aggregation need not coincide for different kinds of differences. The **d**-capitols can exist, not only by explicit declarations, but also implicitly by their focal locations in the structure defined by convergent **d**-pointers. (In the Newell-Simon GPS framework, the "differences" are ordered into a fixed hierarchy. By making the priorities depend on the goal, the same memories could be made to serve more purposes; the resulting problem-solver would lose the elegance of a single, simply-ordered measure of "progress," but that is the price of moving from a first-order theory.)

Finally, we should point out that we do not need to invoke any mysterious additional mechanism for creating the clustering structure. Developmentally, one would assume, the earliest frames would tend to become the capitols of their later relatives, unless this is firmly prevented by experience. For, each time the use of one stereotype is reasonably successful, its centrality is reinforced by another pointer from somewhere else. Otherwise, the acquisition of new centers is in large measure forced upon us from the outside: by the words available in one's language; by the behavior of objects in one's environment; by what one is told by one's teachers, family, and general culture. Of course, at each step the structure of the previous structure dominates the acquisition of the latter. But in any case such forms and clusters should emerge from the interactions between the world and almost any memory-using mechanism; it would require more explanation were they not found!

6.3.6 Analogies and Alternative Descriptions

We have discussed the use of different frames of the same system to describe the same situation in different ways: for change of position in vision and for change of emphasis in language. In the wolf and lamb episode, for example, two frames are used in a before-after situation pair. Sometimes, in "problem-solving" we use two or more descriptions in a more complex way to construct an analogy or to apply two radically different kinds of analysis to the same situation. For hard problems, one "problem space" is usually not enough!

Suppose your car battery runs down. You believe that there is an electricity shortage and blame the generator.

The generator can be represented as a mechanical system: the rotor has a pulley wheel driven by a belt from the engine. Is the belt tight enough? Is it even there? The output, seen mechanically, is a cable to the battery or whatever. Is it intact? Are the bolts tight? Are the brushes pressing on the commutator?

Seen electrically, the generator is described differently. The rotor is seen as a flux-linking coil, rather than as a rotating device. The brushes and commutator are seen as electrical switches. The output is current along a pair of conductors leading from the brushes through control circuits to the battery.

We thus represent the situation in two quite different frame-systems. In one, the armature is a mechanical rotor with pulley, in the other it is a conductor in a changing magnetic field. The same—or analogous—elements share terminals of different frames, and the frame-transformations apply only to some of them.

The differences between the two frames are substantial. The entire mechanical chassis of the car plays the simple role, in the electrical frame, of one of the battery connections. The diagnostician has to use both representations. A failure of current to flow often means that an intended conductor is not acting like one. For this case, the basic transformation between the frames depends on the fact that electrical continuity is in general equivalent to firm mechanical attachment. Therefore, any conduction disparity revealed by electrical measurements should make us look for a corresponding disparity in the mechanical frame. In fact, since "repair" in this universe is synonymous with "mechanical repair," the diagnosis must end in the mechanical frame.

Eventually, we might locate a defective mechanical junction and discover a loose connection, corrosion, wear, or whatever.

Why have two separate frames, rather than one integrated structure to represent the generator? I believe that in such a complex problem one can never cope with many details at once. At each moment one must work within a reasonably simple framework. I contend that any problem that a person can solve at all is worked out at each moment in a small context and that the key operations in problem solving are concerned with finding or constructing these working environments.

Indeed, finding an electrical fault requires moving between at least three frames: a visual one along with the electrical and mechanical frames. If electrical evidence suggests a loose mechanical connection, one needs a visual frame to guide himself to the mechanical fault.

Are there general methods for constructing adequate frames? The answer is both yes and no! There are some often-useful strategies for adapting old frames to new purposes; but I should emphasize that humans certainly have no magical way to solve all hard problems! One must not fall into what Papert calls the Superhuman-Human Fallacy and require a theory of human behavior to explain even things that people cannot really do!

One cannot expect to have a frame exactly right for any problem or expect always to be able to invent one. But we do have a good deal to work with, and it is important to remember the contribution of one's culture in assessing the complexity of problems people seem to solve. The experienced mechanic need not routinely invent; he already has engine representations in terms of ignition, lubrication, cooling, timing, fuel mixing, transmission, compression, and so forth. Cooling, for example, is already subdivided into fluid circulation, air flow, thermostasis, etc. Most "ordinary" problems are presumably solved by systematic use of the analogies provided by the transformations between pairs of these structures. The huge network of knowledge, acquired from school, books, apprenticeship or whatever, is interlinked by difference and relevancy pointers. No doubt the culture imparts a good deal of this structure by its conventional use of the same words in explanations of different views of a subject.

What about interactions that cross many of these boundaries? A Gestalt philosopher might demand some kind of synthesis in which one sees the engine as a whole. But before we demand a general solution, we should remind ourselves that for faults that stem from three-or-more interacting elements, a human auto mechanic will diagnose them, if at all, only after expensive, exhaustive replacement of many innocent components. Thus, the desire for complete synthesis is probably a chimera, and should not be a theoretical requirement. To be sure, there must indeed be some structure linking together the different conceptual engine frames. But this, too, may be relatively simple. Perhaps one must add a fourth engine-superframe whose terminals point to the various electrical, mechanical, and visual representation frames and are themselves interconnected by pointers describing when and how the different subframes are to be used. Presumably every complicated system that is "understood" contains some superframe structures that direct the utilization of subframes.

Incidentally, it is tempting in our culture to believe that a larger view is taken in our subconscious minds. As Poincaré observes, one often comes upon a sudden illumination after a period of conscious formulation, followed by a much longer period of nonconscious activity. I read his further discussion as proposing that the unconscious activity is a combinatorial heuristic search in which the chance of success depends mainly on the quality of the ingredients introduced by the preliminary conscious analysis; these elements are combined in different ways until a configuration is reached that passes some sort of test.

> I have spoken of the feeling of absolute certitude accompanying the inspiration . . . ; often this feeling deceives us without being any the less vivid, and we only find it out when we seek to put on foot the demonstrations. I have especially noticed this fact in regard to ideas coming to me in the morning or evening in bed while in a self-hypnagogic state.
>
> –Poincaré, H.: "The Foundations of Science," 1946

The inspirational product is thus not a fully detailed solution but a "point of departure" or plan, brought to consciousness because it has passed some sort of threshold of "esthetic sensibility."

On this last point Poincaré does indeed seem to subscribe to a holistic conception for he characterizes "elegant" mathematical entities as those "whose elements are so harmoniously disposed that the mind can embrace their totality while realizing the details." It remains to be seen whether the filters that admit new descriptive combinations to the status of fully conscious attention require a complex, active analysis or can be explained by simpler matching and retrieval operations. (It is an unhappy fact that mathematicians have not contributed much to understanding the mechanisms of problem-solving, with the exception of Poincaré, Polya, and a few others. I wonder if this is not largely due to their attachment to the concept of "elegance," passed from one generation to the next as an intangible quality, worshipped but not explained or analyzed.) In any case, I see no reason to suppose that the unconscious is distinguished either along the dimension of massive parallel computation or by extraordinary holistic synthesis. A more plausible function would seem to be rapid, shallow exploration using material prepared by earlier analysis. The unconscious aspect might only reflect the lack of "annotation" and record-keeping that would make the process otherwise accessible to review and analysis. But the question about the complexity of the acceptance filter certainly still stands.

6.3.7 Summaries: Using Frames in Heuristic Search

Over the past decade, it has become widely recognized how important are the details of the representation of a "problem space"; but it was not so well recognized that descriptions can be useful to a program, as well as to the person writing the program. Perhaps progress was actually retarded by ingenious schemes to avoid explicit manipulation of descriptions. Especially in "theorem-proving" and in "game-playing" the dominant paradigm of the past might be schematized as follows:

> The central goal of a theory of problem-solving is to find systematic ways to reduce the extent of the search through the problem space.

Sometimes a simple problem is indeed solved by trying a sequence of "methods" until one is found to work. Some harder problems are solved by a sequence of local improvements, by "hill-climbing" within the problem space. But even when this solves a particular problem, it tells us little about the problem-space; hence yielding no improved future competence. The best-developed technology of heuristic search is that of game-playing using tree-pruning, plausible-move generation, and terminal-evaluation methods. But even those systems that use hierarchies of symbolic goals do not improve their understanding or refine their representations. I now propose a more mature and powerful paradigm:

> The primary purpose in problem solving should be better to understand the problem space, to find representations within which the problems are easier to solve. The purpose of search is to get information for this reformulation, not—as is usually assumed—to find solutions; once the space is adequately understood, solutions to problems will more easily be found.

In particular, I reject the idea that the value of an intellectual experiment should be assessed along the dimension of success-partial success-failure, or in terms of "improving the situation" or "reducing a difference." An application of a "method," or a reconfiguration of a representation can be valuable if it leads to a way to improve the strategy of subsequent trials. Earlier formulations of the role of heuristic search strategies did not emphasize these possibilities, although they are implicit in discussions of "planning."

How can the new paradigm be combined with the classical minimax strategy? In a typical episode, one is located at a certain node A in the search tree, and examines two or more possible moves, say, B and C. Each of these is somehow evaluated to yield values V(B) and V(C). Then these are somehow combined to yield a score

$$S(A) = Mm[V(B), V(C)]$$

where Mm is some function that takes two numbers and yields one. In effect, Mm has to summarize the results of all the search below A and compress them into a single numerical quantity to represent the value of being at node A.

Now, what is the purpose of this? If one were able to search the entire game-tree, we could use S at each node to decide which move is best to make.

Since we cannot search the whole tree, we need information about what next to explore; we want S to tell the move generator what kinds of moves to consider. But if S is a mere number, this is unsuitable for much reasoning or analysis.

If S(B) has a low value, we can assume that B is a bad position. But if we want the move generator not to make the "same kind of mistake" again, the message must contain some additional clue about why B is weak—or better, what to do about it. So we really need a summary explanation of what was found in the search; and since we are in a tree we need further to summarize such summaries recursively.

There is a problem here we might call "summary-divergence." If the summary of the situation at A contains (in general) any explicit mention of B and C, then any recursive description scheme is in danger of containing an explicit copy of the entire move-tree; then to answer a question one might have nearly as bad a time searching the summary as the game-tree itself. One way to prevent this is simply to limit the size of the summary. However, we can avoid such drastic knowledge-destruction; in a frame-description, the important features and relations at the top levels can serve as summaries while the lower-level subsidiary descriptions can be accessed only if necessary. How much of the whole analysis tree remains in long term memory, and how much is left as garbage after the move is made would depend on other aspects of how the game-player uses his general experience.

How are the summaries to be made? Again, the frame idea suggests a flexible approach. Instead of demanding a rigid format, we could build up a collection of ad hoc "summary" frames, each evoked when their terminals fit subordinate descriptions and its frame-markers match the current goals. Thus each does its job when appropriate. For example, one might have a variety of "fork" frames. If a Knight lands on a square that threatens both check and rook capture, a fork frame is activated by its condition that in each of only two plausible moves, the unmoved piece is lost. Once this frame is activated it can make a specific recommendation, perhaps that the generator for the forked player see if a previously available move can apply the additional defense to the forking square.

6.3.8 Frames as Paradigms

> Until that scholastic paradigm [the medieval "impetus" theory] was invented, there were no pendulums, but only swinging stones, for scientists to see. Pendulums were brought into the world by something very like a paradigm-induced gestalt switch.
>
> Do we, however, really need to describe what separates Galileo from Aristotle, or Lavoisier from Priestly, as a transformation of vision? Did these men really see different things when looking at the same sorts of objects? Is there any legitimate sense in which we can say they pursued their research in different worlds?
>
> [I am] acutely aware of the difficulties created by saying that when Aristotle and Galileo looked at swinging stones, the first saw constrained fall, the

> second a pendulum. Nevertheless, I am convinced that we must learn to make sense of sentences that at least resemble these.
>
> –Kuhn, T.: "The Structure of Scientific Revolutions," 1970

According to Kuhn's model of scientific evolution "normal" science proceeds by using established descriptive schemes. Major changes result from new "paradigms," new ways of describing things that lead to new methods and techniques. Eventually there is a redefining of "normal."

Now while Kuhn prefers to apply his own very effective redescription paradigm at the level of major scientific revolutions, it seems to me that the same idea applies as well to the microcosm of everyday thinking. Indeed, in that last sentence quoted, we see that Kuhn is seriously considering the paradigms to play a substantive rather than metaphorical role in visual perception, just as we have proposed for frames.

Whenever our customary viewpoints do not work well, whenever we fail to find effective frame systems in memory, we must construct new ones that bring out the right features. Presumably, the most usual way to do this is to build some sort of pair-system from two or more old ones and then edit or debug it to suit the circumstances. How might this be done? It is tempting to formulate it in terms of constructing a frame-system with certain properties. This appears to simplify the problem by dividing it into two stages: first formulate the requirements and then solve the construction problem.

But that is certainly not the usual course of ordinary thinking! Neither are requirements formulated all at once, nor is the new system constructed entirely by deliberate preplanning. Instead we recognize unsatisfied requirements, one by one, as deficiencies or "bugs," in the course of a sequence of modifications made to an unsatisfactory representation.

I think Papert[35,36] is correct in believing that the ability to diagnose and modify one's own procedures is a collection of specific and important "skills." Debugging, a fundamentally important component of intelligence, has its own special techniques and procedures. Every normal person is pretty good at them or otherwise he would not have learned to see and talk! Although this essay is already speculative, I would like to point here to the theses of Goldstein[37] and Sussman[38] about the explicit use of knowledge about debugging in learning symbolic representations. They build new procedures to satisfy multiple requirements by elementary but powerful techniques:

1. Make a crude first attempt by the first order method of simply putting together procedures that separately achieve the individual goals.
2. If something goes wrong, try to characterize one of the defects as a specific (and undesirable) kind of interaction between two procedures.
3. Apply a "debugging technique" that, according to a record in memory, is good at repairing that specific kind of interaction.
4. Summarize the experience to add to the "debugging techniques library" in memory.

These might seem simpleminded, but if the new problem is not too radically different from the old ones, then they have a good chance to work, especially if one picks out the right first-order approximations. If the new problem is radically different, one should not expect any learning theory to work well. Without a structured cognitive map—without the "near misses" of Winston, or a cultural supply of good training sequences of problems—we should not expect radically new paradigms to appear magically whenever we need them.

What are "kinds of interactions," and what are "debugging techniques"? The simplest, perhaps, are those in which the result of achieving a first goal interferes with some condition prerequisite for achieving a second goal. The simplest repair is to reinsert that prerequisite as a new condition. There are examples in which this technique alone cannot succeed because a prerequisite for the second goal is incompatible with the first. Sussman presents a more sophisticated diagnosis and repair method that recognizes this and exchanges the order of the goals. Goldstein considers related problems in a multiple description context.

If asked about important future lines of research on artificial or natural intelligence, I would point to the interactions between these ideas and the problems of using multiple representations to deal with the same situation from several viewpoints. To carry out such a study, we need better ideas about interactions among the transformed relationships. Here the frame-system idea by itself begins to show limitations. Fitting together new representations from parts of old ones is clearly a complex process itself, and one that could be solved within the framework of our theory (if at all) only by an intricate bootstrapping. This, too, is surely a special skill with its own techniques. I consider it a crucial component of a theory of intelligence.

6.4 CONTROL

I have said little about the processes that manipulate frame systems. This is not the place to discuss long-duration management of thought involving such problems as controlling a large variety of types of goals, sharing time between chronic and acute concerns, or regulating allocation of energy, storage, and other resources.

Over much smaller time spans (call them episodes) I imagine that thinking and understanding, be it perceptual or problem-solving, is usually concerned with finding and instantiating a frame. This breaks large problems down into many small jobs to be done and raises all the usual issues about heuristic programming, the following for example:

Top-down or lateral: Should one make a pass over all the terminals first, or should one attempt a complete, detailed instantiation of some supposedly most critical one? In fact, neither policy is uniformly good. One should usually "look before leaping," but there must be pathways through which an interesting or unexpected event can invoke a subframe to be processed immediately.

Central control: Should a frame, once activated, "take over" and control its instantiation, or should a central process organize the operation. Again, no uniform strategy is entirely adequate. No "demon" or other local process can know enough about the overall situation to make good decisions; but no top-level manager can know enough details either.

Perhaps both issues can be resolved by something involving the idea of "back-off" proposed to me by William Martin in contrast to "back-up" as a strategy for dealing with errors and failures. One cannot either release control to subsidiaries or keep it at the top, so we need some sort of interpreter that has access both to the top level goals and to the operation of the separate "demons." In any case, one cannot ask for a uniform strategy; different kinds of terminals require different kinds of processes. Instantiating a wall terminal of a room-frame invites finding and filling a lower level wall subframe, while instantiating a door terminal invites attaching another room frame to the superior house frame. To embed in each frame expectations about such matters, each terminal could point to instructions for the interpreter about how to collect the information it needs and how to complain about difficulties or surprises.

In any case, the frame-filling process ought to combine at least the components of decision tree and demon activation processes: in a decision tree control depends on results of tests. A particular room frame, once accepted, might test for a major feature of a wall. Such tests would work through a tree of possible wall frames, the tree structure providing a convenient nonlinear ordering for deciding which default assignments can remain and which need attention.

In a demon model, several terminals of an evoked frame activate "demons" for noticing things. A round object high on a center wall (or elliptical on a side wall) suggests a clock, to be confirmed by finding an appropriate number, mark, or radial line. If not so confirmed, the viewer would have "seen" the clock but would be unable to describe it in detail. An eye-level trapezoid could indicate a picture or a window; here further analysis is usually mandatory.

The goal of seeing is not a fixed requirement to find what is out there in the world; it is subordinate to answering questions by combining exterior visual evidence with expectations generated by internal processes. Nevertheless, most questions require us in any case to know our orientation with respect to our immediate surroudings. Therefore a certain amount of "default" processing can proceed without any special question or goal. We clearly need a compromise in which a weak default ordering of terminals to be filled is easily superseded when any demon encounters a surprise.

In the "productions" of Newell and Simon,[2] the control structure is implicit in the sequential arrangement (in some memory) of the local behavior statements. In systems like the CONNIVER language[39] there are explicit higher-level control structures, but a lot still depends on which production-like assertions are currently in active memory and this control is not explicit. Both systems feature a high degree of local procedural control. Anything "noticed" is matched to an "antecedant pattern" which evokes another subframe, attaches it, and executes some of its processes.

There remains a problem. Processes common to many systems ought to be centralized, both for economy and for sharing improvements that result from debugging. Too much autonomy makes it hard for the whole system to be properly responsive to central, high level goals.

The next section proposes one way such conflicts might possibly be resolved. A frame is envisioned as a "packet" of data and processes and so are the high level goals. When a frame is proposed, its packet is added to the current program "environment" so that its processes have direct access to what they need to know, without being choked by access to the entire knowledge of the whole system. It remains to be seen how to fill in the details of this scheme and how well it will work.

I should explain at this point that this manuscript took shape, over more than a year, in the form of a file in the experimental ARPA computer network—the manuscript resided at various times in two different M.I.T. computers and one at Stanford, freely accessible to students and colleagues. A graduate student, Scott Fahlman, read an early draft before it contained a control scheme. Later, as part of a thesis proposal, Fahlman presented a control plan that seemed substantially better than my own, which he had not seen, and the next section is taken from his proposal. Several terms are used differently, but this should cause no problem.

Frame Verfication

by Scott Fahlman

"I envision a data base in which related sets of facts and demons are grouped into packets, any number of which can be activated or made available for access at once. A packet can contain any number of other packets (recursively), in the sense that if the containing packet is activated, the contained packets are activated as well, and any data items in them become available unless they are specifically modified or cancelled. Thus, by activating a few appropriate packets, the system can create a tailor-made execution environment containing only the relevant portion of its global knowledge and an appropriate set of demons. Sometimes, of course, it will have to add specific new packets to the active set in order to deal with some special situation, but this inconvenience will be far less than the burden of constantly tripping over unwanted knowledge or triggering spurious demons.

"The frame begins the verification process by checking any sample features that it already has on hand—features that arrived in the first wave or were obtained while testing previous hypotheses. Then, if the hypothesis has not already been accepted or rejected, the frame begins asking questions to get more information about features of the sample. The nature of these questions will vary according to the problem domain: A doctor program might order some lab tests. A vision program might look more closely. Sometimes a question will recursively start another recognition process: 'This might be a cow—see if that part is an udder.'

"The order in which the questions are asked is determined by auxiliary information in the frame. This information indicates which features are the most critical in the verfication at hand, how these priorities might be affected by information already present, and how much each question will cost to answer. As each new feature of the sample is established, its description is added to a special packet of information about the sample, along with some indication of where the information came from and how reliable it is. This packet can be taken along if the system moves to another hypothesis. Sometimes unsolicited information will be noticed along the way; it, too, is tested and thrown into the pot.

"Of course, the system will practically never get a perfect match to any of its ideal exemplars. Auxiliary frame information will indicate for each expected type of violation whether it should be considered trivial, serious, or fatal (in the sense that it decisively rules out the current frame). Continuously variable features such as size, body proportions, or blood pressure will have a range of normal variation indicated, along with a mapping from other ranges into seriousness values. Sometimes a feature will provide no real evidence for or against a hypothesis, but can be explained by it; this, too, is noted in the frame. If there are striking or conspicuous features in the sample (antlers, perhaps) that are not mentioned in the current frame, the system will usually consider these to be serious violations; such features are evaluated according to information stored in a packet associated with the feature, since the hypothesis frame clearly cannot mention every feature not present in the exemplar.

"Occasionally a feature will have a strong confirming effect: If you see it, you can stop worrying about whether you are in the right place. Usually, though, we will not be so lucky as to have a decisive test. The normal procedure, then, is to gather in sample features until either some satisfaction level is reached and the hypothesis is accepted or until a clear violation or the weight of several minor violations sends the system off in search of something better. (My current image of the satisfaction level is as some sort of numerical score, with each matched feature adding a few points and each trivial mismatch removing a few. Perhaps some more complex symbolic scheme will be needed for this, but right now I do not see why.) The satisfaction level can vary considerably, according to the situation: The most cursory glance will convince me that my desk is still in my office, while a unicorn or a thousand dollar bill will rate a very close inspection before being accepted.

"Sometimes the sample will appear to fit quite well into some category, but there will be one or two serious violations. In such a case the system will consider possible excuses for the discrepancies: Perhaps the cow is purple because someone has painted it. Perhaps the patient doesn't have the expected high blood pressure because he is taking some drug to suppress it. If a discrepancy can be satisfactorily explained away, the system can accept the hypothesis after all. Of course, if the discrepancies suggest something else, the system will try that first and resort to excuses only if the new hypothesis is no better. Sometimes two categories will be so close together that they can only be told apart by some special test or by paying particular attention to some otherwise insignificant detail. It is a simple enough matter for both of the frames to include a warning of the similarity and a set of instructions for making the discrimination. In medicine, such testing is called differential diagnosis.

"Note that this use of exemplars gives the system an immense flexibility in dealing with noisy, confused, and unanticipated situations. A cow may formally be a large quadruped, but our system would have little trouble dealing with a three-legged cow amputee, as long as it is a reasonably good cow in most other respects. (A missing leg is easy to explain; an extra one is somewhat more difficult.) If the system is shown something that fits none of its present categories, it can at least indicate what the sample is close to, along with some indication of the major deviations from that category. A visual system organized along these lines might easily come up with 'like a person, only 80 feet tall and green' or 'a woman from the waist up and a tuna fish from the waist down.' Under certain circumstances, such descriptions might serve as the nuclei of new recognition frames representing legitimate, though unnamed, conceptual categories.

"An important feature of recognition frames (and of the recognition categories they represent) is that they can be organized into hierarchies. The system can thus hypothesize at many levels, from the very general to the very specific: An animal of some sort, a medium-sized quadruped, a dog, a collie, Lassie. Each level has its own recognition frame, but the frames of the more specific hypotheses include the information packets of the more general frames above them; thus, if the system is working under the 'dog' frame, the information in the 'animal' frame is available as well. A specific frame may, of course, indicate exceptions to the more general information: The 'platypus' frame would include the information in 'mammal,' but it would have to cancel the parts about live birth of young. Often a general frame will use one of the specific cases below it as its exemplar; 'mammal' might simply use 'dog' or 'cow' as its exemplar, rather than trying to come up with some schematic model of an ideal nonspecific mammal. In such a case, the only difference between hypothesizing 'mammal' and 'cow' would be a somewhat greater reluctance to move to another mammal in the latter case; the system would test the same things in either case.

"Note that there can be many different hierarchical networks, and that these can overlap and tangle together in interesting ways: A komodo dragon is taxonomically a reptile, but its four-legged shape and its habits are closer to a dog's than to a snake's. How to represent these entanglements and what to do about them are problems that will require some further thought. Some frames are parasitic: Their sole purpose is to attach themselves to other frames and alter the effects of those frames. (Perhaps 'viral' would be a better term.) 'Statue-of' might attach to a frame like 'cow' to wipe out its animal properties of motion and material (beef), while leaving its shape properties intact. 'Mythical' could be added to animal to make flying, disappearance, and the speaking of riddles in Latin more plausible, but actual physical presence less so. Complications could be grafted onto a disease using this mechanism. There is nothing to prevent more than one parasite at a time from attaching to a frame, as long as the parasites are not hopelessly contradictory; one could, for instance, have a statue of a mythical animal."

6.5 SPATIAL IMAGERY

6.5.1 Places and Headings

We normally imagine ourselves moving within a stationary spatial setting. The world does not recede when we advance; it does not spin when we turn! At my desk I am aware of a nearby river whose direction I think of as north although I know that this is off by many degrees, assimilated years ago from a truer north at another location on the same river. This sense of direction permeates the setting; the same "north" is constant through one's house and neighborhood, and every fixed object has a definite heading.

Besides a heading, every object has a place. We are less positive about the relations between places from one room to another. This is partly because heading is computationally simpler but also because (in rectangular rooms) headings transfer directly whereas "place" requires metric calculations.

In unfamiliar surroundings, some people deal much less capriciously than others with headings. One person I know regularly and accurately relates himself to true compass direction. He is never lost in a new city. Only a small part of this is based on better quantitative integration of rotations. He uses a variety of cues—maps, shadows, time-of-day, major landmarks (even glimpsed from windows), and so forth. It seems at first uncanny, but it doesn't really require much information. The trick is to acquire effective habits of noticing and representing such things.

Once acquired, headings are quite persistent and are difficult to revise when one tries to make "basic" changes. When I finally understood the bend in the river, it did not seem worth the effort to rebuild my wrong, large-scale spatial model. Similarly, I spent years in Boston before noticing that its "Central Park" has five sides. A native of rectangular Manhattan, I never repaired the thoroughly non-Euclidean nonsense this mistake created; there is simply no angular sector space in it to represent Boston's North End.

Such difficulties suggest that we use gross, global frames of reference as well as smaller, local structures. The difficulty of rearrangement suggests that the local frames are not complete, transformable, structures but depend on their attachment to "global frames" to deduce inter-object relationships. Below I discuss some implications of using global reference systems; in principle this suggests more powerful and general processes for rearranging parts of complicated images, but in practice people seem quite limited at this, especially when operating under time constraints.

6.5.2 A Global Space Frame System?

I do not like the following model very much, but something of its sort seems needed. A global space frame (GSF for short) is a fixed collection of "typical locations" in an abstract three-dimensional space, and copies of it are used as frameworks for assembling components of complex scenes. One might imagine such a skeleton as a five-by-five horizontal array of "places," each with three vertical levels. The central cells represent zones near the center of interest, while the peripheral cells have to represent everything else. (In effect, one always imagines himself within this universal ghost room in which one's current real environment is also embedded.) Actually, people probably use skeletons more complicated and less mathematically regular than this, emphasizing easily accessible volumes near the hands and face to represent space in ways more directly related to manipulative access than to a uniform physical geometry.

The GSF is associated with a system of view frames; each view frame describes the visual appearance of the GSF from a different observer viewpoint. The system is thus both Copernican and Ptolemaic; the embedding of the current scene in the GSF skeleton does not change when the observer moves, but each viewpoint gives the scene a distinctive appearance because the observer's location (or, rather, his belief about his location) activates an appropriate view-frame.

The view-frame corresponding to any particular place is derived by projecting the GSF cells toward that place; this yields an array of view lists—each of which is an ordered list of those cells of the GSF that would intersect some certain ray emitted from the observer's eye. Thus a view frame is like an ordinary scene frame except that its elements are derived from the GSF skeleton rather than from specific visual features and relations of any particular scene. While view lists correspond to retinal regions, we think of them as three-dimensional zones extending in some general direction out to distant space.

Occlusions are explained or imagined in terms of view-list orderings; one expects not to see all of an object that comes later on a view list than does another object. (Similarly, earlier objects are obstacles to manipulating later ones.) In memory matching, occluded view-list cells should relax the matching constraints on corresponding terminals.

To absorb visual information from multiple viewpoints, we need some sort of "indirect address" scheme in which visual features are assigned to view frames through the GSF skeleton; here is a first-order sketch of such a scheme:

Seeing: A variety of types of visual "features" are detected by retinal or post-retinal "feature demons." Each detected feature is automatically associated with the view direction of the current view list corresponding to its location in the visual field.

Frame-activation: At the same moment, some object frame or expectation is tentatively assigned to some of the GSF cells in the current view list for that direction. This means that each terminal of that frame is associated with the view direction of some active view list. (In other words, scene frame terminals contain spatial-location information by pointing to GSF places. [See below.]) Different scene frames of the same system are selected according to the current view frame. The headings of objects must be appropriately transformed.

Instantiation: When looking in a certain direction we (a) expect to see certain visual features in certain cells, as suggested by the active scene frame, and (b) actually see certain features in certain visual regions. So it is natural to propose a first-order vision theory in which each marker of each terminal actually specifies the signature—and also the proposed GSF location-cell—of some class of visual feature-demons. The observer can also be represented within the system as an object, allowing one to imagine himself within a scene but viewed from another location.

Given all this it is easy to obtain the information needed to assign terminals and instantiate frames. All the system has to do is match the "perceptual" [feature-demon, view-list] pairs to the "schematic" [marker, GSF-cell] pairs. If object-frame terminals could be attached directly to GSF locations and if these were automatically projected into view-lists, these would eliminate almost all need to recompute representations of things that have already been seen from other viewpoints.

6.5.3 Embedding Complications

In our first formulation, the terminals of a vision frame were understood to be in some way associated with cells of the GSF skeleton. The idea is tempting: why not abandon the whole visual frame-system idea and build "3-D" object-frames that map directly into space locations? Then an object-frame could represent almost directly a symbolic three-dimensional structure and the GSF system could automatically generate different view-frames for the object.

For a computer system, this might work very well. For a psychological model, it leaves too many serious problems: How can we deal with translations, rotations, and scale-changes; how do we reorient substructures? A crude solution, for rotations, is to have for each object a few standard views such as embeddings of different sizes and orientations. Before rejecting this outright, note that it might be entirely adequate for some kinds of performance and for early stages of development of others.

But in "adult" imagery, any object type can be embedded in so many different ways that some more general kind of transformation-based operation seems needed. The obvious mathematical solution, for purposes of relocation and scaling, is to provide some kind of intermediate structure: each object-frame could be embedded in a relocatable, "portable" mini-GSF that can be rotated and attached to any global GSF cell, with an appropriate "view note" specifying how the prototype figure was transformed.

Providing such a structure entails more than merely complicating the embedding operation. It also requires building a "uniform structure" into the GSF, straightening out the early, useful, but idiosyncratic exaggerations of the more familiar parts of near-body space. Attractive as such a model might be, I simply do not believe one is ever actually realized in people. People are not very good at imagining transformed scenes; I quoted Hogarth's account of the very special training required, and I noted Piaget's observation that even moderate competence in such matters seems not to mature before the second decade.

We thus have a continuum of spatial mechanism theories to consider. I will not pick any particular point in this spectrum to designate as "the theory." This is not entirely because of laziness; it is important to recognize that each individual probably has to develop through some sequence of more-and-more sophisticated such mechanisms. Before we can expect to build a theory consistent with developmental phenomena, we will have to understand better which mechanisms can suffice for different levels of image-manipulation performance. And we certainly need to see a much more complete psychological portrait of what people really do with spatial-visual imagery.

Since we have come so close to building a three-dimensional analog mechanism, why not simply do that in some more elegant and systematic way? Although this is a popular proposal, no one has moved past the early, inadequate Gestalt models to suggest how a practical scheme might function. The neuronal construction of a non-symbolic three-dimensional representation system is imaginable, but the problems of constructing hypothetical solids and surfaces within it bring us right back to the same computationally nontrivial—and basically symbolic—issues. And the equivalent of the instantiated view-list has to be constructed in any case, so far as I can see, so that the value of an intermediate, analog space model remains somewhat questionable.

6.5.4 Evolution

Our frame theory assumes a variety of special mechanisms for vision and symbolic manipulation. I doubt that much of this arises from "self-organizing" processes; most of it probably depends on innately provided "hardware." What evolutionary steps could have produced this equipment? The arguments below suggest that the requirements of three-dimensional vision may have helped the evolution of frame-like representations in general.

In the early steps of visual evolution, the most critical steps must have concerned the refinement of specific feature detectors for use in nutrition, reproduction, and defense. As both vision and mobility grew more sophisticated, it became more important to better relate the things that are seen to their places in the outer world—to locations that one can reach or leap at. Especially, one needs the transformations that compensate for postural changes. These problems become acute in competitive, motion-rich situations. In predation or flight, there is an advantage in being able to coordinate information obtained during motion; even if vision is still based on the simplest feature-list recognition scheme, there is an advantage in correct aggregation of different features seen at different times.

Many useful "recognition" schemes can be based on simple, linear, horizontal ordering of visual features. One can get even more by using similar data from two motion-related views, or by using changes (motion parallax) in a moving view. Since so much can be done with such lists, we should look (1) for recognition schemes based on matching linear memory frames to parts of such ordered sets and (2) for aggregation schemes that might serve as early stages in developing a coarse ground-plan representation. One would not expect anything like a ground plan at first; initially one would expect an egocentric polar representation, relating pairs of objects, or relating an object to some reference direction such as the sun. We would not expect relational descriptions, sophisticated figure-ground mechanisms, or three-dimensional schemata at early stages. (I know of no good evidence that animals other than humans *ever* develop realistic ground plans; although other animals' behavior can appear to use them, there may be simpler explanations.)

The construction and use of a ground plan requires evolution of the very same motion transformations needed to assign multiple view data to appropriate cells. For a theory of how these in turn might develop we need to imagine possible developmental sequences, beginning in egocentric angular space, that at every stage offer advantages in visual-motor performance. Among such schemata, I would expect to find some structures that would also help to realize multiple memory frames with common terminals—since this is a similar (and simpler) problem. Other visual memory needs demand ways to file assignment sets in long term memory; one wants representations of one's home, nesting area, predation regions, mate, enemies, and "bad places." It would be of value to develop a reliable global orientation within one's territory, if one is that kind of animal.

While the needs of vision point toward frame-like symbol manipulation, they do not so clearly point toward processes in which one makes hypothetical internal substitutions, i.e., imagination. But those operations would be useful in any problem-solving activity that requires planning.

We should consider individual as well as evolutionary development. In an "adult" system one's current view-frame depends on where one thinks his feet are; and this requires accumulating rotations due to body posture, head rotation, and eye-direction. It would be no surprise to find "innate" hardware, perhaps in the frontal visual cortex, through which such postural parameters operate to readdress the signatures of visual feature demons; the innateness hypothesis is supported by the good visual-motor coordination seen in the early infancy of many vertebrates. On the other hand, men could do with less preprogramming, given enough other mechanism to make this evolution within the individual reasonably certain.

Although the "adult" system is Copernican we would expect to find, in babies, more self-centered schemata. Perhaps the infant begins with a system centered around the face (rather than the feet), whose primary function is to relate vision to arm-motions; next one would expect a crude locomotor body image; only much later emerges the global system with a "permanent" sense of heading and within which the "observer" can freely move. This evolution from head through body to space-centered imagery would certainly be very laborious, but the infant has plenty of time. Perhaps one could study such a process, in microcosm, by seeing how people acquire the skill required for map-navigation. At first, one has to align the map with the scene; later this seems less necessary. The trick seems to involve representing both the scene and the map, alike, with respect to an internally defined reference direction for (say) North. Of course, part of this new skill involves improving one's collection of perspective transforms for irregular shapes of landmarks as one's viewpoint moves through extremes of obliquity.

In any case, the question is not to decide between "innate" and "developmental" models but to construct better scenarios of how intermediate systems would operate. The relative helplessness of the infant human does not mean he lacks the innate spatiomotor machinery of the infant horse, but perhaps only that its availability is "purposefully" delayed until the imagery prerequisites are also available for building the more complex system.

6.5.5 Metric and Quantitative Issues

Most people in our culture feel a conflict between (a) explaining thinking in terms of discrete symbolic descriptions and (b) the popular phenomenology in which the inner world seems continuously colored by magnitudes, intensities, strengths and weaknesses—entities with the properties of *continua.* Introspection or intuition is not very helpful in this area. I am convinced that the symbolic models are the more profound ones and that, perhaps paradoxically to some readers, continuous structures are restrictive and confining. We already illustrated this point in the discussion of evaluation functions in chess. To be sure, continuous variables (and "analog machinery") could be helpful in many applications. There would be no basic problem in adding magnitudes, probabilities, utility theories, or comparable mathematical gadgets. On the other side, naive analysts underrate the power of symbolic systems. Perhaps we tend to reject the idea of symbolic descriptions because of our sense of "continuous awareness"—would we not notice any hypothetical processes in which one symbolic description is abruptly dissolved and replaced by another?

There would be no actual power in such a continuous awareness; for only a process that can reflect on what it has done—that can examine a record of what has happened—can have any consequences. Just as our ability to debug a computer program depends on the character and quality of traces and records, self-consciousness itself must depend on the quality and character of one's summaries of his own recent states. The "phenomenological" smoothness or roughness of a sequence of mental states would then reflect only the style of description used in the representation of that sequence.

Many psychologists feel that the experiments of Shepard on matching rotated objects indicate that humans perform continuous operations upon picture-like images.[40] In that experiment it was shown that the time it takes for a person to decide whether two pictures show rotations of the same object increases linearly with the angle of rotation between them. But a time-linear experimental result does not imply that an analog, non-symbolic process is involved. Equally natural explanations include

A large number of quasi-independent activities, or
A transformational structure that is incremental.

So Shepard's result might suggest that a person has no frame transformations for accurate large rotations of unfamiliar objects; he has to apply many small, incremental changes. Essentially this same proposal is worked out in some detail elsewhere and I will not describe my own version here.

In a computer-based robot, one certainly could use metric parameters to make exact perspective calculations. But in a theory of human vision, I think we should try to find out how well our image abilities can be simulated by "qualitative," symbolic methods. People are very poor at handling magnitudes or intensities on any absolute scale; they cannot reliably classify size, loudness, pitch, and weight into even so many as ten reliably distinct categories. In comparative judgments, too, many conclusions that might seem to require numerical information are already implied by simple order, or gross order of magnitude. Consider three objects A, B, and C tentatively assigned, in that order, to a center wall of a room. If we move right and now find B to the left of A, we can reassign B to the foreground. There is even more information in crude judgments of apparent movement, which can be interpreted as (inverse) order of distance from the observer's line of motion.

One thus hardly ever needs quantitative precision; differential measurements are fine for nearby objects while correspondingly gross judgments suffice for objects at grossly different ranges. For most practical purposes it is enough to notice just a few relations between an object and its neighbors. The number of noticed relations need not even grow faster than the number of objects: if two objects are near opposite walls, then this fact is directly represented in the top-level room frame, and one rarely needs to know more; if two objects are close together, there is usually a smaller frame including both, which gives more information about their relation. So we would (correctly) expect people to find it hard to recall spatial relations between objects in distinct subframes because reconstruction through chaining of several frames needs information that is not usually stored—and would be tedious and innaccurate in any case.

There are some substantial objections to the GSF scheme. It is in the nature of perspective that each nearby cell will occlude a number of faraway cells, and the cell-boundary occlusions are so irregular that one would not be able to tell just which parts of a faraway object will be occluded. (So the view-list idea does not work very well, but so far as human imagery is concerned, people have similar problems.) To improve the predictive quality of the system, the view lists could be elaborated to view structures for representing spatial relations more complex than simple "nearer-further." The metrical quality of the system could be dramatically improved, I think, by using "symbolic interpolation": consider together or sequentially two or more view-lists from nearby locations, and compromise between predictions that do not agree. One can thus better estimate the exact boundary of an occlusion by finding out which motions would make it certainly occur.

This idea of interpolation—or, in its simplest form, superposition—may often offer a way to improve the accuracy of an otherwise adequate strategy. If one averages—or otherwise summarizes—the predictions of two or more standard views, one obtains predictions of intermediate views that are better than one might imagine. Thus the calculations for body-image management (which one might suppose require complex vector and matrix transformations) might very well be handled by summing the expectations or predictions from the nearest "stereotype postures"—provided that the latter are reasonably adequate by themselves. It is tempting to generalize this to abstract activities, e.g., processes that can make symbolic use of multiple representations.

Another area in which quantitative methods seem important, at least on the surface, is in memory retrieval. One needs mechanisms for controlling the allowed range-of-variation of assignments. Does one demand "best match," does one require a threshold of fit, or what? No one policy will work well. Consider a request of the form

"Pick up the big red block."

To decide what is "biggest," one has to compare different dimensions. Rather than assign a fixed procedure—which might work in simple problems—one should refer to the current problem-goal. If one is concerned with weight, then *biggest* = *heaviest* should work. If one is propping up a window, then *biggest* = *largest dimension*—that is, *longest*—is appropriate. The situation is more complex with unspecified selection, as in

"Pick up a big red block."

but the same principles apply: divide the world into classes appropriate to the micro-world we are in and then pick one from that class that best fits "big." Normally "big" means biggest, but not in a context that refers also to "enormous" blocks. Again, one must choose from one's collection of clustering methods by using the goal-micro-world context. But here, again, the quantitative aspects should be on tap, not on top, or else the outstandingly important aspects of each domain will not be captured. McDermott[28] discusses many issues about discrete representation of spatial structures in his thesis.

This essay contains quite a few different arguments against quantitative models. Perhaps I should explain the general principle upon which they are based, since I see that separately they are not very compelling. Thesis: the output of a quantitative mechanism, be it numerical, statistical, analog, or physical (nonsymbolic), is too structureless and uninformative to permit further analysis. Number-like magnitudes can form the basis of decisions for immediate action, for muscular superpositions, for filtering and summing of stimulus features, and so forth. But each is a "dead end" so far as further understanding and planning is concerned, for each is an evaluation and not a summary. *A number cannot reflect the considerations that formed it.* Thus, although quantitative results are useful for immediate purposes, they impose a large cost on further and deeper development.

This does not mean that people do not, or even that they should not, use such methods. But because of the block they present to further contemplation, we can predict that they will tend to be focused in what we might call terminal activities. In large measure, these may be just the activities most easily seen behavioristically and this might account in part for the traditional attraction of such models to workers in the behavioristic tradition. The danger is that theories based upon them—response probabilities, subjective probabilities, reinforcement schedule parameters—are not likely to be able to account for sophisticated cognitive activities. As psychological theories they are very likely to be wrong.

At times I may have overemphasized ways in which other kinds of first-order models can be satisfactory. This may be an overreaction to some holism-oriented critics who showed (but did not notice) that if you can always notice one more feature of a situation, then you can make yourself believe that you have already noticed an infinite number of them. On the other side I may have overreacted against colleagues who ignore introspective phenomenology too thoroughly or try to explain behavior in terms of unstructured elementary fragments. While any theory must "reduce" things to simpler elements, these need not be identifiable with behaviorally observable units of learning or doing.

REFERENCES

1. Minsky, Marvin, and Seymour Papert: Progress Report on Artificial Intelligence, *M.I.T. Artificial Intelligence Laboratory Memo* 252, 1972.
2. Newell, Allen, and Herbert Simon: "Human Problem Solving," Prentice-Hall, Englewood Cliffs, N.J., 1972.
3. Schank, R. C.: Identification of Conceptualizations Underlying Natural Language, in R. C. Schank and K. M. Colby (eds.), "Computer Models of Thought and Language," W. H. Freeman, San Francisco, 1973.
4. Abelson, R. P.: The Structure of Belief Systems, in R. C. Schank and K. M. Colby (eds.), "Computer Models of Thought and Language," W. H. Freeman, San Francisco, 1973.
5. Norman, Donald: Memory, Knowledge and the Answering of Questions, in R. L. Solso (ed.), "Contemporary Issues in Cognitive Psychology: The Loyola Symposium," V. H. Winston & Sons, Washington, D.C., 1973.
6. Koffka, K.: "Principles of Gestalt Psychology," Harcourt, Brace, New York, 1935; Harcourt Brace Jovanovich, 1963.
7. Guzman, Adolfo: "Computer Recognition of Three-dimensional Objects in a Visual Scene," Ph.D. thesis, MAC-TR-59, Project MAC, Massachusetts Institute of Technology, Cambridge, Mass., 1968.

8*a*. Waltz, David: "Generating Semantic Descriptions from Drawings of Scenes with Shadows," Ph.D. thesis, Massachusetts Institute of Technology, Cambridge, Mass., 1972 (included as Chap. 2 of this book).

8*b*. Winston, Patrick H.: "Learning Structural Descriptions from Examples," Ph.D. thesis, Massachusetts Institute of Technology, Cambridge, Mass., 1970 (included as Chap. 5 of this book).

9. Minsky, Marvin, and Seymour Papert: "Perceptrons," The M.I.T. Press, Cambridge, Mass., 1969.
10. Roberts, L. G.: Machine Perception of Three-Dimensional Solids, in J. T. Tippet et al. (eds.), "Optical and Electro-Optical Information Processing," pp. 159–197, The M.I.T. Press, Cambridge, Mass., 1965.
11. Huffman, David: Impossible Objects as Nonsense Sentences, in B. Meltzer and D. Michie (eds.), "Machine Intelligence 6," Edinburgh University Press, Edinburgh, Scotland, 1971.
12. Clowes, Maxwell: On Seeing Things, *Artif. Intel.*, 2(1):79–116 (1971).
13. Shirai, Yoshiaki: A Context Sensitive Line Finder for Recognition of Polyhedra, *Artif. Intel.*, 4(2):95–120 (1973) (included as Chap. 3 of this book).
14. Binford, T. O., and B. K. P. Horn: "The Binford-Horn Line Finder," *M.I.T. Artificial Intelligence Laboratory Working Paper* 16, 1971.
15. Nevatia, R., and T. O. Binford: Structured Descriptions of Complex Objects, *3d Intern. J. Conf. Artif. Intel.*, Stanford Research Institute Publications Department, Menlo Park, Calif., pp. 641–657, 1973.

16. Binford, T. O., and G. J. Agin: Computer Description of Curved Objects, *3d Intern. J. Conf. Artif. Intel.,* Stanford Research Institute Publications Department, Menlo Park, Calif., pp. 629–640, 1973.
17. Bartlett, F. C.: "Remembering: A Study in Experimental and Social Psychology," The University Press, Cambridge, England, 1932, 1961.
18. Newell, Allen: Artificial Intelligence and the Concept of Mind, in R. C. Schank and C. M. Colby (eds.), "Computer Models of Thought and Language," W. H. Freeman, San Francisco, 1973.
19. Newell, Allen: "Productions Systems: Models of Control Structures, Visual Information Processing," Academic Press, New York, 1973.
20. Pylyshyn, Z. W.: What the Mind's Eye Tells the Mind's Brain, *Psych. Bull.,* **80**(1):1–24 (1973).
21. Guzman, Adolfo: "Some Aspects of Pattern Recognition by Computer," M.S. thesis, MAC-TR-37, Project MAC, Massachusetts Institute of Technology, Cambridge, Mass., 1967.
22. Piaget, Jean, and B. Inhelder: "The Child's Conception of Space," The Humanities Press, New York, 1956.
23. Gombrich, E. H.: "Art and Illusion," Pantheon Books, New York, 1969.
24. Chomsky, N.: "Syntactic Structures," Mouton, The Hague, Netherlands, 1957.
25. Chafe, D. W.: Contrastive Semantics Project, *First Technic Report,* Department of Linguistics, University of California, Berkeley, 1972.
26. Schank, R. C.: Conceptual Dependency: A Theory of Natural Language Understanding, *Cognit. Psych.,* **3**(4):557–631 (1972).
27. Wilks, Y.: Preference Semantics, *Artificial Intelligence Center AIM* 206, Stanford University, Stanford, Calif., 1973.
28. McDermott, Drew: "Assimilation of New Information by a Natural Language Understanding System," M.S. thesis, AI-TR-291, Artificial Intelligence Laboratory, Massachusetts Institute of Technology, Cambridge, Mass., 1974.
29. Fillmore, C. J.: The Case for Case, in E. W. Bach and R. H. Harms (eds.), "Universals in Linguistic Theory," Holt, Rinehart & Winston, New York, 1968.
30. Celce-Murcia, M.: Paradigms for Sentence Recognition, Department of Linguistics, University of California at Los Angeles, Los Angeles, 1972.
31. Charniak, E.: "Toward a Model of Children's Story Comprehension," Ph.D. thesis, AI-TR-266, Artificial Intelligence Laboratory, Massachusetts Institute of Technology, Cambridge, Mass., 1974.
32. Schank, R. C.: The Fourteen Primitive Actions and Their Inferences, *Artificial Intelligence Center AIM* 183, Stanford University, Palo Alto, Calif., 1972.
33. Martin, William: Memos on the OWL System, Project MAC, Massachusetts Institute of Technology, 1974.
34. Freeman, P., and A. Newell: A Model for Functional Reasoning in Design, *Proc. 2d Intern. Conf. Artif. Intel.,* London, 1971.
35. Papert, S.: Teaching Children to Be Mathematicians vs. Teaching about Mathematics, *Int. J. Math. Educ. Sci. Technol.,* **3**:249–262(1972).
36. Minsky, M.: Form and Content in Computer Science, *J.A.C.M.* (Jan. 1972).
37. Goldstein, Ira: "Understanding Simple Picture Programs," Ph.D. thesis, AI-TR-294, Artificial Intelligence Laboratory, Massachusetts Institute of Technology, Cambridge, Mass., 1974.
38. Sussman, G. J.: "A Computational Model of Skill Acquisition," Ph.D. thesis, AI-TR-297, Artificial Intelligence Laboratory, Massachusetts Institute of Technology, Cambridge, Mass., 1973.
39. McDermott, Drew, and Gerald Sussman, The CONNIVER Reference Manual, *M.I.T. Artificial Intelligence Laboratory Memo* 259A, 1972.
40. Shepard, R. N. and B. Metzler: Mental Rotation of Three-Dimensional Objects, *Science,* **171**:701–703, 1971.

BIBLIOGRAPHY

Agin, G.: "Representation and Description of Curved Objects," Ph.D. thesis, *Artificial Intelligence Center AIM* 173, Stanford University, Palo Alto, Calif., 1972.

Bartlett, F. C.: "Remembering: A Study in Experimental and Social Psychology," The University Press, Cambridge, England, 1932 (revised, 1961).

Berlin, I.: "The Hedgehog and the Fox: An Essay on Tolstoy's View of History," Simon & Schuster, New York, 1953.

Binford, T. O., and B. K. P. Horn: "The Binford-Horn Line Finder," *M.I.T. Artificial Intelligence Laboratory Working Paper* 16, 1971.

Clowes, M. B., A. K. Mackworth, and R. B. Stanton: "Picture Interpretation as a Problem Solving Process," Laboratory of Experimental Psychology, University of Sussex, England, 1971.

Ernst, G., and A. Newell: "GPS: A Case Study in Generality and Problem Solving," Academic Press, New York, 1969.

Falk, Gill: "Computer Interpretation of Imperfect Line Data as a Three-Dimensional Scene," Ph.D. thesis, *Artificial Intelligence Center AIM* 139, Stanford University, Palo Alto, Calif., 1970.

Finin, Tim: Finding the Skeleton of a Brick, *M.I.T. Artificial Intelligence Laboratory Working Paper* 19, 1971.

Gibson, J. J.: "The Perception of the Visual World," Houghton Mifflin, Boston, 1950.

Griffith, Arnold: "Computer Recognition of Prismatic Solids," Ph.D. thesis, MAC-TR-73, Project MAC, Massachusetts Institute of Technology, Cambridge, Mass., 1970.

Herskovits, A., and T. Binford: On Boundary Detection, *M.I.T. Artificial Intelligence Laboratory Memo* 183, 1970.

Hogarth, W.: "Hogarth Essays," Doubleday and Doran, Garden City, N.Y., 1955.

Horn, Berthold K. P.: "Shape from Shading: A Method for Obtaining the Shape of a Smooth Opaque Object from One View," Ph.D. thesis, 1970 (included as Chap. 4 of this book).

Hume, David: "An Enquiry Concerning Human Understanding and Other Essays," Washington Square Press, New York, 1963.

Krakauer, L. J.: "Computer Analysis of Visual Properties of Curved Objects," Ph.D. thesis, AI-TR-234, Artificial Intelligence Laboratory, Massachusetts Institute of Technology, Cambridge, Mass., 1970.

Kuhn, T.: "The Structure of Scientific Revolutions," University of Chicago Press, Chicago, 1970.

Lavoisier, A.: "Elements of Chemistry," Robert Kerr (trans.), *Great Books of the Western World,* vol. 45, Encyclopaedia Britannica, Chicago, 1952.

Lerman, Jerome: "Computer Processing of Stereo Images for the Automatic Extraction of Range," M.S. thesis, Department of Electrical Engineering, Massachusetts Institute of Technology, Cambridge, Mass., 1973.

Levin, J. A.: "Network Representation and Rotation of Letters," Department of Psychology, University of California at San Diego, La Jolla, Calif., 1973.

Minksy, Marvin: Form and Content in Computer Science, *J.A.C.M.,* 17(2):197-215 (1972).

Newell, Allen: Artificial Intelligence and the Concept of Mind, in R. C. Schank and K. M. Colby (eds.), "Computer Models of Thought and Language," W. H. Freeman, San Francisco, 1973.

Orban, R.: "Removing Shadows in a Scene," B.S. thesis, *M.I.T. Artificial Intelligence Laboratory Memo* 192, 1970.

Piaget, Jean: "Six Psychological Studies," D. Elkind (ed.), Random House, New York, 1967.

Piaget, Jean: "Mental Imagery in the Child: A Study of the Development of Imaginal Representation," Basic Books, New York, 1971.

Piaget, Jean, and B. Inhelder: "The Child's Conception of Space," The Humanities Press, New York, 1956.

Poincaré, H.: "The Foundations of Science," The Science Press, New York, 1946.

Rattner, M. H.: "Extending Guzman's SEE Program," B.S. thesis, *M.I.T. Artificial Intelligence Laboratory Memo* 204, 1970.

Rosenfeld, Azriel: Picture Processing by Computer, "A.C.M. Computing Surveys," vol. 1, pp. 147-176, 1969.

———: Picture Processing: 1972, "Computer Graphics and Image Processing," vol. 1, pp. 394–416, 1972.

———: Progress in Picture Processing: 1969-1971, "A.C.M. Computing Surveys," vol. 5, pp. 81-108, 1973.

———: Picture Processing: 1973, "Computer Graphics and Processing," vol. 3, in publication.

Schank, R. C., and K. M. Colby (eds.): "Computer Models of Thought and Language," W. H. Freeman, San Francisco, 1973.

Shepard, R. N., and B. Metzler: Mental Rotation of Three-Dimensional Objects, *Science,* **171**:701-703 (1971).

Simmons, R. F.: Semantic Networks: Their Computation and Use for Understanding English Sentences, in R. C. Schank and K. M. Colby (eds.), "Computer Models of Thought and Language," W. H. Freeman, San Francisco, 1973.

Sussman, Gerald, and Drew McDermott: Why Conniving is Better than Planning, *M.I.T. Artificial Intelligence Laboratory Memo* 255A, 1972.

Thornton, P. R.: The Scanning Electron Microscope, *Science Journal,* **1**(9):66-71 (1965).

Underwood, S. A., and C. L. Gates: Visual Learning and Recognition by Computer, *TR-123,* Electrical Research Center, University of Texas, Austin, 1972.

Wertheimer, Max: "Productive Thinking," Harper & Row, New York, 1959.

Wilks, Y.: An Artificial Intelligence Approach to Machine Translation, in R. C. Schank and K. M. Colby (eds.), "Computer Models of Thought and Language," W. H. Freeman, San Francisco, 1973.

Winston, Patrick H.: The MIT Robot, "Machine Intelligence 7," Edinburgh University Press, Edinburgh, Scotland, 1972.

Winograd, Terry: "Understanding Natural Language," Academic Press, New York, 1972.

INDEX